An
Indonesian Frontier

An Indonesian Frontier

Acehnese & Other Histories of Sumatra

Anthony Reid

NUS PRESS
SINGAPORE

© Anthony Reid

Published by:

NUS Press
National University of Singapore
AS3-01-02, 3 Arts Link
Singapore 117569
Fax: (65) 6774-0652
E-mail: nusbooks@nus.edu.sg
Website: http://nuspress.nus.edu.sg

Reprint 2018
Reprint 2019
Reprint 2020

ISBN 978-981-4722-98-8 (Paper)

All rights reserved. This book, or parts thereof, may not be reproduced in any form
or by any means, electronic or mechanical, including photocopying, recording or any
information storage and retrieval system now known or to be invented, without written
permission from the Publisher.

The first edition was published by Singapore University Press in 2005.

Typeset by: International Typesetters Pte Ltd
Printed by: Markono Print Media Pte Ltd

Contents

Maps, Illustrations and Tables	vi
Acknowledgements	viii
Abbreviations	x
Preface	xiii

1. Introduction: Sumatra as a Frontier — 1
2. The Identity of "Sumatra" in History — 23
3. Inside Out: The Colonial Displacement of Sumatra's Population — 41
4. The Turkish Connection — 69
5. Trade and the Problem of Royal Power in Aceh: Three Stages, c. 1550–1700 — 94
6. Elephants and Water in the Feasting of Seventeenth-century Aceh — 112
7. The Transition from Autocracy — 136
8. The French Connection — 151
9. Chinese Migration into North Sumatra — 194
10. Nineteenth-century Pan-Islam Below the Winds — 226
11. Merchant Imperialist: W.H. Read and the Dutch Consulate in the Straits Settlements — 249
12. The Japanese Occupation and Rival Sumatran Elites — 276
13. Indonesianizing Sumatra: The Birth of the Republic — 294
14. Social Revolution in Three Sumatran Locales — 321
15. Conflicting Histories: Aceh and Indonesia — 335

Notes	355
Glossary	425
Index	427

Maps, Illustrations and Tables

Maps

1. Colonial divisions of Sumatra   25

2. Highland population centres   47

3. The Indian Ocean   76

4. Aceh ports of the 18th and 19th centuries   150

5. Aceh's *ulèëbalang*-ships in the 1930s   283

Illustrations

1. Bhairawa statue in probable likeness of King Adityavarman   4

2. Dutch impression of Palembang city in 1659   9

3. Dutch tourist poster for Sumatra in the 1930s   12

4. P.J. Veth's map of northern Sumatra in 1873   49

5. Sultan Selim II of Turkey   81

6. Acehnese siege of Portuguese Melaka in 1629   82

7. The *Gunongan* in Aceh, built by Sultan Iskandar Thani (1637–41)   96

8. An *orangkaya* (merchant aristocrat) of Aceh   99

9. The funeral of Sultan Iskandar Thani in 1641   118

10. Part of Aceh's *Idul Adh* procession   121

11. Elephant fight at the court of Aceh   130

12. Brau de St.-Pol Lias in Aceh   186

Maps, Illustrations and Tables   vii

13. Arrival of Chinese contract labour at Belawan port,   201
c. 1903

14. Chinese coolies tending Deli tobacco in the 1880s   205

15. a. W.H. Read   262
b. T.M. Arifin   262

16. Turkish and Portuguese guns being transported to   340
Holland in 1874

17. The surrender of the young Sultan Muhammad Daud   342
in 1903

18. The capture of the resistance heroine Cut Nyak Dien   352
in 1905

19. Aceh poster hailing the peace of 9 December 2002   353

Tables

1. Change of population balance in West Sumatra   53

2. Change of population balance in North Sumatra   57

3. Labour contracts for Langkat, Deli, Serdang and   212
Asahan made before the Protectors of Chinese,
Penang and Singapore

4. Demand and supply of Chinese labour   214

5. Labour contracts signed before the Protector of   218
Chinese, Straits Settlements

6. Ethnic composition of East Coast plantation labour   223

Acknowledgements

I am grateful to the following publishers for granting permission to reprint the chapters indicated.

1. "A Portrait of Sumatra", in guidebook *Indonesia West: Sumatra, Java, Bali, Lombok*, n.p., Robertson McCarta/Nelles Verlag, 1990, pp. 61–73. [substantially revised]

2. "The Identity of 'Sumatra' in History", in *Cultures and Societies of North Sumatra*, ed. Rainer Carle (Berlin: Dietrich Reimer Verlag, 1988).

3. "Inside Out: The Colonial Displacement of Sumatra's Population", in *Paper Landscapes*, ed. Peter Boomgaard, Freek Columbijn and David Henley (Leiden: KITLV Press, 1997), pp.61–89.

4. "Sixteenth Century Turkish Influence in Western Indonesia", *JSEAH* 10, 3 (1969): 395–414. [revised]

5. "Trade and the Problem of Royal Power in Aceh: Three Stages", in *Pre-colonial State Systems in Southeast Asia*, ed. Anthony Reid and Lance Castles (Kuala Lumpur: MBRAS, 1975). [revised]

6. "Elephants and Water in the Feasting of Seventeenth Century Aceh", *JMBRAS* 62, 2 (1989): 25–44.

7. (with Takeshi Ito) "From Harbour Autocracies to Feudal Diffusion in 17th-century Indonesia: The case of Aceh", in *Feudalism: Comparative Studies*, ed. Edmund Leach, S.N. Mukherjee and John Ward (Sydney: Sydney Association for Studies in Society and Culture, 1985), pp. 197–213; with permission from Dr Ito. [revised]

Acknowledgements

8. "The French in Sumatra and the Malay World, 1760–1890", *Bijdragen tot de Taal-, Land-, en Volkenkunde* [KITLV, Leiden] 129, ii/iii (1973): 195–238. [revised]

9. "Early Chinese Migration into North Sumatra", in *Studies in the Social History of China and South-East Asia: Essays in memory of Victor Purcell*, ed. Jerome Ch'en and Nicholas Tarling (Cambridge: Cambridge University Press, 1970), pp. 289–320.

10. "Nineteenth Century Pan-Islam in Indonesia and Malaysia", *JAS* 26, 2 (1967): 267–83. [substantially revised]

11. "Merchant Imperialist: W.H. Read and the Dutch Consulate in the Straits Settlements", in *Empires, Imperialism and Southeast Asia: Essays in Honour of Nicholas Tarling*, ed. Brook Barrington (Clayton, Vic.: Monash Asia Institute, 1997), pp. 34–59. [revised]

12. "The Japanese Occupation and Rival Indonesian Elites: Northern Sumatra in 1942", *JAS* 35, 1 (Nov. 1975): 49–61. [revised]

13. "The Birth of the Indonesian Republic in Sumatra", *Indonesia* 12 (Oct. 1971): 21–45. [revised]

14. "Social revolution — national revolution", *Prisma: The Indonesian Indicator* 23 (Jakarta, Dec. 1981): 64–72. [revised]

15. "Conflicting Histories: Aceh and Indonesia". Different versions of this paper were published electronically in the Working Papers Series of the Asia Research Institute (June 2003), <www.ari.nus.edu.sg/wps>; and in hard-copy in *Asian Ethnicities* (forthcoming).

Abbreviations

ANU	Australian National University
API	Angkatan Pemuda Indonesia (Indonesian Youth Force)
ARA	Algemene Rijksarchief (Netherlands national archive)
BEFEO	*Bulletin de l'Ecole Française d'Extrême-Orient*, Paris
BKI	*Bijdragen tot de Taal-, Land-, en Volkenkunde*, issued by KITLV
BPI	Barisan Pemuda Indonesia (Indonesian Youth Front)
C.O.	Colonial Office [records held in Public Record Office, London]
COHA	Cessation of Hostilities Agreement
D.P.V.	Deli Planters Vereeniging
ENI	*Encyclopedie van Nederlandsch Indië*
F.O.	Foreign Office [records held in Public Record Office, London]
GAM	Gerakan Acheh Merdeka (Aceh Independence Movement)
GERINDO	Gerakan Rakyat Indonesia; Indonesian Peoples' Movement
I.C.	Indisch Collectie of the Rijksinstituut voor Oorlogsdocumentatie [National (later Netherlands) Institute for War Documentation], Amsterdam
IPO	*Inlandsche Pers-Overzicht* or *Overzicht van de Inlandsche en Maleisch-Chineesche Pers*
ISEAS	Institute of Southeast Asian Studies, Singapore
JAS	*Journal of Asian Studies*
JMBRAS	*Journal of the Malaysian Branch, Royal Asiatic Society*
JRAS	*Journal of the Royal Asiatic Society*
JSB	Jong Sumatranen Bond (Young Sumatrans' League)
JSEAH	*Journal of Southeast Asian History, Singapore* (continued as *JSEAS*)

Abbreviations

JSBRAS	*Journal of the Straits Branch, Royal Asiatic Society*
JSEAS	*Journal of Southeast Asian Studies*, Singapore
K.A.	Koloniaal Archief (Colonial Archive section of ARA)
KITLV	Koninklijk Instituut voor Taal-, Land-, en Volkenkunde, Leiden
KNI	Komite Nasional Indonesia
Mailr.	Mailrapporten (Official reports from Batavia to The Hague)
M.A.E.	(archives of the) Ministère des Affaires Etrangères, Paris
MBRAS	Malaysian Branch, Royal Asiatic Society
MHSI	Monumentum Historicum Societatis Iesu
NHM	Nederlands Handel Maatschappij
Mr.	Meester in de Rechten (Dutch title of law graduate)
MvO	Memorie van Overgave (parting testament to a successor in office)
NICA	Netherlands Indies Civil Administration
N.I.P.	Nationale Indische Partij
OUP	Oxford University Press
Pesindo	Pemuda Sosialis Indonesia
PPKI	Panitia Persiapan Kemerdekaan Indonesia (Committee for the Preparation of Indonesian Independence)
PNI	Partai Nasional Indonesia
PRI	Pemuda Republik Indonesia (Youth of the Indonesian Republic)
PRO	Public Record Office, London
PUSA	Persatuan Ulama2 Seluruh Aceh (all-Aceh union of Islamic teachers)
PARTINDO	Partai Indonesia
PKI	Partai Kommunis Indonesia
PNI	Partai Nasionalis Indonesia
SETIA	Sarikat Tani Indonesia; Indonesian Peasants' Union
S.M.E.	[archives of the] Société des Missions Etrangères de Paris
SSFR	Straits Settlements Factory Records
SSGG	*Straits Settlements Government Gazette*

SSLCP	*Straits Settlements Legislative Council Proceedings*
SSLCR	*Straits Settlements Labour Commission Report* (Singapore, 1890)
T.	Teuku (title of Acehnese *ulèëbalang*)
T.A.G.	*Tijdschrift van het Aardrijkskundig Genootschap*
TBG	*Tijdschrift voor Indische Taal-, Land-, en Volkenkunde,* issued by the Bataviaasch Genootschap, Batavia
TKR	Tentera Keamanan Rakyat (People's Peacekeeping Army)
TOEM	*Tarihi Osmani Encümeni Mecmuasi* (Istanbul)
VBG	*Verhandelingen van het Bataviaasch Genootschap* (BG Proceedings)
VKI	*Verhandelingen van het Koninklik Instituut* (KITLV Proceedings)
VOC	Verenigde Oost-Indische Compagnie [(Dutch) United East India Company]
WO	War Office (records in PRO, London)

Preface

SUMATRA is a vast and understudied island, which still awaits its historian. The island's importance in the history of the Indian Ocean and Southeast Asia bears no relation to the small number of serious works which have been devoted to its history. Particularly rare are the attempts to describe that history as a coherent whole. The relative inaccessibility of the island's interior, and the exceptional diversity of ethno-political groups into which its 43 million people (in 2000) are divided, have discouraged almost all from undertaking this task. William Marsden set a very high standard with his *History of Sumatra* in 1783, and it would almost be true to say that no-one has sought to repeat the effort. Although there have been a handful of modern works in Dutch, English and Indonesian attempting to survey the ethnography of the island, the best historians who have turned their attention to it have chronicled a particular region or ethnicity.

This book is not the coherent and balanced history the island deserves. It is a compilation of work I have done on different aspects of the island's history over the past 40 years. All except the final chapter have been previously published in some form. Aceh is over-represented, with four chapters wholly and another four heavily concerned with it. This can be justified by Aceh's political prominence in the early modern period, and its critical position for the survival of the Indonesia project today, but Acehnese are only a tenth of Sumatrans and arguably among the least "typical". Southern Sumatra as a whole is particularly inadequately treated. Four chapters (1–3 and 13) do try to establish some coherence for the island as a whole, but this is the barest beginning to that very challenging task.

In the 40 years during which I have been concerned with the history of Sumatra, the island has changed as much as I. In the 1960s it still had an uneasy place within the Indonesian Republic, its transport infrastructure a shambles, with many regions resentful of what

Indonesian rule had done to a richly endowed landscape. Under Suharto's rule the island as a whole prospered. It became much more settled, accessible and tied to Jakarta by a web of bus routes, daily flights, bureaucratic institutions and schools. With the exception of Aceh, its place within a unitary republic seemed more secure than ever before.

That exception was a suppressed one for most of the time since 1967 when I have been a regular visitor to Sumatra. Although Hasan Tiro proclaimed the independence of Aceh from Indonesia in 1976, and an effective guerrilla movement in 1989–91 was suppressed only through a government reign of terror, my less frequent visits at that time (1981, 1988, 1995) did not force me to rethink my assumptions. During most of the period I was studying Aceh I believed I shared the view of my Acehnese friends and contacts that this was a part of Indonesia, albeit a restive and troubled part. This changed rapidly in 1998–9, when the fall of Suharto allowed a free press to publicise military atrocities, and the East Timor referendum opened up possibilities of which few Acehnese had previously dared to think. Brief visits in 2000 and 2003 obliged me to rethink my assumptions about Aceh's future. I have added a final chapter seeking to explain why many Acehnese no longer feel themselves Indonesians, and placing the events of 1945 in a somewhat different perspective.

I have revisited all the essays which now comprise this book, but have made fewer revisions than I would have expected. A number of outstanding historical studies appeared in the 1990s, after most of these essays were written. Barbara Andaya's work on Palembang and Jambi, Mary Somers' on Bangka, Joel Kahn's and Jane Drakard's on Minangkabau, Daniel Perret's on the northeast; Rita Kipp's on the Karo-Batak, John Bowen's on the Gayo, Jorge Alves' and Lee Kam Hing's on Aceh and Timothy Barnard's on Siak should especially be mentioned.[1] The ethnography has grown substantially richer, particularly on the Minangkabau, Batak, Pasemah and Kerinci. My own books on the Social Revolutions of 1945–6 (1979) and on Southeast Asia in the early modern period (1988–93) post-dated some of the writing here. Although I have added references to this more recent literature, and edited all chapters in the interests of consistency, it did not seem

Preface

appropriate wholly to alter the perspective of any chapter except the first and tenth.

I wish to thank Connie Teo, who was very helpful in the final stages of formatting this text, and Tan Ying Ying, who steered me through the digitilization problems. Helen was indispensable, both directly in labouring on this book, and more fundamentally by keeping me on the rails for 40 years.

1

Introduction:
Sumatra as a Frontier

SUMATRA is a frontier. For the ancient civilizations surrounding the Indian Ocean it was always a mysterious eastern island of riches — *Suvarna-dvipa*, the gold-land guarding the entrance·to all the wealth of Southeast Asia. For Indonesia it is the land of opportunity, of vast natural resources and economic dynamism. For the foreign visitor it offers natural beauty, cultural diversity, untamed forests still home to elephants, tapirs, tigers and rhinoceros, and rapidly developing facilities which still offer surprises. Having spent much less of their history under the tutelage of powerful states, Sumatrans frequently admit that they are less cultivated than upper-class Javanese, but they quickly add that they are far more egalitarian, enterprising, and self-reliant.

The world's sixth largest island, more than twice the size of Britain or Honshu, Sumatra has been separated from the mainland of Asia (and Java and Borneo) only for the last 10,000 years. It is dominated by its westerly spine of mountains, the Bukit Barisan, formed by the collision of the northward-moving Indian plate with the Asian continent from 60 million years ago. The uneasy conjunction of plates continues to cause geological instability along this range, including earthquakes and volcanic eruptions. Seventy-five thousand years ago Lake Toba was formed in the ruins of a massive eruption which deposited a thick layer of ash still readily discernible all over Sumatra and the Peninsula and as far away as Sri Lanka. At the other end of the island, in 1883,

Krakatau erupted to provide the modern world's biggest blast, claiming 36,000 lives.

The vastness and physical variety of Sumatra give it a wild, open quality in striking contrast to Java and Bali. Both those islands long ago tamed their vast forests, established efficient internal lines of communications, and unified their densely settled people into a few large linguistic-political units. Sumatra, by contrast, never approached political unification until the Dutch conquest at the beginning of this century, as discussed in the following chapter.

Although its strategic location, its great rivers and its prized exports supplied the basis for a succession of powerful kingdoms, the eastern marshes and western mountains provided protection for interior peoples who developed their own civilizations very little influenced by the outside world. Despite giving Indonesia its national language, its dominant religion (Islam) and its modern literature, Sumatra therefore retained a dozen mutually unintelligible languages and divergent religious and cultural systems of its own.

Srivijaya

Sumatra may have been the Taprobana of Ptolemy; it certainly formed a crucial (though not very distinct) part of the "gold-land" (*Suwarnabumi*) of early Indian epics and the "Jawah" of Muslim travellers. Most seafarers from outside, like the inhabitants themselves, had little sense of the separate unity of this island of many kings so narrowly divided from Java and Malaya. They were, however, aware in early times of the kings who controlled the export of gold and dominated the vital straits of Sunda and Malacca. Chinese records tell of successive shadowy kingdoms in the southeast Sumatran area, but these were all eclipsed by the rise of Srivijaya in the seventh century AD.

Several Srivijaya inscriptions, found within a few kilometres of modern Palembang, provide the earliest record of the use of the Malay language, in the period 683–6 AD. They tell of a Buddhist king responsible for the spiritual and material welfare of his subjects, and extracting from them solemn oaths of loyalty. His capital was a major Buddhist centre. Although it continued to dominate the Straits of

Sumatra as a Frontier

Malacca until the 11th century, Srivijaya left no great monuments to rival the Borobodur in Java. The temples it must have built in stone were destroyed in Palembang, though they survived better in what appears to have been the Srivijayan capital after 1080 at Muara Jambi, on the next major river north, and as far away as the upwaters of the Kampar River at Muara Takus. Moreover, the power of the centre sat lightly upon the scattered interior populations, concentrating on dominating the various international ports of eastern Sumatra and the Malayan Peninsula, in many of which inscriptions and buried Buddhist statuary have been found. Its capital at Palembang was plundered in a south Indian raid in 1025, and during the next century independent trade centres grew up in Java, northern Sumatra and Malaya.

The chief heir of Srivijaya's glory was Minangkabau, the heavily-populated rice and gold producing area in the central mountains. After the 13th-century Javanese conquest of the major ports of Sumatra's eastern seaboard, a prince claiming descent from both Majapahit and Srivijaya established his own kingdom near the headwaters of the Indragiri and Batang Hari Rivers, controlling the gold of Minangkabau. This (Tantric) Buddhist king, Adityavarman (1356–75), left numerous statues and inscriptions suggesting he controlled most of central Sumatra (Fig. 1).

Islam

The north and west coasts of Sumatra long remained a political low-pressure area. Their rivers were not navigable, their ports were exposed to the northwest monsoon, their peoples reportedly stateless, barbarous cannibals. The major attractions of the northwest were its location for Indian Ocean traders and the camphor which was collected as resin from trees in the hills above Barus and Sibolga.

Along the lengthy coast between Barus and present-day Medan were numerous other small river-ports. At one of them Marco Polo waited for the monsoon in 1292, as part of the expedition carrying a princess from the Mongol Emperor of China to Persia. He relates that his expedition disembarked there and "for fear of these nasty and

Figure 1 Bhairawa statue in probable likeness of 14th-century King Adityavarman, found in Minangkabau territory near the headwaters of the Batang Hari

Sumatra as a Frontier

brutish folk who kill men for food we dug a big trench round our encampment ... and within these fortifications we lived for five months". Despite his distaste, Polo and his colleagues lived and traded sufficiently with them to give Europe its first account of sago, of palm-wine, of rhinoceros and of cannibalism itself. This was at the port of Samudra (Sanskrit for "sea"), or Sumatra (near modern Lhokseumawe), which during the ensuing two centuries became sufficiently important to give its name to the whole island, at least for Arabs and Europeans coming from the West. In Polo's time it was still a small kingdom practising shamanistic animism. He reported, however, that already the neighbouring kingdom of Perlak (near modern Langsa) had become Muslim, "owing to contact with Saracen merchants, who continually resort here in their ships".

Samudra itself was Muslim by 1297, to judge from the earliest of the tombstones in the ancient cemetery at Geudong. When it was visited by the greatest of Arab travel-writers, Ibn Battuta, in 1323 it was a sophisticated sultanate with international relations around the Indian Ocean and to China. Under its preferred Muslim name of Pasai, it issued gold coins, sent ships to the major ports of Asia, and developed a Malay system of writing in Arabic script. For subsequent sultanates Pasai represented the great Southeast Asian centre of Islamic scholarship. Pasai was a producer of silk, and in the 15th century grew much pepper for the Chinese market.

Despite its commercial and religious eminence, Samudra-Pasai never united northern Sumatra politically. On the arrival of the Portuguese (1509), there were still separate Muslim port-states at (west to east) Barus, Daya, Lamri, Pidië, Pasai and Aru. After conquering Melaka (Malacca) in 1511, and driving out many of its Muslim merchants, the Portuguese attempted to gain influence in Pasai and Pidië by supporting one side of their numerous succession disputes. The effect was to drive all the anti-Portuguese elements, who included the wealthy Muslim merchant community, to unite under the banner of Aceh, a new sultanate formed around 1500 on the ruins of ancient Lamri at the northwestern tip of Sumatra. Between 1519 and 1524 Sultan Ali Mughayat Syah of Aceh drove the Portuguese out of northern Sumatra and

6   An Indonesian Frontier

began what was to be a century of bitter conflict with these Christian intruders.

On the Portuguese arrival the important ports of Sumatra were all under Islamic authority, and Islam had begun to make inroads on the major interior population center of Minangkabau. Most of these gains can be attributed to the wealth and status of Muslim traders, and the need of an increasingly commercialized people for a portable, universally valid, faith. The Portuguese onslaught against Muslim trade, and Aceh's counter-crusade against the Portuguese, introduced a new element of holy war. In the period 1540 to 1630, Aceh fought a number of wars against interior peoples they called Bataks, in which the acceptance of Islam was a major Acehnese aim. In northern Sumatra a clear line developed between those who accepted Aceh authority, Islam, and the Arabic script, and those who withdrew to mountain fastnesses, accepted the designation Batak, continued to eat pork, use their ancient Indic script and practise the old spirit worship. The Gayo people around Lake Tawar (in modern Aceh) were in the former group, the Toba and Karo in the latter. In south and central Sumatra, by contrast, Islam spread very gradually from the coastal centres to the interior, with no major resistance to it ever developing.

The Aceh Sultanate

Initially the Portuguese succeeded in disrupting Muslim shipments of Indian pepper to Egypt and the West. It was the achievement of Aceh to expand greatly the growing of pepper in Sumatra, and to find a way of shipping it directly to the Muslim ports in the Red Sea, avoiding the areas of Portuguese strength on the Indian west coast. By the 1550s Aceh was supplying Europe with about half of its pepper through this route.

Since Turkey was then the master of Egypt, this brought the Sultan of Aceh into contact with the Ottomans, as discussed in detail in Chapter 4. In the 1560s Sultan Ala'ad-din al-Kahar ("the conqueror") sent his envoys with gifts of pepper to Suleiman the Magnificent, appealing for help against the accursed infidels who had seized Melaka and terrorized Muslim traders and pilgrims in the Indian Ocean.

The Ottomans responded by sending gunsmiths and artillerymen, who contributed much to Aceh's holy wars against the Bataks and the Portuguese. The memory of this assistance from the Caliph of Islam was kept alive by a great Turkish cannon which guarded the palace, by a Turkish-style red flag, and by various popular stories. Economic rivalry with the Portuguese over the pepper trade reinforced a dozen attacks from Acehnese fleets between 1537 and 1629.

For the Dutch (in 1598), English (in 1600) and French (in 1602), Aceh was one of the first Asian targets because of its abundant pepper and its own aversion to the Portuguese enemy. These northern Europeans were welcomed, mounted on elephants for their official reception at the palace, and honoured with gifts of *sarung* and *kris*. They found the Acehnese to be difficult bargaining partners, but continued to visit the busy port. They confirmed the Acehnese popular memory that the peak of power and wealth of the sultanate was reached under Sultan Iskandar Muda ("the young Alexander", 1607–36).

In this popular period Aceh was one of the important powers of Asia, with its authority stretching as far as Tiku and Priaman (near modern Padang) in west Sumatra, Asahan in east Sumatra, Pahang, Johor and Kedah in the Peninsula. Thousands of captives were brought back from its victorious naval expeditions to populate the city, man the war galleys, and conduct the heavy construction work in the sultan's buildings. Yet warfare and the impermanence of wooden buildings have left little trace of its former splendour.

The last years of Iskandar Muda were marred by his 1629 defeat before Melaka and signs of paranoia in which he killed many of those closest to him, including his son. His son-in-law succeeded him as Iskandar Thani, but in turn died in 1641. Anxious to avoid such autocratic extremes the leading men then put four successive women on the throne. This important transition is described in Chapter 7. Foreign traders were gratified by more predictable conditions, and local Acehnese chiefs were able to demand great autonomy. But Aceh was no longer able to counter persistent Dutch attempts to prise loose the pepper-growing regions and the tin-producing areas of the Peninsula. Aceh remained a great Southeast Asia port, and the only major Indonesian state to retain full freedom of action *vis-à-vis* the Dutch. But its major exports were the non-renewable items formerly monopolized by the king — gold and elephants.

Decline of the Harbour Sultanates

While Aceh dominated the coasts of northern Sumatra, sultanates arose on the southern rivers for similar reasons. Pepper-growing spread to almost every suitable part of Sumatra during the boom caused by the exceptional European demand in the 16th and 17th centuries. Much of this was grown by Minangkabau on the higher ground of central Sumatra. When they found Aceh's attempted monopoly on the west coast oppressive, they sought other outlets down the Musi and Batang Hari rivers. At Palembang and Jambi the English and Dutch competed vigorously for this pepper, though the Dutch got the upper hand by the middle of the century (Fig. 2).

The dominance of these port-cities over the vast and varied hinterland of Sumatra was in sharp decline by 1700. The European demand for pepper dropped after 1650, and the Dutch and English companies drove ever harder bargains for guaranteed delivery at fixed low prices. Both companies ended by relying on pepper suppliers over whom they had monopoly control. Female rule was overthrown in Aceh in 1699 on the grounds of being non-Islamic, but this only initiated a period of dynastic conflict in which the autonomy of the many local chiefs (*ulèëbalang*) was confirmed.

During the late 17th and 18th centuries the weight of state authority was even less felt by the majority of Sumatrans, who organized themselves in the highland around kinship-based communities, and in the coastal areas around entrepreneurial chiefs who could open up an area to cultivation or trade. Such conditions made it easy for enterprising outsiders to play a role. Bugis from South Sulawesi, Arabs from Hadhramaut, and Minangkabau adventurers from Sumatra itself formed many of the new dynasties of the 18th century.

Figure 2 Dutch impression of Palembang city on the Musi River, at the moment before they sacked it in 1659

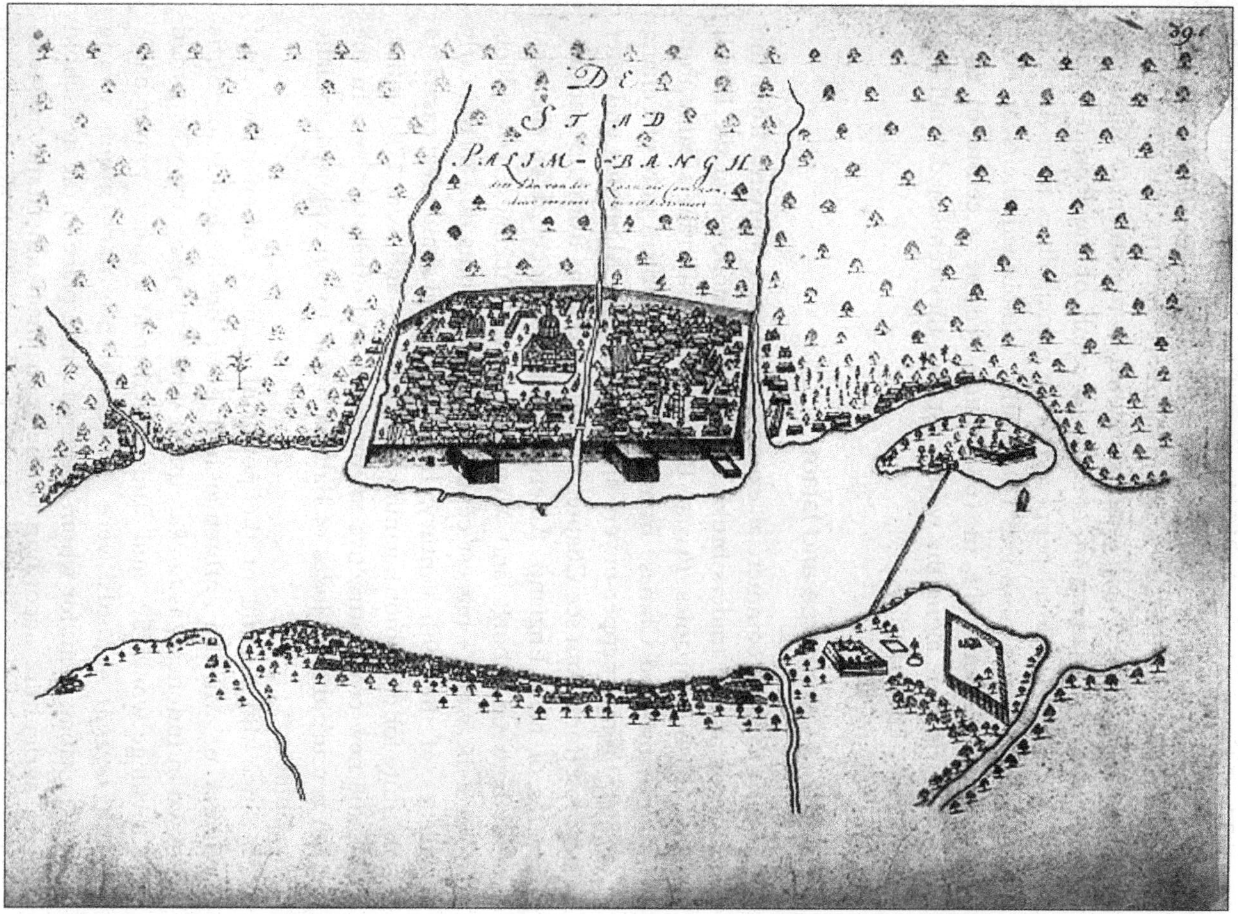

Source: Algemene Rijksarchief.

The biggest players in this league of foreigners were the British and Dutch companies, but for them pepper had become a marginal trade item by the 18th century, and therefore Sumatra was something of a backwater. The Dutch established their own permanent Sumatran headquarters in Padang in 1663, as a result of the Painan Treaty agreeing to protect local pepper-growing principalities from Aceh in exchange for their produce. The British established theirs at Fort Marlborough, Bengkulu, in 1685. Each became a centre of rival networks of trade along the west coast, but they remained small and vulnerable colonies.

Revival of Commerce and Islam

A new phase of commercial expansion affected Sumatra from the 1780s, as private traders broke the fading monopolies of the Dutch and English companies. Private British and Tamil traders came from India, British and Chinese from the new free British port of Penang (1786), French pepper-buyers and slavers from Mauritius and later Réunion (for whom see Chapter 8), and Americans from the maritime centres of New England. American attention focused on the west coast between Sibolga and Meulaboh, where Acehnese river-chiefs created the world's biggest centre of pepper production in the early decades of the 19th century. In the Minangkabau area cassia (a substitute for cinnamon), gambir (for tanning), and from 1790 coffee, became new crops attractive to American and other shippers. In the 18th century the tin lodes of Bangka began to be exploited, initially by Chinese.

Since the decline of the powerful Islamic sultans, the chief bearers of Muslim influence had been brotherhoods of Sufis known in Indonesia as *tarekat*, under whose auspices the young men of a village would live and study together in a *surau* (prayer hall). Such *tarekat* schools were especially popular among young Minangkabau men, for whom there was little place in the household or in agriculture according to the matrilineal inheritance system. These schools provided the basis for a powerful movement of Islamic reform.

The new commercialism had increased the social ills this movement objected to, but also the number of Sumatrans able to make the pilgrimage to Mecca. In 1803, three such pilgrims returned after having witnessed the victory in Mecca of the fundamentalist Wahhabis and set about trying to reform Minangkabau in a similar direction. Society was quickly polarized, as the reformers (known as Padris) tried to ban such beloved traditional pastimes as cock-fighting and betel-chewing, as well as tobacco and opium, and at the same time forced the people to pray and to adopt Arab dress. In 1815 the movement struck at the remnants of the old Minangkabau kingdom centred at Pagarruyung, killing several princes and burning the palace.

Chapter 10 describes the importance of currents of reform emanating from the heartland of Islam in galvanizing Sumatrans and others against Dutch encroachment.

The Dutch Conquest

Despite all their 17th-century treaties with most of the coastal states of Sumatra (notably excluding Aceh), the Dutch had to start almost from scratch when Britain returned to its prewar possessions after the Napoleonic Wars, in 1816. They were in no position to prevent the dominance over Sumatran trade of the British ports of Penang and Singapore, which continued well into the 20th century. Dutch military advances were slow, and usually provoked by the need to exclude other Europeans. Almost nowhere did Sumatrans accept the extension of Dutch authority without a fight.

The basis of the present Malaysia-Indonesia border is the 1824 Anglo-Dutch Treaty, whereby the British withdrew all their claims and possessions in Sumatra, and the Dutch in the Malayan Peninsula. Melaka therefore became British, Bengkulu became Dutch, and the Sultanate of Riau-Johor was divided between British-protected Johor and Dutch-protected Riau. Palembang was considered vital to Dutch interests because of its claim over Bangka tin and its proximity to Singapore, but it required two military expeditions, many casualties and repeated attempts to find a pliable sultan before the Dutch finally

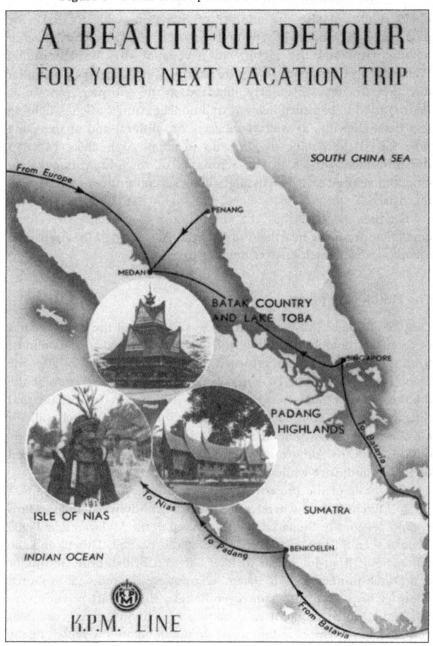

Figure 3 Dutch tourist poster for Sumatra in the 1930s

Sumatra as a Frontier 13

abolished the sultanate and ruled Palembang directly from 1825. Rebellions were frequent throughout the 19th century both here and in neighbouring Jambi, where the Dutch established a garrison in 1834.

But in Padang the returning Dutch inherited the Padri headache from the British. Despite their weakness, they were drawn into supporting the opponents of the Padris in a series of protracted operations from 1820 to 1841 which became known as the Padri War. This made the most densely-populated region of Sumatra also the principal Dutch stronghold. The expenses of the garrison were met by the forced delivery of coffee at fixed prices. Enterprising Minangkabau also took advantage of improved communications and markets to grow their own coffee, as well as tobacco, sugar, cassia and gambir, providing a prosperous commercially oriented middle class in many areas of Minangkabau. The same group responded enthusiastically to modern-style education, funding their own secular schools from the 1840s. By 1872 there were almost 1200 Minangkabau children in such schools — a proportion several times higher than in Java, where education was limited to the aristocracy. This first generation to be literate in Malay (in Roman script) launched Minangkabau into its role of providing Sumatra with a high proportion of clerks, schoolteachers, journalists and political activists.

On the east coast of Sumatra the Dutch advanced slowly, opposed by Singapore merchants as well as local *rajas*. The most valuable Dutch acquisitions proved to be the hitherto insignificant Malay states of Langkat, Deli, Serdang and Asahan in 1865. Jacob Nienhuys began to grow tobacco in Deli with labour brought from Penang, and within a decade this was acknowledged as the finest leaf tobacco for wrapping cigars. British objections were quickly overcome by the opportunities for supplying the burgeoning new "plantation district" from the Straits Settlements. Twenty thousand Chinese labourers each year were brought in to cut down the forests and tend the tobacco plants, as described in Chapter 9. Only in the 1890s did cheaper and more tractable Javanese take their place — there were 260,000 contract workers there in the 1920s. Rubber, tea and oil palm estates followed tobacco. Prosperous modern towns grew up at Medan, Binjei,

Pematang Siantar and Tanjung Balei, and the Malay *rajas* who were held to own the valuable land grew unprecedentedly wealthy on the royalties from it.

Aceh was by far the biggest challenge to Dutch arms and diplomacy. Proud and free, it had wealth and foreign contacts from its pepper and betelnut trade, a self-image as "the verandah of Mecca", and deep suspicion of Dutch advances on both the east and west coasts of Sumatra. In deference to Britain's relations with Aceh, including a treaty of mutual deference in 1819, the Dutch had undertaken in a note appended to the 1824 treaty to respect the sultanate's continued independence. This was annulled by another Anglo-Dutch Treaty in 1871.

The Dutch attack was hastened by energetic Acehnese attempts to form defensive alliances with Turkey, France and the United States, as discussed in Chapter 11. A force of 3,000 men attacked Banda Aceh in April 1873, but withdrew after losing its commander and 80 men. This proved, however, only the first chapter of a war which was to last until 1903, exhausting all Dutch resources of men, money and morale, and leaving a terrible legacy of bitterness in Aceh. By the mid-1880s resistance leadership had passed to *ulama* (religious scholars) who preached the necessity of a holy war at any cost. The Dutch graveyard in Banda Aceh remains as a monument to more than 10,000 who died on the Dutch side. For the Acehnese, who lost at least five times as many, the monument is the crop of war heroes who continued to inspire them, some of whom are now officially recognized as Indonesia's national heroes. At the approach of the Japanese in 1942 the province rebelled and drove out the remaining Dutch presence, as described in Chapter 12.

Much of the credit for the eventual Dutch success in imposing their authority was given to Colonel J.B. van Heutsz, Military Governor of Aceh from 1898 to 1904. His policy of relentless pursuit and emphatic assertion of Dutch power was endorsed by a government that made him Governor-General (1904–9). In that capacity he sent Dutch troops to every corner of the archipelago where independent *rajas* and villages continued to exist. By 1910 the whole of Sumatra was for the first time under a single authority, albeit a much resented foreign one.

Highland and Christian Sumatrans

Thus far the reader will have had the impression that Sumatran history is a matter of the maritime states around the coast, including of course the Dutch Company. Since these were the polities which compiled chronicles and dealt with foreigners, theirs tends always to be the voice we hear speaking for Sumatra in history. Chapter 3 shows, however, that the majority of Sumatra's population for many centuries before the 20th in fact lived in highland valleys largely unknown to the outside world. The Minangkabau of central Sumatra, perhaps because of their gold, were the best connected of these highland peoples to the commercial patterns outside, and they accepted some degree of Islam from the 16th century. Most of the remaining highlanders resisted the claims of both states and scriptural religions until some time in the 19th or early 20th centuries.

The southern inhabitants of the cordillera absorbed increasing elements of Islam from their coastal neighbours in the 19th and 20th centuries; the southernmost Batak group, today known as Mandailing, were more forcefully Islamized in the later stages of the Padri movement. When Christian missionaries made their first concerted efforts to locate promising terrain on this island frontier, it was only the isolated peoples who had firmly resisted Islam — Bataks and the islanders off the west coast — who offered any encouragement.

Though there were several earlier probes, the history of Christian conversion in Sumatra really began with the decision of the German Rhenisch Mission Society to work there in 1861, and the arrival the following year of their dominating figure, Ludwig Nommenson. Winning confidence as a doctor, mediator and teacher, he extended the mission's work northward from Silindung to Lake Toba, always in advance of Dutch control. Protestant Christianity was melded onto Toba Batak identity with great skill, and the reward was the acceptance of Christianity by the majority of the Toba Batak people in the period 1880–1900. Responding to nationalist movements against Western control in the 1920s, an autonomous Batak church was established in 1930, which helped to maintain the identity of Toba Bataks as they began their successful expansion into commercial and teaching roles all over Indonesia. In contrast to the somewhat marginal place of Christians in most of Asia, the 3–4 million Toba Batak Christians are confident and unapologetic about their status as Indonesians.

The other Batak sub-groups were later and less fully Christianized, and all in varying degrees sought to distance themselves from the Christianized Tobas as the largest Batak group. The Mandailing Batak of South Tapanuli saw themselves as Muslim and civilized when the Tobas were still cannibals, and they avoided the term Batak once it became associated with the Tobas. The Simalungun and Karo churches operated in a plural context where substantial proportions of their kinsmen were Muslim (and in the Karo case also still animist). The one million Karo, who on the whole resisted Christianity and modern education until the 1940s, embraced both rapidly thereafter. At the end of the 20th century they had surpassed even the Toba as the most educated Indonesian community, and like them an important diaspora throughout urban Indonesia.

Sumatra and Indonesia

The chapters which follow do not sufficiently cover the transforming nature of Dutch rule over Sumatra in the first half of the 20th century. For the first time the island was under a single authority, albeit an alien one centred in Batavia (Jakarta). For the first time many of the highland people experienced a state structure claiming a monopoly of the means of violence, a tax system and the beginnings of a rule of law. The new elites from a great variety of peoples experienced a common schooling, and with it the discovery that they were Sumatrans and Indonesians. The differences between elites were increasingly seen not as regional conflicts so much as splits between those favoured and those marginalized by the Dutch, as explained in Chapter 12. Acehnese, and to a considerable extent Karo Bataks, typically experienced Dutch rule as defeat and humiliation, but at the other extreme many other highland people found it offered astonishing new possibilities for travel, trade, education and employment.

Economically there were at least three Sumatras in the early part of the 20th century. Each of the three major cities was the centre of a separate rail and road system. Medan in the north was a brash commercial hub, strongly European and Chinese in character, with its closest external links to British Malaya rather than to other Dutch centres. Padang, in the centre, was the oldest but sleepiest of the colonial towns. Palembang was an old city with new oil wealth, linked to Java by history, by Dutch-sponsored transmigrants in its hinterland, and by road and rail systems leading southward to the ferry to Java. The trans-Sumatra highway was first discussed in 1916, but was not finally completed until 1938. In the same year the colonial government erected the first pan-Sumatran administration, with a governor in Medan supervising ten residencies (see following chapter).

In 1917 some Sumatrans formed the Young Sumatran League centred in the high schools of Batavia, and in 1921–2 sponsored Sumatra unity conferences in Sibolga, Bukittinggi and Padang. Most of the support came from Muslim Minangkabaus. Christian Batak students became numerous enough in the 1920s to want their own organization, and by 1926 it was apparent that the only acceptable ideals above the ethno-linguistic level would be national Indonesian ones. In fact Sumatra contributed far more than its share towards the development of Indonesian nationalism, with figures like Mohammad Hatta (later Vice-president), Soetan Sjahrir (first Prime Minister) and Amir Sjarifuddin (second Prime Minister) playing a role in developing the ideas of national unity.

Even more important was the Sumatran role in developing a national literature. For most Sumatrans Malay had always been the principal written language, and its adoption as the language of nationalism involved no such problem as for the Javanese. The development of the modern Indonesian novel was almost entirely a Minangkabau affair, with Marah Rusli, Takdir Alisjabana, Nur Iskandar, Abdul Muis and the Muslim leader Hamka dominating the 1920s and 1930s. Aceh had been the first great crucible of "classical" Malay literature in the 17th century, and its written texts continued to be predominately Malay even while the spoken language was Acehnese.

18   An Indonesian Frontier

Given this strong contribution to Indonesian nationalism in many fields, and its lack of any inherent unity at an island-wide level, it is not surprising that Sumatra rejected all attempts to separate it from Java in the turbulent 1940s. The Japanese in 1945 belatedly fostered the idea of an independent Sumatra centred in Bukittinggi, while the Dutch in 1948–9 tried to foster a Sumatran umbrella for the federal states they had set up in various parts of the island. But Sumatrans themselves had already decided in the 1920s that they could only bring their diverse ethnic groups together at the Indonesian level.

Revolution, Rebellion, and Integration

When independence was declared in Jakarta on 17 August 1945, Sumatra was governed by ten separate Japanese administrations, which had allowed very little Indonesian contact among them. The revolution against first the Japanese, then the British who occupied the three major cities in October 1945, and finally the Dutch, had to be fought separately in each residency, with little beyond radio broadcasts from Java to provide inspiration. Sumatra had to undergo some of the most violent aspects of the revolution before it could fit easily within a nationalist framework. In Aceh the *ulèëbalang* who had ruled under the Dutch and Japanese were violently overthrown in December 1945 by a Muslim-led coalition. Three months later the Malay sultans and Simelungun *raja* who had risen to often flamboyant prosperity were similarly overthrown, in what was dubbed a "Social Revolution" by the Marxists among its supporters. These movements were not controlled by the Republican administration, and they led to a breakdown in authority, especially in east Sumatra where nationalist gangs became a law unto themselves.

Even though these excesses caused a reaction among some groups, who sought Dutch protection in 1947–9, Sumatrans were probably more wholehearted in their rejection of Dutch authority than any other major part of the colony. During the period of six months (1948–9) when the Dutch occupied all the cities and towns of Java, Aceh was the only province which the Dutch thought best to leave alone, and Banda Aceh became the capital of what remained of the republic. Despite Dutch attempts to surround republican Java with a ring of minorities fearful of Javanese dominance, they were forced to accept the reality of republican sentiments in Sumatra.

Nevertheless, the vast island was far from integrated politically or economically when the revolution ended with the transfer of full sovereignty to Indonesia in 1950. Each former residency had its own battle-hardened military force not eager to return to civilian life, and each felt it had earned the right to play a part in the republic on its own terms. The lucrative smuggling trade to Singapore, which had seemed patriotic during both the Japanese occupation and the revolution, was not easy to give up to a central government in Jakarta which had little to offer in return.

The first crisis came in Aceh, which objected to incorporation with Christian Bataks into a province of North Sumatra, to the failure to declare Indonesia a Muslim state, and to the poor rewards for its leaders within the new state. In 1953 the Islamic leadership of Aceh revolted against Jakarta, and declared Aceh part of *Dar ul-Islam*. Troops sent from Java reoccupied the Acehnese towns, but the rebels controlled the hinterlands until 1959, when they surrendered in return for autonomous status for Aceh. Before then Toba Batak and Minangkabau military leaders had allied with national politicians dissatisfied with the centralism, corruption and pro-Communist policies of the central government, in February 1958 forming the Revolutionary Government of the Republic of Indonesia (PRRI). The central government reacted with great vigour, bombing Padang and Bukittinggi and sending a large force from Java. The fighting was over within six months; but it left Minangkabau, like Aceh in the same period, feeling like an occupied province in which locals were no longer trusted with high military or civilian office.

Under President Suharto Sumatran discontents appeared to ease. The anti-Communist and free-market policies of the New Order were those that the Sumatran leaders in the PRRI had advocated, and the central government had the resources to provide a generous return to the Sumatran provinces for their loyalty. The road system was finally restored in the 1970s to pre-war levels and better. Large multi-ethnic provinces were broken up until all except North Sumatra (pre-war East Sumatra plus Tapanuli) returned to the approximate boundaries of the old Dutch residencies. Although in Aceh after 1989 the independence movement became a real threat and the Indonesian military presence consequently oppressive, in other provinces the military presence became less obvious under Suharto. One heard plenty of complaints about the *pusat* (centre), but these were little different from those heard in Java.

The fall of Suharto in 1998 brought profound changes. The press was freed by President Habibie, while under his successor Abdurrahman Wahid the military was gradually moved out of the central political role it had played under Suharto. For Aceh this meant exposure of the atrocities committed by the military forces attempting to suppress the Aceh Independence Movement (GAM) of Hasan Mohammad Tiro, and demands mounted for the trial of human rights offenders. In the climate of East Timor's 1999 independence referendum, more and more Acehnese came to think that they too should have a choice on whether they wished to remain in Indonesia. Serious negotiations with GAM were begun by the Abdurrahman Government, which led under his successor Megawati to a short-lived cease-fire agreement in December 2002, monitored by international observers. Aceh's proud history of handling its own relations with the rest of the world, to which Chapters 4–8 attest, had come into direct conflict with the enthusiastic embracing of Indonesian nationalism described in Chapters 12 and 13.

The democratic *reformasi* mood of the 1988–2001 period brought a greater sense of self-assertiveness among all of Sumatra's peoples. In particular the wealth which Riau Province gained from its oil deposits and its proximity to booming Singapore led to some talk also of Riau independence. Regional autonomy, and the return of resources to the province, effectively gave this movement what it wanted, however. The attractions of regional autonomy also led to new provinces, with Bangka and Belitung splitting off from Palembang, and the Riau Archipelago with Singapore's island hinterlands of Batam and Bintan splitting from Riau. Nobody, however, raised the issue of Sumatran separatism. Even less than in the 1940s did the unity and distinctiveness of Sumatra seem a viable proposition.

Economic Development

Sumatra has often been called the island of Indonesia's future, with unbounded potential for development of its rich agricultural and mineral resources. It is certainly true that since the unification of Indonesia at the beginning of this century, it has been Sumatra that has grown the fastest in population, exports, and wealth. Both by immigration (three million of Sumatra's present population were not born there) and natural increase, Sumatra grew by over three per cent a year for most of the 20th century, while growth in the rest of the country was closer to two per cent. Medan was the fastest growing of Indonesia's cities, from 5,800 in 1893 to over two million today.

Abundant arable land as well as a strong entrepreneurial tradition drew Sumatrans enthusiastically into the rubber boom in the 1920s, and into cloves, pepper, coffee, tobacco, oil palm and other crops since. In addition Sumatra has been Indonesia's biggest provider of oil, with the wells at Langkat and Palembang being followed by newer ones at Pekanbaru and in the 1970s a vast natural gas field at Lhokseumawe.

Whereas Java provided most of Indonesia's exports in the 19th century, Sumatra did so in the 20th, as indeed in ancient times. In the 1930s Sumatran ports handled roughly half the value of Indonesia's exports, but this grew to nearly 70 per cent in the 1950s and 1960s, even without counting the large amount of smuggling. The growth of Java-based manufacturing and the mineral wealth of eastern Indonesia thereafter reduced this dominance, but Sumatra still provided the largest share of Indonesia's ever-expanding exports. Many of those who made their start handling these exports went on to become the biggest *pribumi* (native, i.e. non-Chinese) entrepreneurs of Indonesia in the 1950s and 1960s. However, the centralization of the economy and the importance of political connections tended to reduce the role of Sumatrans in the economy towards the end of the century.

The wealth has given Sumatrans a relatively comfortable standard of living, even though the infrastructure of communications, electricity grids and piped water remains less developed than that of Java.

From the 1920s to the 1960s Sumatrans may have had on average double the income of Javanese, though this gap too narrowed with the industry-based development in Java. The poorer southern provinces — Lampung and Bengkulu — are no longer above the national average as all were in the 1950s. But still, Sumatrans attend school longer, own more cars, bicycles, and TV sets, and spend more on food and clothing than Indonesians on average. The confident spirit of individual enterprise through the centuries will continue to serve them well.

2

The Identity of "Sumatra" in History

ISLANDS like Sumatra, of substantial size and population, might appear to be nature's way of defining a distinct place and people. For Great Britain, Honshu and its offshoot Japanese islands, Madagascar, Sri Lanka or Cuba, this seems so obvious as hardly to need asserting. But the humid tropical islands of Indonesia were not encouraging to land communication and the unification it brings, and were only integrated as part of larger imperial/national units. The question does therefore arise whether Sumatra as a whole should be distinguished as a field of enquiry.

Curiously, William Marsden and his less distinguished contemporaries A. Eschels-Kroon and J.C.M. Radermacher began the scholarly industry on Sumatra as a unit within three years of each other in the 1780s.[1] In the subsequent colonial period there were also impressive scholarly monuments to the proposition that Sumatra is a unit — notably by C. Lekkerkerker, O.J.A. Collet, and Edwin Loeb.[2] The Indonesian period has not produced comparable studies, although in the period 1971–5 the anthropologist Mervyn Jaspan launched the *Sumatra Research Bulletin* in the hope of promoting the coherent study of "one of the most important culture areas of island Southeast Asia". It was the birth of that worthy journal which set my own thoughts moving on the question of Sumatran coherence, although its death four years later led me to wonder whether the question had already been decided in the negative. The degree of objective unity in the language, culture, mythology, prehistory or economy of Sumatra has not yet been adequately researched. Since scholarship often follows political reality, however (though the reverse process also occurs, as we shall see below), it may be of interest to trace the self-identification of Sumatrans themselves during their recent history.

Geography has always made it difficult for Sumatra to manifest a single identity, at least as long as the most effective communication was by sea. The Straits of Malacca united the broad rivers of the east coast with the Malayan Peninsula and beyond, as the Sunda Straits united the south with Java. The great historical achievements of the people of Sumatra, therefore, never remained exclusively Sumatran. Perversely, even some of the names by which Sumatra first appeared on the historical stage — Melayu (in the *Nagarakertagama*) and Java (in mediaeval Arab and European sources, including Ibn Battuta and Marco Polo) — have been appropriated by Sumatra's neighbours.

There are two major historical achievements, in particular, which might have been expected to form the basis for a Sumatran cultural nationalism in modern times. Firstly the Srivijaya empire, centred in Palembang and Jambi, was supreme over all the coastal ports of Sumatra as well as the Malay Peninsula for most of the period from the 7th to the 13th centuries — by far the longest-lived of Indonesia's great powers.

Secondly the Malay language and its literature, now the official language of four countries, was nurtured primarily if not exclusively in a succession of Sumatran centres — Srivijaya, Samudra-Pasai, Aceh, Palembang, Riau-Lingga — and was spoken and read throughout the island. It was the very success of this language in becoming first the lingua franca of the Archipelago and then the language of nationalism which prevented it being seen as "the language of Sumatra".[3]

If we compare the career of Srivijaya with that of Majapahit in nationalist historiography,[4] it becomes clear that the former has been at a disadvantage. Both empires of the past had been largely forgotten by the 19th century, though retaining an indistinct aura of a vanished greatness. Because Dutch scholarship was concentrated on Java,

Map 1 Colonial divisions of Sumatra

Brandes' editions of the *Pararaton* and the *Nagarakertagama* provided the basis, at least by the time of Fruin-Mees'. popular *Geschiedenis van Java* (1919), for incorporating a glorious Majapahit into the textbook view of Javanese, hence Indonesian, history. By contrast Dutch scholarship on Sumatra was modest and uncoordinated. Most of the more ambitious writing on Sumatra was always by non-Dutch scholars, and it was two Frenchmen, George Coedes (1918)

and Gabriel Ferrand (1922), who finally established the claims of Srivijaya to a former greatness. The impact of their findings on Sumatrans was delayed not only by being relatively inaccessible in French (until incorporated into Dutch textbooks, notably by N.J. Krom in the 1930s), but also because the name selected by the scholars, "Srivijaya", had no popular association at all. The legendary greatness of a past Sumatran kingdom was linked in the popular mind with Bukit Siguntang, a small sacred hill at the site of one of the Srivijaya capitals, or with "Andalas" and "Pulo Percha". Both the last two were apparently kingdoms in the headwaters of the Musi or Batang Hari rivers, which must have flourished during the long process by which the aura of Srivijaya moved upriver until it eventually settled on the Yang di Pertuan Sakti of Minangkabau, at Pagarruyung.[5]

On the other hand, once the centre of British interest in Southeast Asia moved from Sumatra to Malaya (in 1824 at the latest), there were no more works like that of Marsden. British scholarship increasingly tended to associate the heritage of Srivijaya and the achievements of the Malay language with the Malayan peninsula, notably Singapore (Tumasek) and Melaka — a tradition which laid a natural basis for Malay cultural nationalism rather than Sumatran.

Nineteenth-century writers are probably correct in reporting that Sumatra was then "without a name familiar to the inhabitants".[6] As an experienced French traveller explained,

> When one asks a native of Sumatra what name he gives his island, one has considerable difficulty making oneself understood. He knows the islands, many of them, around him, but Sumatra, with its innumerable countries, its diverse races, its numerous languages, is a world for him.[7]

For navigators from elsewhere, on the other hand, the name of the whole was taken from the name of a part — in particular from the strongest kingdom of the northwestern corner which was the first landfall for Arabs, Indians, and Europeans. Lamri (Lamuri, Lambri or Ramni), near present Banda Aceh, gave its name to the whole

The Identity of "Sumatra" in History

island for many Arab geographers of the 10th–13th centuries, whereas the rising power of Samudra (or Pasai), near modern Lhokseumawe, had begun to popularize the modern name by the late 14th century (e.g. Nicolo de Conti, Ludovico de Varthema). It is possible, however, as Krom[8] has argued, that the success of Samudra/Sumatra as the name for the whole island also owed something to the older Sanskrit term *Suwarna-bumi* ("gold-land") occasionally applied to Sumatra, notably by a Singasari inscription of 1286.

The Heritage of Srivijaya

The inhabitants of the island only began to call it Sumatra as a result of European influence, for the most part only in the 20th century. It was not the north but the centre of the island which carried powerful associations for most of them. These associations must originate with the mantle of Srivijaya. The Raja Alam or Yang di Pertuan Sakti of Pagarruyung, despite having very little effective power even within Minangkabau itself, was widely believed to have semi-divine powers as one of the three heirs, along with China and Rum (Constantinople/Turkey), of the world ruler Alexander the Great. At least twice a war-leader was able to arouse widespread support in Sumatra on the basis of a real or alleged connection with the dynasty of Pagarruyung. In the 1680s Ahmad Shah ibn Iskandar obtained support from the rulers of Palembang and Jambi, and from many chiefs in the Lampung and Bengkulen regions, for his intended "holy war" against the Dutch.[9] A generation later, in 1717–8, Raja Kecil used a similar claim to be a prince from Pagarruyung to good effect in seizing the thrones of Siak and Riau.[10]

Even the Bataks, relatively more isolated in their mountain valleys, appear to have shared this reverence. According to Marsden,

> Notwithstanding the independent spirit of the Battas ... they have a superstitious veneration for the Sultan of Menangkabau, and shew blind submission to his relations and emissaries, real or pretended, when such appear among them for the purposes of levying contributions ... they think that their affairs would never

prosper, that their padi would be blighted, and their buffaloes die: that they would remain under a kind of spell, for offending these sacred messengers.[11]

This remote but attractive Minangkabau supremacy appears to have been ended by the militant expansionism of the Padris in the first three decades of the 19th century. These Islamic reformers may have sought to unite the whole of Sumatra on an Islamic base, with the central valleys of Central and North Sumatra rather than the coastal cities as the power centres.[12] Their aggressive tactics in South Tapanuli, however, had the opposite effect, changing the sacred but remote image of Minangkabau into a hostile and threatening one similar to the long-standing image of Aceh. A recent Batak author[13] has seen the Padri offensive as a crucial watershed which divided the Bataks from each other as well from the Minangkabau. The subsequent adoption of Christianity by the Toba Batak can be seen as a response to this threat to Toba identity.

By the end of the 19th century, therefore, there was little recollection of any common Sumatran identity or loyalty. Even the anti-Dutch hopes kindled by the Aceh War failed to evoke any such response except among a small group of followers of Singamangaraja XII in the 1880s. The Acehnese leaders wrote to Minangkabau and Batak chiefs for support in 1873, but since their letters were entrusted to a Dutch spy they were unlikely to have reached their destination. Envoys were more successful among the neighbouring Gayo and Karo people, though the envoys to Karo were eventually killed there in 1874, perhaps because of the traditional distrust of Acehnese motives referred to by Singarimbun.[14]

Internal Communication

If there was an economic and communications centre for Sumatra in the 19th century, it was paradoxically in the British settlements of Penang and Singapore. Since it was there that the trade of Sumatra was concentrated, it was only there that Sumatrans from different ends of the island were likely to meet. For the Acehnese, for example,

The Identity of "Sumatra" in History

29

Snouk Hurgronje argued in 1893, "Penang is the gateway to the world; yes, the world itself".[15] If Acehnese used the word *pulau* (island) without further qualification, it meant not Sumatra but Penang.

This same problem dogged the two European powers which, seeing Sumatra as a geographical expression on a map, appointed consuls to it in the 19th century. The French based their Sumatra consul at Padang, the principal Dutch post, in the period 1856–65,[16] and the British based theirs at Ulèëlheuë, the port which supplied the Dutch forces in Aceh, in 1883–5. Both proved "a complete failure", since the commerce they were meant to serve had flourished only by avoiding these centres of Dutch power and trading at scores of tiny independent ports along the Sumatran coast.[17]

The Dutch in the 19th century knew at least two Sumatras — the West Coast and the East Coast — with Palembang as something else again, a little more nearly part of Java. Their earliest newspapers proclaimed themselves Sumatran, but whereas the *Sumatra Post* (Medan, 1889–) in practice circulated among the planters of East Sumatra, the *Sumatra Bode* (Padang 1893–) was limited to the West Coast.

Java was physically united by a trunk railway in 1894, speeding up the long-standing network of the post roads. By contrast railway-building in Sumatra laboured to unite not the whole island, but each of the three distinct regions mentioned above. The northern Sumatra network, begun at different ends in the 1880s, finally joined Aceh with Medan, Belawan, and Asahan only in 1916. Similarly in the South, the Lampung line and the Palembang–Lahat line joined in 1927. Meanwhile a third, smaller network developed in West Sumatra from the 1880s. These three distinct networks were never linked, and it was left to road transport finally to accomplish the economic unification of the island. The major boom in road building and in vehicle import to Sumatra coincided with the high rubber prices of the mid-1920s. The number of trucks and buses imported to Sumatra leaped from 94 in 1924 to 1172 in 1926, while the number of private cars rose in the same period from 539 to 3059. Relative to population, the motor vehicle was playing a larger role in Sumatra than in Java, and at last breaking down the isolation of the island's regions from each other. The first "Sumatra Highway" (*longitudinalen weg*) was planned in 1916, but the last bridge linking the southern networks to those of the north and centre was only completed in 1938. It was not a pure coincidence that Sumatra's decade as an autonomous political/administrative unit also began in 1938, and was therefore enacted at a period when internal communication was easier than at any time before or since. During the 1940s Sumatran officials constantly toured the island by car, something only a very brave and patient person would have done in the 1950s and 1960s.

"Sumatran Nationalism"

The heyday of "Sumatran nationalism" occurred earlier, however — two decades before the structural basis of unity had been laid by this road network. Like so many other Indonesian movements, it began in the Dutch-language school systems, especially the STOVIA Medical School in Batavia. This elite school, which educated the ablest sons of the various Indonesian regions and peoples, had given birth to Budi Utomo and to Jong Java, and it was not surprising that the Sumatran minority of students felt the need of their own vehicle for expressing the common striving for unity and progress. In December 1917 the Jong Sumatranen Bond (JSB) was formed "for Sumatran young people who are undergoing secondary or vocational education", with the primary aim "to strengthen the bond between studying Sumatran youth, by driving out all racial feelings (*rassenwaan*) ... and by posing to each member the inescapable demand that he call himself a Sumatran" (*Jong-Sumatra*, 1918). Its first chairman, the Asahan (East Sumatra) prince and medical student Tengku Mansur, emphasized in his opening speech that Sumatrans would continue to be disregarded until they were united. Nevertheless cooperation was necessary not only among Sumatrans but also with the other ethnic groups of the Indies. The second chairman, the Minangkabau (later Dr) Amir, was still more emphatic in rejecting the "chauvinism" of some who

The Identity of "Sumatra" in History

dreamed of separating "an absolute-Sumatran state and nation" from the Indies bond.[18] As Lance Castles has pointed out,[19] these Sumatran nationalists spoke "the language ... of unity, not division; ...they really had no very cogent reasons why working together should be limited to Sumatra". Sumatran nationalism was a stage in the movement towards Indonesian nationalism rather than a contradiction of it (as Java nationalism, with its deeper cultural associations, sometimes was).

It was not surprising that the sense of Sumatran unity was first felt by students in Batavia, conscious of being outnumbered in an alien environment. However, the JSB initiative evoked a rapid response in Sumatra itself. Branches of the JSB were established in Bukittinggi and Padang (where Hatta was an enthusiastic leader) in January 1918, and in Medan the following May. More remarkably, the popular political movements of West Sumatra and Tapanuli went through a striking period of pan-Sumatran enthusiasm between 1918 and 1922. Newspapers like *Tjahaja Sumatra*, *Sinar Sumatra*, and *Sumatra Bergerak* were founded, and unity congresses pledged their faith in Sumatra as "the island of the future".

The catalysts of the Sumatran unity conferences were young political activists who happened to have a foot in more than one ethnic group. Xarim M.S. (the later leader of the Sumatran PKI) was a Minangkabau who had grown up between Aceh and East Sumatra; Manullang was a fiery Toba Batak, who as leader of the radical Hatopan Kristen Batak frequently cooperated with the Muslim southern Bataks of Sarekat Islam; and the Angkola Batak journalists Abdulmanap and Parada Harahap both worked with the Sibolga radical newspaper *Hindia Sepakat*, which drew its readers from Aceh, Tapanuli, and West Sumatra. They staged two preliminary unity congresses, at Sibolga and Padang respectively, in the last two months of 1921, campaigning among other things for the removal of the headquarters of the Sarekat Sumatra from Batavia (where it acted primarily as a lobby for the Minangkabau Volksraad members, Abdul Rivai and Abdul Muis) to Sumatra itself.[20]

The high point of this Sumatra Unity movement was a well-attended conference in Padang in July 1922, with Manullang as chairman and Xarim as secretary. The most active political parties in Sumatra at the time, Sarekat Islam and NIP (the former Indische Partij), as well as many local associations in West Sumatra, Tapanuli, East Sumatra and Aceh, sent delegates to the conference. Its radical tone was expressed in a number of resolutions, including one calling for "a speedy grant of autonomy to Sumatra, because Sumatra hopes for a liberation of the Indies from the tutelage of the Netherlands".[21] Thereafter, however, the movement declined very rapidly. One reason was the radicalism which brought imprisonment to some of the activists and which frightened some established leaders. Another was the difficulty in agreeing to a headquarters or a leadership which was truly representative. More important still was the fact that the more reforms were demanded of the Dutch government, the more the community of interest with nationalist organizations throughout the Indies became apparent.

Like most of the politicians involved in the Sumatra unity movement, the JSB also moved increasingly into the mainstream of Indonesian nationalism. From 1926 it attended a series of national youth conferences, and it had lost any real dynamic of its own long before it fused into Pemuda Indonesia in 1931. One of the factors which delayed this fusion was the splitting away of a Jong Batak organization in 1926. The Toba Batak students had decided that they would develop their own relationship with Indonesian nationalism as Bataks, rather than through the mediation of what they saw (with some justification) as a Minangkabau-dominated organization. In the more intense spirit of nationalism after 1926 that seemed for many others the obvious path to take.

A sceptic might reasonably point out that the Dutch took up the question of Sumatran autonomy only once they were quite sure that Indonesian political leaders had laid it down. By 1930 the locus of popular politics was firmly that of Indonesian nationalism, and it was the colonial government which moved cumbrously towards establishing a single "Province" of Sumatra as one of six large units for the colony. Although the government now said that it wanted to encourage the feelings of "Sumatranness" which it discerned,[22] nothing was done to this end. The creation of the

The Identity of "Sumatra" in History

province, legislated in 1936 and made effective in 1938, was entirely a matter of reorganizing administrative functions. Nothing was done to establish any representative element — even to the extent of the powerless provincial councils in Java. As with every discussion of Sumatran unity, the most difficult question in these colonial debates was that of the capital. Padang was first chosen, and Palembang was considered, but eventually it was at Medan that the first Governor of Sumatra established his residence and offices.[23] The choice emphasized the primacy of European commercial and administrative interests.

Sumatra in Isolation, 1943–5

As is well known, the Japanese occupation began with a complete denial of Indonesian unity. Instead Sumatra and Malaya were regarded as a unit, "the nuclear zone of the Empire's plans for the Southern Area", and administered as such by the Japanese 25th Army. The capital of this new unit was Syonan (Singapore), reflecting the economic realities of the 19th century better than the political and cultural ones of the 20th century. This experiment broke down mainly as a result of increasing Japanese communications difficulties between islands, but also because the legal and political systems on the two sides of the Straits were by now far apart. In May 1943 the link with Malaya was broken, and the 25th Army took charge of Sumatra alone. Now the capital was shifted to Bukittinggi, not so much in deference to the "cultural centre" of Sumatra, as some Minangkabaus liked to claim, as out of strategic calculations.

The slogan favoured by the 25th Army thereafter was "Sumatera Baru" — New Sumatra. All links between Indonesians in Sumatra and those in other islands were cut, and no talk of Indonesian nationalism was allowed. Until the last moment, however, the Japanese did virtually nothing to develop a positive Sumatran identity to fill this gap. The administration was very decentralized, with each residency (*shū*) having to develop its own economy and its own consultative bodies. Only in a few pan-Sumatran specialist schools and a couple of all-Sumatra delegations to Japan could Sumatrans from different residencies gather to develop a common strategy or feeling. It cannot have helped encourage a Sumatran political leadership when the outspoken leader of the all-Sumatra delegation to Japan in October 1943, T.M. Hasan (of Glumpang Payung, Aceh), was executed by the *Kempeitai* less than a year later.

Only in the last four months of the Occupation did the 25th Army leadership bestir itself at all to develop a pan-Sumatran leadership, and then only as a way of resisting unwelcome pressure from Tokyo to move towards Indonesian independence. On 24 March 1945 it was announced that a Sumatran Central Advisory Council (*Chuo Sangi In*) would be set up — almost two years after its Java equivalent. At the end of May the *Gunseikanbu* (Military Administration) in Bukittinggi announced its choice of leaders for this council. The chairman would be Engku Mohammad Sjafei, the Minangkabau educational reformer who had become the most prominent politician in West Sumatra under the Japanese. Its secretary was another Minangkabau, Djamaluddin Adinegoro, probably the leading Indonesian journalist of his day. He was moved from Medan to Bukittinggi to take up his duties. The two vice-chairmen were Teuku Njak Arif and Mr. Abdul Abbas, chairman of the representative councils in Aceh and Lampung respectively. During June and July these men began to be promoted in the Japanese controlled press as the *empat serangkai* (four-in-one) of Sumatra, comparable to the better-known quadrumvirate in Java.[24]

The single meeting of the Sumatra Central Advisory Council, for five days ending 2 July 1945, was of considerable significance as the first ever conference representing all major social and political forces in Sumatra. It made a number of demands for rapid development of popular, military, and educational bodies at Sumatran level, and it undoubtedly helped to legitimize for the first time a genuine Sumatran leadership — in which Dr. A.K. Gani, a Minangkabau politician resident in Palembang, and the Toba Batak leader Dr. Ferdinand Lumbantobing joined the *empat serangkai* above. The spirit of the meeting appeared to favour a stronger and more self-governing Sumatra, but to oppose the 25th Army's attempts to separate the island altogether from the independent Indonesia decided upon by Tokyo.

The Sumatran Province of the Indonesian Republic

Despite the crudeness and belatedness with which the 25th Army went about preparing an autonomous Sumatra, the Sumatra government would have amounted to something had these preparations been built upon in the Republic which followed. But for reasons which are still unclear, the three delegates of Sumatra sent to the independence preparation meetings in Jakarta in mid-August 1945 were not the leaders who had been groomed in Bukittinggi. Instead the Japanese sent Mr Abbas from Lampung, and two Medan intellectuals who had played little part in the Sumatran preparations, Dr. M. Amir (the guiding light of JSB in its most flourishing years) and Mr. T. Hasan. In the hasty arrangements after the independence proclamation in Jakarta, Dr. Amir was able to ensure that Medan, not Bukittinggi, was designated the capital of the Republican Province of Sumatra, and that the little-known Acehnese, Mr. Hasan, was appointed as Governor. Dr. Amir, a non-active member of Sukarno's first cabinet, was named Deputy Governor of Sumatra in December.

Neither West Sumatra nor Palembang was impressed with the decisions made in Jakarta, nor with the leadership provided by Hasan and Amir in Medan. In the first months of independence Sjafei and Adinegoro in West Sumatra and Dr. Gani in Palembang both issued proclamations on behalf of Sumatra as a whole, leaving no doubt of their impatience at the slowness of Hasan to do anything to set up a Republican Government. Their claims to rival leadership were given some legitimation by Gani's appointment to represent the PNI State Party and later the Republican Army in Sumatra, and by Adinegoro's to represent the Republican Information Ministry in Sumatra.

In short, the all-Sumatra leadership of the Republic had very little support in the island as a whole. In this it contrasted with the Japanese-designated leaders in each Residency of Sumatra (except East Sumatra, where there was none), who were all able to assume control fairly smoothly after independence. It was an accident which turned out to be extremely fortunate for the eventual unity of Indonesia that no strong Sumatran leadership had been developed by the Japanese and confirmed by the Republic.[25]

Hasan and Amir, particularly the latter, did appear to seek "autonomy concerning internal and external affairs" for Sumatra.[26] After a visit to Java in December 1945 Amir gave a press conference declaring that "the government of the Republic in Java considers Sumatra as being politically and economically independent of Java, and at liberty to take any action which does not run counter to the interests of the Republic".[27] He appears to have been thinking of a loose Indonesian confederation. However, he was forced to repudiate very quickly statements such as these by youth activists (*pemuda*) who were suspicious of any signs of separatism on the part of the older generation. Particularly during the first half of 1946 *pemuda* organizations in East Sumatra regularly intimidated the official Republican leadership, and denied it much real power. Dr. Amir himself was so dismayed by his own ineffectiveness that he defected to the Allies in April 1946, complaining, "There is not the least unity in Sumatra — There is not one instrument of authority."[28]

In fact an all-Sumatran government was beginning to assume some substance at about this time, but more as a link between the Residencies and the Republican capital than as an independent power centre. Stirred by reports of chaos in Sumatra, particularly East Sumatra, the first Central Government delegation toured the island in April led by Amir Sjarifuddin. The ministers attended the first meeting of the all-Sumatra representative council (KNI) in Bukittinggi, which helped provide some legitimacy for Hasan as Governor, and elected a working committee to assist him. In June and July the members of this working committee began to converge in Pematang Siantar, which had been selected as the new Sumatran capital to replace Allied-dominated Medan. Heads of various all-Sumatra Departments were also appointed to reside there. Thereafter missions from Jogjakarta were repeated regularly in an attempt to strengthen the Republican position by working through this all-Sumatra government. Since the Dutch government had announced in early May that it could not recognize Republican claims over Sumatra in view of the chaos reigning there, it became a high priority of the Republic to demonstrate stability and control.

Vice-President Hatta himself began a tour of Sumatra with Governor Hasan in June 1947, and remained there throughout the first Dutch military action.

While Jogjakarta attempted to strengthen the weak Sumatra Province government, politicians within Sumatra itself consistently demanded its abolition. For Central and South Sumatra the capital was far too remote, and even in the North *pemuda* groups took more notice of central government delegations than of the Sumatran governor. The plunder of the East Sumatran *rajas* and the lucrative smuggling trade to Singapore gave a smell of corruption to many levels of government in Republican Sumatra, so that a preference developed for government which was either close enough to be controlled, or remote enough (in Java) to be assumed guiltless. The first meeting of the Sumatran KNI began the process of devolution by deciding for three sub-governors, in North, Central and South Sumatra, to be responsible to the governor. These sub-governors had hardly begun to function, however, before they were overtaken by the Dutch military action and a shift to military zones (*Daerah Militer*). The military action also speeded the return of the Sumatran capital to Bukittinggi under Hatta's guidance.[29]

The complete dismemberment of the Sumatran Province into three provinces of North, Central and South was proposed by the all-Sumatra assembly at its May 1947 meeting in Bukittinggi. Given the crisis caused by the Dutch military action, however, nothing was done to implement this until April 1948, when a law (*UU* 10 of 1948) was passed by the Republican parliament bringing an official end to Sumatra's decade as an administrative unit. Three provinces were established in Sumatra, each under a Governor assisted by an executive board elected by a representative assembly (DPR). Mr S.M. Amin, a lawyer of Mandailing origin but Acehnese residence, became the first Governor of North Sumatra on 19 June 1948. Despite much debate between Tapanuli and Aceh over the site for the North Sumatran capital (given the Dutch occupation of most of East Sumatra), Amin remained at Kutaraja (Banda Aceh).[30]

Federal / Dutch Hopes

The Dutch strategy for outflanking the Republic through a federally constituted Indonesia had also involved from the beginning a pan-Sumatran entity of some sort. Dutch plans called for large states in Sumatra, Borneo, and Eastern Indonesia (the only one successfully created), each made up of an elaborate configuration of smaller autonomous ethnic units. As early as February 1947, however, a perceptive Dutch memorandum[31] acknowledged that the Dutch were powerless to woo Sumatra away from Java since it was precisely the common opposition to Dutch influence which drove the two islands together. Even were the anti-Dutch struggle to end, Idenberg conceded, "it would in practice be very difficult to bring a government of its own into being in Sumatra which had the support of the Sumatran people".[32] For none of the four major groupings in Sumatra was the idea of a strong Sumatran government really attractive. The South Sumatrans on the whole feared Minangkabau domination more than they feared Java; the Minangkabau, although seeing themselves as natural leaders of Sumatra in a general way, could not bring themselves to accept the legitimacy of any state structure or leadership; the Batak and the Acehnese, the other two groupings, could not be very enthusiastic about any political structure in which they were not dominant. All, in other words, "would rather relate to the half-magical idea of an Indonesian Republic than to the much more real character of a Greater Sumatra in which they would have to accept the influence of other Sumatrans".[33] The Director of General Affairs concluded that it would be extremely difficult to involve a Sumatran unit of any sort in a federal structure, in which Sumatra would pay most of the bills but Sumatrans would be outnumbered.

> As soon as one comes to the substantial ordering of Indonesian relationships one comes up against contradictions, which are easier to resolve in a provisional sense through an emotional phenomenon like the Indonesian Republic than in an organized political structure.[34]

The Identity of "Sumatra" in History

The all-Sumatra conferences organized by the federalists in 1949 seemed destined to fulfil this prophecy. Dr. Tengku Mansur, the first JSB chairman, had become the head of the Dutch-backed State of East Sumatra (NST) in January 1948, governing the area which had been occupied by Dutch troops the previous year. He was predictably enthusiastic about a strong and united Sumatra, and he was well supported by his counterpart in the State of South Sumatra, Abdul Malik. On 29 March they succeeded in bringing together for a "Muktamar Sumatera" in Medan, 84 delegates from 16 regions. Only Aceh and Nias, neither of which had been occupied by Dutch troops in the "Second Police Action", were unrepresented.[35]

Dr. Mansur's opening speech was remarkably reminiscent of the emphasis of JSB, stressing unity rather than division. His metaphor for Sumatra was a pillar on which the great building of federal Indonesia had to rest. But "a pillar which is built of stones will fall apart and lack strength ... we must work to provide the cement to bind those stones".[36] Yet the conference was unable to agree on anything more than an intention "to create a Sumatra which is strong and united", and a decision to meet again.[37] Ethnic and regional rivalries dogged the whole conference, with most delegations more concerned to strengthen the autonomy of their respective regions than to sacrifice any powers to a Sumatran government. The second "Muktamar Sumatera" did meet in Medan on 28 May, and opted for a "provisional federation" in Sumatra as part of federal Indonesia. Yet only a week after this hesitant decision was taken it was torpedoed by the principal sponsor of the whole movement, the State of East Sumatra, whose assembly rejected NST participation in a Sumatran federation because this would comprise its own independence.[38] Even those who in principle believed in federalism, in other words, could not construct a Sumatran unit.

Conclusion

In the long run the Republic found that even the smaller Provinces of North, Central and South Sumatra were too full of contradictions to stay together. Each split until provincial boundaries came to replicate for the most part the old ethnic boundaries which had formed Residencies under Dutch administration. North Sumatra is the principal exception. Its two pre-war constituents, East Sumatra and Tapanuli, were each so ethnically divided that a more complex multi-ethnic North Sumatra appeared to have fewer objections. Perhaps partly for similar reasons, Medan retains some ambitions to act as a focus for all of Sumatra.[39]

The history of the PRRI rebellion only confirms the theme of this chapter, that it has been easier for Sumatrans in modern times to relate to a distant government in Java than a close one in Sumatra. There are many advantages from a scholarly point of view in looking at Sumatra as a whole, but we will never be able to see it in isolation from its neighbours — any more than Sumatrans themselves have done.

3

Inside Out:
The Colonial Displacement of
Sumatra's Population

> The traveller of yesterday was almost entirely confined to the
> plains, the gardens, the dazzling shores and teeming life of the
> sea. To tell the truth, the historian is not unlike the traveller. He
> tends to linger over the plain, which is the setting for the leading
> actors of the day, and does not seem eager to approach the high
> mountains nearby.[1]

THE present occupants of the Indonesian archipelago do not appear
to have a very long history there. Linguistic and archaeological evidence
suggests the movement of Austronesian languages southwards from
Taiwan within the last five thousand years, carried by peoples also
noted for rice agriculture and pottery.[2] Many important maritime
migrations took place much more recently. Should we not then expect
these people to colonize first the fertile lowland valleys and coastal
plains we now see covered in ricefields, close also to fish-stocks? Only
as population pressures or internal conflicts drove some pioneers out
of the coastal lowlands would we expect to find them penetrating the
mountainous cores of the islands.

Yet the origin myths of many Indonesian peoples speak not of the
sea, the coast, and gradual migration inland, but of a kind of
ethnogenesis in the mountains.[3] In islands like Bali and Nias there

seems to be a positive aversion to the sea, and a habit of building villages on ridgetops rather than near waterways. Even small islands which have played intensely maritime roles in historic times often hark back to an older tradition of settlement high up in the interior. Tidore (North Moluccas), for example, sent *kora-kora* expeditions as far as New Guinea and received tribute from dozens of islands, but its first capital was not at the coast where Soa is now but six kilometres up the mountain at Gurabanga.

During the rapid population growth of the 20th century, the most significant migrations in Indonesia have not been of lowlanders into the sparsely-settled highlands, as has been a marked feature in China and Vietnam (and to some extent the goal of successive Indonesian governments through the transmigration scheme), but the reverse. Bataks, Minangkabaus, Banjarese, Minahasans, Toraja, and Atoni moved from their relatively crowded and impoverished highland valleys into the coastal cities and lowland plains.

How should we explain this paradoxical feature of what is usually considered Asia's most "maritime" region? Were pre-colonial conditions more congenial to highland settlement, with the lowland cities becoming attractive only under high-colonial and modern conditions? Did colonialism distort a more "natural" highland development we would have expected without it? Or is this a false paradox, based on unreliable origin myths associated with sacred mountains? Before considering possible explanations, I will very briefly review the pattern in the larger Indonesian islands, and then assemble the evidence on Sumatra.

Broader Indonesian Patterns

Borneo as a whole has been exceptionally sparsely populated even by Southeast Asian standards throughout recorded history. Its vast coastal swamps and deltaic regions were largely uncultivated until about a century ago, and many of the people who now populate these lowlands have come from outside the island — notably from South Sulawesi, South China, the southern Philippines, and Java.[4] Even the Iban and related groups which now form a large proportion of the "Dayak" or

The Colonial Displacement of Sumatra's Population 43

indigenous non-Muslim population of Sarawak and West Kalimantan have a language very close to Malay and traditions which suggest immigration to Borneo from the Malacca Straits area within the last millennium.[5]

Though Borneo has a relatively small area of true highlands favourable to the early stages of agriculture, these appear to have played a disproportionate role in the development of the oldest settled agriculture. The Kelabit of North-Central Borneo in particular have apparently practised wet rice agriculture for centuries in alluvial valleys above 1,000 metres around the northeastern end of the current Sarawak-Kalimantan border, and developed a complex culture there of metalworking and pottery, as well as creating carved stone graves and monuments perhaps thousands of years old.[6] The more numerous Kayan and Kenyah groups in adjacent areas near the headwaters of the east and northwestern Borneo rivers are swidden cultivators, but also developed a high level of craftsmanship, stone monuments, and hierarchic social structure. According to Raymond Kennedy all Kayan groups trace their genealogy back to the ancestral homeland in the Apo Kayan. He believed this "lofty rolling plateau country" was the centre of diffusion for Borneo's more "civilized" peoples.[7]

The more numerous Kadazans (or Dusuns), who dominated the fertile west coast of today's Sabah at the beginning of Chartered Company rule, trace their origins to Nunuk Ragang (literally "red banyan tree"), which is today understood to be at the junction of the Liwagu and Gelibang Rivers well to the east of the Crocker range which forms the backbone of Sabah. According to the legend, population pressure caused a dispersal from these uplands towards the valleys of the west coast.[8]

By far the most dense population of pre-colonial Borneo was in the Hulu Sungai, some hundred kilometres up the Barito above Banjarmasin. Exploiting the alluvial basins of the eastern tributaries of the Barito, flowing down from the Meratus Mountains, or around the lakes and swampy areas where retreating floodwaters provided fine conditions for wet rice growing, the Banjarese of this small area probably represented almost half of Borneo's population in the early 18th century.[9] Banjar outmigration began during the 1850s, first around southeastern Borneo and in the 1870s into the middle Mahakam River of East Borneo. By 1890 they had begun to colonize East Sumatra and the Malayan Peninsula. At the 1930 census there were still 551,571 inhabitants of the Hulu Sungai at a density of 47 per km^2 (as well as another 200,000 downstream in the Banjarmasin District), as against a population density for the whole of Dutch Borneo of only four persons per km^2. But by then there were nearly 80,000 Banjarese migrants in Sumatra and 45,000 in Malaya.[10]

In Sulawesi one must distinguish between the Bugis, Makassar, and Mandar peoples of the southwestern peninsula, who appear to have developed rice agriculture in the coastal lowlands by the 16th century, and most of the rest of the island where agriculture was primarily a highland activity. The heartland of Minahasa rice growing and demographic development appears to have been in the high intermontane basin which contains Lake Tondano.[11] Other highland lakes such as Lake Poso and Lake Lindu were important centres of sedentarization, although the main centre of the mysterious megalith remains of Central Sulawesi is in an upland valley mid-way between these two lakes. The Toraja of the central massif also developed a complex stateless civilization at elevations above 1,000 metres.

Even for the cultures which cannot be considered either highland or interior, lakes merit attention as early population centres and foci for some of the first states. Lake Limboto appears to have played a role in the development of the fish and rice culture of Gorontalo, while C. Pelras[12] argues that it was Lake Tempe in Wajo (South Sulawesi) which enabled the Bugis to develop as a distinct culture. The iron and nickel deposits around Lake Matano appear to have had a role in the early development of Bugis kingship at Luwu.[13]

Timor has a relatively narrow coastal belt below 300 metres in height, and until recently it remained little cultivated. The dominant agricultural pattern was a highland one, producing rice and maize through shifting cultivation which became increasingly difficult to sustain in the dry conditions of most areas. The Atoni Pa Meto ("people of the dry land") who comprise three-quarters of the population of West Timor considered themselves inherently agricultural highlanders. Like many peoples of the eastern Indonesian islands, they have resisted

The Colonial Displacement of Sumatra's Population 45

government efforts in this century to bring them down to the coastal lowlands where they can be controlled and transformed.[14]

Java is the large island most difficult to fit into the "Sumatran" pattern I am proposing. West Java does have physical and climatic similarities with Sumatra, and its extensive upland valleys probably have more agricultural potential than the lowlands. Moreover in the 16th century a coastal Islamic kingdom, Javanese-speaking Banten, created a sharp cultural dichotomy with the quasi-stateless Sundanese of these highland valleys. But unlike the Sumatran uplands, the Priangan struck the earliest 18th-century Dutch visitors as surprisingly unpopulated, which F. de Haan[15] attributed to epidemics, notably smallpox, and an uncertain food supply. Since Dutch control generally preceded adequate Dutch reporting in this area, however, it may be a case of a highland people valuing their independence and retreating eastwards before the Dutch coffee-sergeants.

The Sumatran evidence assembled below may suggest a need to look again at the understudied history of West Java, and perhaps to question older assumptions that Sundanese civilization began around the Bogor-Jakarta area, where the main evidence for some kind of state is focused. Did "the westward expansion of Muslim Javanese along the north coast cut off the Sundanese from the sea, forcing them to settle in the Priangan highlands", as Th.G.Th. Pigeaud[16] argued, or were they there all along, with the "kingdom" of Pajajaran acting only as the mediator between this mountain civilization and the outside world, as Batak "kings" did in the same period?[17]

Central and East Java are not the model for Indonesia so much as the exception, in that there, "unlike neighbouring areas of Southeast Asia, there was [...] a remarkable degree of ethnic homogeneity from an early period".[18] Lowland and deltaic irrigated rice agriculture was practised since the 14th century and probably earlier, eventually driving out the malaria-carrying *Anopheles sundaicus* from the cultivated regions. Although the Javanese were very seldom politically united during their long history, the relatively easy movement along the Solo and Brantas Rivers appears to have created a greater degree of cultural and economic interaction between coast and interior than applied in the other large islands.

46   An Indonesian Frontier

Java does, however, provide the model which enables us to understand how the "age of commerce"[19] affected the balance of population in some other areas. The oldest Hindu-Javanese centres were far from the coast, around wet rice cultivating areas of the Mataram plain and the headwaters of the Solo and Brantas Rivers. From about 1300 to 1600, however, when the advantages of trade pulled population and rice production towards the coast, first Majapahit and then Demak, Cirebon, Gresik, and Surabaya all flourished while we hear almost nothing of the interior areas. This phase is comparable to the change brought about in the same period in the northern (Aceh) coast of Sumatra and in the South Sulawesi peninsula, where lowland irrigated rice also expanded to feed the burgeoning port-cities.

The complex crisis of the 17th century, in which the forced monopolies of the VOC were the most obvious if not the most fundamental element, appears to have restored the comparative advantage of the upland interior.[20] The rulers of the new Mataram unified the fertile interior plains of Surakarta and Yogyakarta, and Sultan Agung assaulted the *pasisir* (northern coastal belt) and moved much of its remaining population inland. When the Mataram court explained the number of its arms-bearing subjects to Rijklof van Goens in the 1650s, 630,000 were inscribed for the Mataram heartland and other interior areas as against only 290,000 (30 per cent) from the *pasisir* districts (including Cirebon).[21] When *cacah* (households) were counted in 1755 for the division of the realm, there were still more than twice as many in the interior heartland as in the then VOC-controlled *pasisir* — though Ricklefs has shown that these were probably conventional figures which ignored losses of population in the war-torn interior.[22] When the first Dutch count took place in 1795 the *pasisir* and Madura together already equalled the (possibly underestimated) *cacah* counts of interior Central and East Java.[23] More confidently we may use the first Dutch population count for the whole island, in 1831, when the interior, which Peter Boomgaard calls the *kejawen*, and the *pasisir* each held about 2.2 million people, with the predominantly lowland and coastal Oosthoek a further 0.8 million.[24]

Map 2 Highland population centres

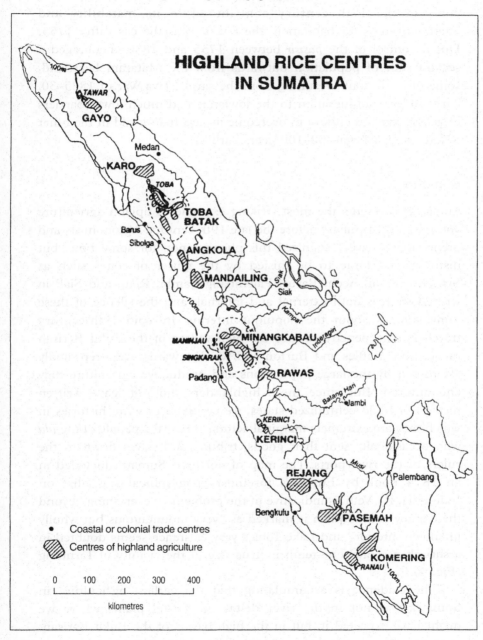

We can reasonably conclude that while Dutch intervention on the coast in the 17th century contributed to its instability and unattractiveness for habitation, the reverse was the case after 1755. Dutch control of the *pasisir* between 1755 and 1830 encouraged a second shift of population outwards from the Mataram heartland, some of it no doubt resulting from the savage Java War of 1825–30. The modern outmigration to the lowlands had much lower barriers of geography and culture to overcome in Java than it did in the other islands, and it began 50–100 years earlier.

Sumatra

Sumatra represents the most striking example of upland agriculture and lowland emptiness before the late 19th century. Agronomists and prehistorians have recognized this phenomenon for some time, but historians continue to be misled by the glitter of states such as Srivijaya, Pasai, Aceh, Barus, Palembang, Jambi, Riau, and Siak in written sources both external and internal, and the silence of these same sources about the populous interior. Intrepid 19th-century travellers who penetrated into the high valleys of the Bukit Barisan range, from Raffles and Burton and Ward onwards, were repeatedly astonished by the large populations and productive agriculture they encountered. But since these highlanders did not leave written records or build centralized states, we continue to write histories in which they are extremely marginal actors, at best the people of the *ulu* who occasionally sent their goods, tribute, and slaves down to the rulers of the river-ports. The map of northern Sumatra included in an 1874 book by Europe's foremost geographical specialist on Indonesia, P.J. Veth, is indicative of the problem — everything beyond the narrow coastal plain is marked as "very mountainous but wholly unknown interior" and Lake Toba's very existence seems doubted in a shrunken scrawl one-tenth its true size in the vicinity of Tarutung (Fig. 4).[25]

The evidence is accumulating that the earliest agriculture in Sumatra was not in the river deltas or coastal plains where we might have expected it, but in the high basins of the Bukit Barisan,

The Colonial Displacement of Sumatra's Population

Figure 4 P.J. Veth's map of northern Sumatra in 1873, marking the interior as "very mountainous and wholly unknown".

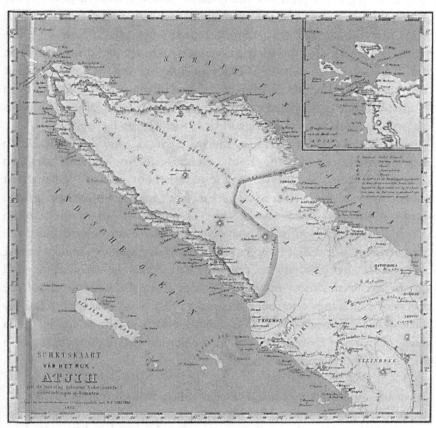

Source: P.J. Veth, *Atjeh* (Leiden: Kolff, 1893).

generally above 500 metres. Pollen analysis of cores taken to the south of Lake Toba and around Lake Kerinci have shown evidence of rice agriculture as much as 5,000 years ago in the first case and 3,000 in the second.[26] Japanese agronomic historians have made clear that the intramontane basins of highlands in Sumatra, as in Thailand, are particularly suitable for the early stages of rice cultivation, and one has judged the Besemah (Pasemah) basin as exhibiting features of low-technology wet rice agriculture (no plough, mini-*sawah* fed by streams, harvesting by *ani-ani*) also found two thousand years ago in

Japan and Yunnan.[27] Most of Sumatra's pre-Islamic monuments are found in highland plateaux many days' journey from a port — the extraordinary stone statues, cists, and menhirs of Besemah (0–500 AD), the Tantric Buddhist temple remains of Padang Lawas (10th–13th centuries), and the inscriptions and statuary of Adityavarman in Pagarruyung (14th century). Dongson-like bronzes have been found near the mountain lakes of Kerinci and Ranau in highland South Sumatra, while one of the Besemah stone statues at Pagaralam includes the representation of a Dongson drum of Heger I type.[28]

The coasts of Sumatra, on the other hand, were inhospitable to early agriculture, with the single exception of the narrow northern littoral of Aceh, where since about the 16th century permanent ricefields were built to feed an urban and coastal population grown large in the age of commerce. The east coast south of the Asahan River was ringed with tidal peat swamps, and even behind these the permanence of rainfall (with no significant dry season), made shifting agriculture very difficult to practise. Cities such as Palembang and Jambi were fed almost entirely with rice from the headwaters of the rivers of which they controlled the outlet.[29] The west coast had relatively little flat land, much of it also abandoned to swamps in the delta areas. Christine Dobbin described the settlements of the coast north of Padang in the early 19th century as:

> small, drab-looking coastal villages which differed markedly from those of the uplands. They were small in terms of both size and population; even the leading ones, such as Ulakan [...] presented "a wretched appearance" (Nahuijs). Behind these villages stretched sparsely peopled, marshy plains [...] Even where the plain was broadest, large tracts of marshy swamp and *alang-alang* grass separated one village from another.[30]

In 18th-century Bengkulu the British constantly worried why the area under their domination was so underpopulated. They blamed poor soil, disease, frequent abortion, a discouragingly difficult marriage system, and the flight of people from British labour demands, but some argued that the coastal strip could still support 50 times its population.[31]

The Colonial Displacement of Sumatra's Population 51

By contrast the upland valleys occupied by (south to north) the Ranau, Komering, Rawas, Besemah, Rejang, Kerinci, Minangkabau, Mandailing, Angkola, Toba Batak, and Karo Batak were all reportedly heavily populated at the point at which they were first seen by Europeans in the 19th century. Much of the population that did exist on the coast had migrated there in recent times from relatively heavily-populated highlands — like the Besemah and Rejang in parts of the Bengkulu coast, the Minangkabau who went down to the west-coast ports to trade, the Toba Bataks who had settled in the ports of Barus and Tapanuli (Sibolga) on the west coast, and in agricultural areas of Asahan on the east coast (where genealogies suggest immigration from the highlands in the 18th century), or the Karo Bataks who were growing pepper in the Deli Langkat area of East Sumatra by the early 19th century. Some of these peoples' origin myths include reference to a contact of the founding ancestors with Java (sometimes as Majapahit) or India, but all believe that they became distinctive peoples in their own highlands, at some sacred origin place from which all have subsequently dispersed.

Population figures are scarce and unreliable before the modern transformation, but tend to confirm this picture. Thomas Stamford Raffles' visit to Pagarruyung in the Minangkabau highlands in 1818 had convinced him that the population within a radius of 50 miles "cannot be estimated at less than a million", while Burton and Ward in 1824 reckoned the "whole Batak country" to contain 1.5 million people.[32] In 1817 an English visitor had claimed 100,000 people in Besemah Lebar alone,[33] and the following year Raffles thought the Pagaralam area of Besemah which he visited "one of the finest countries in the world", with many villages having more than 500 inhabitants and rice costing one-fifth what it did on the coast at Bengkulu.[34]

Population pressure in the Besemah ricelands at the end of the 18th century was beginning to push Besemah to colonize other upland basins in the headwaters of the Ogan, Komering and Musi Rivers on the eastern side of the divide, and the Manna and Alas Rivers on the west side, as well as further south into Ranau and Lampung. But in general the Besemah avoided moving below 500 metres because their

52   An Indonesian Frontier

system of *sawah* irrigation required a drop of water off the hills. "We can only cultivate at the foot of mountains with running water for our *sawah*", as one told a Dutch official.[35]

By comparison with the seemingly abundant 19th-century population of the highlands, the coastal strip of Bengkulu had only 60,000 inhabitants when the British surveyed it in 1819,[36] though in the censuses after 1960 between two-thirds and three-quarters of Bengkulu Province's population lived in that strip. The 1920 census still listed only 61,000 *orang Palembang*, but classified 212,000 South Sumatrans as *orang ulu*, which included Ogan, Komering, Semendo, Rejang, Besemah, and Serawai.[37]

For West Sumatra it is possible to construct a table (Table 1) of highland and lowland population over a somewhat longer term, though with the usual caveats about the earliest figures. Highland population was concentrated in the three intramontane valleys of Tanah Datar, Limapuluh Kota, and Agam, together with the Solok basin to the south of Lake Singkarak, which was less important an agricultural area but has been the site of much modern development.

The earliest figures are such rough estimates that they might be discarded were it not that they predate the devastating Padri War, which may well have been a factor in beginning the remarkable modern phase of outmigration from the Minangkabau highlands where it was fought. Even if we consider the pattern only from the more reliable 1852 figures, the change in the balance of population in the colonial period is evident. Between 1852 and 1990 the highland population increased only four-fold (and that in the original three rice-bowls only threefold), while the lowland population increased 14-fold. By comparison the population of Java increased 11-fold in the same period. Even more highland Minangkabau migrated to lowlands on the eastern coast of Sumatra or in Java or Malaya than to the west-coast lowlands which remained within the provincial boundaries of West Sumatra. By the time of the 1930 census 211,000 Minangkabaus or 11 per cent of their population already lived outside their homeland — the largest groups being in adjacent Jambi (58,000), Riau (51,000), East Sumatra (51,000), and Malaya (14,000 — not including the Negri Sembilan migrants of the 18th century).[38] After independence

TABLE 1
Change of population balance in West Sumatra

	ca 1830[a]	1852[b]	1920[c]	1990[d]
Tanah Datar	{ between 200,000	153,604	260,835	380,709
Solok	{ and 600,000	70,752	221,316	782,551
Limapuluh Kota	300,000	103,567	182,672	387,847
Agam	100,000	197,217	246,890	491,520
Total highlands	ca 800,000 (91%)	556,980 (80%)	958,784 (64%)	2,042,627 (51%)
Coastal lowlands	ca 80,000 (9%)	138,937 (20%)	546,777 (36%)	1,956,050 (49%)

Notes: [a] Dutch figures of 1824 and 1833 cited by Dobbin.[39] The lowland figure is my estimate based on Dutch figures of 13,000 for Padang and 50,000 for the coastal plain to its north.

[b] 1852 Dutch census cited by E. Graves.[40] The "Total highlands" figure is greater than the sum of the four key districts because of the addition of Ophir and Rau, minor highland areas to the north.

[c] Figures derived from Graves.[41] Again the total highlands figure is higher for the same reason.

[d] Biro Pusat Statistik.[42] *Kabupaten* boundaries are somewhat different from those of the Dutch *onderafdelingen*; city populations now administratively separate have been added to *kabupaten* totals.

Jakarta and the other major cities of the Republic became the greatest magnet for Minangkabau migrants. Lance Castles already estimated 60,000 Minangkabaus there in 1962 and Minangkabau leaders claimed as many as 10 per cent of the Jakarta population in the 1970s (though undoubtedly with exaggeration).[43] Modern censuses show not ethnicity but place of birth, which of course catches only the first generation of migrants. By that measure, 15 per cent of those born in West Sumatra were no longer there at the 1990 census, with the largest groups of migrants being in Jakarta (154,000), Riau (146,000) and West Java (88,170).[44]

The Batak Highlands

Toba Batak oral tradition, and that of many *marga* of the other Batak subgroups, trace their origins back to the divine ancestor Si Raja Batak, who descended on the slopes of the mountain (Pusuk Buhit) dominating the western shore of Lake Toba. There he built the village and wet ricefields of Sianjur Mula-Mula, and gave birth to two sons who became ancestors of the Batak moieties — Lontung and Sumba. Today, no doubt influenced by the elaborate *marga* lineages published in the 1920s,[45] Toba Bataks relate to each other by tracing common ancestry back to these founding figures. The longest genealogies do not extend beyond 25 to 30 generations, however, whereas it seems likely that peoples related to the Batak were occupying the shores of Lake Toba for more than 2,000 years.[46]

The concentration of Batak peoples around Lake Toba, at an elevation of around a thousand metres, cannot simply be explained by the unsuitability of the lowlands of North Sumatra for settlement. Both coasts of Sumatra have rich soils and safe harbours at the latitude of Lake Toba, and the East Coast in particular has become in the 20th century one of the outstanding agricultural regions of Indonesia. Nevertheless these lowlands too remained a scarcely-populated jungle until the 1860s, while the Bataks developed complex agricultural civilizations in their highland valleys around the lake, gradually spreading southwards and eastwards to other highland locations, but seldom cultivating near the coast.

The estimate of Burton and Ward in 1824 of 1.5 million Bataks in total is generally regarded as much too high, since even today the population of the central Batak highlands has barely crawled to such a figure. Lance Castles' careful estimates are now the most useful for the 19th century, based on an extrapolation of Junghuhn's detailed figures of 1840. He thereby arrives at a figure of 352,000 for the 1840 population of Tapanuli Residency, about two-thirds of it in the present Toba Batak *kabupaten* of North Tapanuli. Junghuhn himself believed, however, that the population may have been twice as large before the terrible destruction wrought by the militant Islamic Padri movement which invaded the Batak area between Burton and Ward's visit and his own.[47]

On any reckoning, the small area comprising the island of Samosir and the highland valleys to the south of Lake Toba contained several times the population of the lowlands eventually incorporated into the Residency of East Sumatra. When the latter's population was first counted in 1880 there were only 119,000 people there,[48] of whom about 30,000 were recent migrants and contract labourers from outside Sumatra, while some (probably too few) must have been Karo and Toba Bataks already attracted down to the lowlands by the growing opportunities represented by the estates. Even allowing for undercounting of the interior, in the mid-19th century there are unlikely to have been more than 100,000 people in the 90,000 km^2 of the East Sumatran lowlands. The small island of Samosir (670 km^2) within Lake Toba alone had almost as many people. Its population when first counted in 1907 was 74,000 at a density of 110 per km^2 (the highest anywhere outside Java and Bali), despite soils and rainfall much inferior to those of eastern Sumatra.[49] Given its high outmigration we can assume it was already extremely thickly populated by Sumatran standards in the 19th century.

Once the East Sumatran plantation district began to import labour on a massive scale, the change in the balance of North Sumatran population was even more striking than that of West Sumatra (Table 2). The biggest influx in 1870–90 was of Chinese and in 1890–1930 of Javanese contract labourers, but there was also, at first as a trickle and since 1940 as the overwhelmingly

56 An Indonesian Frontier

dominant factor, an internal flow of Bataks, coming down to the lowlands.

The Bataks were slower than the Minangkabaus to leave their mountain fastnesses. The early directions of outmigration from the crowded Toba Batak heartland around Lake Toba were predominately to other highland valleys, in Dairi and Alas to the north and Silindung, Angkola, and Asahan in the south.[50] The first large-scale Toba migration to the lower slopes was facilitated by the colonial government, anxious to develop wet rice agriculture in the Simalungun area when it became a new frontier for plantation development. From 1915 onwards Toba Batak cultivators opened *sawah* in lower Simalungun where irrigation facilities were provided by the government. By 1930, 12 per cent of the Toba Batak population lived in East Sumatra's lowlands, 49,000 of them in Simalungun and 18,000 in Asahan.[51]

In total, the 1930 census showed "Bataks" already as the leading outmigrants of Indonesia, with 15.3 per cent of their number living outside the original Batak Province of Tapanuli, as against comparable figures of 14 per cent for the Banjar, 11 per cent for the Minangkabau, 10.5 per cent for the Bugis, and 9.5 per cent for the Menadonese — and at the other end of the scale only 3.4 per cent for Javanese, despite all the official encouragement for them to transmigrate, and 0.1 per cent for Balinese and Sasak.[52]

At the same time Mandailings from South Tapanuli, quicker to profit from colonial education opportunities and as Muslims more readily fitting into the Malay establishment of the East Coast, began to occupy clerical and commercial positions in the eastern lowlands. There were 45,000 of them in the east coast in 1930, more than half as many as the Mandailings remaining at home.[53]

The revolution of 1945–9 with its destruction of the authority of not only the Dutch colonial state, but also the Malay sultanates and the Western plantations, opened the floodgates to more extensive Batak migration to the lowlands. Although there are again no census figures by ethnicity, Cunningham (1958:95) has shown that an average of 17 Toba Batak churches a year were opened in East Sumatra in the period 1950–5, as against barely two a year in the 50 preceding years. The strength of the flow of outmigration is illustrated by his study of

TABLE 2
Change of population balance in North Sumatra (excluding Nias)

	Mid-19th century[a]	1930[b]	1990[c]
North Tapanuli highlands	ca 200,000	418,736	695,777
South Tapanuli	ca 140,000	276,681	954,245
Karo highlands	ca 60,000	86,411	257,981
Dairi	ca 20,000	54,053	276,980
Total highlands	ca 420,000 (79%)	835,881 (33%)	2,184,983 (23%)
East Sumatra minus Karo	ca 100,000	1,587,272	7,192,773
Sibolga and Barus	ca 10,000	92,036	285,912
Total lowlands	ca 110,000 (21%)	1,679,308 (67%)	7,478,685 (77%)

Notes: [a] The Tapanuli figures are based on Castles,[54] who estimated populations roughly half what they were in 1930, which was the scale of increase suggested by Junghuhn's partial figures. I have however assumed a rate of population increase slightly above this norm for Dairi, because it was a frontier for Toba Batak immigration well before 1930; and somewhat below it for Karo, which was throughout the 20th century distinguished from other Batak areas by its low rate of population increase, and which suffered more than other areas from the Dutch conquest. Joustra's population estimates in 1906–8 were 84,000 for the Karo highlands (thought to be relatively well documented), 25,000 for Dairi, 75,000 for Samosir and 248,000 for the remainder of the North Tapanuli highlands.[55]

[b] *Volkstelling 1930,* IV.

[c] Biro Pusat Statistik, *Penduduk Indonesia,* p. 19.

one village of the Meat valley running down to Lake Toba. Of the 59 people in the village in 1950, no less than 34 (58 per cent) had left for the East Coast by 1955, though the high Batak fertility had brought the remaining population up to 42.[56]

Although the Karo Bataks of the Karo plateau (at roughly 1,300 metres elevation, to the north of Lake Toba) were closest to the Medan area and may at one time have dominated it, their 20th-century descent to the plains is the most recent of all. Only after the revolutionary experience of 1945–9 did Karos massively embrace the opportunities of education and modernization, as well as joining the Toba in occupying former plantation land near Medan. By 1981 there were 52,000 Karo in Medan — much fewer than the absolute numbers of Toba (183,000), Mandailing or Minangkabau, but a bigger proportion (say 10 per cent) of the whole Karo Batak people.[57]

The trend of the last 20 years has been for migration not to the local coastal cities, where opportunities tend to be limited by the ethnic niche each occupies, but to Jakarta. The number of North Sumatra-born migrants in other provinces has increased dramatically at the three censuses: 188,326 in 1971, 417,659 in 1980, and 770,093 in 1990. Of the last figure, 200,000 were in Jakarta and 116,000 more in West Java, meaning that North Sumatrans (predominantly Bataks of various sorts) were the third largest group in the capital after Javanese and Sundanese.[58]

The most recent migration trends are better shown by the question asked in the last two censuses as to where people were five years ago. This showed that 177,289 people had left North Sumatra in the five years before the 1980 census and 277,647 before that of 1990. Both the absolute figures for 1990 and the pace of increase show that Bataks (in the broadest sense) are now the ethnic group most likely to emigrate outside their province, even though that province is now defined to include the original area to which they migrated (East Sumatra).

In 1995 I conducted similar surveys in Tiga Binanga (Karo) and Samosir (Toba) to those which Cunningham carried out in 1956. These showed that the pace of migration has accelerated further to the point where virtually all youth leave the village in their late teens, with a tiny fraction returning after marriage to care for the old people.

The Colonial Displacement of Sumatra's Population   59

But where Cunningham's outmigrants headed almost exclusively for the East Sumatran lowlands, they are now destined for Jakarta, Bandung, and the new industrial estates of Batam, near Singapore.

The nine households of the hamlet (*huta*) of Lumban Tonga-tonga (Pangururan, Samosir) produced 69 children since the 1950s. Sixty-one of these are old enough to have migrated, of whom only four (7 per cent) remain in the village. Forty-five people, or 73 per cent of the whole generation, have left the province of North Sumatra, the largest concentrations being in Bandung (23) and West Sumatra (7). This group is not distinguished educationally, with only three appearing to have tertiary qualifications of any kind.

Toba Batak, especially in Samosir, continue to have large families, for whom outmigration is the only real option. By contrast Karo Bataks have the lowest birth rates in North Sumatra and the highest education rates. With Karos the motive for migration is their exceptional commitment to using education to push the next generation into a better life.

In the much larger Karo, village of Gunung, 90 per cent of the youngest generation born to parents now under 60 had left the highlands by the time they were 20 years of age, compared with 58 per cent of those born to parents aged 60–75. In the youngest generation, the favourite destination was Jakarta (40 per cent), followed by Medan, Batam, and Bandung. The educational record of these children would be high for a developed industrial country, and is astonishing for children born in an Indonesian village with no educational opportunities at all before 1950. Ninety-five per cent of the younger generation and 41 per cent of the older one finished high school, while 45 per cent and 22 per cent had tertiary education.

In the 20th century, and particularly after political independence removed their peculiar alienness under Dutch rule, the cities have become the great poles of attraction for ambitious highlanders. As one Toba Batak clergyman who lived through the transition pointed out: "When I was a boy in Tapanuli and left to study in Singapore [...] the women in the family moaned and cried, fearing that I would fall off the earth [...] Today the women will moan and cry if a son does not have ambition and does not want to leave the *huta*."[59] The

60 An Indonesian Frontier

urban Indonesian population of just 4 million or 7 per cent in 1930 became 14 million (15 per cent) in 1961 and 55 million (31 per cent) in 1990.[60] With the interesting exception of Bandung in Java, all the urban growth centres were in the lowlands. Although the Sumatran highlands sustained the bulk of that island's population up to 1900, they now contain no major city, no airport (to the dismay of tour operators), and no state university. More than ever, the path to modernization is to leave the highlands.

Hypotheses

Why did pre-modern Sumatrans, and many other Indonesians, for the most part cluster in upland valleys? If we can establish these reasons, can we explain why they have been so reversed in the course of the 20th century that highlanders are now rushing to the lowland cities and leaving their pleasant cool valleys to become depopulated museums? Are these changes a necessary part of the modernization process, or to some extent a distortion introduced by colonial control?

Five factors appear to have played some part in the attractiveness of the highlands in the past: agriculture, health, statelessness, security, and culture.

1. *Agriculture*

The lowland valleys and deltas where most of Southeast Asia's current rice production is concentrated was not in fact hospitable to earlier generations of cultivators. Floods were a constant problem, ruining crops, endangering cattle, and threatening households and their fresh water supplies. Only large-scale irrigation and drainage works could control the large volumes of water in the lowlands and direct it to maintaining the permanent, inundated ricefields which we know today to be highly efficient. As Odum has pointed out, the wet rice agriculture of lowland valleys and deltas is "one of the most productive and dependable of agricultural systems yet devised by man", but it requires a complete alteration of the natural environment and very high inputs of labour.[61] With relatively simple technology and small family units

The Colonial Displacement of Sumatra's Population

of labour, highland valleys with small but permanent streams of water are far easier to manage. While it is conventional to draw a sharp line between upland rain-fed shifting cultivation and lowland permanent wet ricefields, in reality both types have long operated together as part of a spectrum of different agricultural strategies. Small plots of irrigated *sawah* were relatively easy to construct even without ploughing if adjacent to natural streams, and highlanders used them in addition to shifting plots on higher slopes.

Secondly, the density of the rain forest in most of Sumatra, Borneo, West Java, and northern Moluccas presents particular problems for pioneer cultivators. In most of these regions (unlike eastern Java and Nusa Tenggara) there is a minimal dry season, little light penetrates the dense forest canopy, and soils obtain few nutrients from decaying vegetable matter. The forest is difficult to fell, and never really dries out enough to burn easily. Unsuccessful burning is the major cause of swidden failure in such areas, and is especially likely in thick primary forest.[62] Such dense forest also has little game for hunting. The areas with a more pronounced dry season are at a distinct advantage for the development of settled agriculture, both of dry and wet type. As it happens some of the mountain valleys of the Bukit Barisan do have such a dry season when the southwest monsoon drops its heavy rain on the high western range close to the coast, sparing the protected valleys behind them. No more than 50 mm falls each month on average in June, July, and August in the Lake Toba area and the valleys to the north and south of it.[63] To a lesser degree the same phenomenon occurs in the valleys of West Sumatra. This season is critical for shifting cultivators to burn off, and for the rice to ripen satisfactorily.

For these reasons agrarian historians are unsurprised that the high valleys produced the earliest concentrations of settled rice agriculture. These highland farmers moved to the coastal areas chiefly in the late 19th and 20th centuries. Some, like the Banjarese at the end of the 19th century, appear to have extended their cultivation to the swampier delta areas when the pressure of humans on resources was such as to make the draining and cultivation of those swamps cost-effective. Elsewhere it was colonial intervention in the form of

62   An Indonesian Frontier

drainage and irrigation, often intended in the first instance to serve Western plantations, which was the stimulus for opening new lowland areas for rice. At the end of the colonial period some of the most heavily populated parts of Indonesia were the Brantas delta and the northern coast of Java from Cirebon to Demak, where Dutch engineers had regulated the flood-prone lowlands.

2. Health

It is too easy to point to malaria as the chief reason why highlands were relatively healthier than lowlands until modem times. Pierre Gourou is the most emphatic proponent of the view that all Southeast Asia's problems were caused by the anopheles mosquito.

> It attacks something like one-third of the human race, but in practice all the inhabitants of the hot, wet belt may be considered to be more or less infected [...]. [After citing horrific figures for deaths] the most serious fact perhaps is that one death from malaria corresponds to at least 2,000 days of illness. Undoubtedly, malaria is largely responsible for the poor health, small numbers, absence of enthusiasm for work, stationary demographic character, and backwardness of tropical peoples.[64]

A.W. Nieuwenhuis in 1930 also believed that centuries of exposure to malaria was the reason Indonesians were smaller, sicker, and less dynamic than Polynesians, with each generation becoming physically and intellectually weaker.[65]

But even Gourou conceded that among the peasants of the Tongking delta malaria was not a great problem, since most of the anopheles vectors in Southeast Asia did not breed in muddy ricefields. The same applied to heavily populated rice-bowls in Java. But the most fatal seemed indeed to be the lowland areas of the "empty centre" of pre-colonial Southeast Asia in Malaya, eastern Sumatra and southern and western Borneo, where *Anopheles umbrosus* ruled the coastal swamps, and *Anopheles sundaicus* took over as soon as the swamp forests were cleared. In this region one was really safe from malaria only above 2,000 feet or 600 metres — where most of the

Sumatrans made their homes. A recent thesis by Peter van der Brug has shown convincingly that the appalling mortality of Batavia between 1733 and 1776, when 50 per cent of VOC soldiers died within a year of reaching the city, was caused by the depredations of *Anopheles sundaicus* once brackish fish-ponds were developed immediately adjacent to the city. Those élite Dutch who could afford to build their mansions only a few kilometres inland survived the epidemic.[66]

There were other factors than malaria. Water-borne diseases such as typhoid and cholera must have killed far more in the lowlands, where clean water sources were rare and floods particularly dangerous, than in highlands where the clear water of mountain streams could often be piped or carried to settlements. Coastal and river-mouth cities were the worst death-traps of all. Certainly the historical sources for 19th-century Sumatra suggest that highlanders were healthier and better formed.[67] Even well into the 20th century highlanders believed their homelands far healthier than the coasts. "Coolness is associated [by the Rejang] with fertility, peace and sound health. The Malays, by contrast, live in a warm climate [...] there is much disease and the people are poor and miserable. These images conform in most respects to the facts."[68]

These relative advantages were reversed in the 20th century. The "taming" of the lowlands through drainage of swamps, the felling of forest, and the extension of rice paddies, together with the much better provision of clean water and health facilities in cities and more accessible areas, has made the lowlands much healthier places to live today.

3. *Statelessness*

In Indonesia the state has always been essentially coastal and sustained by foreign resources, while the highlands have been miracles of statelessness, tenuously held together by kinship systems and ritual obligations rather than bureaucracy.

In the Mediterranean context Fernand Braudel sought to explain why mountains were the "asylum of liberty" by reference to their

64 An Indonesian Frontier

relative emptiness: "the population is so inadequate, thinly distributed and widely dispersed as to prevent the establishment of the state, dominant languages, and important civilizations".[69] This cannot be the reason in the pre-colonial archipelago, where I have shown population densities to have been relatively high in upland valleys and plateaux. The Batak, Minangkabau, and Rejang certainly did establish complex civilizations in these valleys, with their own writing systems, but without giving rise to a recognizable state. Minangkabau and Batak kings were charismatic or magical figures who projected their power outwards but did not *rule* their own people.[70]

So persistently has each step towards stronger states in the archipelago arisen from trading ports, with external aid and inspiration, that one is inclined to seek the indigenous political dynamic in a genius for managing without states. Indic, Chinese, Islamic, and European ideas and actors each inspired state forms more ambitious and effective than those that went before.[71] With some exceptions in Java and Bali, all states in the archipelago have been based at river mouths or strategic coastal locations. They absorbed some of the interior people and established loose relations of tribute with others, but most highland populations defended their autonomies by a mixture of guerrilla warfare, diplomatic flexibility, and deliberate exaggeration of myths about their savagery. Masashi Hirosue (1996) has recently revived persuasively an argument that the ferocity of Batak cannibalism was deliberately exaggerated by Bataks to ensure that they were left in peace by coastal rulers and alien adventurers. Some of the highlanders of South Sumatra consciously designated themselves as freemen *(orang mardika)*, who paid no tax and owed no obligations to the *raja* of the river-mouths, nor to the Dutch and British.[72]

In the 17th and 18th centuries the establishment of European colonial power at fortified coastal strongpoints probably tended to drive Indonesian populations further into highlands beyond their reach. The VOC discouraged the local population from settling near Batavia and other forts for strategic reasons. Villagers sought to escape labour burdens imposed by the Dutch or British Companies, as well as periodic retribution, by retreating further inland. This

The Colonial Displacement of Sumatra's Population

factor was gradually reversed in the 19th century as the Pax Neerlandica spread in the lowlands. The low-level war and raiding endemic to the stateless highlands was an increasingly high price to pay for freedom once a novel kind of rule of law became available in the 20th century. Although few surrendered their independence to the colonizer without a fight, the highlanders were fortunate to encounter him at a late period when he also offered positive opportunities for modernization.

4. Security

Those who followed the option of statelessness had to find other means to defend themselves. Mountain barriers and sheer distance were a major asset. State power, particularly in its colonial form, operated primarily by sea. In local warfare hilltop villages had particular defensive advantages.

Coastal communities with weak states or no states suffered terrible depredations from maritime raiding expeditions. Best documented (since the careful work of James Warren) is the Iranun/Balangingi raiding of the 18th and 19th centuries, estimated to have taken 200,000–300,000 captives from coastal areas of the Philippine and Indonesian archipelagos in the period 1770–1870.[73] In the Straits of Malacca area *orang laut* also carried off many people in coastal communities for sale to the prosperous sultanates of Jambi, Palembang, and elsewhere.[74] These raids undoubtedly discouraged people from settling in any areas accessible to raiding vessels.[75]

Lakes are associated with the ethnogenesis of many interior peoples: Toba for the Bataks; Kerinci for the Kerinci; the central Kapuas Lake system for the Ibanic peoples, Tondano for the Minahasa, Limboto for Gorontalo; Poso and Lindu in Central Sulawesi, Tempe and Matano for the origin of Bugis states, and Lanau for the Magindanao and Illanun of Mindanao. The lakes must have been a source of inexhaustible fresh water and of fish, but there may also have been a strategic factor — most apparent in Samosir Island in Lake Toba. When the enemy had to attack by water one could see him coming long beforehand and there was less fear of real surprise.

5. *Culture*

Those who participate in states and live in cities are inclined to categorize those who do not as uncivilized, barbarous, and pagan (in the literal as well as the religious sense). This savage/civilized dichotomy is an ancient one in Southeast Asia, and visitors like Marco Polo, Ibn Battuta and Ma Huan relayed it to wider audiences. In the 16th and 17th centuries Islam in Indonesia (like Christianity in the Philippines) became the major boundary-marker between the civilized and savage, urban and upland, and wars to extend this boundary made it a strongly felt one. The success of this first phase of Islamization among upland Minangkabau and Javanese, on the other hand, eroded the cultural boundary almost completely.

Where it remained strong this cultural boundary no doubt prolonged the highlanders' sense of distinctiveness and apartness from the modernizing state project. Until the 20th century interior Bataks, Torajans, Alfurs, Dayaks, and Dusuns knew that they would be looked at with contempt when trading or migrating to the lowland towns unless they adapted Malayo-Muslim dress, language, diet, and behaviour. As long as that cultural barrier remained high, highlanders seldom migrated voluntarily to the lowlands, which they associated rather with the involuntary movement of enslavement or exile from their own community. For some the domination of lowlands by Europeans was a further reason to avoid them.

The conversion of highlanders to Islam or Christianity marked a crucial breakdown of this cultural barrier in the long term, even if in the short term it sometimes strengthened it. As Mandailing or Besemah became Muslims and Toba Batak, Torajan or Dusun turned to Christianity they embraced the modernizing project of the 20th-century cities. They had an identity they could use effectively in the cities, whether or not a distinctive highland one. The Karo Batak example is instructive here. Although inhabiting the immediate hinterland of Medan, and growing vegetables for it and other lowland cities from virtually the moment a road was put through to the Karo plateau in 1909, they remained suspicious of the lowland and its power structures. Colonial attempts to expand education, notably through the Dutch Protestant Mission, were met with little enthusiasm and even hostility.

The Colonial Displacement of Sumatra's Population 67

Only with the Japanese occupation and the Indonesian Revolution in the 1940s did Karos on a large scale accept that their destiny too lay in the modern state, education, urbanization, and all the associated cultural changes. Having once made that decision, they could not leave their highlands soon enough. Karos are today probably the best-educated of Indonesia's ethnic groups, and one of the most urbanized.[76]

Urban Progress or Colonial Distortion?

The modern world of nation states has no place for mountain "asylums of liberty" which were also pockets of insecurity of life and property. There was no question that the present century would see the highlands of Indonesia, as of other parts of the world, incorporated into a nation state with the usual demands for monopoly of the use of force within fixed borders. The colonial means by which this incorporation came about, for the most part at the turn of the last century, would, however, determine much of what followed.

The Dutch colonial state, the agent of this incorporation, was an extreme form of the sea-based coastal polity. It had been built by naval power, and until the end of the 19th century remained wary of venturing far from the reach of that power. On the one hand this made it possible for highlanders to keep their statelessness longer than their equivalents in other parts of the world. By the time they were forcibly incorporated into the colonial state it was shedding its predatory quality in favour of a modernization project. This undoubtedly enabled highlanders to perceive the positive opportunities embedded within the disaster of colonial conquest, and to seize them more enthusiastically than lowlanders embittered by centuries of conflict. Minahasans, Minangkabaus, Mandailings, and Toba Bataks became the best-educated Indonesians of the first half of this century, joined by Karos and Torajans in the second half.

On the other hand the incorporation of highlands by lowlands was as one-sided a process as could be imagined, with all centres of power, influence, capital, and knowledge being firmly on the coast. No interior or highland centres developed to provide foci of modernization like a Mexico City, Bogota or La Paz; a Delhi or

Lahore; a Nairobi, Entebbe or Johannesburg. Even in areas such as Tapanuli (North Sumatra), Central Sumatra, South Sumatra, and Timor, where the bulk of population, agriculture, and economic opportunity was still in the highlands in 1900, colonial centres remained firmly in Sibolga, Padang, Palembang, and Kupang. The reasons were in part the realities of Dutch military power mediated over three centuries. When one considers the significantly different pattern of Spanish and British colonies, however, it is difficult to avoid a sense that the heritage of the Low Countries lay too heavy on Dutch statesmen for them to conceive a successful city not accessible to ships. Even the attraction of a base among Christian or potentially Christian highlanders could not outweigh the lure of the sea.

Independence did nothing to break this pattern. Officials living in their coastal capitals continued to distrust the highlands, where comforts were few and the reach of government tenuous. Many upland villages continued to be relocated to valley floors, where the people could be reached by government, schools, police, and religious institutions. Once the colonial communications networks were in place, linking highlands to the ports rather than to each other, it was never likely that the pattern could be broken. Aeroplanes and buses did not have to follow the same coastal and lowland routes as ships and railways, but airports and roads were built as if they did. Indonesia's highlands still enjoy a pleasant climate and scenery and the heritage of ancient civilizations. Their most thriving industry is now tourism, but poor communications continue to hold back this industry like all others. Even the low-cost expedient of flying tourists to the highland lakes by seaplane has so far been passed up by established urban interests.

Highlanders are convinced that the route to the modernization they all desire is in leaving the land of their ancestors. The peculiar shape of Indonesia's modern history, and the prominence of the colonial factor in it, helps to explain why the highlands are now assuming the peripheral quality in fact which they always had in the European imagination.

4

The Turkish Connection

THE existence of diplomatic and military relations between Ottoman Turkey and Aceh has been known for centuries. The Portuguese chroniclers, notably Couto and Pinto, kept the memory alive in the West; oral traditions and a few chronicles kept it more vividly before the imagination of the Acehnese; and in Turkey there was a revived interest in the connection at least from 1873. An attempt therefore seems overdue to seek greater precision on these remarkable events, by considering at least the most notable of the sources from the three sides.

For the peoples of Indonesia and Malaysia, the *Raja Rum* has figured as one of the great kings of the world since the earliest Muslim literature. Since the 16th century this title clearly referred to the Ottoman Sultan, the strongest of Muslim monarchs and heir presumptive to the dignity of the Caliphate. Long before the Ottoman rise, however, Persian and Turkish literature used Rum to designate the Byzantine, and occasionally also the Roman Empires.[1] It is clear that the legendary greatness of this distant kingdom owed something to the lustre of all three imperial occupants of Constantinople.

Many traditions of Malaya and Sumatra, in particular, associate *Raja Rum*, the great king of the West, with *Raja Cina* (China), the great king of the East. A typical origin myth is that of Johor, as quoted by William Marsden.[2] Iskandar Dzul Karnain (Alexander the Great) had three sons by the daughter of the King of the Ocean. After a contest between the three brothers in Singapore Straits, the eldest went to the West to become Raja Rum, the second East to become

70 An Indonesian Frontier

Raja China, while the third remained at Johor, to begin the later Minangkabau dynasty. Even as late as Marsden's own time in Sumatra (1771–9) the Sultan of Minangkabau styled himself younger brother of the rulers of Rum and China.[3]

A similar origin myth is that of Kedah, contained in the *Hikayat Marong Mahawangsa*.[4] The story goes that Garuda, the bird of Vishnu, who inhabited the island Langkapuri, made a wager with Suleiman (Solomon — lord of the animal world in Muslim literature) that he could prevent the destined marriage between the son of Raja Rum and the daughter of Raja China. Garuda succeeded in capturing the Chinese princess and bringing her to Langkapuri, and then sank the fleet which was bringing the prince of Rum together with his escort, the hero Marong Mahawangsa. The prince, however, drifted to Langkapuri and there married the princess from China, bringing frustration to Garuda. Meanwhile Marong Mahawangsa established the Kingdom of Langkasuka. Soon after he returned to Rum, leaving Langkasuka to his son, who was the progenitor of the dynasties of Siam (the eldest), Kedah, Patani, and Perak.

Equally fanciful tales are current among the Gayo, who now inhabit the interior of Aceh in Northwest Sumatra though they appear to have come from the coast. They relate that a young child of Raja Rum was conveyed to Sumatra, where the child was brought up by a local fisherman, and in time became the progenitor of the Gayo people.[5]

The list of such traditions could certainly be lengthened. Suffice it to say that when first Ottoman Turkey emerged as a power in the Indian Ocean it became the focus of a considerable heritage of tradition about a mighty kingdom in the West.

Only in Aceh, however, do we find written accounts of contact with Turkey which bear a historic character. The most reliable chronicle of 16th-century Aceh is the *Bustanu's-Salatin*, written in the Acehnese capital by the Gujerati Nurud-din ar-Raniri in 1638. In his usual factual manner, Nurud-din ascribed the opening of relations with Turkey to the Acehnese Sultan Ala'ad-din Ri'ayat Shah al-Kahar (1539–71):

> He it was who created the system of government of Aceh Daru's-Salam and sent a mission to Sultan Rum, to the state of Istanbul,

The Turkish Connection   71

in order to strengthen the Muslim religion. The Sultan Rum sent
various craftsmen and experts who knew how to make guns. It
was at that time that the large guns were cast. It was also he who
first built a fort at Aceh Daru's-Salam, and he who first fought
all unbelievers, to the extent of going to attack Melaka (Malacca)
in person.[6]

The most famous of the "large guns" to which Raniri referred was
known to the Acehnese as *lada sa-cupak* — one (bamboo) measure of
pepper. It lay at the mouth of the Aceh-river until taken to Holland
in 1874 (see Fig. 16 on p. 340), and still bears a Turkish star-motif
along the barrel.[7] Most of the oral traditions which have been strongly
preserved in Aceh about a mission to Turkey are woven around this
fine piece of artillery. At least one chronicle, the Acehnese epic poem
Hikayat Meukota Alam,[8] has preserved this tradition in writing. It
attributes the mission to Iskandar Muda (1607–36), the Acehnese *roi-
soleil* traditionally credited with many of the spectacular achievements
of the early Sultanate. He decided to send an envoy to Istanbul with
money for the support of the holy places, because the Sultan of
Turkey was the greatest among Muslim rulers and had the care of
Mecca and Madina. He sent three ships, laden with *padi, beras* and
pepper respectively. But the crew had such difficulties that they only
reached Istanbul after three years, by which time they had eaten all
the rice, and sold most of the pepper to support themselves. Only *sa-
cupak lada* remained. The envoys were mortified, but Sultan Rum was
magnanimous, and sent them back in state with the great cannon,
which he named himself. He also sent to Aceh twelve *pahlawans*
(war-leaders). These were so skilful that they enabled Iskandar Muda
to build the great fort of Aceh, the palace, and even the famous
Gunongan [more reliably credited to Iskandar Thani (1637–41)].
Sultan Rum had advised Iskandar Muda to kill the *pahlawans* when
they had finished their work. He was at first reluctant to do so, but
the Turks finally alienated everybody by their arrogance, and were
stoned to death.[9]

The story of the *pahlawans* appears to be a special touch of this
poet, but in other respects the story is similar to those which have
been recorded more recently from oral traditions. The latter versions,

72   An Indonesian Frontier

recorded by Snouck Hurgronje in 1891[10] and by Saffet Bey in 1911,[11] have the Acehnese envoys wasting two years in Istanbul rather than at sea. They also stress the existence of a Turkish village in Aceh named Bitay, which the Acehnese derive from Bait ul-mukaddis (Jerusalem). Its inhabitants were said to be the descendants of Syrian artisans from that city, who were sent out by the Sultan of Turkey. According to the version of Snouck Hurgronje, the Ottoman Sultan exempted the Acehnese from sending regular tribute to him as their sovereign. Instead they should honour him by observing the feast of Mohammad's birthday with special zeal. In this way the latter-day Acehnese explained their exceptional devotion to this *Mo'lot* feast. Saffet's version also gives a religious character to the authority of the Turkish Caliph. He was alleged to have sent a sermon to be read in the Acehnese great mosque every Friday.

This oral tradition was strong enough to form an important element in the Acehnese diplomatic offensive in 1873, when their country was invaded by the Dutch. It even entered briefly into the calculations of the Powers. Aceh appealed to Turkey for protection on the strength of the ancient connection between the two countries. The Porte took the idea seriously, and stated in an official offer of mediation in the war, communicated to the Netherlands and other Powers:

> When Sultan Selim[12] carried his victorious arms to the extremities of the Arabian peninsula, of which he made the conquest, the echo of his victories reached as far as the island of Sumatra. The Acehnese sent a deputation to the feet of the conqueror, recognized the supremacy of the powers inherent in his title of Khalif, made an act of submission into the hands of the famous Sinan Pasha, raised the Ottoman flag in their ports and on their vessels, declared themselves vassals of Sultan Selim and asked in return for his high protection. Sultan Selim received these offers favorably. By his orders the Vezir Sinan Pasha sent to the vassal Sultan the cannons and swords of honor which are still to be seen in Aceh.[13]

While the date of the mission thus seems to have been pushed back by the Turks to a period before Aceh's appearance on the international scene, other Acehnese accounts prefer to credit it to the

The Turkish Connection

reign of the great Iskandar Muda. But the mission takes on different shapes to suit the chronicler's purpose. Thus the *Hikayat Atjeh,* a hymn of praise to Iskandar Muda written during his lifetime, makes the incident an opportunity to show how "the account of Djohan Alam [Iskandar Muda] became famous throughout all nations of the earth".[14] The Turkish incident is made to follow the story of an embassy from Siam, which resulted in the greater glory of Iskandar Muda among the nations of the East. Then a delegation arrived from Rum, via Yemen and Mocha, seeking oriental balms to cure the illness of Sultan Muhammad (Mehmed III, 1595–1603). The envoys arrived while Iskandar Muda was warring against Deli (thus 1612), but they were splendidly received on his return. Later the envoys reported back to Sultan Rum on the wonders of Aceh, whereupon the Ottoman ruler declared:

> ...in former times in the providence of God there were two great kings in the world, the prophet Solomon and Raja Iskandar ... Now in our time also in the providence of God there are two great kings in the world. In the west we are the great king, and in the east Sri Sultan Perkasa Alam [Iskandar Muda] is the king who is great and who upholds the religion of God and his Prophet.[15]

Later the Pasha of Yeman confirmed the envoys' account of Aceh from some Acehnese pilgrims in Medina. It was these hajis who brought back to the great Acehnese religious teacher Sheikh Shamsuddin of Pasai the story of all that had occurred in Turkey.[16]

For a yet more fanciful account we might turn to the ever-popular Malay romance of Hang Tuah. This legendary hero of the last years of the Melaka Sultanate is pictured on a variety of adventurous missions for his Sultan. After visits to Majapahit, India and China, he is finally sent to Rum to buy cannon for Melaka. Though much embroidered, the basic story may well be borrowed from the *Bustanu's-Salatin.*[17]

Thus the notion that diplomatic relations were established with Turkey, and cannon received in exchange for tribute, is well established in the indigenous literature. Of the sources mentioned, the *Bustanu's-Salatin* is much the most reliable in matters of chronology. It would

74 An Indonesian Frontier

therefore be reasonable on the basis of the Indonesian materials alone to assume that a relationship of this type was established during the reign of Sultan Ala'ad-din Ri'ayat Shah al-Kahar (1539–71), and that this became the basis for differently dated stories in the other sources. As Charles Boxer made clear, the Portuguese (as well as Turkish) sources regarding this contact also focus almost exclusively on the reign of al-Kahar.[18]

This Portuguese material, and the Turkish archival data now available,[19] make clear that Turkey played a substantial role in the fortunes and alliances of the Muslim states of Southeast Asia during the 16th century. What follows is an attempt to relate Southeast Asian developments to the wider sphere of Turkish and Islamic politics.

As explained in the previous chapter, Aceh emerged as a strong local power by the conquests of Sultan Ali Mughayat Shah (1516?–30). These conquests involved the defeat of substantial Portuguese forces, and made North Sumatra safe from the Western challenge for several centuries to come. Acehnese power during this early period rested in large part on weapons captured from the Portuguese, and probably also on the support of the Muslim commercial element from the old trading centres of Pasai and Pidië. But Aceh was not yet in a position to threaten overseas enemies such as Portuguese Melaka. The relatively inactive decade following the capture of Pasai may have been a period of consolidation, or of internal dispute under Salah-ad-din (1530–9) — "a weakling, not fit to rule", according to Malay sources.[20]

Meanwhile Muslim trade in the Indian Ocean was recovering from the Portuguese onslaught, which had incapacitated it almost completely during the first two decades of the century.[21] The date 1534 given by Boxer,[22] or "a few years" after 1526 by M.A.P. Meilink-Roelofsz,[23] for the first documented Acehnese pepper shipment to the Red Sea forms the background to a new burst of expansion in the late 1530s. It seems more than likely that the Muslim shipping of this period was centred not at Banda Aceh, the capital of the weak Salah-ad-din, but at Pasai, where his energetic brother Ala'ad-din (later Sultan) held local authority.[24] The valley of the Aceh river, behind Banda Aceh, had never produced much pepper, the cultivation of

The Turkish Connection
75

which had long been centred in Pasai and Pidië. F. Mendes Pinto's reference to a treaty giving the Turks a factory at Pasai about 1540 (below) is evidence that the trade continued to be centred there for some time after the shift of the political centre. If the first Acehnese attack on Melaka, in 1537, predated Ala'ad-din's assumption of the throne, it is likely that the expedition was nevertheless launched by Ala'ad-din from Pasai.

The exact date of Ala'ad-din's overthrow of his elder brother is unclear, though it cannot be later than 1539 and may have been as early as 1537.[25] The events leading up to this coup and the beginning of a more energetic period of expansion thus coincide with the major Turkish enterprise in the Indian Ocean — Suleiman Pasha's abortive expedition to Diu in 1537–8.

Following Pinto's account,[26] the major antagonist of Aceh during the late 1530s would have been an extensive Batak state which had access to the north as well as the west coast of Aceh, but whose centre was probably in the region of the Singkil river in the still-Batak area of Tapanuli. The first war between Aceh and the Bataks was ended by a peace favorable to the Bataks.

> The blessings of this peace treaty lasted for only two and a half months, which was all the time the Achinese [king] needed for the three hundred Turks he had been expecting to reach him. They arrived from the Straits of Mecca in the four *naos* [large ships] he had originally sent there with a cargo of pepper, and on their return their holds were filled with many crates of muskets and other arms, including some heavy artillery made of bronze and caste iron.

These hardy warriors with their up-to-date arms enabled Aceh to drive the besieging Bataks back to the hills with considerable losses. A Batak emissary was thereupon sent for help to Melaka, where he awaited the new Governor de Faria and Pinto in June 1539.[27]

This first recorded instance of substantial Turkish help for Aceh must have taken place sometime in 1537 or 1538: thus either just before or just after the great Turkish attempt to smash the Portuguese fleet under Suleiman Pasha, Governor of Egypt. We know that Suleiman

Map 3 The Indian Ocean

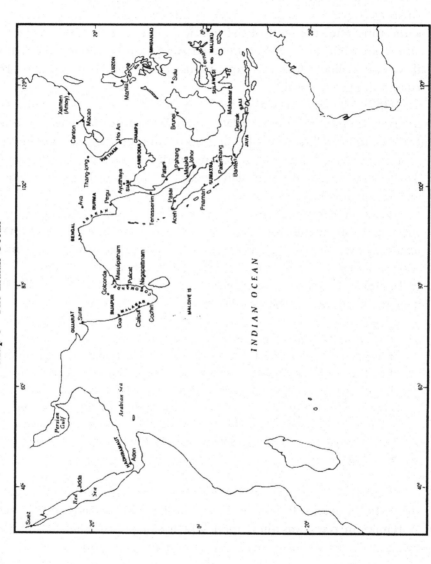

The Turkish Connection 77

despatched envoys to Gujerat and the Arabian ports in 1537 to gain their support for the attack on the Portuguese.[28] Did he also send envoys to Aceh, which must have been well known to him from its pepper shipments? If so, this might have served as a stimulus for the first Acehnese attack on Melaka in September 1537, and also for a correspondence between Johor and Aceh in the autumn of 1538 about a joint attack on the infidels at Melaka.[29] It might, on the other hand, be argued that the Turkish troops noted by Pinto were a more fortuitous windfall for Aceh from Suleiman Pasha's unwieldy army of 20,000, many of whom "dispersed because the people of India had induced them away" during their abortive siege of Diu in September, 1538.[30] In that case the dating of the events described by Pinto would have to be compressed into a few months preceding his arrival in Melaka. Whatever the dating, it also seems likely that the Turkish contact may have provided legitimation in Ala'ad-din's eyes for his seizure of the throne from his elder brother.

The defeat of the 1538 expedition and his own inability to control his agents so far away must have decided the "Grand Turk", Sultan Suleiman the Magnificent, to concentrate his major designs on Europe. Later Turkish initiatives in the Indian Ocean were of minor significance, with the possible exception of the fleet of Piri Bey, smashed by the Portuguese in the Persian Gulf in 1551.[31]

In Aceh itself the influx of Turkish men and weapons enabled Ala'ad-din Ri'ayat Shah al-Kahar to defeat the Bataks and then to turn his forces against Aru, a once-mighty state in northeastern Sumatra. In this he was again successful, according to Pinto's account, because of the continued receipt of Turkish soldiers and weapons from Egypt. One of Aceh's war leaders, Pinto recounts,

> was an Abyssinian by the name of *Mamedecan* [Mahmud Khan] who had arrived from Jidda less than a month before to ratify and swear allegiance to the new league and treaty arranged by the Pasha of Cairo with the King of Aceh in the name of the Grand Turk, in exchange for which he was granted the exclusive rights to a trading factory in the Port of *Pazem* [Pasai]. Leading a company of sixty Turks, forty Jannisseries, and some other Moors from the Malabar coast, this Abyssinian captain gained control of the river fortifications.[32]

Shortly afterward, however, probably still during 1540, the Acehnese were expelled from Aru by a combined force of Malays from Johor, Riau, Siak, Perak and elsewhere led by the Sultan of Johor, who had married the widow of the slain ruler of Aru. In the course of the battles of 1540 for possession of Aru most of the Turkish elite troops on the Acehnese side appear to have perished.[33] Thus once again, Aceh's expansion was halted. During the 1540s and 1550s we hear less of Sultan Ala'ad-din al-Kahar, whose main concern appears to have reverted to strengthening his economic position as the major supplier of pepper for the Muslim trade. Pepper growing spread down the west coast of Sumatra to the south of Minangkabau, and Aceh's commercial control followed with it.

The only major blow by Aceh against the Christian intruders during this period was an attack on Melaka in 1547, but this was not large by Acehnese standards. A detachment of Turks was again noted among the assailants, but the Portuguese chroniclers do not mention any specific alliance. These Turks may be explained in the context of the steadily expanding numbers of traders from the Red Sea who must have been calling at Aceh during the period.

Indeed it was the ruler of Johor, rather than Aceh, who appeared to the Melaka Portuguese as "the man most feared in this fortress", or "our capital enemy" during these two decades.[34] The sources do not provide evidence that the forces of international Islam began to look to Johor to rally their eastern flank. But on a local level Johor did take this role upon itself. In 1550–1 it organized an anti-Portuguese coalition in the name of Islam, which included Japara, Portugal's main rival in the Moluccan spice trade, as well as the smaller Malay states of the Peninsula.[35]

The 1560s, on the other hand, saw Aceh suddenly re-emerging as the formidable eastern bastion of the Muslim counter-crusade against the Portuguese. Charles Boxer warns us against seeing this political connection as the result of a wholly new commercial link with the Red Sea ports. The 1560s were merely the peak period for a trade which had steadily been gathering strength at the expense of the Portuguese since the 1530s. Its growth is explained in part by the increasing volume and strength of Gujerati and Arab shipping in

The Turkish Connection

the Indian Ocean in relation to the Portuguese. In part, also, it relates to events in Indonesia. By the 1560s the rich new pepper plantations must have been established around Tiku, Pariaman and Indrapuri on Sumatra's west coast, and brought under Acehnese control.[36] Moreover, the Muslim merchants of Japara and Banda were steadily eroding Portuguese control of the Moluccan spice trade, especially since the 1550s. Much of their spice was carried to the West through Aceh.

While we can safely assume the existence of a stable and expanding commercial connection between Turkey and Aceh from 1540 onwards, the evidence for political connections is markedly discontinuous. Throughout the 1560s there are Turkish, Portuguese and Venetian references to political relations between the two countries, where there had been silence for the previous two decades.

The Venetian sources are the earliest in documenting a military alliance between Aceh and Turkey. The Venetian ambassador to Constantinople reported as early as June 1562 that an Acehnese ambassador was in the city to ask for artillery to fight the Portuguese.[37] In 1564 Venetian sources already stated that Turkey had sent arms and gunners to Aceh.[38] This early contact is supported by Portuguese reports of a sea battle off the South Arabian coast in March–April 1561. According to Diogo Do Couto's version, the large ship from Aceh which the Portuguese attacked was laden with gold and jewelry for the Sultan of Turkey — suggesting a major Acehnese overture in the early 1560s.[39]

The Turkish sources are fortunately more specific. They include a petition of January 1566 from the Aceh Sultan Ala'ad-din Ri'ayat Shah al-Kahar addressed to Sultan Suleiman as Khalifa of Islam. The Aceh ruler acknowledges the safe arrival of eight Turkish gunners sent earlier by Suleiman, thus confirming the success of the 1561–2 embassy referred to by the Venetians. It appeals repeatedly to the Turkish Sultan to come to the aid of Muslim pilgrims and merchants being attacked by the infidel Portuguese as they travel to the Hejaz. The Muslims of Calicut and Ceylon, who are also harassed by the Portuguese, promise that the non-Muslim rulers of their states will be willing to fight the Franks if the Ottoman Sultan leads the campaign. "If Your Majesty's aid is not forthcoming, the wretched unbelievers will continue to massacre the innocent Muslims."[40]

The ambassador who carried this appeal, named Husain, arrived after a new Sultan, Selim II, had succeeded Suleiman on the throne (Fig. 5). Selim showed extraordinary enthusiasm for assisting the Muslims of the Indian Ocean, and projecting Ottoman power into that region. His initial response, dated 16 Rabi'ul-awal 975H (20 Sept. 1567), accurately summarizes the petition brought by the Acehnese envoy. It conveys Selim's decision to grant the request by sending a fleet of 15 galleys and 2 barks, with numerous master gunsmiths, soldiers, and artillery. The Admiral of Suez, Kurtoglu Hizir Reis, was instructed to command the fleet, to crush Aceh's enemies, and to take the "old fortress" (Melaka?) from the hands of the *kafir*. This letter was sent to Ala'ad-din by the hand of a Turkish envoy, Mustaffa Camus.[41]

Another letter of approximately the same date gave instructions to Kurtoglu Hizir about the expedition. Salaries and provisions for the men would be provided for a year, after which the Sultan of Aceh would have to support them if he still required them.[42] The scale of Selim's ambitions in the Indian Ocean are indicated by another *firman* to the Governor of Egypt in January 1568, which sketched a similar picture of the depredations of the Portuguese against innocent Muslim pilgrims and traders. In order to facilitate the movement of the great fleet Selim intended to send out to crush the Portuguese, the Governor should have a canal dug between the Mediterranean and the Red Sea. This project may have been 300 years too early in terms of technology, but reflects the global vision of the Ottomans at this moment.

Only a few days before that remarkable authorization of a Suez canal, however, on 5 Rajab 975H (5 Jan. 1568), Selim had to write apologetically to the Acehnese envoy Husain. The Sumatra campaign had had to be delayed because of a rebellion in the Yemen, which the fleet of Kurtoglu Hizir had been diverted to suppress. It would nevertheless take place "next year" (i.e. the Hijra year 976 beginning June 1568).[43]

Beyond this the primary sources do not go. We know about the suppression of the Yemen revolt, finally completed by Sinan Pasha in 1571, but not whether any ships of the fleet did ever proceed to Aceh.

Figure 5 Sultan Selim II of Turkey

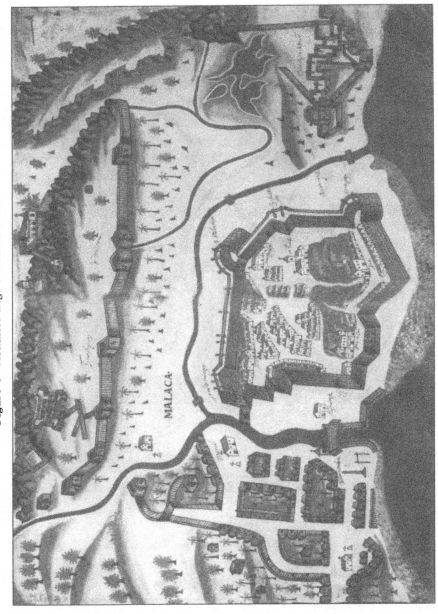

Figure 6 Acehnese siege of Melaka in 1629

The Turkish Connection 83

It is not clear whether the large cannon and the gunsmiths whose arrival in Aceh made an impact on Acehnese and Portuguese sources were relics of this more ambitious expedition of Selim II, or whether they were those sent around 1563 by Suleiman and acknowledged in the 1566 petition.

The most quoted of the Portuguese sources, Couto's *Decade Eight*, clearly refers to the earlier mission. This passage describes the preparations of Sultan "Alaharadi" [Ala'ad-din] to take Melaka, which alone stood in his way to becoming emperor of the Malays after mastering Aru and Johor (generally understood to have been conquered in 1564). He sent rich presents to the Grand Turk, and promises of all the spices of the Indonesian region once Melaka was back in Muslim hands. The Ottoman Sultan responded immediately to his request for aid, sending "500 Turks, many large bombards, abundant ammunition, many engineers and masters of artillery".[44] Other Acehnese ambassadors were sent to "Baroche" [Bijapur?], Demak, Calicut, and the Coromandel coast rulers seeking assistance. All sent help except Demak, which was so afraid of the insatiable ambition of the Sultan of Aceh that it put his ambassadors to death.

All this, Couto continues, was communicated to the Viceroy Antonio Noronha when he assumed office in 1564. He immediately ordered reinforcements for the Melaka fortress, to defend it against the Acehnese attack which eventually took place from 20 January to 25 February 1568. Couto then immediately continues, in the following chapter, to relate the major Acehnese attack of 1568.[45] It may therefore be reading too literally to assume all the preparations attributed by him to Aceh took place before 1564.[46]

It seems clear that the earlier Turkish assistance around 1563 had assisted Aceh's campaigns against Aru and Johor (relative friends of the Portuguese) the following year, and encouraged planning for a more ambitious assault on Melaka. According to Jesuit sources, a Turkish ambassador was in Aceh when some Portuguese vessels arrived there to trade during 1565. Although Aceh had previously not been at war with Melaka, the intervention of the Turk resulted in the Portuguese being given the choice of conversion to Islam or martyrdom.[47] The same Jesuit letters, written in Melaka at the end of

84   An Indonesian Frontier

1566, indicate that an attack on Melaka was expected, and that men and artillery for it had been supplied from Turkey, "for the Turks merchandise with this king, who, every year, sends him many loaded vessels to Mecca".[48]

Couto is quite clear that during the attack of January–February 1568 the Acehnese were aided by about 400 Turks, as well as some help from Japara and Calicut. But the Jesuits insist that Turkish assistance to Aceh continued after the failure of that attack. A letter from Melaka at the end of 1568 reported that the Melakans were still living in fear, because the Sultan of Aceh was continuing his warlike preparations, and his alliances with Muslims in India, Malaya and Java. Because of his great commerce with Turkey, "the Turk provides him with men, gunners and artillery with which he makes war against us".[49] This pressure was maintained, and gave the Portuguese some of their most anxious moments in Asia, until in 1570–1 Bijapur, Ahmadnegar (Gujerat), Calicut and Aceh launched a concerted offensive against Portuguese possessions. This offensive was halted in a series of notable battles, particularly at Melaka on 21 October 1570.[50]

Combining our various sources, the following reconstruction of the events of the 1560s appears the most probable. The growing commerce between the Red Sea and Sumatra must have brought a steady trickle of Turkish traders and adventurers to Aceh, whose military expertise often proved useful to Aceh. The Portuguese attacks against this commerce from 1554 encouraged plans for larger scale attacks against the Portuguese menace. From as early as 1561–2 Aceh was sending envoys to Constantinople to procure supplies and men, and to try to interest the Ottoman Sultan in a major military operation. These efforts succeeded in obtaining substantial reinforcements of Turkish gunners at least by 1564, when they may have helped Aceh to make a military comeback by conquering Aru and Johor. Some arms were probably also purchased. The Acehnese embassy of Husain, which probably covered the years 1565–8, came close to achieving a more spectacular success. After the delay caused by the death of Suleiman in 1566, Selim II was sufficiently impressed by the opportunities in the

The Turkish Connection

Indian Ocean to decree a major expedition. His decision, taken in the autumn of 1567 soon after he had established himself in power, appeared to presage a historic change of direction for Turkish policy, as indicated by the Suez canal project. The positive outcome of the mission must have been known in Aceh well before the end of 1567, and produced immediate preparations for an attack on Melaka. On January 20th the attack began without the expected Turkish fleet, probably because Ala'ad-din had already heard the bad news that Kurtoglu Hizir had been diverted to Yemen, but could not delay his own plans once the preparations for an attack had been finalized.

Kurtoglu Hizir and his fleet never reached Aceh. But the importance the Acehnese give to the cannon, the flag, and the gunsmiths makes it reasonably certain that these at least were sent, along with some sort of imperial message. They probably reached Aceh during 1568 or 1569, and strengthened her considerably in relation to her Indonesian rivals. They must also have encouraged further thoughts of a pan-Islamic front against the Portuguese, which had its culmination in the manoeuvres of 1570–1.

The burst of Islamic solidarity with Indian states soon faded, but its effects in the Indonesian region were felt for another decade. Indeed the death of Ala'ad-din Ri'ayat Shah al-Kahar in 1571 appears to have reduced some of the fears of Aceh among her neighbours. His successor Ali Riayat Shah (1571–8) showed a more genuine desire to win Johor round to an alliance against the *kafir*. It was probably in the early 1570s that he sent one of the great cannon he had received from Turkey to Johor to symbolize this alliance.[51] In 1573 Aceh appealed successfully to the militant Queen of Japara for a joint attack on Melaka, which took place in stages during 1573 and 1574. The Japara fleet arrived before Melaka only after the Acehnese had retired. Johor, too, played a supporting role in this alliance, as the Japara ships were reported to have called there on their way to the attack.[52] The alliance with Johor appears to have flourished thereafter for the remainder of Ali Riayat Shah's reign in Aceh. According to one Portuguese account it was sealed by a royal marriage between the ruling houses.[53]

The two decades from 1560 to 1580 must be seen as the highest point for the military fortunes of Islam in Southeast Asia. During this period the Portuguese were consistently on the defensive. Aceh dominated the Straits of Malacca, with fitful support from Johor and Japara, while the Muslim traders of Japara, Gresik, Ternate and the Banda islands gained the upper hand in the eastern archipelago. How much weight should we give to Turkish intervention in bringing about this greater militance and cohesion on the part of the Muslim states?

The failure of the Muslim powers to unite in the 16th century should not surprise us. There were no precedents in Southeast Asia, and few in the Muslim world, for states to undertake a joint enterprise on a basis of mutual equality and respect.[54] Boundaries were not clearly defined, and the strongest states were influenced by notions of universal empire inherited from the older Indianized states. Given in addition the basic commercial rivalry of many of the states, it is small wonder that the ambitions of the strong were always suspect.

More remarkable than this background of disunity, it seems to me, are the tentative ventures that were made during the 1560s and 1570s towards a Muslim alliance. Islam was the only basis for such an alliance. Nineteenth-century evidence supports the conclusion that the ideal of the unity of the ummat under a sole Caliphate had particular weight for otherwise disunited Muslims in Southeast Asia. The Malay literature suggests that this was no less strong in the 16th century. At a point in time when the illustrious name of Rum and the prestige of the Caliphate were supported by the immense military power of Suleiman the Magnificent, the possibility of a common crusade under Turkish leadership need not have seemed absurd.

Of course we should not press this too far. The only Muslim powers in Southeast Asia which appeared susceptible to the pan-Islamic ideal were Aceh, Japara, Ternate, Gresik, and to some extent Johor. As Meilink-Roelofsz has reminded us, these were all states which participated in the Muslim spice trade from Ternate through Java and Aceh to the west. Consequently they shared the international currents of the Muslim world.

It was otherwise with the agrarian heartland of Java, whether this was centred politically at Demak, Pajang or Mataram. Except for a

The Turkish Connection

brief phase under Demak at the beginning of the 16th century, this region was economically and culturally more self-sufficient. Banten, however, is an odder omission from the list of Muslim allies. Founded by the crusading Falatehan, who had left his native Pasai in protest against Portuguese control there, it remained a part of the cosmopolitan Muslim maritime world. Yet like Brunei and a few smaller states it was seldom at odds with the Portuguese. This must be attributed to Portuguese commercial rivalry with Aceh for access to Sumatran pepper and supremacy in shipping it to Europe. Probably because of Aceh's obstructionism in the West, Banten seems to have sent most of its pepper to China and Portuguese Melaka.[55]

If we accept the importance of Turkish intervention on Southeast Asian alliances, should we agree with the Jesuit who argued that the Sultan of Aceh was "vehemently opposed to all Christians, spurred on to this by the Turks?"[56] The above account would lead rather to the conclusion that the Acehnese took the initiative for the Turkish alliance. During the early 1560s Sultan Suleiman was fully occupied with his push to the west, and can have had little thought of eastern adventure. Indeed it seems possible to argue that it was precisely this Acehnese initiative which drew Turkish attention once more to the Indian Ocean, after Suleiman had abandoned it in 1540. An historian of Ottoman expansion has suggested 1570 as a date when the abler Turkish statesmen were considering a shift in emphasis from the Mediterranean in view of the newly realized importance of oceanic strategy.[57]

This new-found emphasis came to naught because it coincided with the beginning of the decline in Turkish power. Suleiman was the last of the really masterful Ottomans. The empire was kept in order for a considerable time after his death in 1566 by the talented ministers he had gathered around him — especially the Vezir Sokolli. At the latter's death in 1578 the empire became a prey to weakness and corruption at the centre, leaving the Janissaries as the effective power.[58] The last Turkish enterprise in the Indian Ocean was the very individualistic one of Ali Beg (1580–9) who relied more on bluff than power in gaining brief recognition from a number of East African states. His capture by the Portuguese in 1589 ended Ottoman naval power east of Aden.[59] The deterioration of Ottoman power in the

88   An Indonesian Frontier

Yemen, complete by 1635, removed even the base from which earlier fleets had set out.

In Aceh, too, a period of weakness was inaugurated by the death of Sultan Ali Riayat Shah in June 1578. After a rapid succession of three rulers, Ala'ad-din Mansur Shah was called from Perak to assume a more shaky throne, and was not well obeyed by his new subjects, according to a Portuguese source.[60] The alliance with Johor collapsed, and war had broken out again by 1582. The Portuguese could again rely on the passive support of one or the other of their Muslim neighbours.

In India the Portuguese were able to establish cordial relations with the Moghul ports in Gujerat towards the end of the century, and to dominate even more the trade of the western Indian ocean. The traffic in Gujerati ships between Aceh and the Red Sea survived at least to the end of the century,[61] but quickly dwindled with the coming of English and Dutch shipping to Aceh. In their dealings with Aceh both Britain and Holland were careful to stress their opposition to Spain/Portugal, and their friendship with Turkey.[62] Thus the simple opposition between the forces of Islam and the "Franks", which had been fought for a century on so many fronts, no longer matched the realities of the period.

Though the political link with Turkey appears to have been almost completely broken after 1580, Aceh at least retained a measure of Turkish influence for some time to come. This was most notable in the military field. Acehnese military tactics, military engineering and artillery were famous long after their Turkish tutors had departed. An example was their capture of Deli in 1612 by the use of trenches, even though the town was skilfully defended by the Portuguese.[63] The palace guard maintained by Iskandar Muda (1607–36) was remarkably similar to the Turkish body of Janissaries. It was composed of military slaves, captured from the enemy when young and trained rigorously in the arts of war.[64]

The control of these remarkable military resources on the Turkish model placed Acehnese rulers on a perilous pinnacle of power. They were in a position to tyrannize over their subjects to a greater degree than most Indonesian rulers. In the case of Iskandar Muda in

The Turkish Connection

particular, the picture we have of a court riddled with suspicion and intrigue, of a closely guarded palace reserved for the numerous royal women, is more reminiscent of a Middle-Eastern state than the more patriarchal style of Indonesian sultanates. It was clearly force, rather than the proverbial loyalty of the Malays, which kept the Acehnese state together.[65]

Culturally, too, Aceh retained a closer contact with the Muslim countries of the West — though here it was the Arabs rather than the Turks who had something to offer. From the 1570s the chronicles are dotted with the names of eminent theologians from Egypt, the Hejaz, Yemen and Gujerat who had come to teach in Aceh.[66] Schools flourished, and a knowledge of Arabic was widespread among the upper classes. Many of Aceh's diplomatic letters in the early 17th century appear to have been written in Arabic, including the one sent to Queen Elizabeth with Lancaster.[67]

To conclude, then, it is possible to discern two distinct periods at which Turkish intervention was significant in Southeast Asia. The first took place in connection with Suleiman Pasha's expedition to Gujerat in 1538; the second during the peak of the commercial contact with the Red Sea in the 1560s. In both cases Turkish influence was applied through, and to the benefit of, Sultan Ala'ad-din al-Kahar. But in both cases, and particularly the second, this encouraged an unusual degree of cooperation among some Muslim states of Southeast Asia. The diplomatic contact of the 1560s between Turkey and Aceh reached the highest level and was important in the subsequent direction of both Turkish and Acehnese policy. It has been commemorated in a variety of forms in Malay and Acehnese literature.

90   An Indonesian Frontier

Appendix

Some Turkish Sources for the "Sumatran Expedition"

The existence of Turkish references to the "Sumatran expedition" of the 1560s was first brought to the attention of Southeast Asian historians by the article by Juynboll and Voorhoeve in the new edition of *Encyclopedia of Islam*.[68] Unfortunately the effect of condensation and the misprint in the conversion of the only Muslim date given make it in some respects a misleading reference. Salih Ozbaran of the School of Oriental and African Studies (SOAS) in London and the University of Istanbul was patient enough to go through some of the Turkish articles with me, providing a rough translation. As few Southeast Asian historians have a knowledge of Turkish, it may be useful to expand here on the content of the various sources. I am very grateful to Mr Ozbaran, and also to Professor Bernard Lewis, for the help they have given.

Much the most important source is an article by the naval historian Saffet Bey, which appeared in two parts in the standard journal of Ottoman history during 1912.[69] Though not in scholarly form, it is based on some letters in the Ottoman archives as well as some published sources available to him. The article begins by retelling the *lada sacupak* story from "European sources" — which can hardly be other than the English translation of Snouck Hurgronje's *The Achehnese*. Saffet then quotes in full the text of Sultan Selim's first *firman* on the subject, dated 16 Rabi'ul-awal 975 (20 Sept. 1567). The *firman* first recapitulates the petition of the Acehnese "Vezir", Husain. Aceh, it is claimed, has been left alone to fight the kafirs up till now, and requests the help of Turkey's experienced soldiers. In the regions around Aceh there are 24,000 islands, whose Muslim inhabitants are oppressed by the kafirs. The Portuguese have also bombarded and taken prisoner merchants trading between Aceh and Mecca. Furthermore "the kafirs of Calicut and Ceylon" are harming the Muslim inhabitants of those places. Husain believes that an Ottoman fleet in those parts would be able to crush the kafirs. He also requests that gunsmiths be sent to Aceh, and that orders be given to the governors of Yemen, Aden, Mecca and elsewhere to assist Turkish soldiers on their way to Aceh. The *firman*

The Turkish Connection

concludes by granting Husain's petition. Fifteen galleys (*kadirqa*) and two barks (*barça*) are ordered to proceed from Suez, with a master gunsmith, seven other gunsmiths, some soldiers, cannon, and smaller guns (*tüfenk*). The High Admiral Kurtoglu Hizir is given command of the expedition, with orders to crush Aceh's enemies, to defend the Muslim religion, and to take the old fortress belonging to the kafirs. Kurtoglu should make arrangements for paying the salaries of his men.

The remainder of the first part of Saffet's article is taken up with some comments on this letter, followed by a description of Suleiman Pasha's 1538 expedition and of Turkish-Portuguese relations.

The second part begins with some further comments about the Acehnese embassy, which appear to be based on some unnamed Turkish books and the evidence of "a man here called Lutfy, who went to India and returned". Saffet states that the Acehnese ambassador stayed in Istanbul for two years, in a special place for foreign envoys, while Suleiman was away on the Szigetvar campaign. Selim II, however, welcomed the envoy after his father's death, and sent him on a Turkish vessel to Alexandria. From there he was accompanied to Aden by other Turkish officials. Later the Aceh expedition was prepared in Suez, consisting of altogether 19 galleys and three barks. Kurtoglu Hizir Reis was to be commander and Mehmet Bey deputy commander. They were to be at the disposal of the Acehnese Sultan for as long as he required them, though they had salary and provisions for only one year.

To reinforce this last information Saffet quotes two further letters from the Ottoman archives. The first instructed Kurtoglu to besiege the kafirs' fort by land while his deputy Mehmet remained with the ships. The second, dated 5 Rajab 975 (5 Jan. 1568), advised Sultan Ala'ad-din Ri'ayat Shah that the expedition had been delayed because of the rebellion in Yemen. "God willing the rebellion will be crushed, and the expedition will proceed next year."

These are the only archival sources given. Saffet goes on to describe Kurtoglu's activities in the Yemen, about which, he says, there is abundant literature.

He quotes two later Turkish writers of the mid-17th century who refer to Aceh. These are the geographers Katib Celebi and Ebu Bekr

Dimiski, in their works respectively entitled *Cihannùa* and *Cografya*. They appear to say little about the Acehnese save that they were good fighters, who had learned how to make guns and swords from the Turks.

Saffet closes his article with two interesting informants of his own time. The first is a member of the Acehnese royal family who met Saffet in October 1911, and told him the following story: Long ago Acehnese ambassadors went to Turkey seeking help. Two ships were sent in return to Aceh, with many soldiers and craftsmen. The guns and flags from these two ships remained in Aceh until the war against the Dutch. Neither ships nor men ever returned to Turkey. They established a Turkish village in Aceh, whose inhabitants still regard themselves as Turkish, though they have assimilated completely into the Acehnese culture. With the two ships there also came a *firman*, which was still in the hands of the last Raja.[70] There also came with the ships a sermon, subsequently read in the mosque every Friday. There were numerous guns, large and small. A Turkish ambassador named Seyyid el-Kemal was subsequently made commander of an Acehnese province. Some *ulama* also came with the ships, among them Sheikh Abdur'rauf, Teungku Kuala.[71]

Finally, Saffet quotes a Turkish traveller, Abdul Aziz, who visited Aceh in 1898 and met the *uleëbalang* of Meureudu, Teuku Suleiman. This *uleëbalang* told him that there was one old Turkish cannon in the Governor's residence, and one in Java. Abdul Aziz related further, "I saw in Aceh a Turkish cemetery and other people resembling Turks, though they know unfortunately little about Turkey they still say they are Turks. I saw nothing else of interest."

The other Turkish historians who have noted the Aceh affair appear to rely on Saffet. But what is hypothesis in Saffet's work has become fact for the later writers. I.H. Uzuncarsili, in his standard *Osmanli Tarihi*,[72] relates that Aceh sent an embassy to Istanbul in 1565. The ambassador had to wait for two years, until Selim II accepted his appeal and decided to despatch over 20 ships. After the expedition was diverted to Yemen, the equipment and gunsmiths were sent on to Aceh in two ships. The Turks who were sent to Aceh settled there.

The Turkish Connection

The nationalist historian Danismend[73] goes further in asserting the certainty of the expedition to Aceh, and does not even mention the diversion of Kurtoglu's fleet to Yemen. He stresses the sovereignty which Selim assumed over Aceh, and concludes by pointing out that after Ottoman rule expanded to much of Europe, Asia and Africa, it finally reached as far as Aceh.

5

Trade and the Problem of Royal Power in Aceh: Three Stages, c. 1550–1700

The Problem

BETWEEN about 1400 and the mid-17th century there was a remarkable development of organized trading networks in southern Asia, from the Red Sea in the West to Canton in the East, embracing much of the maritime Malay world. This dynamic force provided the economic base not only for the Islamization of the Malay world, but for the rise of the various maritime kingdoms, which have given that world much of its modern character.

What foreign trade had provided, foreign trade could take away. The more effective Dutch monopoly of the 17th century, supported by local Chinese trade, had a reverse effect to the commercial stimulus, which small Gujerati, Malabari, Coromandel, Arab, Portuguese and Chinese traders had provided in the 15th and 16th centuries. Yet the maritime states of Southeast Asia were much more than the passive victims of this process. Their success or failure depended much on their capacity to grow with their commercial environment, to provide it with the stability, the legal machinery, and above all the "protection of person and property ... against the whim of an arbitrary sovereign", which Meilink-Roelofsz[1] saw as essential to the nascent capitalism of the same or earlier periods in Antwerp and Venice, Cairo and Aleppo, or even Ahmedabad and Golconda. Insofar as foreign trade remained

Royal Power in Aceh

"foreign" in various Southeast Asian states, the major reason seems frequently to have been the lack of security and autonomy for the domestic merchant *vis-à-vis* the state.

It is this relationship between commercial power and state power, which I wish to explore in the particular case of Aceh. How far was the role of the ruler limited by convention, contract, or ideology? Was the state conceptually and organizationally separable from its ruler? What power and prerogatives within the system were enjoyed by the merchants of the capital on the one hand, and territorial barons on the other? It seems to me these questions lie close to the heart of the problem of transition to the modern world, at least as that is understood in our capitalist tradition. The answers to them, if they could be found, would have more than historical interest.

The Historical Legacy in Northern Sumatra

Although this is no place for further speculation about the origins of the Acehnese state, a few of the peculiar features of north Sumatra may usefully be recapitulated.

1. Prior to 1520 the north Sumatran coast was divided among a number of completely distinct port-states, none of which appeared even to claim suzerainty over the others. Marco Polo's fascinating picture of the region in 1292 includes the insistence that "There are eight kingdoms on the island [all of those described lying in northern Sumatra], and eight crowned kings...each of the eight kingdoms has its own language."[2] Despite the subsequent commercial and cultural flowering of Pasai and Pidië in particular, they remained, like Lamri in what would become Aceh Besar, essentially port-states in conflict with the less civilized people of the interior. The Aceh Sultanate created by Sultan Ali Mughayat Syah's conquest of the whole northern coast (1520–4) was essentially a new beginning, made possible only by the intolerable intervention of the Portuguese. Although some chronicles do attribute supernatural origins to the ruling dynasty, the most reliable, the *Bustanu's-Salatin*, begins abruptly: "The first to rule the kingdom of Aceh Darus-Salam was Sultan Ali Mughayat Syah."[3]

2. Even within the separate north Sumatran states before Aceh, cosmic Indian-influenced conceptions of the state appear less well established than in South or Central Sumatra or in Java. Even when account is made of the underdeveloped study of several promising pre-Islamic sites around Banda Aceh, Hindu-Buddhist concepts appear a more distant part of Aceh's heritage than in Java, and the Islamic experience correspondingly longer. North Sumatrans became notorious for their sceptical attitude to kingship, to the extent that Tomé Pires (1515) could write of Pasai kings:[4]

> The grandees of Pase have from time to time agreed that whoever kills the king becomes king; and they say that on one day there were seven kings in Pase, because one killed the other and another the other; no disturbance whatever in the city or among the people and merchants whether king be killed or live.

Figure 7 The *Gunongan* in Aceh, built by Sultan Iskandar Thani (1637–41)

Royal Power in Aceh

3. The valley of the Aceh river itself, which became the political centre of Aceh after 1520 — known as Aceh Besar (Groot-Atjeh or Acheen Proper) — was not itself an important source of export produce. Pepper, and later betelnut, was grown on the northern coast; pepper, camphor, gold and other exports came from the ports of the west coast; tin was exported from Perak. Aceh's consistent policy was to dominate these regions politically, deny their produce to the enemy Portuguese, and as far as possible direct their foreign trade through its capital. It seems likely that Pasai continued to be the major Acehnese export port as late as 1539,[5] but thereafter strenuous and largely successful measures were taken to ensure the political and commercial subordination of these production centres.

Stage 1: The Great Mercantile *Orangkaya* — to 1589

Much of the credit for the viability of the Acehnese state, fashioned as it was from diverse peoples and traditions, must go to its great 16th-century ruler, Ala'ad-din Ri'ayat Syah al-Kahar (1539–71). He conquered Aru on the east coast and Pariaman on the west, establishing his sons as vassal rulers of these regions. He presided over the revival of the Muslim spice trade between his port and the Red Sea, which by the end of his reign was carrying as much as the Portuguese route. He forged an alliance with Turkey and became the scourge of the Portuguese in Melaka (Malacca). The commercial emporium of Banda Aceh must have grown up around his palace.

The Portuguese sources make clear the importance of Acehnese shipments of pepper and other spices to the Red Sea throughout his reign, reaching a peak during the 1560s as described in the previous chapter. After reporting the arrival in Jidda in 1564 of 1,800 quintals (90 tons) of pepper and 3,000 quintals of other spices, carried in 23 Muslim ships, a Portuguese report continued, "These Acehnese are those who most frequent this commerce and navigation."[6] The sources do not reveal how this trade was organized or how much share in it was taken by the ruler. It is difficult to conceive how this spectacular growth could have been achieved, however, unless by attracting wealthy Islamic traders from the whole Straits of Malacca area and

98 An Indonesian Frontier

beyond to shelter under the powerful protection of al-Kahar. For some time to come the city of Banda Aceh was noted for its polyglot population, and the language of the city was Malay rather than Acehnese. A probable picture is of a trade largely financed and organized by a varied group of Muslim merchants whose origins were in Pasai, Pidië, Melaka, Gujarat and South India, but who increasingly became involved in Aceh's state system, its court ceremonies and its wars.

Following the death of al-Kahar and of his son Ali Ri'ayat Syah (1571–9), the powerful men of the capital appear to have established complete domination over the throne. Five rulers were dethroned in the space of ten years, without apparent disapproval from later court chroniclers of the 17th century. At three points during this period the *Hikayat Atjeh* describes the decision of "all the rajas and *hulubalang*" to overthrow a ruler or appoint a successor. Sultan Sri Alam was overthrown in 1579 because he too recklessly disposed of the treasury to his followers;[7] his successor Zainal Abidin was killed a few months later because of his cruelty and his obsession with hunting and animal-fights;[8] the *rajas* and *hulubalang* finally offered the crown to Ala'ad-din Ri'ayat Syah Sayyid al-Mukamil in 1589 (the chronicler having overlooked two intervening kings).[9] The chronicles do not help us to identify these rajas and *hulubalang*, to whom the *kadi* is sometimes added, although leadership was attributed to the Maharaja Lela and someone called Malik az-Zahir. It is too early to see in the reference to *hulubalang* (Acehnese *ulèëbalang*) the territorial aristocracy of the 18th and 19th centuries.

Western sources are more informative about the great men of the country, whom they invariably call *orangkaya*. The Malay sources use *orangkaya* as part of the title of the great officers of state, but for European visitors of the 17th century the expression appeared to designate a top class of nobles, courtiers and officials. Francois Martin remarked that they distinguished themselves by growing a long nail on their thumb and little finger "showing that they do not do manual work".[10] Both Best[11] and Beaulieu[12] were given the title and status of *orangkaya putih*, entitling them to privileged access to court.

Royal Power in Aceh

Beaulieu, describing a period 30 years before his own residence in Aceh, gives a vivid picture of the *orangkaya* in the days of their great wealth and power before 1589; in this period,

> the Orangkayas lived extravagantly, and following the affections of their nature were addicted to novelties, insolent, and proud. The great wealth their predecessors had left them, in lands and houses in the city, as well as gold and silver, supported this life; no kings have oppressed them nor foreign nation plundered them. The town was six times as populous as it is at present, and so crowded that it was difficult to move in the streets. The wealth of the island being scattered in diverse hands, there was such a great number of merchants that there was no city in the Indies

Figure 8 An *orangkaya* (merchant-aristocrat) of Aceh, sketched by Peter Mundy in the 1630s

where trade so flourished. Moreover there was no *Alfandegue* [customs office], or other duties than that of the *tjap*, so that merchants could do their business in a fortnight ... The orangkayas had beautiful, large, solid houses, with cannon at their doors, and a large number of slaves, both as guards and servants. They went out superbly dressed, with large retinues, respected by the people. Such great power very much diminished royal authority, and even safety, for the principal orangkayas had such authority and power, that when they tired of the domination of one king, they massacred him in order to install another. Thus a king was very lucky if he enjoyed his crown for two years. If he lasted longer it was with such exertion and such obligations towards several orangkayas, that nothing remained of his dignity except the title.[13]

No doubt this picture was exaggerated, at least in the scale of commercial decline it depicted. Nevertheless there is sufficient corroboration from other sources to suggest a situation in which the merchant-officials of the city had considerable autonomy and power, without succeeding in establishing a stable, institutionalized basis for the state.

Stage 2: (1589–1636): Royal Absolutism

After two successive foreign-born rulers had been installed by these *orangkayas* an Acehnese dynasty regained the throne in 1589 in the person of Ala'ad-din Ri'ayat Syah Sayyid al-Mukammil (1589–1604). We know that this man was a descendant of the dynasty of Dar al-Kamal, which had ruled in the Aceh valley before its unification: that he was already old, and a distinguished naval leader (perhaps the Orangkaya Laksamana); and that he was initially elected as guardian of a young royal candidate, Raja Asyem, whom he quickly killed.[14] Beaulieu states that the *kadi* (or "great bishop") was among his strongest promoters, and later sources describe a very powerful *kadi*, probably Sheikh Shamsud-din, at his court.[15] The *Hikayat Aceh*, written for his grandson and protégé Iskandar Muda, praises his justice and the prosperity of his realm.[16] Certainly he ended the unstable period when the throne was a plaything of the *orangkaya*. Beaulieu goes

Royal Power in Aceh

much further than this, graphically depicting a complete royal *coup* upon al-Mukammil's accession to the throne. The new king massacred a large number of leading *orangkaya* by stratagem at a feast, justifying this to his people on the grounds that:

> in the past they had made and unmade so many kings at their whim, that they had abolished the whole line .... That as King, he did not wish to be only a shadow, nor to be the plaything of the fickle humours of the Orangkayas, who after having massacred him, would have relapsed into their former disputes, into which they would gradually have drawn the masses, who would have suffered the most; that moreover his intention was to preserve peace for all, impose severe justice on evildoers, and reign equitably.[17]

Having thus broken the power of the *orangkaya*, the new Sultan took steps to ensure they would not rise again:

> he had all the houses of the executed Orangkayas demolished, took their cannon, arms, and most of their furniture into the castle; forbade anyone to build in stone, to have cannon at their houses, or to make defensive trenches within or without ... he provided an example of how future houses should be built, which was of only one story, with matting walls, as they are today....
>
> He treated the Moorish merchants very badly, but was extremely courteous to the English and Dutch, who settled there in his time.[18]

Even if Beaulieu exaggerated the dramatic suddenness of this shift in the balance of power, its occurrence is beyond doubt.[19] The early English and Dutch accounts suggest an autocracy in which there were no major Acehnese merchants except the Sultan himself.

Al-Mukammil's centralizing policy was carried to new heights by his brilliant protégé, ruling as Iskandar Muda (1607–36). Under this mightiest of Acehnese sultans, an absolutist strategy appears to have been conducted deliberately and with astonishing success.[20] A series of military victories in East Sumatra and Malaya achieved the objective of earlier rulers to monopolize the export produce of the region and destroy his major rivals. Tight control was established over the pepper-producing centres of West Sumatra, with Acehnese *panglima* (governors) being replaced every three years and annually called to account.[21] Foreign merchants were forced to come to terms with the Sultan in his capital before they could proceed to any other port. The ruler himself controlled a very large percentage of the pepper for sale within his dominions, and insisted on selling this at a high price before allowing foreigners to buy on the "open" market.[22] Both European and Muslim traders appear to have become increasingly frustrated at the hard bargains the Sultan drove. In 1620–2 the English and Dutch were ejected altogether.

Internally, too, Iskandar Muda's control was extraordinarily complete. His permanent army was only a royal guard (*biduanda* or *hamba raja*)[23] of about 500 men around the *dalam* (royal enclosure), used for carrying out sentences and overawing the populace. Beaulieu describes them as a corps of foreign "slaves", trained in war since their youth in the manner of Turkish Janissaries.[24] Massive armies were raised when needed through the *orangkaya*, each group of men being made answerable to a certain *orangkaya* in time of war. They marched at their own expense and with their own provisions, unless the campaign lasted for more than three months. Royal control was reinforced by a strict check on all firearms, an indication of how the introduction of artillery can tend towards centralization of authority: "The King provides them with arms, of which a register is kept, they being obliged to restore them at their return."[25] Moreover, the families at home were held accountable for the performance of their menfolk in the field.

Beaulieu also informs us that "each of the Orangkayas has a territory (*continent de terre*) under his jurisdiction, the inhabitants of which are under their authority and justice".[26] If the purpose of their territorial role was to ensure men for Iskandar Muda's constant wars, as the paragraph above suggests, then we may reasonably see in such *orangkaya* the *ulèëbalang* (Malay *hulubalang*) who were to come in time to form the territorial aristocracy of Aceh. "He has exterminated almost all the ancient nobility, and has created new ones."[27] During

Iskandar Muda's lifetime, however, such new *orangkaya* were kept under very tight control. According to Beaulieu each was obliged to keep watch, unarmed, in the palace every third night, so that if there was an anti-royal plot at any time at least one-third of the nobility would be in the king's hands.[28]

The accounts we have of Iskandar Muda's Aceh can leave little doubt that we are facing here a true peak of royal power and centralization in the pre-colonial Malay world. Some of the factors which had brought about this situation — commercial expansion of the mart-capital; command of artillery; a particularly masterful ruler — had contributed to the rise of what might be considered modern states on the ruins of feudalism in Tudor England, Capetian France or, perhaps more relevantly, the Venice of the Doges. At this peak of royal absolutism in Aceh, can we see the emergence of truly bureaucratic administration, a developed legal system, financial institutions and the other hallmarks of an impersonal territorial state?

That Iskandar Muda codified and enforced a complex legal system is beyond doubt. Even if surviving versions of the *Adat Aceh* are all more recent, Iskandar Muda's name is always attached to them as the legendary father of the law. Drewes and Voorhoeve's text explicitly attributes the origin of the codified laws to the instructions given by Iskandar Muda to *orangkaya* Sri Maharaja Lela and a number of scribes in the year of his accession.[29] Several foreign accounts mention the working of courts of justice, Beaulieu as usual providing the most detailed picture. He describes four distinct courts with separate jurisdictions: one for the settlement of debts and punishment of defaulters, which sat six mornings a week near the Great Mosque; a criminal court presided over by different *orangkaya* in rotation, where theft was punished by the loss of a limb, or in petty cases by the lash; a religious court under the *kadi;* and a court in the *Alfandegue,* under the Orangkaya Laksamana, for establishing and enforcing commercial laws, especially those touching royal commercial interests.[30]

The scale of Iskandar Muda's operations naturally demanded a relatively large body of officials, though progress towards a professional bureaucracy was very slight. The most powerful officials were the Orangkaya Laksamana (probably the naval genius from whom the

Hikayat Malem Dagang takes its name); the *orangkaya* Maharaja Sri Maharaja, also called Perdana Mentri by the *Bustanu's-Salatin;* and Sheikh Shamsud-din, by now very old, and sharing his religious jurisdiction with a Kadhi Maliku'l Adil.[31] Four *syahbandar* (port officials) and a number of *kerkun* (scribes) were assigned to the administration of commerce, while other *kerkun* had court duties. Four *Penghulu Kawal* were in charge of patrolling the city, particularly at night.[32] These officials were probably not salaried. Commercial officials had on the contrary to make a valuable annual present to the king. They drew their wealth largely from the presents they in turn demanded from merchants.[33] The apparent arbitrariness of such exactions from merchants, and the total dependence of officials on royal favour, does not suggest any substantial development towards professionalization of the bureaucracy.

A more critical deficiency of Iskandar Muda's absolutism in comparison with that which brought European states out of feudalism, however, was its apparent incompatibility with private commercial enterprise. If foreign merchants were invariably disgruntled by the demands the Sultan made of them, the position of local Acehnese trade was very much worse. Iskandar Muda's objective appeared to be to draw as much as possible of the local trade into his own hands, so as to enjoy a monopolistic position towards the foreigners. About 1616 he began to be able to take most of the West Coast pepper to the capital in his own ships, cutting out the local traders who had performed this function.[34] His intense interest in trade as the basis of his whole regime appeared to make him less tolerant of domestic commercial enterprise than even his counterparts in states Wittfogel might have called hydraulic, such as Ayutthaya.

Acehnese tradition, as reflected in all the Malay and Acehnese chronicles, puts Iskandar Muda on a pedestal of glory. Foreigners who moved among the merchants and officials of the capital, however, leave no doubt of the terror the ruler inspired in this class. Beaulieu stressed the frequency with which Iskandar Muda killed the wealthy in order to confiscate their property: "He draws great profit by confiscating the goods of those he daily puts to death ... two causes in particular cost various Orangkayas their life; viz. the good reputation

Royal Power in Aceh

they have among the people, and secondly their wealth";[35] "He has depopulated the whole territory of Aceh, and drained everybody of their money, even all the foreigners who have been there."[36] Thomas Bowrey, visiting Aceh several decades after his death, recorded the dread the leading men still held for Iskandar Muda, "and indeed, by the account they give of him, he was the cruelest Tyrant that many ages afforded".[37] In fairness to this great ruler, we should also quote his own classic defence of his absolutism in a passionate speech to Beaulieu:

> he said his Orangkayas were wicked and cruel, and failed to realise that it was their own wickedness which drew upon them the wrath of God, who made use of him to punish them; That they had no occasion to complain of him, since he had let them live with their wives, children, slaves, and sufficient wealth to nourish and sustain themselves, maintaining them in their religion, and preventing neighbouring kings from taking them as slaves from their homes, or foreigners from robbing them; That he had known Aceh formerly as a haven for murderers and brigands, where the stronger trampled on the weak, and the great oppressed the small; where one had to defend oneself against armed robbers in broad daylight, and to barricade one's house at night; That the reason they hated him was that he prevented their wickedness, extortion, massacres and theft; That they would like to make kings at their own whim, and have them killed when they grew tired of them.[38]

Stage 3: Decline of the Crown; Rise of the Three *Sagi*

The end of royal absolutism was a gradual process. Externally at least, the power of the Acehnese throne already began to decline slowly from its peak after the first major defeat of Iskandar Muda's forces — the disaster before Melaka in 1629 (see Fig. 6 on p. 82). The reduced skill and authority of the rulers who followed Iskandar Muda, and the rapidly growing commercial power of the Dutch after their capture of Melaka (1641), speeded this process. Internally, no change in the system of government was immediately obvious following the

106   An Indonesian Frontier

great king's death in 1636. The style, however, was quickly transformed. Both foreign sources and the chronicles stress the mildness of the rule of Iskandar Thani (1636–41) and the first Queen, Taj al-Alam (1641–75), and the prosperity of the capital under them.[39] In the course of Taj al-Alam's long reign, moreover, fundamental changes were taking place in the balance of power which would ultimately produce a radically different state structure.

The decision to place a woman on the throne was not in itself an attack on absolutism, although its subsequent retention certainly was.[40] Iskandar Muda had killed all his male heirs before his own death, leaving his son-in-law, a prince from Pahang, as the most obvious successor. On this ruler's premature death there was again no male heir. The *orangkaya* appeared to have thrown the capital into confusion for several days, "for each one wanted to be king". Eventually they resolved to crown Iskandar Thani's consort (Iskandar Muda's daughter) as queen in her own right.[41] The great ministers of state quickly established greater power and security than in the past, yet the last say remained with the ruler. The *Bustanu's-Salatin* written during her reign describes her as loving and caring for her subjects "as a mother loves her children".[42] In practice, however, few men were allowed access to her, particularly if it was thought conceivable they might pose as suitors. There were some Elizabethan qualities in the reverence in which her subjects held her, the intense rivalry among her chief ministers which appeared to leave her unscathed,[43] and the recognition that the satisfactory balance within the state would be seriously jeopardized if the Queen were to marry. Even though the political and commercial authority of Aceh in West Sumatra and Perak was rapidly being eroded by the Dutch, the capital was more favourably depicted by travellers than before. Bowrey (1675) tells of its fame "as the place of residence of theire virgin Queene ... as alsoe for theire good laws and government, and the great Traffick and Commerce from most parts of India, China, and South Seas".[44] The impression given by these reports is of a situation satisfactory to the city merchants, where the legal and administrative system developed under absolutism continued, without the royal jealousy which had made life so hazardous for the great and wealthy.

Royal Power in Aceh

It is not surprising, therefore, that the *orangkaya* decided to continue the system by crowning three more queens in succession after the death of Taj al-Alam in 1675. These later queens, however, had none of the status the first had enjoyed as daughter of one mighty king and widow of another. With each new queen, the power wielded by the leading *orangkaya* became more apparent.

It is to the short, otherwise unremarkable, reign of the second queen, Nur al-Alam (1675–8), that the chronicles attribute the creation of the three *sagis* (literally "corners") of Aceh Besar, the most important element in the political structure of 18th and 19th century Aceh.[45] Most Dutch writers followed Snouck Hurgronje[46] in discounting this clear statement, on the presumption that the *sagis* and the system of *ulèëbalangs* must be older than the Sultanate itself. All the available evidence nevertheless confirms the record of the chronicles, as we will attempt to show below, and with different evidence in Chapter 5. While the merchant officials were establishing a congenial regime in the capital, a powerful new force was arising in the agricultural hinterland.

There were three levels of supra-village organization in 18th- and 19th-century Aceh Besar: the *mukim* (parish); the grouping of *mukims* ruled by an *ulèëbalang*; and the *sagi*. The chronicles attribute the original division into *mukims* to Iskandar Muda, who was also a great mosque-builder. Seven Acehnese mosques are attributed to his reign, and the first *mukims* may have been grouped around these. The *Imams* of the *mukims* must, as their name implies, have begun as religious officials, but quickly became secular, hereditary rulers of the *mukim*, distinct from the *imam sembahyang*.[47] The *ulèëbalangs* responsible for a number of *mukims* may, as suggested above, owe their origin to Iskandar Muda's system of mobilizing men for war. The chronicles are silent on this point. Nor do any foreign sources, except Beaulieu's single reference, mention a system of territorial rule in the interior of Aceh Besar. The state was the city and its coastal dependencies.

The oral traditions and genealogies of the Polem family, *panglimas* of the powerful upland *sagi* of the 22 *mukims*, confirm the Chronicles' statement that the *sagis* began under female rule. The progenitor of

108   An Indonesian Frontier

the family was Teuku Itam, an illegitimate son of Sultan Iskandar Muda, who adopted the title *Pólèm* (literally, "elder brother") because he was older than his half-sister, Queen Taj al-Alam. He became the *Imam* of Gle Yeueng, at that time one of the furthest *mukims* up-river from the capital. His son succeeded him as *Imam*, and became famous as a warrior. Soon he was chosen by neighbouring *mukims* as their military leader, giving rise to the *sagi* of the 22 *mukims*. The other two federations of *mukims*, the *sagis* of the 26 and 25 *mukims*, on the east and west banks respectively of the lower reaches of the Aceh river, were formed in reaction to the power of the upland *sagi*.[48]

Thomas Bowrey was in Aceh in 1675, to witness the accession of the "young queen", Nur al-Alam, to whose reign the chronicles attribute the establishment of the sagis. He noted that female rule was accepted in the city, but

> The inhabitants up in the Country not above 20 or 30 miles off Achin are for the most part disaffected to this sort of Government, and Scruple not to Say they will have a Kinge to rule and beare dominion over them, and that the true heire to the Crowne is yet alive and hath Severall Sons, and him they will obey. He is one that liveth amongst them, a great promoter of a Rebellion, and oftentimes much prejudice both in Citty and Countrey.[49]

This description fits very neatly the Polem family, whose capital, Gle Yeuëng, was about 20 miles above the capital.

The reasons for the emergence of this new political force in the interior of Aceh Besar were partly economic. The relative power of the port-capital was reduced along with its trade, and especially the royal share in trade. At the same time there appears to have been a striking increase in rice cultivation in Aceh Besar. Foreign observers throughout most of the 17th century stressed the total dependence of Aceh Besar on rice imports from Pidië, or even from Malaya and South India, even though there was land suitable for rice cultivation being put to little use.[50] Dampier, in 1688, had the same impression, but added that:

Royal Power in Aceh

of late they have sown pretty large Fields of Rice, This thrives here well enough; but they are so proud, that it is against their Stomach to work: neither do they themselves much trouble their heads about it, but leave it to be managed by their Slaves: and they were the Slaves brought lately by the English and the Danes from the Coast of Coromandel, in the Time of a Famine there, I spoke of before, who first brought this Sort of Husbandry into such Request among the Achinese. Yet neither does the Rice they have this way supply one Quarter of their Occasions, but they have it brought to them from their Neighbouring Countries.[51]

It would be difficult to place much credence in such a large-scale movement of Indian slaves into agriculture in Aceh Besar, were the point not made even more explicitly by Charles Lockyer,[52] and unwittingly confirmed two centuries later by Snouck Hurgronje:

> There have been within the memory of man a large number of Klings in the highlands of Great Acheh (XXII Mukims) living entirely as Achehnese and engaged in agriculture.[53]

Whatever the Indian role, the population of the 22 *mukims* expanded rapidly, so that it was the most populous of the three *sagis* in the 19th century. Rice was not among the important imports of Aceh Besar in the 18th century. The relative strength of urban and rural Aceh Besar was being rapidly reversed in the late 17th century.

The political threat from the 22 *mukims*, which Bowrey had observed in 1675, was much better established in 1688 when the fourth queen, Kamalat Syah, was installed. The twelve "guardians" of the Acehnese throne, comprising four *ulèëbalangs* from each *sagi*, appeared already to have established their claims. Dampier described the government of the Queen, "under whom there are twelve Oronkeys, or great Lords. These act in their several precincts with great power and authority". At the election of the new queen, "Four of the Oronkeys who lived more remote from the court [presumably those of the 22 Mukims] took up Arms to oppose the new Queen and the rest of the Oronkeys, and brought 5000 or 6000 men against the City."[54] The men of the 22 *mukims* continued to demand a return to male rule.

Although they were narrowly defeated on this occasion, they won their point in 1699, aided by a letter from Mecca forbidding female rule as contrary to Islam.

In the 18th and early 19th centuries the 22 *mukims* under Panglima Polem repeatedly plunged the kingdom back into civil war as they opposed one sultan after another. Their power was nominally accommodated within the formula of the "twelve *ulèëbalangs* who appoint and dethrone princes". In reality these twelve were far from equal. The *sagi* of the 22 *mukims* and its Panglima Polem represented one pole of Acehnese power, a constant challenge to the Sultans of the port, who were frequently beholden to foreign traders and troops for their survival.[55]

* * *

The 18th and 19th century diffusion of power among *sagis*, *ulèëbalangs* and coastal rajas was a peculiarly Acehnese problem. The vicissitudes of the Sultanate in its heyday were representative of a much larger dilemma. Aceh is a useful model not only because of its historic role, but also because of its synthetic character: a new nation initially owing more to economic, political and religious forces than to cosmic tradition or ethnic solidarity. In its first two centuries of existence as a state it underwent a number of profound changes, which could be viewed in various lights. If my categorization can be sustained, Aceh flourished first as a centre for large merchants of foreign origin, underwent a period of royal absolutism which centred commercial, as well as political, life in the palace, and then a reaction against this absolutism by merchant-officials who sought to find their requirements of stability without tyranny in a system of female rule. Although prosperity continued, the state under this last arrangement was not strong enough to prevent either the loss of its outer dependencies or the rise of a new, disruptive challenge from the interior of Aceh Besar. The promising movement towards institutionalized government broke down.

Should the more fundamental causes of this breakdown be sought in a lack of consensus about the nature of the state; in particular administrative or financial weaknesses; in the inability of the trading

Royal Power in Aceh

city to develop a life separate from that of the state; or in the monopolistic nature of the western economic threat, to which royal monopoly was the only appropriate answer? These questions continue to demand the attention of historians of Aceh, and of the region in general.

6

Elephants and Water in the Feasting of Seventeenth-century Aceh[1]

WHEN we read either the elaborate provisions of the *Adat Aceh*, or the accounts of the numerous traders and ambassadors who visited the Sultanate of Aceh in its heyday, it seems almost incredible how much of the time and effort of the state went into organizing royal processions, shows and entertainment. In this preoccupation with splendid public rituals, however, Aceh was not alone. All of the other great courts of Southeast Asia in the 17th century — Siam, Burma, Cambodia, Banten, Patani and Mataram — competed with each other in the magnificence of their processions and entertainment. The courts of such contemporary rulers as Louis XIII of France, James I of England, Shah Abbas in Persia or Akbar and Jahangir in India, were similarly concerned to show the king as the centre of a magnificent drama in which he represented not only power but also wealth, vigour, piety, generosity and illumination.

In his description of the "theatre state" of Bali, Clifford Geertz[2] has argued that these "performances" were not simply extravagant indulgences by the state — they were the state itself. Through splendid rituals centring on the person of the king, the pre-modern Southeast Asian state showed its subjects and its neighbours that its *raja* was truly a *raja*, whose power on earth was in some sense based on the divine order of the cosmos.

Feasting of Seventeenth-century Aceh

Important events in the life of the court and the state were always accompanied by processions, music, dance and entertainment. The biggest such events were the important religious festivals and the *rites de passage* of the royal family — circumcisions, weddings and funerals. Even the reception of foreign envoys, however, was the occasion for processions and feasting on a grand scale. Foreign visitors to the courts of Southeast Asia were constantly surprised by the frequency and the magnificence of these occasions. The Siamese nation, said one, "is a great lover of shows and splendid ceremonies".[3] In the Burmese capital envoys were exhausted by the theatrical performances which "continued from day to day almost uninterruptedly".[4] In Banten "the dancing goes on all night, so that in the evenings there is a great hubbub of gongs and instruments".[5] In Patani the Queen's court entertained envoys and visitors with dances and theatrical performance, "very pleasaunte to behold, so as I doute not to have seene the lyke in any place".[6]

At least during the first half of the 17th century, Banda Aceh was one of the wealthiest maritime cities of Asia. Ambassadors and traders came to Aceh from Siam, Banten, Pegu (Burma), the Moghuls in India, Golconda (in South India), Persia, England, Holland, and France. Envoys from the last four of these powers have left graphic descriptions of their reception and of the ceremonies of the court, Dutch descriptions of the 1630s and 1640s being particularly detailed. More than for any other Muslim court in Southeast Asia in this period, therefore, it is possible to check the ceremonial prescribed in court chronicles (notably the *Adat Aceh* in this case) against external observations of what happened. The result is largely to confirm the magnificence of court rituals and ceremonies throughout the first half of the 17th century, when Aceh was at its commercial and political peak.

In Siam and Burma the most majestic processions were on the river, with hundreds of magnificently arrayed galleys carrying local and foreign dignitaries to the palace.[7] In Malaya and Sumatra, on the other hand, it was with elephants — a pan-Southeast Asian symbol of dignity and honour — that the court constituted its most impressive royal processions and brought important visitors to the court. In the

114 An Indonesian Frontier

Melaka sultanate, according to the *Sejarah Melayu*, the protocol was that people of sufficient rank were brought to the palace by elephant.[8] The same procedure was followed in early 17th-century Patani.[9] Even in Java, where elephants had to be imported at great expense, the king of Tuban had a collection of many around 1600, which he used for royal processions and receiving envoys.[10]

Elephants were abundant in the forests of Aceh in the 17th century, and the sources refer to many elephant hunts quite near to the coastal centres of the kingdom. The *Bustanu's-Salatin*,[11] for example, describes how Sultan Iskandar Muda paused to hunt elephants at several points in his journey along the coast from Pidie to Pasai in 1638. Elephants were regarded as an important part of the Acehnese army, and also as an indication of the highest status. For that reason, both Iskandar Muda and his successor Iskandar Thani (1637–41) exercised a kind of monopoly over all the captive elephants in the land. Iskandar Muda was said to have had 900 elephants in his possession, and his son-in-law Iskandar Thani 1,000.[12]

At least in the 1630s and 1640s elephants were as important a symbol of the majesty of Acehnese as of Siamese kings. Sultan Iskandar Muda in his early letters appeared to regard his possession of incredible quantities of gold ornaments as the principal symbol of his *daulat* (sovereignty), and mentioned his elephants primarily in terms of the gold decoration they wore.[13] Iskandar Thani (1637–41), however, placed as much emphasis on his elephants as any Thai ruler. His very formal letter to the Governor-General in Batavia in 1640 announced that the King was:

> King of the whole world, who is like a god over it, shining like the sun at midday, a king whose radiance is like the full moon, chosen by God ... who has a white elephant, the eyes of which shine like the morning star, also elephants with four tusks, purple and spotted elephants, *Sawak* as well as *Binloka* and *Queen* elephants, for which God has given me so many gold cloths of different sorts, enamelled and encrusted with various precious stones, to dress these elephants, as well as so many hundred elephants to use in war, with iron, bulletproof armour, which

Feasting of Seventeenth-century Aceh

cover their tusks with steel and their feet with copper, also so many hundred horses....[14]

The *Hikayat Aceh*, written in the time of Iskandar Muda (1604–37), credited the bravery of the elephants of Aceh to the God-given healthiness of the Acehnese climate.[15] Aceh needed no physical defenses because of:

all the elephants which are very strong and very brave and whose number is beyond counting... And that city is not walled as is the custom of other fortified cities because of the quantity of war elephants there are in that city.[16]

Royal Marriages and Funerals

Among the most important occasions in any kingdom of the time were the key rituals of transition for members of the royal family, such as marriages, circumcisions and coronations. These provided an opportunity to make known as publicly and grandly as possible who the future ruler would be. The festivities in 1765 when Raja Ismail of Johor married a Trengganu princess "lasted about three months, during which there was entertainment like *wayang* and *mendora*".[17] The *Adat Raja-raja Melayu* specifies in great detail the elaborate gifts, processions, entertainment (*topeng, wayang, joget, tandak, mendora Siam*) and games [*jogar* (like checkers), chess, gambling, cock-fights, etc.] which had to accompany a royal wedding. There are many other examples in both the court literature and foreign descriptions of extravagant royal celebrations at Southeast Asian courts.[18]

Acehnese court chronicles celebrate a number of opulent weddings, especially those central to the legitimacy of the royal patron of the chronicle-writer in question. In the *Hikayat Aceh* it is the betrothal and subsequent wedding of the parents of Sultan Iskandar Muda, which gain the most attention. The grandeur of the processions, gifts, decorations, and entertainment on that occasion presumably helped to compensate for any deficiencies in Iskandar's claim to the throne through his mother.[19] The ceremony arranged by Sultan Iskandar

116 An Indonesian Frontier

Muda for his daughter and the young prince of Pahang who was to become Sultan Iskandar Thani was similarly essential to the latter's claim to the throne. Nuru'd-din ar-Raniri devoted nine pages of his *Bustanu's-Salatin* to a description of these ceremonies. First when he reached the age of nine the prince was married in a lavishly decorated palace, in front of all the great men of the court, with the Kadhi Malikul Adil officiating.[20] A year later an even grander celebration was held, after 40 days of feasting throughout the whole land. There was singing and dancing:

> All the singers with good voices sang while striking their *dap* drums which were encrusted with jewels and made of gold, *suasa*, [gold-copper alloy], and silver, and their *repana* drums were the same. The various types of singers of zikir [religious chants] all wore gold studded with jewels, lapis-lazuli and *suasa*. Then they all danced each one according to their special training. Some did the *tari*, some the *tandak* [Javanese-style dance] and some the *rakat* [a form of masked theatre].[21]

The central rituals on this occasion were the firing of all the great guns, followed by a procession from the *dalam* (citadel) twice around the Masjid Baitu'r-Rahman, with the young couple surrounded by all the court notables and lavishly dressed elephants and horses:

> All the people and the humblest folk all gathered together. All the caparisoned elephants were equipped with their golden howdahs, and some had howdahs of *suasa* and silver, or of iron covered with gold and *suasa*. There were various fine horses of Arab and Iraqi stock, and some also of Turkish and Byzantine [*rumi*] stock, complete with every adornment, their coats embroidered with gold, jewels, and lapis-lazuli, inlaid with jems of all kinds, and fringed with pearls.[22]

The young couple, dressed so splendidly that eyes had never seen the like, then presented themselves to the Sultan, who ceremonially bathed the prince in holy water which the Sultan had seen in a dream being

Feasting of Seventeenth-century Aceh

brought from heaven by angels. Meanwhile there was such a noise as ears had never heard from the playing of various gongs, drums and flutes.[23]

Since Raniri must have been anxious to show the legitimacy of the succession of his royal patron Iskandar Thani, it is possible that he allowed himself some poetic licence in describing the grandeur of the occasion. But we know from outsiders that such events were indeed celebrated on a grand scale designed to demonstrate the supernatural symbols of the dynasty's right to rule. When Sultan Iskandar Thani died in February 1641, Nicolaus de Graaff was there to record the ceremonies (see Fig. 9):

> the funeral procession was carried out with royal magnificence: it consisted in a great following of Princes, Lords and Nobles, as well as 260 elephants, all hung with costly silks, gold cloth, and embroidered cloths. Their tusks were covered with gold, others with silver; others had little square houses and lavish tents on their backs, which had many banners hanging from them, worked with silver and gold. Also some rhinoceros and Persian horses with silver and gold bridles, equipped with costly cloths. And so the body was carried in a chest of *tembaga suasa*, that is half gold and half copper, to the grave dug by his forefathers... The King's body was not put in its grave before two silver double-cannon were fired, after which all the guns in Aceh were fired off during the whole night, with continual shouts of "God protect the new Queen".[24]

Such specifically royal occasions were probably the grandest of any in Aceh, since they were essential to upholding the sacred majesty of the ruler. Yet the calendar was generously sprinkled with occasions of great pomp, and few weeks can have gone by without some opportunity for the populace to witness some piece of magnificent royal theatre.

The great feasts of the Islamic year were among the biggest occasions for royal display in most parts of the Muslim world in the 17th century. One might speculate why in Turkey, as in Southeast

Figure 9 The funeral of Sultan Iskandar Thani in 1641, as depicted by a contemporary Dutch engraver

Asia, such public celebrations were much less in evidence in the century which followed.[25] According to the Raffles' (1612) edition of the *Sejarah Melayu*, the Sultans of 15th-century Melaka were solemnly borne in procession to the mosque on three Muslim feast days — *Idulfitri*, *Idul Adh*, and 27 *Ramadan*.[26] For 17th-century Aceh the *Adat Aceh* sets out the way in which four Islamic feasts were publicly celebrated in the 17th century, that is: the eve of the fasting month (*hari memegang puasa*); the night of revelation on 27 *Ramadan* (*malam lailatulkadar*); the end of the fast (*hari raya puasa* or *Idulfitri*); and the festival of sacrifice during the month of pilgrimage on 10 *Dhulhijja* (*hari raya haji* or *Idul Adh*).[27]

Three other royal ceremonies are described in which Islam played a minor part — the day of pledging allegiance (*hari raya junjung duli*); the Saturday ritual on which war-leaders (*hulubalang*) came to the palace; and the king's ritual bath (*mandi Safar*). It is interesting that *Maulud*, the Prophet's birthday, was not mentioned in the *Adat Aceh* or other sources of this period as a significant festival, despite the 19th-century tradition reported by Snouck Hurgronje[28] that the celebration of *Maulud* was especially extensive in every village of Aceh because it had been so commanded by a 16th-century Turkish sultan as a token of Acehnese vassalage to the Caliph.

Idul Adh

On the other hand, European sources confirm that the festivals before and after the fasting month and *Idul Adh* were celebrated on a great scale. *Idul Adh*, the "major feast" required by Islam, appears indeed to have been the most important day of the Acehnese year, whether we judge from the space devoted to it in the *Adat Aceh* or from the accounts of foreigners.[29] For both it was the great procession from the palace to the Masjid Bait ur-Rahman which drew the most attention. The *Adat Aceh* listed the 30 groups comprising the procession, with the Sultan himself in the 24th group on the royal elephant Lela Manikam. The foreign traders take their place in the 27th group, but the largest numbers are in the last three sections of the mighty

120 An Indonesian Frontier

procession. In the 28th group 30 decorated elephants and 7,000 soldiers of different types, all carrying arms and splendidly dressed; in the 29th the same; in the 30th 50 elephants, many of which are named, and thousands more soldiers. At the mosque the Sultan and the leading figures go inside for the prescribed prayers, and then the Sultan goes out onto the terrace to make the first cut on the ritually prepared animals to be sacrificed. Finally the whole procession goes back to the *dalam* accompanied by various kinds of music.[30] The scene was splendid, but the enormous crowds of participants and spectators were not easy to manage, for:

> of the many pregnant women who went to see Johan 'Alam go out on that *hari raya*, some gave birth along the road and in the market, and some of the crowds of people did not find the place because of all the people who were scattered about.[31]

There may be some poetic exaggeration in the numbers listed in this court work — indeed it is difficult to see how so many men and elephants could be accommodated in the roughly 500 metres between the palace and the mosque. Yet the outline of this description is confirmed by Peter Mundy, who witnessed the first *Idul Adh* ceremony under Sultan Iskandar Thani in 1637 (see Fig. 10). As Ito has pointed out[32] the ranks of military in the procession may have been reduced by Aceh's heavy losses in 1629, and by Iskandar Thani's relatively weaker position than his predecessor. Even so Mundy witnessed an extraordinary procession from the palace to the mosque:

> ... Then came a squadron of elephants with certain things like little low turrets on their backs, and in each of them a soldier in red with a lance in his hand standing upright... The first rank of elephants (they going four in rank) had each of them two great swords, or rather long iron scythes fastened to their tusks...
>
> Next after these came another number of elephants with little turrets... whereon were placed small guns... After these other elephants with more turrets with 2 men in each... Then other

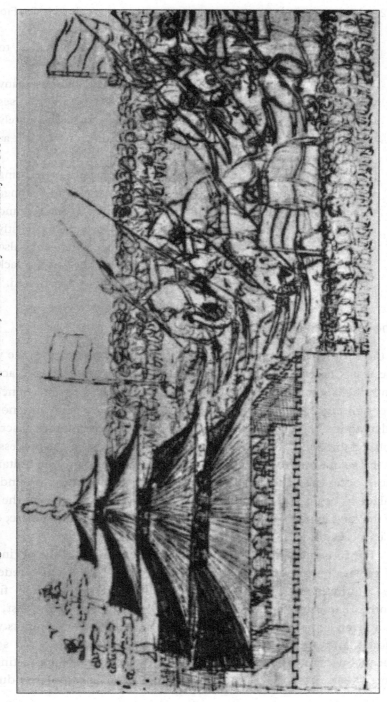

Figure 10 Part of Aceh's *Idul Adh* procession, sketched by Peter Mundy in 1637

elephants with long flags ... ; others covered from their head to their feet...

After these came a multitude with guns, and then as many with very long pikes... Amongst all were led many good horses with rich saddles... Then comes the King on a great and stately elephant, richly adorned and covered all over down to the feet as beforementioned...

The march was also very confused and on heaps, there being scarce room or time for order. However it was all rare and strange to behold, viz., the multitude of great elephants accoutered and armed after several manners, weapons and ornaments, costly furniture, etc., there being near as many more elephants also fitted for this show (that could not march with the rest for lack of room) which stood in sundry places by while others passed.[33]

The Feasts of the Fasting Month

If the feast of sacrifice was evidently the most magnificent of the year, the feasts before and after the fasting month were also spectacular. Both the beginning and end of the fasting month were determined by the sighting of the moon, as required by *Shafi'i* law, and not by calculation.[34] The most elaborate features of the ceremonies described both on the eve of the fast and on *Idulfitri* are, however, the processions to the palace and to the mosque, the tribute brought to the Sultan on these occasions, and the fanfare of music and firearms around the palace to begin and to end the fast. In all of this, once again, the cult of the king appears to be the central aim of an elaborate theatre, even if its occasion is an orthodox Islamic feast.

For foreigners in Aceh, the most striking feature of the beginning of the fasting month was the bedlam of noise. In 1600, Frederick de Houtman noted how all the nobility dressed in their finest clothes came to the palace on 29 *Sha'ban*, the eve of the fast, and at a given signal "all the drums were beaten, and the trumpets were blown, and finally all the flintlocks were fired, so were seven harquebuses outside the palace. This is the advent of their fasting."[35] Forty years later the cannon which had been accumulated during

Feasting of Seventeenth-century Aceh

Iskandar Muda's reign played a larger role, and the noise was still more deafening:

> A cannon was fired from Inderapurwa, and immediately there [were] set off cannons from the palace and all the forts, cannons were limbered; and to these shots replied [from Inderapurwa], besides 300 or 400 arquebuses.[36]

For the *Adat Aceh*, on the other hand, the key ceremonies appear to be the bringing of tribute to the king by various types of official, the elaborate processions to carry the regalia into the palace, the offerings on the royal tombs, and the centrality of the ruler in the whole ceremony.[37]

Similarly in its description of the ceremonies for *Idulfitri*, the *Adat Aceh* is most concerned with the precedence of different ranks of officials in the royal procession by elephant from the citadel to the mosque and back again, and the different types of music and drumbeat to be played at each stage of the procession. Inside the mosque, the Imam led the prescribed prayer, and the Khatib gave the sermon.[38]

Foreign accounts were naturally most impressed by this procession, the purpose of which was clearly so that all could see the grandeur of the king on this joyous occasion:

> a great elephant gracefully adorned was brought into the courtyard. The young king [Ali Ri'ayat Syah, 1604–71, wearing a kind of gilt helmet, mounted the elephant and seated himself under a magnificent canopy; in front of him sat one well dressed and wearing a gold coronet, who controlled the elephant, and also the other handsomely dressed behind him... Thus the young prince went to the mosque, accompanied by many nobility, a great number of elephants and a small number of horses; in addition several thousand people, carrying arms, standards, arrows and flintlocks, also followed on foot. There was tremendous noise of various instruments, such as horns, trombones, kettle-drums and cymbals.[39]

Friday Prayer

These ceremonies for the great occasions of the year must certainly have been spectacular, for even the regular Friday prayer was an opportunity for the king to overawe his subjects and visitors — at least during the reign of Iskandar Muda. Even for this routine weekly event the *Adat Aceh* provides a lengthy description of how the procession of elephants, dignitaries and soldiers must assemble, and which rhythms must be played on the drums as the procession moves along.[40]

It appears to have been such a routine procession which the English merchants under Thomas Best were summoned to participate in on Friday, 2 July 1613. It seems scarcely credible that about 5,000 men should be mobilized for a procession every week of the year, but the fact that Croft described two successive Friday processions (26 June and 2 July) suggests that at this period it was a regular event. This procession may have been especially grand because the occasion was used also as a farewell to the Siamese ambassador.

> We met his majesty in most royal state on the way to the church with great solemnity. He had, for his guard [that] went before him, 200 great elephants, 2000 small shot, 2000 pikes, 200 lances, 100 bowmen; 20 naked swords of pure gold carried before him. 20 fencers went before him, playing with swords and targets. A horse [was] led before him, covered with beaten gold, the bridle set with stones; at his saddle crutch a sheaf of arrows, the quiver of beaten gold, set with precious stones. Before him went his two sons, of 8 or 9 years old, arrayed with jewels and rich stones. His Majesty rode upon an elephant, his saddle of pure gold; his slave behind him in rich array, with his betel box and a fan of pure gold in his hand, to keep the flies from the king. The king's robes were so rich that I cannot well describe them. He had a turban upon his head, set with jewels and precious stones invaluable; kris and sword of pure gold, the scabbard set with stones. Before him went an elephant with a chair of state, covered all with beaten

Feasting of Seventeenth-century Aceh

silver, that, if it should chance to rain, he might change elephants. This elephant had cases made of pure gold, to put upon his tusks.

From the church he returned to a place of pleasure prepared for his entertainment. Where his majesty being seated, all his nobles, according to their custom, were called, and all foreign ambassadors, as the fame of their country did deserve, were seated among the nobles; which being done, we saw the fighting of wild and tame elephants, buffaloes and rams.[41]

As we noted above, Iskandar Muda prided himself even more on his magnificent treasures of gold than on his elephants, and these processions to the mosque were an opportunity to dazzle his people and his visitors with their display as part of the theatre of kingship. Part of the purpose of the show was entertainment, however, as indicated by the animal fights so regularly staged, which we must assume to have been eagerly attended every week by the people of Banda Aceh.

Reception of Diplomats

Such massive spectacles every week must have been enough to keep the court busy and the large population of Banda Aceh entertained. In addition, however, there were frequent receptions of foreign envoys, which involved not only massive banqueting within the palace, but also a procession of the envoys through the streets of Banda Aceh by elephant, and often an animal fight which the populace may have been allowed to witness. When the envoys carried a letter from their sovereign the reception was particularly ornate. The letter itself would be carried on a velvet cushion on the largest and most magnificent of elephants, while the envoys rode behind on other elephants,[42] from their lodgings to the palace. Among the earliest European monarchs to communicate with a Sultan of Aceh was Queen Elizabeth, whose letter was delivered by James Lancaster in 1602. The elderly Sultan Ala'ad-din Ri'ayat Syah:

126 An Indonesian Frontier

sent six great elephants, with many trumpets, drums, and streamers, with much people, to accompany the [English] general to the court, so that the press was exceedingly great. The biggest of these elephants was about thirteen or fourteen feet high; which had a small castle (like a coach) upon his back, covered with crimson velvet. In the middle thereof was a great basin of gold, and a piece of silk exceedingly richly wrought to cover it, under which Her Majesty's letter was put. The general was mounted upon another of the elephants. Some of the attendants rode; others went on foot.[43]

This procedure appears to have been common in Malay courts. The *Sejarah Melayu* specified that letters to Melaka from kings of appropriate rank should be carried by elephant, while in Patani Floris reported that the letter he carried was put in a golden basin to be carried to court on an elephant.[44]

In subsequent negotiations for access to trade, Europeans often found it very difficult to come to a definite agreement with the Acehnese, especially in the time of Iskandar Muda. Nevertheless their missions always began well, as the lavishness of the royal reception was as impressive as anything they had ever seen. The feast served for Thomas Best by Sultan Iskandar Muda contained "at least 400 dishes, with such plenty of hot drinks as might have sufficed a drunken army"; all the meat dishes for James Lancaster's reception were "either of pure gold or of another metal ... of gold and brass together [i.e. *suasa*]".[45]

All of this was of course intended to impress both the envoys and the Acehnese public. It was not that a splendid show was put on for the foreign envoys, but rather that the envoys themselves were given minor roles to play in the ongoing theatre of the court.

It is fortunate for the historian that in this way foreign envoys had a glimpse into the life of the court which they recorded in their letters and reports of their missions. In particular they were often allowed to witness the entertainments of the court. Some of these were held in the vast front court of the palace, which Beaulieu states had space for 300 elephants or for 4,000 armed men. These

Feasting of Seventeenth-century Aceh

must often have been accessible to a large crowd of Acehnese onlookers. Other entertainments took place in the inner courtyard, to which only a more privileged group of nobles and court women had access.

The emphasis of these entertainment changed somewhat with each monarch. The earliest Dutch and English envoys who were received by Ala'ad-din Ri'ayat (1589–1604) often saw him watching cock-fights — "one of the greatest sports the king delighteth in".[46] At his feasts and receptions there was a great deal of *arak* drunk, and usually some of the court ladies danced and played music for the guests. With Sultan Iskandar Muda and his short-lived successor Iskandar Thani the principal entertainment seemed always to be spectacular contests of the larger animals — elephants, buffaloes and rams — though we know that Iskandar Muda also enjoyed cock-fighting. In the period of Queen Taj al-Alam, on the other hand, these contests appeared gradually to give way to quieter pursuits in royal pleasure-houses built over or near the water — fishing, music, and gambling.

Contests of Animals

Fights between animals were so prominent a part of the public theatre arranged by the court of Aceh in the late 16th and 17th centuries that some particular explanation seems required. In this respect, as in others, Aceh exemplified a marked feature of Southeast Asian culture in this period. The *senenan* of Java are well known, during which nobles would joust on horseback, and then tigers would be set to fight against buffaloes or against a phalanx of men armed with spears. Similarly in Siam and Laos in the 17th century the king frequently arranged public fights between elephants, or between a tiger and a number of elephants. The elephants would always succeed in killing the tiger by repeatedly throwing it high in the air, just as the *banteng* almost invariably killed the tiger in Java. Similar contests between tigers and either elephants or buffaloes were staged by rulers in what is now southern Vietnam, and in Malaya.[47]

128   An Indonesian Frontier

Given the deep hold that cock-fighting had throughout Southeast
Asia in this period, and the religious associations which cock-fighting
once had in Java and still has in Bali, it may be that the origins of
these animal contests lie far back in some pre-Islamic belief in the
importance of blood-sacrifice. Perhaps some such feelings were still
alive in the mind of Sultan Zainal Abidin, who was killed in 1579
because he was "very quick-tempered, and a killer. Unless he saw
blood, he didn't even want to eat."[48] The *Hikayat Aceh* gives more
detail about the cruel enthusiasm of this ruler for blood sports:

> that sultan always went out to enjoy himself on the parade-ground,
> pitting against each other wild elephants and tame elephants,
> and several people died as a result of stab-wounds from the
> elephants, and the verandah of the Bunga Setangkai palace was
> damaged;... and buffaloes, cattle and sheep were made to charge
> each other. When the buffaloes charged several people were killed,
> injured, crippled and blinded. And he had men engage in
> swordfights, defending themselves with shields... and among the
> Acehnese and Indian swordsmen several were killed and several
> others wounded.[49]

In the 17th century, however, animal fights seem to have entirely
replaced human ones, and the fights seldom got out of control as in
these cases.

The dominant motives for these contests appear to have had to do
with warfare and with the symbolic victory of the king. Since elephants
were regarded as an important part of Aceh's military strength, staging
fights between them was probably intended as both display of this
strength and training for the elephants and their handlers. At least for
Iskandar Muda, the regular elephant fights were probably seen in the
same light as the Javanese *senenan* (or indeed Mediaeval European
jousts) — both as training for war and as a kind of symbolic
representation of military success. The young Iskandar Muda was
himself much given to athletic feats with elephants. If the *Hikayat
Aceh* can be believed, he engaged in the sport (*bermain*) of skillfully
riding elephants and horses every Monday and Thursday.[50] When he

Feasting of Seventeenth-century Aceh 129

became ruler, therefore, it is easy to imagine that he enjoyed watching this kind of sport, and that he believed it would strengthen his army.

In other parts of Southeast Asia, the defeat of the tiger by an elephant or buffalo was a symbolic defeat of the forces threatening the good order of the state. Raffles pointed out that the Javanese identified the tiger with the Europeans in his day, and so rejoiced in the repeated victory of the buffalo which they identified with themselves.[51] In Aceh there must have been a similar concern that the tiger had to be defeated, since it was handicapped by being tied to a stake and having to fight four elephants at once.[52]

Most often, however, animals appeared to have fought their own species in Iskandar Muda's Aceh. In 1608 the Dutch saw 58 elephants pitted against each other, one pair after another fighting.[53] In 1613 the Sultan showed the English envoys a fight of 6 elephants one against the other, then of 4 buffaloes, and then 10 or 12 rams.[54] Under Iskandar Thani these contests continued. Peter Mundy described in some detail the elephant fight he witnessed at the beginning of his reign, in which about 150 elephants were ranged in a circle to form part of the vast arena, while 12 or 13 pairs of elephants in turn engaged in furious battle. Mundy distinguished the most vigorous fights which began and closed the day's entertainment, which were by bull elephants in their rutting season, aroused by the presence of females nearby (see Fig. 11). Buffaloes, "antelopes" (perhaps meaning deer) and rams were also set to fighting.[55] Under Sultan Taj al-Alam foreign envoys were still being regaled with such animal fights at least as late as 1644.[56]

Water Feasts

One of the most intriguing aspects of the feasting of the Aceh court in the 17th century is the role which water appears to have played. Here again there are similarities almost everywhere in Southeast Asia, with the prominence of *mandi Safar* or other purificatory rituals in the island world matching the water throwing hilarity at New Year in mainland Southeast Asia. The 15th-century Melaka Sultans enjoyed a marble swimming pool fed by springs which may have been similar

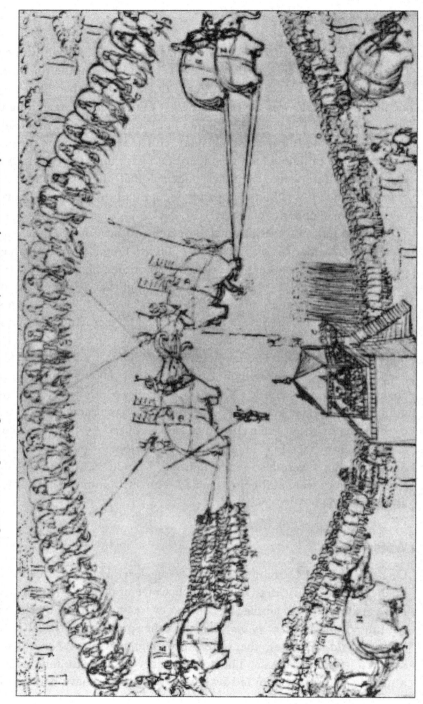

Figure 11 Elephant fight at the court of Aceh, sketched by Peter Mundy

Feasting of Seventeenth-century Aceh

to the later Acehnese pattern.[57] In 17th-century Aceh foreign envoys were frequently invited to join the ruler in some feast at the river, and it is from them that we have most of our information.

The first such report is that of Frederick de Houtman, confirmed by the English pilot Davis who formed part of the same expedition. De Houtman attended a royal feast on 10 July 1599 (16 Dulhijjah 1007H), at which there was dancing by two magnificently dressed women. "After that I went into the river with the king, and stood there in the water with all his nobles. There everybody ate and drank lavishly, such as very strong brandywine."[58] Subsequently on 19 September de Houtman attended another such feast at which everybody stood in the river while eating. Since this corresponded to 28 Safar, this second feast may have been occasioned by a *mandi Safar* ritual.[59]

Iskandar Muda also engaged in such water-feasts, and it seems likely that he was already frequenting Mata Ië [cf. Malay *mata ayer*], the pleasant spot 8 km southwest of the *dalam* where the clear water of the Krueng Daroy stream flows out from two adjacent points at the base of a cliff. On 2 May 1613 he invited the English general Thomas Best:

> to his fountain to swim, it being some 5 or 6 miles from the city. And sent me two elephants to carry me and my provision. And having washed and bathed ourselves in the water, the king presented us with an exceedingly great banquet, with too much arak; all to be eaten and drunk as we sat in the water; all his nobles and great captains being present. Our banquet continued from one of the clock till towards five, at which time the king released me; and half an hour after all strangers.[60]
>
> Here were all the dishes brought by water; the boys holding the dish with one hand and swimming with the other (so did they carry the strong drink also); whereof when they had tasted (which they must of all) they threw the rest into the river.[61]

As described by some of the other Englishmen, this feast resembled even more a *mandi Safar*, since the Sultan sat in a special place in the middle of the river with the chief *orangkaya* surrounding him, while his nephew ceremonially poured water over him from a golden bucket.[62] However, 2 May fell on 12 Rabi'al awal, which was in fact the feast of Maulud al-Nabi, the Prophet's birthday — two weeks after the time for the Safar ritual. It may be that the ruler's illness or some other problem had necessitated the postponement of the *mandi Safar*, since the sultan had been reported to be sick just a few days before, but equally this may be our best evidence for the early celebration of *Maulud* in Aceh. It would not be surprising if here, as in Java, the Prophet's birthday was celebrated primarily as a festival of kingship and the renewing of loyalty. Whatever the effect on the king, however, this water feast had a far from beneficial effect on the Europeans, for the Dutch captain and two of Best's Englishmen died within a few days, which the English considered a consequence of sitting too long in the water and drinking too much *arak*.[63]

The next information we have about such excursions is in 1642, when Iskandar Muda's daughter, Sultana Taj al-Alam, several times invited foreign envoys to join her in the water. There were at least two places favoured by the Queen — one at Mata Ië, where "a stream flowed out from two caves", and another near the mouth of the river. In July 1642 Pieter Sourij and the other Dutch factors, along with prominent Indian merchants and the leading officials of the court, accompanied the Queen with her numerous elephants to Mata Ië, which the Dutch called a *speel hoff* (pleasure garden). The Dutch were placed on a beautifully carved stone ledge beside the water, where they could watch thousands of carp swimming in the water, while they were served an enormous banquet of seven courses. Between courses there was entertainment, while some of the Acehnese nobles prayed and washed. Among the entertainment was "a song of praise" (perhaps the Acehnese verse epic form known as *hikayat*) for the Queen's father, Sultan Iskandar Muda. This brought tears to the eyes of many Acehnese since "although dreaded in his life, he has however left for good among the Acehnese nation an immortal name".[64] Subsequent entertainers included a Javanese comedian, and Siamese, Indian and other musicians and actors. Having arrived at this pleasant spot at about ten in the morning, the whole party did not return to

Feasting of Seventeenth-century Aceh

the city until six o'clock that evening.[65] Five days later there was another excursion to a "bathing place lying in an extraordinarily beautiful situation", probably a different one. Again there was bathing and fishing, and a meal was served of the fish caught at the spot, along with various fruits.[66]

Later in the year two similar royal processions took place to the coast at Indrapura, where there was a "large handsome stone fort", but also "a large *speelhuijs* built over a great river". Here it was not a question of bathing, but of fishing, and also gambling games between the Queen, her royal women, and some of the court eunuchs.[67]

Other Acehnese and foreign sources shed a little light on these pastimes. Bathing in the clear water of the Aceh River was regarded as very healthy by Acehnese. A number of foreign visitors noticed that people who were suffering from various diseases were always brought to the river to bathe. François Martin thought that the clear river water may have acquired its healing properties from the medicinal plants, such as camphor and benzoin trees, which lined its banks.[68] The *Hikayat Aceh* explained that:

> There is a river in the town of Aceh Dar as-Salam. which arises in a spring coming out of a hill and then flows to the sea. Its water is wonderfully sweet and healing. Many sick people when they bathe in that river.... [or] when they drink its water, are cured by God of their illness. And many of the merchants from the Arab world, Turkey, the Mughal Empire and the whole of India,... after feeling the effects of bathing in that river and drinking its water,... declare: "Ah, in all the countries which we have visited and observed, there is no river like this Sungai Aceh Dar as-Salam in terms of its taste or its physical benefits to man."[69]

For the rulers and their circle, however, it was the Sungai Dar al'Isyki ("the abode of love"), later known as Krueng Daroy, which was of primary interest. This must have been the river flowing out from under two caves which Pieter Sourij had visited, for the *Hikayat Aceh* says the same thing:

134 An Indonesian Frontier

there is another river which arises from a spring in a rock cave. Its water is exceedingly cool and sweet. The name of that river is Dar al'Isyki. And the drinking water of all the rajas was the water of this river.[70]

Sultan Iskandar Muda had diverted this beautifully clear river to the northeast in 1613, so that it flowed right through the middle of the royal citadel (Kota Dar ad-Dunia) from south to north as well as providing the water for the moat which surrounded it.[71] Later it was his son-in-law Iskandar Thani who had the banks of the river further beautified and formed into a garden, Taman Ghairah, surrounded by walls and containing the *Gunongan Menara Permata* (see Fig. 7 on p. 96), evidently a place of meditation, as well as a mosque called Isyki Musyahadah ("love of the mystic vision").[72] The extraordinary length of Raniri's description of this garden, and especially of the Dar al'Isyki, its ornamented banks, the marble island within it, and the pools into which its water flowed, make clear that this was a garden not simply for pleasure, but for that highest form of pleasure represented by the mystic communion with God. Many of its features were intended to evoke that heavenly garden which is the conventional Islamic vision of paradise. As Lombard, Brakel and Wessing have pointed out,[73] the Taman Ghairah was one of many royal gardens originally intended for mystical meditation in the palaces of Indonesia, of which Taman Sari in Yogyakarta and Cirebon are the best known. Even more than in Java, however, water appears to have been central to Acehnese ideas of spiritual and physical health. Bathing was pleasurable but it also had a healing, purifying function. It appears that rituals involving bathing were not limited to *mandi Safar*, although that, too, was certainly an important occasion on the Acehnese royal calendar.[74] Perhaps many important moments in the life of the court required the purificatory ritual of a wash in the Dar al'Isyki, followed by entertainment of various kinds.

* * *

Aceh in the 17th century was not simply a centre of trade and of military power. It was a large and wealthy city which had the means

Feasting of Seventeenth-century Aceh 135

and the culture to develop an agreeable life-style, with a great deal of time devoted to sport, entertainment and pageantry. Much of this activity was orchestrated by the court and was designed primarily to represent in striking visual terms the greatness and the supernatural aura of the ruler.

7

The Transition from Autocracy
(co-authored with Takeshi Ito)

WHILE comparative historians must be extremely cautious about transferring the "big" categories of European history like feudalism (or antiquity, slavery, middle ages) to Asia, it remains true that some major transitions have encompassed a number of disparate societies, and therefore demand explanations that rise above the parochialism of culture or nation. In this chapter we wish to focus attention on one such transition in Aceh, which has echoes in other kingdoms of Southeast Asia. It is the shift from a pattern of autocratic states dominated by their commercial port-capitals to one of power diffused among chiefdoms or domains which recognized the aura of the earlier kingdoms without replicating their centralized military or legal coherence. Although the most important phase of this transition occurred in the late 17th century, its European parallels are rather those of the passage from Antiquity to Feudalism.

A Southeast Asian Transition

The late 16th and still more the early 17th centuries witnessed a striking array of powerful city-centred kingdoms inspiring the admiration of European observers — the Burma of Kings Bayinnaung (1551–81) and Anaukhpetlun (1606–29); the Ayutthaya (Siam) of Kings Songtham and Prasat Thong (1610–56); the Mataram (Java) of Sultan Agung and Amangkurat 1 (1613–77); the Makassar of Sultans

The Transition from Autocracy

Mohammad Said and Hasanuddin (1639–69); and the Aceh of Sultans al-Mukammil and Iskandar Muda (1589–1636). The key features of these autocratic kingdoms might be classified as:

1. Enormous armies mobilizing a large proportion of total available manpower. A small standing army of palace guards, foreign mercenaries, etc. Strict royal control of firearms. Numerous state captives resulting from wars of conquest.
2. International trade centred at a single port under royal control (the capital in all cases except Mataram). Revenues of the crown largely dependent on the flourishing port, including a large sector of royal trade.
3. Forced attendance at court for leading nobles of the realm.
4. Some bureaucratization of government, with officials appointed at intervals rather than hereditary.
5. Codification of laws and institutionalization of legal structures, frequently using Indic or Islamic models to justify centralized law-making by the court.
6. Development of an urban cosmopolitan culture, which completely dominated the countryside and provided the cultural model for later periods.

Most historians, like most contemporary observers, have looked at these developments from the point of view of a single country, and have therefore explained the powerful autocracies in terms of the capacity of individual rulers, and subsequent diffusion of power as the result of internal conflict, external pressure, or the ineptitude of 18th-century rulers.[1] Having pointed to a similar phenomenon in a number of countries, we are obliged to look for some underlying structural factors. The most important would appear to be international trade, firearms, and the role of Europeans in Asia.

Until the middle of the 17th century, the role of European traders and trading companies appeared to work in favour of strong rulers, apart perhaps from the disruptions caused by the first few years of the Portuguese onslaught. In their pursuit of stable supplies of spices and other tropical goods, the Europeans preferred to make monopolistic agreements with rulers who appeared to control a large proportion of pepper or clove supplies, thereby often getting the better of the Indian merchants or of European rivals. As the VOC took root in Asia, however, it fought hard for a total monopoly of Southeast Asian spices, eventually succeeding in destroying militarily the remaining indigenous ports of greatest significance in the spice trade — Banten and Makassar — while detaching the main pepper-producing areas from their allegiance to Aceh. The English, French, and Danes, who had been more active in encouraging the state trading of powerful rulers of Banten, Ayutthaya and Makassar, were expelled either by Dutch arms or by internal revolutions by the end of the 17th century.

The earliest firearms to be adopted into Southeast Asian warfare were cannon. In the 16th and 17th centuries, they were generally presented to, bought by, or made for the king alone. Certainly the stronger rulers made a point of controlling both the artillery and the gunpowder — a considerable departure from tradition in an area where no man considered himself adequately dressed without a *kris* or knife of some sort. As hand-held guns became more common and more effective, however, it became increasingly difficult for rulers to maintain such a monopoly on firearms. While the manufacture of cannon appears to have been limited to craftsmen working under royal patronage, muskets in the 18th century were being made and exported by craftsmen in Bali, the Bugis area, and Minangkabau — all areas with markedly fragmented political structures.

More opaque than such external factors are the internal ones, having to do with the effectiveness and durability of the administrative structures built up during the period of autocracy. In this paper we can do no more than invite the attention of other scholars to investigate the problem further. At first glance it appears difficult to develop a general explanation which will work for all the following cases, but we ought to remember that there is a similar diversity in the range of European transitions from antiquity to feudalism, and from feudalism to capitalism, which has never prevented the search for general explanations.

The Transition from Autocracy

Java: The military success of Sultan Agung (1613–45), followed by the tyrannical excesses of Amangkurat I (1645–77) produce rebellion, Dutch intervention, and eventual permanent division of Java into competing kingdoms (1755).

Bali: The "Kingdom" of Bali, with its capital at Gelgel, fragments permanently into eight kingdoms at the end of the 17th century.

South Sulawesi: The domination of Makassar over the whole of South Sulawesi endures from 1610 to 1669, with steadily increasing centralization, until the Dutch/Bugis conquest of Makassar brings about a fragmentation into numerous states and sub-states.

Banten: This sultanate was conquered by the Dutch in 1684, and thereafter lost its international trade and its ability to control tightly its Sumatran dependencies.

Banjarmasin, Palembang, Ternate, Johor, Brunei: Loss of international trade makes it increasingly difficult in the late 17th and 18th centuries to control dependencies of these kingdoms.

Siam: The revolution of 1688 expels European state-trading partners of the King, and the early 18th century witnesses progressive loss of manpower from King to the aristocracy.[2]

Burma: The capital of Burma moves inland from Pegu to Ava 1635, after which there is no strong royal role in international trade; and a steady decline of central control from the death of Tha-lun (1648) to the fall of Ava (1752).[3]

There is a significant recovery in central authority in the 19th century, beginning earlier in Siam and Burma but also affecting the still independent Indonesian states of Aceh and Lombok in the second half of the 19th century. In general, however, there is still an enormous gap between the picture given by the standard literature on 19th-century Southeast Asian states — J.M. Gullick on the Malay States; D.E. Brown on Brunei, C. Snouck Hurgronje on Aceh, John Crawfurd on Siam, H.J. Friedericy on South Sulawesi,[4] etc. — and that on the states of the 16th and 17th centuries.

Aceh

Aceh may be the only Sumatran case that fits this more general process of transition. At least among Indonesian states it has the unique advantage of a continuous history uninterrupted by direct outside intervention until the late 19th century.

As in the cases sketched above, the contrast is extreme between Aceh in its period of "royal absolutism" as described in Chapter 5 above, and the picture given by Dutch scholars in the late 19th century. According to Beaulieu in 1629, Sultan Iskandar Muda could raise an army of 40,000 men within 24 hours. The armoury, containing over 2,000 cannon, was under strict royal control, with firearms issued to the army only at the time of a campaign. The king's writ ran throughout northern and western Sumatra and much of the Malay Peninsula, and foreigners could trade for the coveted pepper only on his terms.[5] Internally, the image of Iskandar Muda's power among later generations of Acehnese was such that all laws were conventionally ascribed to him, and his name was invoked on the seals of all subsequent sultans. By contrast, power in 19th-century Aceh, as portrayed by the Dutch Islamicist Snouck Hurgronje, was dispersed among dozens of *ulèëbalang* (108 were eventually recognized by the Dutch) who were hereditary "governors, judges and military leaders in their own country, in which they admit no higher authority".[6] The effective power of the Sultan was limited to his palace, even though he was honoured everywhere in Aceh.[7] Although the Sultan had no capacity to affect the succession of *ulèëbalang*, the twelve leading *ulèëbalang* were authorized by tradition to confer the throne on the royally born candidate of their choosing.

As explained in Chapter 5, there is an external cause of this transformation in the steady decline of Aceh's role as a major international port in the Bay of Bengal and one of the leading suppliers of the world's pepper — a decline which continued with few interruptions between about 1630 and 1820. Although Acehnese pepper-exports revived strongly in the 19th century the capital no longer had enough control over the pepper exporting areas to draw more than a token share of the revenue thus produced. The decline in trade is a consequence as well as a cause of internal transformation,

The Transition from Autocracy 141

however, and does not suffice as an explanation of the profound structural change internally.

Although there has been considerable speculation on the origins of the 19th-century Acehnese system of *ulèëbalang*, together with the smaller *mukim* units below them and the federations of *ulèëbalang* called *sagi* above them, there has been insufficient data to resolve the issue. Snouck Hurgronje, a dominating influence on all subsequent scholarship, is particularly unhelpful on this issue. He was determined to portray the Sultanate as weak and irrelevant in order to kill any further attempts at peaceful negotiation with it in his own day, and he assumed without historical evidence that the *ulèëbalang* and *sagi* predated the Sultan. By contrast the argument we present here is that the key features of the "diffuse" Acehnese political system of the 19th century took shape essentially in the half century which followed the death of Iskandar Muda in 1637.

The first reference we have to *ulèëbalang* is in a military context — among the Acehnese troops assaulting Portuguese Malacca in 1547.[8] This Portuguese reference confirms the original meaning of *ulèëbalang* as war leader, a usage which still occurs in Malay (*hulubalang*) though retained in Acehnese only through the old literature.[9] Acehnese chronicles already refer to the leading men of the kingdom as *ulèëbalang* by the 1570s,[10] that is following the warlike reign of Sultan Ala'ad-din Ri'ayat Syah al-Kahar (1539–71). It seems likely therefore that by this time *ulèëbalang* had a dual function as war leaders and territorial chiefs, having been rewarded with grants of land in the areas conquered by earlier expansionist Sultans. The most valuable land of the time was undoubtedly along the northern coast, especially around Pidië and Pasai, since this was the main source of pepper exports in the 16th century.[11] Such grants would have provided the means whereby *ulèëbalang* could furnish the men and resources needed for further military campaigns. Despite this development, the large pre-conquest states appear to have retained some identity as tributary fiefdoms, since we know that a number of 16th-century rulers appointed their sons as *raja* (rulers) of Pidië, Pasai, Deli (in East Sumatra) and Periaman (in West Sumatra).[12] One of the earliest lists of the great men of the realm,

142   An Indonesian Frontier

referring to 1579, begins "all the *raja*, and *kadi* [religious officials] and *ulèëbalang*".[13]

We do not know whether the appointments of *raja* and of the *ulèëbalang* who were presumably subordinate to them were intended to have a permanent, hereditary character. They may well have begun to assume such rights for themselves in the 1570s and 1580s when four successive Sultans were deposed or killed by the nobles of the capital. It is quite clear, however, that the two strongest rulers of the early 17th century had no time for any such hereditary claims, and went to great lengths in creating new local elites dependent wholly on themselves. The first of these exceptionally authoritarian rulers was Ala'ad-din Ri'ayat Syah Sayyid al-Mukammil (1589–1604) who reasserted royal power in no uncertain terms, as described in Chapter 5.

The grandson and protegee of al-Mukammil, Sultan Iskandar Muda (1607–36), took this tough policy to new heights. It was also reported of him that "He has exterminated almost all the ancient nobility, and has created new ones."[14] As we have seen, this Sultan also devised very effective means of retaining the loyalty of his new appointees. A complex administrative and judicial hierarchy developed under his authority, while the slightest hint of disloyalty or failure on the part of the *ulèëbalang* elite was punished with exemplary cruelty.[15]

Some evidence of the way in which Iskandar Muda created new benefices for those he raised to office occurs in two surviving *sarakata* (royal decrees), one dating from the early 18th century and the other from the 19th century. Both record that in 1613 Sultan Iskandar Muda granted a certain *orangkaya* a territory in Samalanga (on the north coast bordering Pidië) consisting of six *mukim*. Thirty or more years later, in the reign of Iskandar Muda's daughter, this grant was confirmed to the same beneficiary who now had the title of Orangkaya Seri Paduka Tuan Seberang.[16] The validity of these documents is confirmed by Dutch reports,[17] which identify this same man as Panglima Bandar or port administrator until his death in 1663 (or 1658 according to the *sarakata*), continuing to serve under the Sultana Safiyyat al-Din. As the *sarakata* also tells us that the land grant passed

The Transition from Autocracy

to his son, we may conclude that the benefice granted to a retainer by Iskandar Muda had become hereditary under his successors.

There appears to be no reference to the *mukim* in Aceh earlier than this 1613 grant. The origin of the division of Aceh into *mukim* (from Arabic *muqim*, an adult male resident in a particular parish, and perhaps, by extension, the parish itself) may therefore be due to the initiative of Sultan Iskandar Muda, as suggested by some earlier writers.[18] Iskandar Muda was known as a great mosque builder, a patron of *ulama* (especially those of the Wujuddiya mystical school), and a promoter of Islamic law.[19] He may therefore have appointed *imam* to be in charge of *mukim* throughout Aceh, in part to improve the practice of Islam, but also to act as a check on the power of those *ulèëbalang* who enjoyed benefices comprising several *mukim*. Under subsequent, weaker rulers, these *imam* became hereditary, secular chiefs of their *mukim*, sometimes themselves assuming the title *ulèëbalang* as well as that of *imam*. Already in a decree of 1640 two *imam* were listed among a list of royal officials or vassals in Pasai and Samalanga who had to pay a specified annual tribute to the king.[20] By the 19th century the *imam* who presided over Friday prayer at mosques throughout Aceh were entirely distinct from these chiefs of the *mukim*.[21]

The benefice granted by Iskandar Muda in 1613 discussed above was almost certainly not an isolated one. For the following reign, that of Iskander Muda's son-in-law Iskandar Thani (1636–41), the better evidence available to us shows a pattern of regular grants of land to retainers. One Dutch report in 1640 noted that one of the palace eunuchs, Seri Bijaya, was in charge of "revenue from lands", and had to decide which lands would be granted as benefices to the officers in charge of the royal bodyguard.[22] A decree probably from the same reign, recorded in the Acehnese compilation of edicts and law codes, the *Adat Aceh*, lists nine territories in the Pasai region with their approximate territorial limits. Many of these belonged to the great men of the capital, including the Sultan himself, the *orangkaya* Maharaja and the Laksamana.[23]

It is clear from the tight control Sultan Iskandar Muda exercised over his vassals and courtiers that any benefices granted were at his pleasure, and in no sense intended to be hereditary or permanent. It

144   An Indonesian Frontier

seems significant in this context that the royal decree or *sarakata*, which in the 19th century was taken as proof of an *ulèëbalang*'s hereditary right to his territory, as late as 1660 described as an unsealed ordinance given by the ruler "until its recantation", in contrast to an *eseuteumi* — a sealed decree of "everlasting validity".[24] In the decades after his death in 1636, however, the nature of these benefices appears to have changed fundamentally and become permanent.

The choice of successors to Iskandar Muda is indicative of the ambivalent attitude of the court elite towards his reign. On the one hand the aura of his greatness continued; on the other nobody wanted to have to endure such a reign of terror again. Iskandar Muda appears to have left no legitimate male heir alive, but he had shown great favour to a captured Malay prince from Pahang, who as a boy of nine had been allowed to marry the Sultan's daughter and to occupy a prominent place at court. This foreign prince succeeded as Sultan Iskandar Thani, and his rule appears to have been peaceful and prosperous, though Aceh's external power *vis-à-vis* the Dutch was allowed to erode somewhat.

At his death in 1641 the powerful *orangkaya* jockeyed for position for some days "for each one wanted to be king", according to a Dutch eye-witness.[25] Eventually they resolved to crown the bereaved queen, Iskandar Thani's widow and Iskandar Muda's daughter, as the first female ruler of the country. Although she was held in great respect as the final arbiter in matters of state, the Sultana Safiyyat ad-Din Taj al-Alam Syah (1641–75) had much less power *vis-à-vis* the half dozen most powerful men of the realm than did her father. The horrendous executions and punishments for disloyalty which marked the reign of Iskandar Muda and even to a lesser extent that of Iskandar Thani seem to have been wholly absent from her style of government. Both internal and external sources suggest that Aceh under this queen was well ordered and prosperous, with a climate very favourable to foreign commerce.[26] At her death in 1675 the experiment with female rule was deemed so successful that it was repeated three more times. "The very name of kinge is long since become nautious to them, first caused through the Tyrannical Government of theire last king" [sic] (i.e. last but one — Iskandar Muda).[27] Female rule, in other words,

The Transition from Autocracy

145

had come to seem synonymous with a quite different political order, attractive to the dominant elite in the capital.

It is not surprising that the leading *orangkaya*, most of whom had been courtiers or officials at the end of Iskandar Muda's reign, should have been reluctant to return to such a regime. At the very beginning of Taj al-Alam's reign, four of these *orangkaya* formed a kind of executive council which took many political decisions.[28] Whereas tribute from Aceh's dependencies and exactions on trade went overwhelmingly to the ruler in Iskandar Muda's day, a large share now began to be channelled to these *orangkaya*.[29] Dutch reports note that the great latitude the Queen allowed to her *orangkaya* gave rise to conflicts among them, so that the Sultana's remaining authority was largely derived from a careful balancing act between two major factions at the court.[30] The diversion of resources into the hands of a numerous oligarchy, however, unquestionably reduced Aceh's military capacity to resist the rising threat from the Dutch. The VOC became the dominant naval power in the Straits of Malacca after its capture of Malacca (1641), and Aceh seemed powerless to resist Dutch demands, carried out through a blockade in 1647–50, for a dominant share in Perak tin exports and West Sumatran pepper.[31]

The conflicts between these *orangkaya* incidentally shed valuable light on changes in the attitude to royal benefices. In 1642, the resident Dutch factors reported that a dispute arose between the major court factions over rights to land in the rich rice growing Pidië area. The Maharaja Sri Maharaja was alleged by his rivals to have acquired some of his lands in the region improperly during the reign of Sultan Iskandar Thani.[32] Eventually the Queen resolved the question by ruling that only grants of land made by her father, Sultan Iskandar Muda, would be recognized as valid.[33] The charisma of the great Sultan, in other words, was invoked to support a policy very different from his — making land grants permanent and hereditary. Part of the reason for the installation of a relatively weak ruler, indeed, must have been to prevent a repetition of the carnage and the attendant reallocation of benefices which had occurred under al-Mukammil and Iskandar Muda.

The *ulèëbalang* and *orangkaya* who had once been granted land to assist them to fulfil their obligation to the king quickly became hereditary rulers of these territories, where possible tracing their claim to a grant from Iskandar Muda. By the time of the *Hikayat Pocut Mohammad*, written in the early 18th century, the term *ulèëbalang* carried its modern meaning. It represented the hereditary ruler of a number of *mukim*, needing to be wooed by any Sultan or aspirant Sultan before any action could be undertaken.[34] Many of these hereditary dynasties bore titles betraying their origins in officials of the royal court — *Maharaja* in Lhokseumawe (Pasai); *Laksamana* in Ndjong (Pidië); *Mantroe* (Malay Mantri, minister) in several other Pidië districts.

We have explained above that 16th-century Acehnese kings appointed their sons as *raja* of conquered states — Pidië, Pasai, Deli and Periaman. This indicates that these large satraps remained as units above the level of the *ulèëbalang* benefices. The last such appointment appears to have been Iskandar Muda's of his only legitimate son as Raja Pidië in the early part of his reign.[35] Iskandar Muda was intolerant of anybody, including his relatives, building a significant power base which might eventually be used against him. He therefore developed the institution of *panglima* (governor) as a means of controlling his provinces. The principal function of a *panglima* appears to have been to ensure that the tribute, port duties, and commercial regulations imposed by Iskandar Muda were implemented to the letter, so that the resources of the important export centres flowed to his treasury. We therefore hear most of *panglima* in the pepper exporting areas on the west coast of Aceh. By 1621 the coast as far south as Padang was tightly controlled through two *panglima* placed at Tiku and Periaman. Beaulieu tells us that these officials were replaced every three years to ensure that they did not escape his control. While in office they had to report personally to the court every year.[36] In 1633 Inderapura, further south, was added to Acehnese territory and a *panglima* appointed there.[37] More *panglima* were appointed after Iskandar Muda's death, and in the 1660s they were reported at seven west coast ports — Barus, Pasaman, Tiku, Periaman, Padang, Salida and Inderapura.[38] Each *panglima* had a small staff

The Transition from Autocracy   147

comprising two writers (*kerkun*), a weigh-mast (*penghulu dacing*), and a port security official (*penghulu kawal*), emphasizing the role of the office in controlling trade.[39]

In the provinces to the east of the capital export production was less crucial and the role of *panglima* accordingly less clear. Tin-rich Perak on the Malay Peninsula was under Acehnese authority for decades after 1620, and an Acehnese *panglima* does at times appear to have been based there.[40] In such non-Acehnese territories, however, more attention appears to have been given to manipulating the indigenous *raja* or if necessary replacing him. A local Malay, Minangkabau or Batak hereditary elite continued to govern these territories even when Acehnese officials kept a tight control of the export trade.[41]

In the inner areas of the north coast, which must by this point be considered ethnically assimilated to Aceh, *panglima* may have been experimented with as a replacement for the role once taken in Pidië and Pasai by royal princes. There is a Dutch report as late as 1649 of a "Panglima Pidië" presenting the Queen with a tribute of rice, coconuts, sugar and betel,[42] and an earlier "Panglima Pidië" was a hero of the *Hikayat Malem Dagang* set in the reign of Iskandar Muda.[43] In such areas, however, the *ulèëbalang* benefice-holders appeared to have had direct relations with the court, and left little scope for a *panglima*. In the wars of the early 18th century many regional leaders carry the title of *panglima*, suggesting descent from one of these 17th-century officials, but none had any special relationship with the capital.[44] It seems safe to assume that the office of *panglima* as a device for controlling the provinces disappeared with the loss of the west coast pepper growing dependencies in the 1660s.

During the two decades following the death of Iskandar Muda, then, *ulèëbalang* benefice-holders appeared to have established permanent claims to estates made up of several *mukim* in Acehnese areas of the North Sumatran littoral. As the trade of Banda Aceh (the capital) and the ruler's share in it both declined steadily, such estates must have assumed gradually greater importance as against an advantageous place at court. The pepper exports which had been the key to Aceh's prosperity vanished with the loss of the West Coast ports and Deli under Taj al-Alam. The valuable tin exports of Perak were lost at about the same time, leaving Banda Aceh dependent on the relatively modest export of gold, elephants, horses and forest products. Having always been affluent enough to import rice for its substantial urban population, Aceh towards the end of the 17th century had to expand greatly its own production of foodstuffs -- particularly in the hitherto neglected Aceh River Valley adjacent to the capital.[45] This in turn meant that *ulèëbalang* arose there with large numbers of men under their control, close enough to the capital to have direct influence on its politics.

Although the first of Aceh's four queens, Taj al-Alam (1641–75), was still strong and respected, this was less true of each of her successors in turn. In 1688, near the end of the reign of the third, an Italian missionary noted that "they elect no more kings but Queens, though in fact it is seven of the nobles who rule the kingdom".[46] Ten years later a French visitor was sceptical whether the Queen even existed, since power was divided among the nobles of the court.[47] This type of oligarchy was favoured in the cosmopolitan commercial environment of the city, but these new *ulèëbalang* of the interior were increasingly intolerant of it. Their leader was the first Panglima Polem, reputedly an illegitimate son of Sultan Iskandar Muda and elder half-brother of Taj al-Alam, who had settled at Gle Yeueng about 30 km above the capital. He and his son emerged during the period of female rule as the chief opponents of its continuation. At the death of each of the queens their followers demanded that the throne pass to this Panglima Polem dynasty. In 1675, 1678, and 1688 they mobilized men from what became known as the *sagi* (corner) of the XXII *mukim*, centred on Gle Yeueng, to march on the capital in a vain attempt to decide the succession.[48] When female rule was finally abolished in 1699, however, the throne passed to new men of Arab origin and then to men of Bugis extraction who competed for support among the *ulèëbalang*. In these struggles Panglima Polem became not king but king-maker, or more frequently king-unmaker. By the time relative stability returned in the 1730s, various aphorisms had become current asserting that Panglima Polem, either himself,[49] or acting as one of three or twelve leading *ulèëbalang* of the Aceh

Valley area (known as Aceh Besar),[50] had "the power to enthrone and dethrone Sultans".

In little more than half a century, an autocracy centred in a flourishing port had been transformed into a diffuse polity of hereditary nobles bound together by the memory and heritage of a common past. Just as the European vernacular emerged from the domination of Latin with the transition to feudalism, Acehnese emerged in the early 18th century from the hegemony of Malay, in which all known texts had been written during the literary "golden age" which accompanied autocracy.[51] Another congruence with the European transition to feudalism was the rapid decline of slavery, which had relied, in autocratic Aceh as in ancient Rome, on a successful urban culture with a high level of new slave recruits through warfare.[52] Cultural assimilation, with the excessive cost of maintaining slaves, transformed the bottom class of Acehnese society into peasants owing numerous services to their *ulèëbalang* lord, yet perhaps not serfs in the sense that that category was juridically defined in Europe.

Conclusion

The social and cultural differences between Europe and Southeast Asia are sufficiently obvious to make anyone beware of applying the label "feudal" to the diffuse political system we have described. Even though some classic characterizations of the key features of feudalism[53] are compatible with Aceh and other Southeast Asian societies in the 18th century, there are crucial features of the latter which remain very different — the autonomous role of cities, of the Church, and of law have no real equivalent in Southeast Asia, for example. We prefer to emphasize here that a *transition* of similar magnitude as that from Antiquity to Feudalism appears to have taken place in many parts of Southeast Asia, centring in the late 17th century. It is to such transitions, rather than to the pursuit of static equivalence, that the attention of historians should be primarily directed.

Map 4 Aceh ports of the 18th and 19th centuries

8

The French Connection

WHEN a large Dutch Army finally conquered the *dalam* (citadel) of Aceh in January 1874, after two costly campaigns, it found little documentary evidence within Aceh's illustrious past. The exception was a beautifully written letter within a blue and gold border, signed by Louis Philippe of France and his Foreign Minister Guizot in January 1843. The French Consul in Batavia confirmed its authenticity, but could shed no further light on why it should have been addressed to the Acehnese Sultan. Writing 40 years later, E.S. de Klerck reproduced it "as a curiosity — the letter lacks any political importance".[1]

The present attempt to unravel the motives behind this letter, and other mysterious French appearances on the Sumatran scene, has not entirely succeeded in removing the air of unreality about them. France never had an important share in the riches of the Archipelago spice trade, and appeared slow to understand the importance of Portuguese, Dutch and British commerce there. Consciously or otherwise she appeared drawn rather towards policies and commitments on the Asian mainland. The ambitions the French occasionally entertained for the Archipelago tended to focus at its extremities, Sumatra or the Sulu-Basilan area, which they perceived as serving more important activities in the Indian Ocean and China respectively.

Such initiatives as were taken in the Archipelago were motivated as much by the desire to maintain the status of a great power, or to pursue chimerical visions both material and spiritual, as by a sober calculation of practical advantage. The boldest ventures were all left to languish after a few years. The more modest ones (the French Catholic Mission in Malaya, and some minor commercial enterprises), which did build an unobtrusive basis for permanent French influence in the Malay world, appeared incapable of exciting the French imagination.

Nevertheless, such intermittent activities could not fail to produce an impression on some of the Indonesian rulers concerned. In the 18th and especially the 19th century, France appeared to many Malay and Indonesian rulers as a powerful alternative to their threatening neighbours, Holland and Britain. The British and Dutch themselves, moreover, frequently invoked the threat of French interference to justify further expansion. The long term French contribution to the colonial history of the Malay Archipelago was more important in the shadow than the substance.

France's first contact with the Malay world was characteristic of all that followed, as much by the boldness of its conception as by the pathos of its outcome. The gifted Parmentier brothers of Dieppe led the first non-Portuguese expedition from Europe around the Cape to Indonesia. Hoping to reach China, they landed at Tiku, on the West Coast of Sumatra, in November 1529. Within a month both brothers had died there, and there was nobody to follow their footsteps.[2]

Frenchmen joined the 17th-century wave of northern Europeans, which took the pepper and spice trade between Indonesia and Europe out of the hands of Portuguese and Muslim traders. A number of expeditions sailed from the Breton ports of St. Malo and Dieppe in the period 1601–30, to trade in such ports as Aceh, Banten and Makassar. They are better remembered for their literary than their economic significance. The first of them, two ships under Michel Frotet de la Bardelière, reached Aceh from St. Malo in 1602. One Breton merchant in the fleet, Francois Martin, left a fascinating account of his five months in the sultanate, unfortunately much less used than the English and Dutch ones.[3]

The difficulties of coping with both Dutch naval predominance and with the political intricacies of the region, however, quickly discouraged the financiers of these voyages. Although a factory of St Malo traders maintained a tenuous existence at Banten from 1617 until 1684, a Dutch historian could rightly conclude that the V.O.C. "had little to suffer from the competition of the French".[4]

The French Connection 153

Among the most ambitious of the early voyages was that of Augustin de Beaulieu, who supplies the first record of a letter from an Indonesian ruler to a French king. The mighty Sultan Iskandar Muda of Aceh received Beaulieu well, in 1621, and bestowed on him a letter for Louis XIII: "Since God has made us great kings in this world, it seems reasonable that we should be friends and communicate with one another."[5] A century later another letter in Malay was received at the court of France, from a Malay ruler in very different circumstances. Sultan Abdul Jalil of Johor had been chased from his capital by Raja Kechil in 1718, but hung on in Trengganu until murdered by the victors in 1721. From Trengganu he appealed in vain to the Dutch, the English, and finally the French, to help him regain his fortunes. An English trader, Alexander Hamilton, and a French one, Pierre Villaumont-Gardin, happened both to call at Trengganu in 1719, the Frenchman en route to China. When Sultan Abdul Jalil was discouraged by Hamilton, he asked Villaumont-Gardin:

> if he thought the French nation might be induced to settle in his Dominions and the French Gentleman gave him Hopes that the King of France might be induced to accept his Friendship, and settle a Colony, providing he would certify his Request by a Letter, which the King of Johore readily agreed to.[6]

The Sultan's letter, which offered in return for assistance as much freedom for French subjects "as for my own" to trade, settle, and build fortifications, now rests in the Bibliothèque Nationale.[7] It appears to have aroused no interest in France.

By this time French interest in Asia had retreated to the limited Far Eastern trade of the *Compagnie de Chine*, the activity of the Missions Etrangères, and above all the long losing battle with the British for control of India. The decisive 18th-century wars for hegemony in Bengal and the Carnatic depended on the naval strength the rival powers could muster in the Bay of Bengal. As the Indian coast of the Bay became unsafe during the stormy November–December monsoon, the British fleet habitually "wintered" and refitted in Bombay. French fleets, on the other hand, repeatedly retired either to Mergui or Aceh, whence they were able to return to the fight in India before the

154 An Indonesian Frontier

British fleet could beat around Ceylon. At least as early as 1746 a French fleet made use of Aceh in this way.[8] The most famous such visit, however, was in 1782, when de Suffren arranged a rendezvous in Aceh with de Bussy.

Even though the two fleets failed to meet in Aceh because of de Bussy's late arrival, de Suffren's fleet alone must have been one of the largest ever to anchor off Aceh, with eight ships and several thousand men. The reigning Sultan, Ala'ad-din (1781–95), in fact spoke some French and possessed a considerable knowledge of French military tactics, as a result of having spent a month working in the arsenal of Ile de France (Mauritius) as a young man.[9] Nevertheless the Sultan and his subjects were understandably alarmed at the French arrival, "never having seen such substantial forces in their port".[10] Only by spending freely and keeping a tight control of his crew did de Suffren avoid hostilities. The Acehnese, the French noted, "are very jealous of their women, who are nevertheless not temptingly beautiful".[11]

De Suffren's brilliant campaign was the last to threaten British naval superiority seriously in the Indian Ocean. The French nevertheless continued to harass British shipping in Indian and Indonesian waters through daring raids mounted from the Ile de France. Not content with making prizes of British trading vessels, these raiders attacked the East India Company's factories on the West Coast of Sumatra. So poorly defended were most of these that they could be seized for ransom or plunder with hardly more difficulty than an armed vessel.

The way for later privateers was shown by the Naval Admiral Comte d'Estaing, during the Seven Years' War. In 1760 he seized the principal British post in Indonesia, Fort Marlborough (Bengkulu), as well as its string of dependent settlements along the west coast of Sumatra. The French occupying force was so afflicted by disease, however, that it abandoned Sumatra within a few months.[12]

It was during the Revolutionary War, when the French Navy was no longer a force in the Indian Ocean, that Ile de France acquired its reputation as a *nid de corsairs* through the dashing exploits of privateers like the famous Surcouf brothers.[13] One of the first in the field was Le Même, who crowned two enormously lucrative privateering expeditions with the capture of Padang in December 1793. The leading

The French Connection

Dutch establishment in Sumatra, Padang was still presumed loyal to the Stadtholder. Le Même departed after two weeks' occupation, with a heavy ransom from the burgers and Chinese of Padang.[14]

Earlier in the same year three privateers from Ile de France had already attacked the British posts of Bengkulu and Natal while on an abortive expedition against Batavia.[15] In 1794 Natal and Tapanuli were again briefly taken by privateers.[16] When the Napoleonic war began the French Admiral Linois was again quick to attack Sumatra, seizing Bengkulen in December 1803 by the ruse of entering the port under false colours. In four days of occupation he burned the warehouses and all the vessels in the harbour he was unable to take with him.[17] Even as late as 1809, when the balance of naval power was hopelessly against the French, Admiral Hamelin was able to sack the small but prosperous British post at Tapanuli, burning and plundering the whole town.[18]

This vigorous French activity came to an end with the British capture of Ile de France in December 1810. This was the last and strongest French base east of Suez, and it was not returned after the war. Neighbouring Réunion, returned to French control in 1815, was only gradually developed as an alternative in the 1830s.

Neglected Opportunities

The size and frequency of these naval expeditions must have made Sumatra relatively familiar, at least to French Naval and Colonial circles. Yet it is striking how negligible was the permanent French influence which survived into the 19th century. A number of individual Frenchmen, flotsam of the wreck of empire, lived on in Sumatra as renegades[19] or adventurers, but France possessed neither the strength nor the interest to make use of them.

The most intriguing, unconfirmed report of individual French survival in Sumatra appeared in the official *Le Moniteur* in 1858. The report stated that some members of a family de Molac left the service of de Bussy (presumably in February 1783 when his fleet called at Aceh) to establish themselves in "the wildest part of Sumatra". They built magnificent "agricultural establishments" on the coast, and eventually acquired great influence among the Bataks. In the 1850s one of the family was allegedly elected a "Batak chief". Though the report was emphatically denied by the French Consul in Padang, the factual basis which gave rise to it remains a mystery.[20]

Like the adventurers, French "country traders" had virtually no contact with their government in the late 18th and early 19th centuries. Based on the ports of the Coromandel coast, they played a minor role with British country traders and Chulia (Tamil Muslim) merchants in trading Coromandel cloth and Bengal opium for the pepper, spice, betel and tin of the Malay Archipelago. Such merchants came to dominate the commercial affairs of several contemporary states in Sumatra and the Malay Peninsula.

Between about 1806 and 1810 a small group of "French" country traders, in close commercial association with Chulias, obtained a commanding position in the Aceh Sultanate. Their leader, Francis L'Etoile, was considered to have "the entire control of the state and unlimited influence over the King" shortly before his death in 1810.[21] British fears on his account, however, were unnecessary. Far from being an agent of France, L'Etoile had changed his nationality from French to Danish at Tranquebar, after serving some time on French, British and Danish ships. His policy was to prevent any Western power gaining a foothold in Aceh, although in an emergency he appeared more willing to rely on British than French assistance.[22]

At no point, therefore, did France gain any advantage from the activity of its errant sons in Sumatra. J.E. Heeres[23] records an abortive French plan in the early 18th century to establish trading relations with Aceh. Subsequently it appears not to have impressed the French Government as it did the British that a permanent base in the Straits of Malacca region would be invaluable both for naval operations in the Indian Ocean and for intra-Asian commercial activity. The first of these assets was sufficiently demonstrated by de Suffren; the second had been pointed out as early as the 1740s by the enterprising and persistent Pierre Poivre. Other prominent Frenchmen, including the conqueror of Bengkulu, D'Estaing, echoed Poivre's insistence that in addition to obtaining spice plants for cultivation in Ile de France and Bourbon, the French needed a permanent base in Southeast Asia. Only this could provide the goods needed for trade with China, and avoid a ruinous drain of specie from France.[24]

The French Connection

In contrast to the other Powers, however, France consistently preferred to seek such a base in mainland Southeast Asia. To serve the needs of the French fleet in the Bay of Bengal Dupleix established a connection with Burma, which was renewed by some of his successors.[25] The proponents of a commercial entrepôt to serve the China trade were attracted rather to Vietnam, mainly because of the existing French missionary stake there and the false assumption that island Southeast Asia was already under Spanish or Dutch control. The archipelago remained virtually out of the reckoning, save for an ephemeral interest in Mindanao and Sulu in the 1760s and 1770s.[26]

Exaggerated fears of French activity in the Straits of Malacca nevertheless affected British policy at some vital points. During the War of American Independence fears that the French might occupy Aceh, or destroy Bengkulu once more, led to the appointment to Aceh of a British "commercial resident" in 1784. Although this move was unproductive it was an important step towards the decision to occupy Penang two years later.[27]

L'Etoile's influence over the young Sultan Jauhar al-Alam aroused new British fears during the Napoleonic War. These appeared to be confirmed in June 1809 by the capture just south of Bengkulen of Lt. Col. Leon de la Hussaye, an aide-de-camp of Marshal Daendels in Batavia. Daendels had despatched de la Hussaye to the court of Burma, to see what advantage could be gained from the powerful King Bodawpaya's designs on Bengal.[28] Such was the weakness of French seapower that he was sent up the west coast of Sumatra in a small Indonesian prahu, which leaked so much it was forced to land near Bengkulen. De la Hussaye carried letters to the Sultan of Aceh, presumably designed to facilitate his passage on to Burma. When captured, however, he appears to have thrown the British off his real objective by "admitting" that he had a special mission to Aceh. The Penang Governor, Macalister, wrote angrily to Sultan Jauhar reporting the capture of "documents proving the negotiation that has existed between Your Majesty and the French".[29] It was only a year later that missions sent to Aceh by the Penang Government revealed the complete lack of interest which even L'Etoile and his fellow Frenchmen had in any connection with France.[30]

158 An Indonesian Frontier

No doubt these fears in Penang sustained Raffles, when in 1810 he insisted that British troops occupy Aceh as part of his grand strategy for the Malay world.[31] Raffles also used the French bogey more broadly in his attempt to stimulate an energetic British policy in Southeast Asia.

> That the attention of the French Government has been particularly directed to Java and the Malay States from the time of their losing all hopes of establishing a solid footing on the Continent of Hindostan, may be inferred from a variety of circumstances, one of which is the cultivation of the Malay language in Paris under the celebrated Professor Langlis.[32]

Raffles was wide of the mark. When Louis-Mathieu Langlès became first administrator of the new *Ecole Spéciale des Langues Orientales Vivantes* in 1795, it was indeed intended that Malay should be taught there. But the fact that neither Langlès nor any other French orientalist apparently took the trouble to master this language until 40 years later is testimony to the limits of French interest.[33]

Whatever very limited capability France had to the East of the Cape of Good Hope was eliminated with the British capture of Ile de France and Réunion in 1810, to which the capture of Java was a mere appendix. Ile de France, which had proved such a dangerous base for privateers, was retained by Britain under its earlier Dutch name, Mauritius. The French factories in India (Pondichéry, Chandernagore) were returned in 1816 on the condition that they could not be fortified. Thus the only strategic base left to the French in the Indian Ocean was Réunion, renamed Bourbon by the restored monarchy. It was slowly built into a naval base, though not until the late 1830s did France attempt to use it to return to a position of influence in Southeast Asia.

It was the missionaries and the private pepper-traders who began a more intensive French contact with the Malay world in the 19th century.

French Missionaries in Sumatra

The Société des Missions Etrangères, organized in Paris in 1663 in response to Alexander de Rhodes' appeal for missionaries for Indo-China and Siam, had maintained a tenuous, occasionally interrupted

The French Connection

159

hold there ever since. The first venture of the French missionaries of the society into the Malay world was a mere extension of their work in Siam. Following the short-lived banishment of missionaries by King P'ya Taksin in 1781, shortly before his death, a mission station was established at Kedah to serve about 80 Siamese Christian refugees from Junk Ceylon (Phuket). Far from seeing it as an entry to the Malay world, the Vicar Apostolic Coudé thanked God for "the consolation of being in Siam, and of having a Church of Siamese in Kedah, where the lord has never been praised in that language".[34] However, within a year Fr. Garnault was already hoping to work among Chinese and Malays. When the British settled Penang in 1786, Garnault rapidly made this island the southern centre of his Bangkok Vicariate, because of its ready communications with the area.[35] The island came to seem such a centre of stability in an uncertain environment that in 1806 Penang was chosen as the new site for the Collège Général, the sole seminary of the Society in the Far East, which had led a precarious, shifting existence since its establishment in Ayutthaya in 1665.[36] However, this decision came during the most critical period for the French Missions, curbed and demoralized by Revolutionary anti-clericalism. At times it was struggling to find three priests to cover the whole of Siam and the Malay Peninsula. Only after the Bourbon restoration and the Catholic revival of the 1820s was it possible for the mission in Penang to consider new activities.

Although the French missionaries steadily expanded their work among the non-Malay population of Malaya throughout the 19th century, Sumatra was the first part of the Malay world to attract the enthusiasm of the missionary revival. In 1826 a new Vicar Apostolic, Florens, was asking for a priest to be sent to Aceh. This peculiar idea came from the bishop of Pondichéry, who must have picked up some loose talk from French pepper-traders.[37] But the isolated, still animistic island of Nias, off Sumatra's west coast, attracted more serious attention.

It was Jean-Baptiste Boucho, later to become the first Vicar Apostolic of the Malayan Peninsula (1845), whose enthusiasm gave rise to the Nias venture. He came into contact with Nias slaves and ex-slaves soon after his arrival in Penang in 1824, and baptized about 30 of them. Almost half were the windfall of the British judicial system:

Last year some Chinese traders brought a large number of these unfortunate Nias here to sell them; as this trade is forbidden by the English laws the dealers were arrested and put into prison, but to condemn them witnesses were necessary, and there were only these very Nias who could testify to the fact. The difficulty was that the Nias knowing nothing of a future life or of the punishments reserved for pagans could not be admitted by the law to the oath.... Without losing time, I asked the government for authority to instruct these people, which was given me the more easily because the government had no other means than that to bring the affair to a successful conclusion. By means of the Nias who were already Christian, these new compatriots were so well instructed, to the great satisfaction of the court which had them examined by the grand jury. All got their liberty. There were 10 girls and 3 boys. The girls are already Christian, and 4 of them are married to 4 new Chinese Christians. The boys will be baptised at Pentecost.[38]

Boucho could not sufficiently praise his Niassers, "good, simple, faithful, and very attached to their faith once Christian". From them he learned enough to compile half a Nias dictionary and write a few prayers in the language. Boucho was delighted to discover that they already recognized a beneficent creator God, "Laubalangi", although they directed most of their ritual to placating the evil spirit, named "Cekhou". Their moral code was very strict, adultery and fornication being punished with death.[39]

Despite Boucho's keen desire to go to Nias, however, he could not be spared from the College at Penang, and the task fell to two young priests. Jean-Pierre Vallon, ordained only after his arrival in Penang in August 1831, caught Boucho's enthusiasm to such an extent that the Vicar could not oppose "so obvious a vocation" for Nias. His companion, Jean-Laurent Bérard, appears to have joined the mission partly because of difficulties experienced in Penang.[40]

On 14 December 1831 the two priests left Penang in a small Malay vessel belonging to the Raja of Trumon, accompanied by a Nias catechist named Francisco and his wife Sophie. Their journey to Trumon by way of seven Acehnese ports was slow and difficult. The

The French Connection 161

Malay *nakhoda* and some *haji* passengers returning from Mecca did their best to convert Vallon and his party to Islam. At Trumon they encountered a state of war between the Raja and his subjects. By the time they reached the first Dutch port, Tapanuli (now Sibolga), the whole party was ill and Sophie was out of her mind.[41]

The original plan had been to travel first to the main Dutch centre at Padang, to establish a Christian bridgehead among its five or six thousand Nias (mainly slave) residents. Having returned to health in Tapanuli and neighbouring Natal, however, Vallon was eager to go straight to Nias rather than risk further mishaps in travel. Bérard alone therefore continued the journey south to Padang.[42]

Ignoring warnings from the Dutch military, whose experience in Nias had been particularly dismal, Vallon sailed with Francisco for the main trading and slaving port, Gunung Sitoli, in March 1832. Vallon improved his knowledge of the language, travelled through several villages and baptized a few children, before dying of unknown causes in June 1832. Bérard, "tout écrasé", received this mournful news as he lay with fever in Natal preparing to rejoin his colleague.[43] Nevertheless he proceeded to Gunung Sitoli, where he died within a few days. Both priests were just 30. A sympathetic merchant, Bérard's host in Padang, described what little was known of their death:

> Our friends already spoke enough Nias on their arrival in that island to make the poor islanders understand that their mission was entirely peaceful — that they in no way came to oppress them — on the contrary that it was for their spiritual & temporal good. They were well received by the inhabitants, who are not as bad as people say, which aroused the jealousy of their chiefs and of the Muslims, and *it is supposed* that as a result they were poisoned.[44]

The accusation of poisoning was treated with great scepticism by this merchant, Embrecht. Subsequently, however, it assumed the status of fact in the official record[45] by the efforts of Dutch officials anxious to emphasize the violence of Nias, and pious recorders seeking to add the halo of martyrdom to the heroic mission of these young priests. Poison is not mentioned by the American Congregationalist Lyman, the only other contemporary missionary to visit Nias. Lyman was in

162   An Indonesian Frontier

and around Gunung Sitoli for two weeks of June 1834, just before his own death among the Bataks. Despite his fear of "the curse ... of papal delusion", Lyman gave an endearing picture of Vallon and Bérard:

> They were, from all we learn, monkish, clownish enthusiasts. Their pay was but one hundred Spanish dollars per annum, and they were miserably fitted out. They, however, refused all assistance for themselves, but willingly received old clothes from the officers, to give to the Nyas.[46] One of them embarked at Padang,[47] in a little open boat, which, after he had put in his own baggage, scarcely contained room for himself. He arrived at Gunung Stollis [Gunung Sitoli], and was kindly received by Messam [a Christian from Tapanuli, resident in Gunung Sitofi and married to a high-born Nias], who offered him his own house. But he chose rather to erect a little miserable open shed, on the hill, near the house of a petty chief. He visited among the people, and obtained a child of that chief as his pupil; but in a short time took a fever, and died. His servant, also, had the same fever, but returned soon after to Padang, and resided a while with Mr. Embrecht. This man was hardly dead, and his goods sealed up, ere the other came, having embarked at Natal, where he had been to visit the upper stations of the Dutch. But the fever was already upon him, and he only landed at Gunong Stolis, to linger out eight or ten days, and go to his final account.[48]

The Société des Missions Etrangères did not abandon hope of Nias. It sent three more French priests to renew the work on better-prepared foundations in 1834. Problems of ecclesiastical jurisdiction had already arisen, however, and the priests sailed to Padang via Batavia, where they became involved with the Dutch Vicar Apostolic of Batavia and the colonial bureaucracy. Roman Catholic clergy had been officially permitted to enter Netherlands India only since 1808, and then under stringent conditions, They were forbidden to proselytize among Indonesians under Dutch control. The three priests encountered consistent official pressure to divert their attentions from Nias to the European population of Sumatra.

Until the French missionary initiative, no Dutch priest appears to have visited Sumatra. Vallon and Bérard had discovered that over half

The French Connection 163

the 2,000 or more Dutch soldiers in West Sumatra for the "Padri" War were Roman Catholic, mainly of Belgian origin. Most lived with Indonesian women, but according to Bérard they were prepared to regularize these unions if their mistresses could be instructed and baptized. Dutch law prevented their marriage to non-Christians.

Bérard had spent some three months ministering to these soldiers and their women before his ill-fated journey to Nias. He had travelled as far south as Padang and Painan to visit them, and inland as far as Batu Sangkar, where he had climbed a mountain (Merapi?) barefoot![49]

This scattered European parish therefore provided a ready diversion from the dangerous challenge of Nias. The heroic enthusiasm for Nias of Vallon and Bérard appears in any case not to have been shared by their successors. One of the three priests returned immediately from Padang to Batavia to plead for more money. The other two, Candalph and Galabert, accepted uncritically the hostile picture of Nias provided by embittered Dutch officials:

> it is impossible for foreigners to penetrate the island without suffering death or at least being sold into slavery; and until this island is occupied by troops, any foreigner who wants to enter it will perish without fail.[50]

Worse still, Fr. Candalph proposed the "almost certain alternative method of buying Nias slaves in Padang, to be educated in servility as priests or catechists". While awaiting approval, Candalph and Galabert remained in Padang serving the European Catholics and baptising their illegitimate children. The Dutch Vicar Apostolic of Batavia made his first visit to Sumatra in November 1834, and formally appointed Candalph Vicar of Padang. The French priests left Sumatra six months later, however, when the Dutch Governor-General continued to oppose their presence.[51]

This close identification with an unpopular colonial power brought to an end not only French but all effective Catholic missionary work in Sumatra for a century.

The Dutch duly occupied Gunung Sitoli in 1840, and brought fire and sword to the surrounding area in 1863. Not surprisingly the process

164   An Indonesian Frontier

of Christianizing Nias, begun by the Rhenische (Lutheran) Mission in the wake of this conquest, was painfully slow.[52]

Traders and Gunboats

The French Government appears to have had no connection whatever with this missionary initiative in Sumatra. It was only the rapid expansion of French commercial activity in the area in the 1820s and 1830s which attracted serious official interest in Paris.

In the closing years of the 18th century a remarkable development of pepper cultivation had begun in the southernmost dependencies of the Aceh Sultanate on the west coast of Sumatra. By 1820 this region had come to furnish about half the world's supply of pepper. While the Dutch and British still struggled to extract smaller amounts from their declining stations farther south under conditions of monopoly and forced labour, private traders flocked to buy this Acehnese pepper. New England vessels took the lion's share, but Arab, Indian, Penang (British and Chinese), and French ships were all participating by the 1820s. In 1823 four large French ships were reported to have taken cargoes of pepper from the coast, as against 27 American vessels.[53] Twenty years later the French were considered to occupy third place behind Americans and British. Nine or ten of their vessels visited Penang each year, and most of them went on to Aceh to collect pepper.[54]

Successful trading on the Aceh coast depended on fluency in Malay, if not Acehnese, familiarity with the dangerous coast and its numerous tiny ports, and contacts with the Acehnese rulers and traders who controlled the pepper. Those who acquired this special knowledge tended to spend a good part of their lives in the trade. With the development of Penang as an entrepôt they often used it as a base for multiple trips to Aceh during one voyage from France. One example is provided by the most well-known and respected French trader of the period, Captain Martin of Marseilles.[55] Leaving Marseilles in March 1838, he sailed to Sumatra via Bourbon for a lading of pepper, which he sold in Penang. He then returned for a second cargo of pepper, which he disposed of in Singapore. Finally he loaded 80,000 kg of tin

The French Connection

in Penang, filled his holds with a third cargo of pepper in Aceh, and sailed back via Bourbon to arrive in Marseilles in November 1839 — a total voyage of twenty months.[56]

The fact that the Aceh "pepper coast" comprised numerous autonomous petty states, which acknowledged the sovereignty of the Aceh Sultanate but paid little heed to its commands, made the coast a classic area of western "gunboat diplomacy". Captains who showed reasonable tact, patience, and fairness experienced few difficulties, and indeed established credit arrangements requiring a high degree of trust with the Acehnese sellers. The rapid fluctuations of price in this unstable market, however, did give rise to conflicts which no political authority was in a position to resolve. Few foreigners sought any more centralized control, either Acehnese or colonial, which might have put restrictions on their trade. Instead their ultimate recourse if attacked while trading in Aceh was to ask their respective navies to destroy the village where the offence occurred. As a "system" for the protection of trade it was arbitrary and barbaric, but at least it caused only temporary destruction when practised in moderation. The Acehnese always withdrew inland until the avenging gunboat had completed its destruction, and rebuilt their wooden houses quickly on its departure.

British and Dutch warships had long used these methods in the Malay world, even including other parts of the Aceh coast. It was the Americans, however, who introduced this form of chastisement to the West Aceh pepper trade. American warships destroyed the coastal village of Kuala Batëë in 1826, and the same village together with neighbouring Meuké (Muckie) in 1838, in retaliation for the murders of Captains Endicot and Wilkins respectively. Soon after the second incident, in May 1839, the French Captain Van Tseghem of Nantes was fatally stabbed in a quarrel with a wealthy Acehnese trader at Meuké. The Governor of Bourbon, where the French now had a strong naval presence, immediately sent *La Dordogne* to burn Meuké, just as it was getting on its feet after the American attack.

With this negative gesture began a brief period of French official interest in the West Aceh pepper coast. It was visited by four warships from Bourbon in as many years. Much of the impetus for this came from reports by Captain Martin on the Van Tseghem affair, first to

166   An Indonesian Frontier

the Governor of Bourbon and subsequently to naval officials in France. After describing the attacks on Wilkins, Endicot and Van Tseghem, Martin continued,

> Should we not naturally conclude ... that these are atrocious people, with whom all relations should cease? Nevertheless it is the case that we would be mistaken in so judging them. It is not that I wish to be their defender or apologist, but I am persuaded and I have been able to verify by experience that in proportion to its population the West Coast of Sumatra does not provide many more evil subjects than other parts of India. Captains Wilkins and Endicot were assassinated by order of the Rajas; and they would not have ordered these barbarous acts without having asked and begged these very captains, over several years, not to behave fraudulently, loading half their cargoes at night. As for the Captain Van Tseghem business, there was no premeditation on their part; this was only the unfortunate consequence of a brawl.[57]

Martin recommended that instead of burning market villages, which caused little loss to the Acehnese, the gunboats should seize and destroy the boats of the offending port, which were always well-stocked with arms and money. On the positive side, the captain suggested that the French should capitalize on the fear of retribution of the Acehnese around Meuké to demand the cession of part of the coast as a trading base. The Acehnese, he claimed, were convinced that, in contrast with the upstart Americans, the French, "first among the white races", would exact a terrible punishment. Moreover, the contemporary Dutch attacks on Acehnese border settlements just south of this pepper coast made the need for protection clear to all.[58]

The Governor of Bourbon received Martin's suggestion with some enthusiasm, sending the brig *Le Lancier* a few months behind *La Dordogne* to show the flag on the Aceh coast and investigate the prospects for some sort of base. Stressing the poor state of French commerce in the Malay world, and the rapid expansion of British and Dutch territories there, he urged Paris to move quickly to establish a base on some part of Sumatra not yet occupied by Holland.[59]

The French Connection 167

This opportunity struck France at a moment of greatly revived interest in the Far East in general and the Malay world in particular. As her economic and naval strength gradually returned, France was alarmed to discover the extent and continued growth of British commercial predominance in the East. The "well-nigh desperate concern" of the regimes which ruled France after 1830 to recover international greatpower status gave rise to an unaccustomed eargerness to come to the aid of French traders and missionaries.[60] So limited was the existing French stake in Asian trade that the pepper-traders of the Aceh coast were seized upon with gratitude. In Bourbon the Chamber of Commerce claimed wistfully that French commerce predominated on the Sumatra coast.[61]

Nothing did more to bring home to the French the growing value of the Far Eastern trade, and the key role which Singapore played in this for the British, than the activity of Adolphe Barrot as first French Consul in Manila (1835–8). He proved a splendid propagandist for the commercial attractions of Southeast Asia. On leave in 1839 he succeeded in winning his Government and a number of leading commercial houses throughout France to a broad strategy to break into the burgeoning trade of the East. He was sent back as Consul General for "Indochine" (meaning all Southeast Asia), based at Manila. His deputy Eugène Chaigneau, a veteran of lengthy and abortive negotiations in Annam, was to be based in Singapore, where he did not obtain an exequatur as first French Consul until 1840. The Dutch would allow no Consul in Batavia, but Barrot appointed a French merchant there as "correspondent". Another agent was installed in Macao. From all of these sources, but particularly from Chaigneau in Singapore, a stream of information was provided about the commercial possibilities of the region. Barrot and Chaigneau agreed, however, that the best way to compete with the British in Singapore and the Dutch in Batavia was to establish a comparable French base in Southeast Asian waters.[62]

For a few months following the receipt of Martin's report and that of the Bourbon Governor, the possibility of acquiring territory in Sumatra for a French naval and commercial base was actively considered in Paris. By early 1841, however, the Ministries involved

168   An Indonesian Frontier

(Affaires Etrangères, Marine et Colonies, Commerce) had all agreed that this was impracticable in view of French cordiality towards the Netherlands, which had already manifested its "pretensions ... for the integral occupation of Sumatra".[63] Interest turned further East, where the Opium War would soon open the Treaty Ports in China, bringing about a general redirection of commerce in that direction. Various possible bases were considered on the fringes of the Dutch and Spanish empires in the Malay Archipelago — Sulu, Basilan, Sumbawa, Borneo, as well as Pulo Condore or Tourane in Vietnam. When Lagréné's large-scale attempt to occupy Basilan for France ended in fiasco in 1845, French interest shifted away from the Archipelago altogether in favour of the East Asian mainland. France became ever more deeply embroiled in the affairs of Vietnam and China, and the conquest of Saigon in 1859 provided the needed *point d'appui* for French commerce there.

The period of official French concern with the Malay world was thus fairly brief, between about 1839 and 1845. Initiatives taken during this period were of more lasting significance, however. The chair of Malay which had been neglected at the beginning of the century was finally established in 1844, as a result of the Foreign Minister's insistence on the necessity "of facilitating the teaching in France of a language as widespread as Malay is from the Cape of Good Hope to New Guinea and the north of the Philippines", especially when France was engaged in strengthening its commercial and political links with Southeast Asia.[64] Edouard Dulaurier, an Arabist whose interest had shifted to Malay during a visit to London in 1838, thus became one of the first professors of that language in any country. Throughout the remainder of the 19th century he and his successors Favre and Marre made the Oriental Languages School in Paris one of the world's leading centres for Malay scholarship.[65]

Official Relations Between Aceh and France

The diversion of official French interest from Sumatra to Basilan and then Indo-China did not prevent a growing interest on the part of

The French Connection

169

Aceh in this potential new ally. Acehnese could not but be impressed with the succession of French warships suddenly reinforcing the French pepper-traders between 1839 and 1843. The first visits were not particularly friendly. *La Dordogne* had destroyed Meuké in 1839, and *Le Lancier* did the same for Seunagan in February 1840 after the murder there of the first mate of the Marseilles trader *Comte de Paris*.[66] This second attack, before any attempt was made to investigate the cause of murder, had reportedly infuriated the vigorous Acehnese Sultan of the period, Ala'ad-din Mansur Shah, popularly known as Ibrahim (1838–70).[67]

On the other hand Captain Martin, on a visit to the Acehnese capital in August 1840, was able to assure the Sultan that the chastisement of Seunagan had not been approved in Bourbon and did not imply any official French hostility toward Aceh. Indeed the Governor sent the frigate *La Magicienne* to Seunagan in September 1840, expressly to restore the good relations interrupted by *Le Lancier's* over-hasty bombardment.[68]

Before *La Magicienne's* arrival, Sultan Ibrahim had already given Captain Martin a letter for King Louis-Philippe, "who rules with justice the city of Marseilles". The Sultan appealed to an alliance between France and Aceh which he had heard existed in the time of his grandfather.[69] He sought to revive this imaginary alliance in view of the seemingly relentless Dutch advance on the West Coast, where they had already taken Singkil and Barus (1839–40) at Aceh's expense. Ibrahim was convinced:

> we will have to fight the Dutch because they want to occupy our Kingdom. Nevertheless, with the help of God, we will yield them no part of it. What concems us particularly in this matter is the ability of the Dutch on the sea, whereas we do not know how to fight there. We therefore come to ask help of our friend... If he helps us to gain the victory, we will give him a base wherever it suits him.
>
> We make known further to our friend, regarding the merchant ships which come from the Kingdom of France, which is under his dominion, that he should order them to visit our Kingdom [i.e. the capital, Banda Aceh] so that we can give them the

permission and the facilities to sail wherever they wish to trade. If, after having come to Aceh, they are subsequently robbed, we undertake formally to be responsible to them for the value of all the goods lost. This is what I have to say to our magnificent ally.[70]

Ibrahim's demand that the European powers invoke the authority of the Acehnese sovereign, rather than settling matters directly with his vassals, was a consistent one throughout the 19th century. Although perfectly within his rights in pointing this out to the French, British, American and Dutch alike, the Sultan was too weak to enforce it. It suited the Western traders to avoid entanglements with the Sultanate and remain free to play off the powerless pepper-producing tributaries of the West Coast against one another. The Americans, despite the great value of their trade with Aceh throughout the first half of the 19th century, appear never to have had any formal relations with the Sultanate in this period. The French similarly preferred to avoid the capital until after receipt of Ibrahim's letter. Only in February 1843 did the Corvette *La Fortune* call at Banda Aceh in the course of a detailed investigation of North Sumatra and Pegu, called for by the Minister of the Navy and the Colonies. The Governor of Bourbon had also commissioned its commander, Le Comte, to encourage French commerce, in particular by obtaining Acehnese acceptance of the French five franc piece.

On his preliminary tour of the West Coast ports Le Comte was repeatedly referred to the capital on the question of currency — mainly, one may assume, as a polite way of avoiding having to point out the difficulty of disposing of French coins, in contrast to the popular Spanish silver dollar. On the other hand he found the rulers of the states nearest to the Dutch garrison of Singkil more emphatic than ever in their desire for French protection. Bulo Samah and Trumon, where the leading men of Singkil had settled after failing in its defence, had a particular hatred of the Dutch:

They told me formally that their greatest desire is that France should take them under its protection, and that they wanted to be French.[71]

The French Connection   171

In Banda Aceh Le Comte was received with great formality but little warmth. Sultan Ibrahim undertook to do his best to have French coins accepted, and replied to Le Comte's greeting in the name of the Governor of Bourbon by saying:

> *That formerly* there had been good relations of friendship between his country and France, and that it did not depend upon him to have them re-established.[72]

The question of the sack of Seunagan was discreetly sidestepped at the royal audience on February 25. The following day, however, the Shahbandar and the Sultan's secretary made clear to Le Comte that Ibrahim remained upset about the attack on Seunagan, and repeated the demand that French vessels call first at Banda Aceh before trading on the coast.[73]

Le Comte would have fared much better had he brought some answer to Sultan Ibrahim's letter of 1840. Consistent with the arbitrariness which appeared to govern all France's actions in Sumatra, however, a reply was written only in January 1843, when *La Fortune* was already on its way to Aceh. Louis-Philippe himself then signed a gracious letter expressing his desire for closer relations, and for the Sultan's continued protection of French trading vessels.[74]

Ibrahim was accustomed to receiving letters from the British Governor of the Straits Settlements, or the Dutch Governor of Padang. This was the first time that he, or any of his predecessors since the 17th century, had received a friendly letter from a European Head of State. Not surprisingly the impressive letter, which appears to have been delivered by a warship, was one of the few documents safely preserved in the Acehnese palace until the Dutch conquest of 1874. It appears also to have disposed Ibrahim to regard the little known French as perhaps his most promising potential ally.

Well before the French monarch had signed this letter, the Quai d'Orsay had decided against the possibility of establishing a naval station in Aceh. Yet the short-lived period of official interest had made an impression on some of the French pepper-traders, who may in addition have been sounded out by the Sultan when they visited

172 An Indonesian Frontier

Banda Aceh. In 1845 Noel Berchou of Nantes, an Aceh pepper-trader for 15 years, resurrected the issue with the foreign ministry. He claimed to possess great influence in Aceh, where the Sultan and his chiefs "have often manifested to me the desire they have to be under the protection of the French King".[75] Berchou was politely turned down, and seemed to be growing more desperate by the following year, when the Minister of Agriculture and Commerce was informed that Berchou was planning to "sell" his interests in Aceh to the British, having been rejected by his own government.[76]

Sultan Ibrahim did not reply formally to Louis-Philippe's letter until early 1849. Taking advantage of the intended pilgrimage to Mecca of Muhammad Ghauth, a wealthy nephew of the *ulèëbalang* of Meulaboh distantly related to the ruling house, Ibrahim entrusted him with two further important missions. He was to carry to Constantinople an appeal for diplomatic and military support on the basis of Aceh's strong sentimental and religious ties with Turkey. At the same time he was to journey to Paris to present a letter to Louis Napoleon, whom he addressed as "Paduka Sri Sultan Republic Peranchis".

Ibrahim's letter to the French President began with gratitude for the letter of Louis Philippe, promised that French coins would be accepted, and repeated the request that French traders call first at Banda Aceh for a safe conduct. But Ibrahim had pressing needs of his own:

May you give me a warship or if possible two, so that I can control the people of each state and town. If there is a warship all the ulèëbalangs will certainly be afraid of me. Regarding payment for this ship I have the necessary goods, but I wish to postpone payment if possible for two years. Once this period is up I will pay you the price. Please ensure the ship is complete with equipment.

Furthermore I ask your great mercy, because my country has been taken by the Dutch. There are two or three towns, beginning with Airbangis and extending to Singkil as well as the island Nias, which have been taken by the Dutch because these countries are rather far from Aceh. May it be by your prayer and your decision that the Dutch are removed from all these states.

The French Connection

173

The Sultan's letter ended with a statement of complete confidence in Muhammad Ghauth as his plenipotentiary.[77]

The embassy of Muhammad Ghauth produced striking results at both the French and Turkish courts, each of which appears to have seized eagerly upon this exotic evidence of its international status. The envoy proceeded from Mecca to Constantinople sometime in 1850, to find Sultan Abdul Mejid highly gratified with the homage he brought from such a distant "vassal". The Turkish Sultan issued two *firmans* renewing his ancient "protectorate" over Aceh. To facilitate his homeward journey Muhammad Ghauth was given a recommendation to the Khedive in Egypt, while the Turkish Governor of Yemen was instructed to send the envoy on to Aceh.[78]

This royal treatment must have precluded the continuation of Muhammad Ghauth's mission to Paris, quite apart from practical difficulties of money and language. While in Cairo on his return journey in 1852, therefore, he entrusted Sultan Ibrahim's letter to the French Consul, along with his own apology for his "inability to come in person".[79]

Louis Napoleon, however, was obviously flattered to receive a letter from this obscure oriental kingdom, particularly in the honorific French into which the orientalist Desgranges rendered the rather casual original.[80] He authorized Ghauth's journey to Paris as a guest of the government, while 5,000 francs were set aside for his expenses in France.[81]

Whether the envoy was still in Cairo to receive this reply is not clear. However, the Acehnese who took advantage of the offer, who was escorted around Paris by Foreign Ministry officials, and who was finally received by the Prince-President on 31 October 1852, was clearly not Muhammad Ghauth. It was his young writer Teuku Nyak Adum, who became known in France as Sidi Muhammad. Perhaps the French did not care. In any case they did not appear to realize the mistake until after the envoy's departure. Meanwhile he and an Acehnese companion lived in France at government expense for almost a year, before being sent back to Aceh in January 1853 with a magnificent sword as a present from Napoleon to Sultan Ibrahim.

174   An Indonesian Frontier

The incident naturally created some alarm in The Hague, which was little accustomed to such flamboyant imperial gestures. The Dutch need not have worried. As they were told, the Acehnese visit was simply "a matter of curiosity".[82] Its only political significance was the exotic embellishment it was intended to give to the court of the Prince-President — soon to be Emperor.

The honour of transporting "Sidi Muhammad" back to Sumatra was given, in January 1853, to Noel Berchou, the Nantes pepper-trader who had earlier claimed such influence in Aceh. He became increasingly suspicious about the envoy's credentials, and finally discovered his real identity upon arrival in Aceh. Berchou appeared not to be amused, complaining that "Sidi" had even tried to swindle him in a pepper transaction.[83]

The Sidi Muhammad affair ended official French relations with the independent rulers of Sumatra. Like the missionaries earlier, the French Government henceforth conducted its relations exclusively through the Dutch as overlords. In 1856 a full-time French Consul for Sumatra was sent to the seat of the Dutch Governor at Padang, over thirty years earlier than any other foreign consul in the island. The appointment to a small Dutch garrison town must have originated with the interest of the previous decade in the Acehnese pepper trade. It is characteristic of French relations with Sumatra, however, that the only period of official French representation was also one of exceptionally low French involvement. During the 1850s French pepper ships virtually ceased to visit Sumatra as the market for Aceh pepper shifted to Penang, served by regular steam lines. Until the Consulate's abolition in 1865, successive Consuls had nothing with which to fill their time except an occasional report on Dutch military activity and a continuing squabble to establish their diplomatic privileges.[84] The task of reviving French commercial interest was obviously hopeless. The last and most interesting of the Consuls, Le Comte A. de Pina, pointed out that Dutch policies made it impossible for any European merchant to survive in their Sumatran possessions.[85]

Although de Pina collected some interesting material on Sumatra, it was only after the revival of French interest during the 1870s

The French Connection

that he was able to find a publisher for it. His book was remarkable for its final chapter, in which he advanced the cause of Malay as the great *lingua franca* of Asia. Instead of struggling to master Vietnamese, Thai and Chinese, de Pina argued, France should promote Malay:

> expand it in our East Asian possessions, encourage its study at home, and make it obligatory for officials destined for colonial service.[86]

The Aceh-Dutch War, 1873

The interest France had shown in Aceh in the early 1850s was ephemeral, like that of Turkey. Both countries had forgotten Aceh's existence within a few years. But despite the absence of continuing relations, Aceh continued to regard these two Powers as the most promising potential source of help against the Dutch. About 1862 Sultan Ibrahim asked an Italian adventurer at his court, Cesar Moreno, to look to France in the first instance for a defensive treaty against the Dutch.[87] When Habib Abdur-Rahman az-Zahir came to guide Aceh's foreign relations after 1870, it was again France and Turkey that he looked upon with greatest favour. The Habib even claimed in his memoirs to have been twice in France, once in his youth and once as Acehnese envoy in 1873.[88]

When in November 1872 it became clear to Acehnese leaders that the Dutch were determined to establish their power over Aceh by one means or another, there was a considerable burst of diplomatic activity. The royal favourite Muhammad Tibang was sent to Singapore to try to delay Dutch overtures while sounding out the representatives of the major European powers. Britain had already proved a disappointment. The importance of France in Acehnese hopes was indicated by the fact that Tibang carried one royal letter specifically addressed to the Consul of France, and another open letter to serve the consuls of all the other powers. However, Tibang appears to have been persuaded in Singapore to bypass the unsympathetic French Consul in favour of the American.[89]

Soon after Habib Abdur-Rahman az-Zahir, regent of Aceh, arrived in Penang on the French steamer *Patty* owned by his friend Edouard Roura. Early in January 1873 he took the mail steamer for Jidda and Europe, letting it be known that he intended to appeal to both French and Turkish Governments. When Holland declared war on Aceh on 26 March he was still no further than Mecca. His first thought on hearing of the Dutch invasion appeared to be France, and the French Consul in Jidda reported early in April that the Habib was on his way to Paris.[90] However, like Tibang he seems to have discovered France's real attitude quite quickly, probable in Cairo, and he decided instead to concentrate solely on Turkey.

In the panicky mood into which the Netherlands was thrown prior to the declaration of war on Aceh, and still more after the Dutch expedition had retreated from Aceh in defeat on 25 April, the slightest indications of foreign support for Aceh were wildly exaggerated. France, along with Italy, America, Turkey and Britain, was momentarily suspect. But of all these states France went to the greatest lengths to assure The Hague of full support in the war. While Britain and America attempted to pursue at least a formal neutrality, President Thiers wrote personally to The Hague to convey his confident prayers, "that Dutch arms may establish their legitimate ascendency in the Indies". If, he added, "the Sultan of Aceh had the singular idea of addressing himself to us, he would be abruptly repudiated".[91]

Consistent with this policy, Thier's successor MacMahon refused to reply to a written appeal of July 1873 from Teuku Paya, an Acehnese leader in Penang, complaining about the false accusations of the Dutch. The letter was immediately shown to the Dutch Govemment.[92] The French Ambassador in Constantinople, similarly, was instructed to advise Turkey to drop its plans for mediation in the war.[93]

Having at last recovered its role as a colonial power in Asia, France was no longer interested in flirting with the peripheries of the Dutch empire. The Government could now find no particular French interest in North Sumatra beyond the "chaos of piracy", which it feared would result from an Acehnese victory.[94] Policy was therefore governed exclusively by friendship with Holland and "solidarity among all the countries of Europe in regard to their eastern policies", to see that European "prestige" was maintained.[95]

The French Connection

The Geographical Movement

For French governments of the 1870s Continental strategy was paramount. The pursuit of effective colonial schemes had to be sacrificed to the all-consuming demand to make good the humiliation of 1871, and to heal the wounds of the Paris commune. The overwhelming public sentiment was against wasting on expensive colonies resources which could be used for the task of national survival in Europe.

A minority of French intellectuals and businessmen, on the other hand, reacted quite differently, seeking salvation overseas from the disaster suffered in Europe. The vehicle for such views was the geographical movement. Geographical societies blossomed throughout Europe in the 1870s, but in France they became an obsession. The hitherto austere *Société de Géographie* in Paris opened the way by announcing in 1871 that it would no longer limit itself to pure scholarship, but would pursue the more urgent imperative of demonstrating a new and successful foreign role for French enterprise. Within three years the society doubled in membership, and before the end of the decade it had spawned a dozen geographical societies in the provinces. The recipe under which these societies flourished was a blend, as Mackay puts it, of "national honor, scientific interests, and commercial prosperity".[96] Frenchmen must be made aware of the dazzling commercial and civilizing opportunities that awaited them in Africa and the East. By supporting exploration and colonization, Frenchmen were serving science, commerce and the Fatherland all at once.

One of the most interesting off-shoots of the movement was the Société de Géographie Commerciale, which resulted from a commission formed in 1874 by the *Société de Géographie* on the one hand and the Paris Chambers of Commerce on the other. By 1876 it had assumed a separate life, dedicated to placing the latest scientific knowledge of foreign places at the disposal of French commerce. Among its first projects was to prepare a map of the globe showing every place where Frenchmen resided and where the French government was represented.[97]

Although the principal emphasis of the movement was Africa, the opportunities for France in the Far East were not forgotten. The most ambitious Asian venture arising from the Paris *Société de Géographie*

178   An Indonesian Frontier

was the formation of a task force called the *colons explorateurs,* to establish an experimental commercial colony in the East as a base for further scientific and commercial work. The founder and moving spirit of this project, Brau de St.-Pol Lias,[98] proclaimed the manifesto of the group as follows:

> the true way to study a country seriously is to support exploration upon colonial establishments which allow it all the length of time, all the continuity which it must have, all the security which it must enjoy; just as the way to harvest all the fruits of exploration is to have the exploration radiate from these establishments, to place, behind the explorers, colonists of which they are the avant-garde, who can profit from their discoveries, take root were they have penetrated, and push them yet further afield.[99]

The enthusiasm of Brau de St.-Pol Lias for his vision of a revived expansionist France was tireless and infectious. One of the instigators of the *Société de Géographie Commerciale,* he was convinced that France could only return to her traditional place of honour among nations by forging a new vigour in the fires of overseas adventure:

> Colonization is the most effective spring from which the powers of a people can be refreshed. It not only produces wealth: it makes men vigorous and energetic; it tempers characters.[100]

He never ceased to denounce the argument that Frenchmen lacked the aptitude for colonization, or the adaptability to foreign languages and customs. Every example to the contrary is emphasised in his books. Indeed, he argued in a fascinating extension of Hobsonian logic, it was not only the need to dispose of excess manufactures which demanded that Europe acquire Asian colonies, but the problem of excess talent, education and leadership. Capable men "finding nothing to organize at home ... are led by a fatal necessity into disorganising something".[101] The disastrous deficiency in France was not talent, but a firm colonial policy.

Unlike many of his colleagues in the geographical movement, however, Brau's concern was not limited to the expansion of French

The French Connection

territory. Colonization to him was the work of individuals and firms as much as governments. France, like Germany before her, would draw great benefit from the commercial ventures of her sons in foreign colonies. Equally, like Holland, she would gain from possessing colonial territories even if they were exploited by foreigners.[102] Resentful of British attempts to curb French expansion while fattening on her own Empire, Brau was nevertheless a Europeanist in his approach to colonization. His bitterest denunciations of Britain were because of her refusal to co-operate with the "patriotisme de race" which was his vision for Europe in its dealings with Asia.[103]

For these reasons Brau's first commercial adventures were directed to the newest and apparently richest possessions of the Netherlands and Britain, rather than to French territory. Brau saw himself as a French pioneer at the colonial frontier, whose efforts would bring wealth, prestige, and the growing stimulus of foreign adventure to France without necessarily extending her territory.

As an initial experimental base for the *colons explorateurs* Brau selected the booming new plantation district of East Sumatra, centred around the minor sultanate of Deli. The remarkable suitability of this area for tobacco growing had been demonstrated just a decade earlier by the Dutch planter Nienhuys. Despite numerous last-minute defections Brau eventually brought together half a dozen enthusiastic Frenchmen, who subscribed their own capital for the expedition of which they formed the members. There was a young mining engineer, Wallon; an even younger "agriculturalist", Tabel, and his assistant; a doctor; and a few non-specialists. After two difficult months in Java obtaining the necessary Dutch official backing, they succeeded in marking out a plantation in the last months of 1876. Their concession was in remote Bedagai, bordering Batu Bara and Simelungun Batak territory. At that time it was to the south of the recognized frontier of the tobacco plantation area of Deli.[104]

For two years this tobacco plantation cut from the virgin jungle at Bedagai struggled on. The first crop was good, the second disappointing. But it was not the continuing routine of finding labour, planting, and harvesting that called to these romantic French hearts,

180 An Indonesian Frontier

but the lure of discovery. Within six months of arrival the *colons-explorateurs* had already fallen out with each other in their rush for the fabled gold of Sumatra.

The Quest for Aceh Gold

Gold is present at many points of the mountain ridge running down the western side of Sumatra, and has been exploited throughout historic times. For the early Portuguese Minangkabau had been the best known centre of gold production. Further north, Aceh had also exploited the alluvial gold of the mountain ridge since at least the 17th century. The richest area in Aceh was the federation of *ulèëbalangships* known as Kawaj XII, at the headwaters of the Teunom and Wojla rivers, whose population had been principally occupied in panning for gold until the 19th-century pepper boom drew them nearer the West coast. About 1840 the ruler of Seunagan, further south, also encouraged 200 Chinese to work the alluvial gold in the higher reaches of his river, although their efforts were ultimately thwarted by disease.[105] The existence of gold in these areas had never been a secret. In 1877 a brochure was published in Amsterdam arguing that the gold in the mountain backbone of Sumatra was potentially as rich as the Californian and Australian fields, though since it had been worked for centuries there would be no windfalls for the casual surface prospector.[106] However, the dramatic and widely-reported Dutch setbacks in attempting to conquer Aceh after 1873 tended to inflate the idea of spectacular riches awaiting the conqueror.

The *colons-explorateurs* probably had their attention drawn to West Aceh gold by Edouard Roura, the only French sea captain still operating in Sumatran waters. Although of Spanish origin Roura had been naturalized in Marseilles, and had traded in Aceh pepper since the 1850s with his base in Penang. At the outbreak of the Aceh war he was considered to be the European trader best acquainted with Aceh, speaking Acehnese and having close relations with the *ulèëbalangs* of the West Coast pepper growing states — especially Paté. Habib Abdur-Rahman, the regent of Aceh, was his friend. The Dutch wooed

The French Connection

him with special exemption from their blockade, and later by chartering his vessel the *Patty*, in return for his information and his influence. But Roura was too well aware of Acehnese determination to resist to give the Dutch much pleasure. He constantly stressed the need for negotiation, and fell increasingly out of favour with a government committed to military victory. By 1876 he was very embittered against the Dutch, whom he felt had given him inadequate compensation for the loss of his pepper trade and the help he had provided.

During the early months of 1877 the mining engineer of the *colons-explorateurs*, Wallon, toured Teunom and Woyla, possibly with the help of Roura who made a voyage to the coast in late January.[107] Wallon must have obtained the support at least of Teuku Imam Muda of Teunom, the most important *ulèëbalang* of the area, who was just then negotiating his submission to the Dutch.

Despite his inability on this visit to cope with water seepage into his experimental diggings, Wallon became insatiably eager to return to exploit the fabled gold.[108] He immediately set about organizing a large-scale expedition on his own account, setting off a bitter disagreement with Brau de St.-Pol Lias, "which ended all relations between us".[109] By November of 1877 Wallon had found his own financial backing in Paris and returned to Singapore with another engineer, Moulle, and a businessman, Pillard. In a clumsy attempt to deceive the Dutch, the group claimed to be going to West Aceh to buy pepper and establish an agricultural enterprise. Evidently they were foolish enough to think that if they succeeded in negotiating mineral agreements with the local rulers, the Dutch would then be reluctantly obliged to accept their preemption of the fabulous wealth they envisaged there.

In reality Dutch officials in West Aceh had no illusions about Wallon's intentions, and commended his enterprise.[110] Nevertheless, the Frenchmen were not allowed in to the Teunom area in late 1877, to their intense annoyance, because the Dutch could offer no security whatever.[111]

The *colons-explorateurs* did not survive the dispute over gold. Brau left the East Sumatran plantation for Paris about March 1877. He hoped to find additional finance to enable him to use the plantation as the base for exploiting West Aceh gold. However, he had little

182   An Indonesian Frontier

control over the other *colons-explorateurs*, who had contributed their
own funds and envisaged more spectacular roles for themselves than
planting tobacco. Most of the group drifted back to France. Brau
failed to find in Paris the money to keep Tabel going, and when his
own resources were exhausted in 1878 the experiment had to be
abandoned. Tabel remained in Deli as the chief assistant on the only
other French plantation in Sumatra — that of the two brothers De
Guigné, from Réunion.[112] In 1886 Tabel organized finance in Paris
for his own *Société de tabac de Deli*, but this, too, failed within a few
years because of the poor location of its concession.[113]

The experience with his *colons-explorateurs* modified Brau's
colonial theories considerably. The romantic assumptions, which had
led the original *colons* to pool their resources and energies, now
seemed hopelessly unrealistic for a permanent business operation.
Above all the *colons-explorateurs* had failed to reinforce the authority
of the leader with a single source of capital. The objective therefore
had to be the formation of a large-scale *Compagnie coloniale d'études
et de préparation d'entreprises commerciales, industrielles, et agricoles*,
similar to the great British Chartered Companies being formed at
this time.[114]

By the beginning of 1880 Brau had succeeded at least in forming
"an embryo of this company", the aims of which would be to
demonstrate the practicability of his new vision.[115] The most spectacular
profits now seemed to be in minerals rather than agriculture, however.
Brau's only companion was therefore a mining engineer, M.J. Errington
de la Croix, with whom he left Toulon in January 1880. The first
objective was the gold of Aceh, "one of the richest countries in the
world, and still one of the least known".[116] Failing this, they would
explore the tin resources of Malaya or the minerals of Borneo.

Although conditions in West Aceh were hardly very different in
1880 from 1877, the Dutch attitude had changed. Desperately short of
men, money, and national will to go on killing Acehnese, the Netherlands
was anxious to prove to itself and the world, despite most of the evidence,
that the war was really over.[117] In response to Dutch statements to this
effect, Brau's party and that of Wallon began at the end of 1879 a race
to reach the hitherto forbidden *eldorado* in West Aceh.

The French Connection

Wallon made sure he was the winner. Accompanied by Guilhaume, another mining engineer, and Courret, the son of the principal financier of his party, he arrived in Singapore a few weeks before Brau. After a short period obtaining the necessary approval in Batavia, Wallon took a steamer to Padang and then a small Acehnese prahu from there north to Meulaboh, instead of following the orthodox steam route via Penang and Ulèëlheuë. When Brau and Errington de la Croix reached Singapore on 1 March 1880, Wallon's party was already at Meulaboh.

Wallon's relationship with Dutch officialdom was a crude caricature of Brau's. Brau and Errington, although officially entrusted by the Ministry of Public Instruction with a *mission scientifique*, made clear to Dutch officials that they regarded the quest for an economically viable enterprise as the more important object of their journey.[118] Wallon lacked these scholarly credentials, but engaged in an elaborate pretence that his haste to reach Aceh and explore the gold-bearing regions was "animated by a fervent love for science".[119] The French Consul was alarmed lest in being discovered, Wallon would involve the French in great embarrassment, especially as he was smuggling several rifles in as gifts for the *rajas* with whom he wanted to sign contracts.[120] Dutch officials, however, appear to have decided to play along with both French teams.

Although suffering the effects of their wretched voyage from Padang, Wallon and Guilhaume stayed only a day in the Dutch post at Meulaboh. Courret, however, was too ill to proceed with them to Bubun, Teunom and Woyla. Wallon negotiated at Woyla with Teuku Dy-Blanc, one of the *ulèëbalangs* reputed to control the gold-bearing area, but this chief wanted more than the fifth of the revenue Wallon offered him. The Frenchmen then decided to explore upper Teunom. Teuku Imam, the influential *ulèëbalang* of Teunom, tried to persuade them to wait until he could accompany them himself. Failing in this he provided a few men to smooth their path among the suspicious highlanders. It was to no avail. One Panglima Lam Ara of the Kawaj XII area cut down Wallon and Guilhaume at Tui Peuria, two days' journey up the Teunom river, on 11 March. "You coastal people have already become infidels", he told their Acehnese

184   An Indonesian Frontier

companions, by attempting to make sophisticated distinctions between Dutch and French *kafirs*.[121]

Far from terminating the French quest for Aceh gold, the death of these two rash explorers increased the certainty of their colleagues that the forbidden fruit was of surpassing delicacy. Brau and Errington arrived in Aceh at the beginning of April, hot on the heels of their ill-fated rivals. They were in time to join the expedition, which the Dutch military Governor had sent to the area to "avenge" the death of the Frenchmen. As usual with such expeditions, the principal result was simply to worsen relations between the Dutch and Teuku Imam Muda of Teunom, who by the strange logic of accessibility was held responsible.[122] It also meant that the Dutch forbade further French ventures into the politically uncertain interior of West Aceh.

Brau de St.-Pol Lias, always assiduous at cultivating his connections in high places, quickly re-established good relations with the local Dutch officials. The Assistant-Resident for the West Coast, Van Langen, took the two Frenchmen with him to all the important West Coast ports as far south as Tapak Tuan, and described in grandiose terms the gold reported by Acehnese to lie up some of the rivers. He could not, however, allow Brau and his colleagues to proceed into the interior over which he had no control. After a month's travel on the coast, the two men turned their attention to Lohong, the northernmost river state on the West Coast of Aceh and one of the most pro-Dutch. After examining the very limited goldworking carried on there by a dozen Chinese, Brau decided to attempt to make an establishment, if necessary on an agricultural base, in order to be on hand when the great gold rush he still expected became possible.[123] While awaiting government approval for more extensive operations in Lohong, Brau and Errington de la Croix accepted in August 1880 an invitation from Hugh Low to visit Perak. De la Croix remained for seven months investigating Chinese and Malay tin mining methods there. He obtained two tin concessions which became the basis of the *Société des Etains de Pérak*, formed in Paris for the purpose.[124]

Brau de St.-Pol Lias, however, remained obsessed with the elusive promise of Sumatra. He left Perak after a few weeks to tour the Deli

The French Connection   185

area once more, until permission arrived to explore Lohong without
Dutch escorts. Then he rushed back to stay with "*mon ami le
kedjourouan*" at Lohong, and to stake out a concession intended to
become his Aceh base. Seldom can such enthusiasm have been lavished
on less promising prospects. Fortunately for Brau de St.-Pol Lias the
Governor-General refused to ratify his concessions despite three
months of urgent lobbying in Batavia at the beginning of 1881. The
Frenchman appears finally to have abandoned the project in favour
of the much more realistic Perak venture, and was thus spared the
certainty of disaster as Dutch authority was gradually eroded in Aceh.[125]
Brau's later interests shifted to mainland Southeast Asia, with a mission
to Burma and Indo-China in 1884. His continuing fascination with
Aceh gold, however, is evident from the fact that in the plethora of
writing with which he publicized his 1880–1 expedition after his return
to Paris there is scarcely a mention of the gold which was the principal
object of his quest. Only in 1891 had his own hope of returning
dropped to the point that he published details about the gold in his
last book, *La Côte du Poivre,* for the benefit of "those who will come
after us".[126]

The fascination aroused in Paris by Wallon and Brau de St.-Pol
Lias was a long time dying. Only nine months after Wallon's death,
his two brothers-in-law were in Singapore, hoping to continue the
gold-hunt under the pretext of searching for his body. The French
Consul in Batavia, still suffering from the trauma of concealing the
small armoury in Wallon's luggage from Dutch eyes, ensured that
they did not reach Sumatra.[127]

By the end of 1882 another *Compagnie Malaisienne* was formed in
Paris, and sent three men out to continue the gold hunt. The same
formula of elaborate subterfuge was adopted. The leader, Paul Fauque,
obtained a *mission gratuite* from the Minister of Public Instruction to
continue the "scientific" work of Wallon and Guilhaume and investigate
their death. However, "*certains affaires delicates*" upset the financing of
the project after arrival in Singapore. Fauque's two companions returned
directly to Paris, and Fauque followed them after filling in two months
exploring the commercial potential of Siak in East Sumatra.[128] The
following May (1884) he returned to Sumatra, however, with Burlaud,

Figure 12 Brau de St.-Pol Lias in Aceh with the pro-Dutch ruler of Lhong, his betel-carrier (left) and attendant (right), from *Chez les Atchés. Lohong* (1884).

who had already worked on a Deli plantation for two years. Fauque spent about two months in West Aceh, at a time when the Dutch were hopelessly at odds with Teuku Imam Muda of Teunom, who was holding captive the British crew of the wrecked steamer *Nisero*. Fauque could not reach the Woyla area which was his principal aim, but he did explore Meulaboh, reporting optimistically about its coal and copper, though carefully avoiding any mention of gold.[129]

The French Connection

Not to be left out, Edouard Roura, quite probably the originator of this enduring French dream, managed to organize his own mission in France, where he had lived since 1878. Carrying the usual official commission, this time a hydrographic one from the French Naval Ministry, Roura reached West Aceh in October 1883 with a French companion, Denis Richards. Once again, however, the French Consul was convinced:

> that the scientific mission of M. Roura was a mask, and that he was charged by some French capitalists to study the mineral and other resources in the interior of Sumatra; perhaps even to obtain from the indigenous princes some concessions.[130]

Roura's friendship with the *rajas* of Teunom and Woyla put him in a better position than his predecessors to negotiate concessions, but not to earn the approval of the Dutch.

By a curious chance, Roura and Richards were negotiating with the Raja of Woyla on the very day the *Nisero* was shipwrecked nearby. Roura accepted a Dutch request to use his influence with Teuku Imam Muda of Teunom to negotiate the release of the 29 crew members. However during the three days Roura was at Teunom, 29–31 November, the Raja evolved terms which included a British guarantee for the freedom of his trade, a brilliant stroke which immediately internationalized the issue and brought a powerful Penang mercantile lobby on to his side. In a fury at this escalation of the issue Dutch officials immediately suspected Roura, not without reason, of having assisted Teuku Imam to produce these terms. He was immediately banned from the coast by the Dutch.[131] More bitter than ever, Roura went to Singapore to offer his services to the British in trying to free the crew. In face of Dutch hostility, however, Sir Frederick Weld reluctantly declined to use him.[132]

Roura returned to Europe in 1884, but when the West Coast ports were re-opened a year later he hastened back to his search. By an intriguing coincidence he was also involved in the second great affair of captured European mariners in Aceh. On 14 June 1886 he disembarked at Rigas as the sole passenger on the S.S. *Hok Canton*, to conclude a pepper deal with Teuku Umar, the famous Acehnese

188   An Indonesian Frontier

war leader who at that time was effective warlord of the West Coast north of Teunom. A few hours later Teuku Umar's men attacked the five Europeans remaining on the ship, evidently with a view to capturing them and re-creating a *Nisero* situation. Roura re-appeared in time to conduct the *Hok Canton* back to Ulèëheue after two of its officers had been killed and the other two captured, together with the captain's wife. The probability seems great that Umar's action was connected with remarks made by Roura, but no evidence has appeared to suggest any motive Roura can have had for involvement.[133]

For the inveterate gold seekers the total absence of Dutch control on the West Coast of Aceh between 1885 and 1893 put paid to further hope of exploration. When the area was eventually pacified at the turn of the century the Dutch mining engineer Jansen did investigate the best known areas of the Kawaj XII and Lohong, and came to largely negative conclusions about commercial possibilities.[134] Not until 1939 was a serious attempt made to work the gold of Kawaj XII on an economic scale. Brau de St.-Pol Lias' patriotic wish was eventually fulfilled. It was a French enterprise, the "Marsman Concern" which began commercial mining of Aceh's gold.[135]

The King of the Sedangs

It is, perhaps, unfair to end this chronicle of false starts on a note of pathos, particularly as Charles David de Mayréna[136] appears never to have set foot in Sumatra. Yet in the magnificence of his style, the quixotic heroism of his preoccupations, and the unreality of his financial basis, there is something characteristic of nineteenth century French ventures in that island. "Good-looking, a crack shot ... intelligent and energetic",[137] Mayréna was a French caricature of James Brooke, with all of the style but little of the substance. He had a dashing military career until wounded in the Franco-Prussian war. Later in 1883, he had to leave France suddenly when he was accused of embezzlement, and from that point on sank ever deeper into a fantastic world of his own devising. He made his way to Java, where he lived on credit for almost a year before being deported in August 1884 on another charge of embezzlement.[138]

The French Connection

However, his experience gave him good value on his return to Paris, where he let it be known that he had deserted from the Dutch army in Aceh (as dozens of European soldiers of fortune had done) and obtained the complete confidence of the Sultan of Aceh. The exaggerated optimism about Aceh raised in Paris financial circles by Brau de St.-Pol Lias and Wallon played into his hands. The Acehnese, moreover, were just celebrating the great triumph of a Dutch retreat to a "concentrated line" occupying only a few square miles of Aceh territory. Mayréna was able to persuade a Paris broker, baron Sellière, to advance him 30,000 francs to return to Aceh and take over the lucrative sections of the Sultanate's economy, including mining, arms manufacture, and the minting of money. Despite his dubious past, he also received a commission from the Ministre de l'Instruction Publique for scientific exploration in Aceh.[139] On arrival in Saigon in May 1885, however, Mayréna and his brother Henri made no serious attempt to reach Sumatra, but used Sellière's money profitlessly in Saigon. Sellière's backing and the Government commission were both withdrawn in 1886.[140]

Nevertheless, Mayréna had a phenomenal success in Indo-China. By January 1888 he had persuaded the colonial government to entrust him with a semi-official political task among the Moi tribes living near the southern Laotian border, in what is now Kontum province. Under the guise of a prospector for gold Mayréna was to attempt to woo the Montagnards away from Siam and into the arms of France. At Saigon's request Fr. Gerlach of the Kontum mission put his enormous prestige among the Moi behind Mayréna. The results were astonishing. Within a few months he persuaded numerous mutually hostile villages of Sedangs, Hamongs and Balmars to unite. On 3 June 1888 they agreed to form a Kingdom of the Sedangs, with Mayréna as King Marie the first.

Having achieved this unique feat of unification, however, Mayréna was more interested in magnifying his royal office than giving way to rule from Hué or Saigon. To raise revenue for his new state he issued stamps and bestowed royal titles and decorations on amused or credulous businessmen in Saigon and Hong Kong. When the French challenged these practices and prosecuted him for fraud, he threatened to sell his kingdom to the Germans.[141]

190   An Indonesian Frontier

In 1889 the King of the Sedangs returned to Paris in the hope of winning official recognition and money. He obtained neither, despite the regal style with which he graced society functions and issued high-sounding titles. In July 1889 he moved to Belgium for greater security against law suits. There at last he found another credulous financier. The young Belgian industrialist Somsy paid all his debts and financed his return to his kingdom with 5 well-connected young Belgians, 11 cases of arms and ammunition, and plentiful supplies.[142]

On arrival in Singapore, however, in February 1890, Mayréna's arms were seized by the police. France and Siam both made clear that he would not be allowed to reach his kingdom through their territories. Rapidly Mayréna's world began to collapse and his companions to desert him. He began to talk again of going to Sumatra to lead the Acehnese armies against the Dutch. Even though he became a Muslim and took a Malay wife (his fourth), named Aisa, he had little success raising an army among the Muslims of Singapore. As his fantasy world began to appear ridiculous, he left Singapore in March to live out his dream in the isolation of Pulau Tioman, a tiny island off Rompin, in Pahang. He died under mysterious circumstances on 11 November 1890, leaving only the *anjing peranchis* (French dogs) of Pulau Tioman as a permanent mark of his sojourn in the Malay world.[143]

Mayréna appears to have been the last French adventurer to consider intervening directly in Indonesian affairs at the periphery of the Dutch empire, in defiance of Dutch claims to authority. Subsequent French interest in the area, in the shape of planting and commercial concerns as well as a fine scholarly tradition, operated through the Dutch colonial framework. Indeed many French scholars and officials, like Angoulvant and Bousquet, were attracted to Dutch rather than British colonies in search of parallels with their own.

The chronicle of French activities in Sumatra remains a disjointed one, with no connecting thread beyond the persistence with which bold ventures were left to languish or diverted into profitless paths. The name of France nevertheless remained formidable, if mysterious, to many of the coastal peoples, and played a role in their diplomatic calculations.

The French Connection 191

Appendix

Sultan Ibrahim to President of France
15 Rabi 1, 1265H (8 February 1849)
(Romanized Malay Text)[144]

Bismi'llahi 'l-rahmani 'l-rahim

Al-hamdu li'llah wahdahu wa'l-salatu wa'l-salamu 'ala rasuli'llah wa anna Isa ruhu'llah wa 'ala alihi wa sahbihi ridha Allah. Amma ba`du, adapun kemudian dari itu maka inilah warakat al-ikhlas wa tuhfat al-ainas yang termaktub dalamnya dengan beberapa sembah salam serta ta`zim dan takrim yang keluar daripada kalbi yang nurani dan fu'ad yang hakiki dan sir yang khafi dan rahsia yang terbuni, ya'itu ialah yang datang daripada pihak hamba yang hina dina lagi fana lagi tiada menaruh daya dan upaya lagi dhacif dan miskin serta dengan tiada mengetahui 'adat dan majlis, ya'itu yang bernama Sultan Mansur Syah ibni al-marhum Sultan Jawhar al-'alam Syah yang ada jabatnya memerintahkan cadat yang kuat dan hukum yang 'adil, ya'itu dalam daerah negeri Aceh bandar Daru'l-salam. Maka barang disampaikan Allah subhanahu wa ta'ala datang mendapatkan kebawah kadam sahabat hamba yang mahamulia lagi acla dan fudhla yang telah dikurniai daripada Tuhan yang bernama rabbukum al-a`la, ya'itu sayyidina wa rnaulana Paduka Seri Sultan Republik Peransis yang ada jabat takhta kerajaan daripada emas kudrati yang sepuluh mutu lagi yang bertatahkan ratna mutu macnikam daripada intan dikarang dan berumbai2-kan mutiara dan zabarjad yang telah terseradi dalam daerah negeri Pari makam Daru'l-ma`mur wa'l-masyhuriah serta dengan memerintahkan 'adat yang kuat dan hukum yang 'adil dengan ke`adilannya, ya'itu dalam daerah negeri Peransis Daru'l-amen. Maka tiadalah hamba perpanjangkan kalam melainkan sekadar hamba mengatakan hal dengan ahwal yang maksud sahaja. Amin.

Syahadan hamba beri ma'lumlah kepada Tuan yang sahabat hamba lagi syaudara hamba: Adapun karena tatkala dahulu zaman Louit Pilib (Louis Philippe) adalah dikirimkan surat kepada hamba serta dengan kapal perang dan adalah khabarnya dalam surat itu dianya hendak bersahabat dengan hamba dan serta dengan disuratkan kepada hamba mengambilkan rial Peransis kepada sekalian negeri hamba dalam makam Sumatara bak jadilah rial Peransis jual beli dalam tiap2 negeri dan tiap2 bandar. Sudah itu maka hamba berfikirlah dengan segala hulubalang dan segala syaudagar dan serta dengan segala ra'yatnya fasal rial itu. Maka sudahlah ridha sekalian orang yang dalam negeri Sumatara menerima rial Peransis itu pada tiap2 negeri dan tiap2 bandar yang dalam perintah hamba. Sudah itu dengan takdir Allah tacala maka gaduhlah Louit Pilib dengan segala orang Peransis dan berperanglah dianya dengan segala ra'yatnya, maka Louit Pilib pun larilah kenegeri yang lain. Sekarang sudahlah jadi yang memerintahkan 'adat yang kuat hukum yang 'adil dengan sifat ke'adilannya Sultan Republik dan daripada hamba sama juga Sultan Republik sahabat hamba lagi syaudara hamba. Dan hendaklah sekarang Tuan suruh kapal Peransis berniaga kenegeri Sumatra dan hendaklah mula2 datang kepada hamba kenegeri Aceh, kemudian maka berlayarlah kepada tiap2 negeri dan tiap2 bandar serta, 'alamat daripada hamba kepada segala hulubalang surat satu pucuk. Dan hendaklah mula2 bak banyak kapal sekali itu dan lain kali miski satu kapal pun jadi juga karena sebab setelah macruf banyak rial Peransis pada tiap2 bandar. Dan hendaklah Tuan beri kapal perang kepada hamba al-kadar dua buah karena sebab hamba dha'if sedikit pada menghukumkan ra'yat pada tiap2 negeri dan bandar; jika ada kapal perang niscaya takut segala hulubalang kepada hamba dan tentangan harga kapal itu barang yang patut adalah diatas hamba tetapi hendaklah hamba bertangguh pada Tuan kadar dua tahun. Jika sudah sampai hadnya maka hamba bayarlah akan harganya itu kepada Tuan. Dan hendaklah dengan siap alatnya kapal itu sematanya. Sebagai lagi hamba minta' kasihan banyak2 pada Tuan karena negeri hamba sudah diambil oleh orang Belanda adalah dua tiga buah bandar, mula2 negeri Airbangi hingga sampai kenegeri Singkil dan serta dengan satu pulau Nias sudah diambilnya oleh orang Belanda itu karena negeri itu jauh sedikit daripada negeri Aceh dan hendaklah dengan do'a Tuan serta dengan ikhtiar Tuan bak maulah berpindah orang Belanda pada tiap2 negeri itu. Itulah hal ahwalnya dan yang lain dari itu tiadalah hamba sebutkan melainkan hendaklah Tuan periksa pada orang yang membawa surat ini namanya Muhammad Ghauth karena dianya hulubalang hamba lagi nasab dengan hamba. Apa2 khabarnya, sungguhlah khabar hamba

The French Connection

dan apa2 pekerjaannya maka sungguhlah pekerjaan hamba karena dianya badal ganti hamba, yang mutlak menyuruh pergi berjalan kepada Tuan kenegeri Peransis karena harap hamba seharap2, kecil laut besar harap, rendah bukit tinggi harap. Demikianlah harap hamba akan Tuan, janganlah Tuan beri putus harap, dan tiadalah tanda hayat hamba melainkan do'a sahaja fi kulli'l-lail wa'l-ayyam. Dan hendaklah dengan segara2 Tuan kurnia perintah dan niat, seperti Muhammad Ghauth hendaklah lekas2 kembali kenegeri Acch serta dengan kapal dan orang2 daripada Tuan, dan hendaklah Tuan berikan apa2 yang dipinta' oleh Muhammad Ghauth, janganlah syak waham akan dianya. Itulah khabarnya.

Tersurat2 ini pada tatkala lima belas hari bulan Rabi'u'l-awwal pada hari Khamis pada waktu zuhur pada tarikh sanat 1265.

Bibarakat al-Syaikh Macruf al-Karkhi. Tammat kalam.

Al-Sultan Mansur

(seal)

9

Chinese Migration into North Sumatra

THE most sizeable Chinese Indonesian community of Sumatra, and indeed anywhere outside Java, is that in the province now called North Sumatra. This province includes two former Residencies of Netherlands India, the sparsely populated Residency of Tapanuli, and the former Government of the East Coast of Sumatra, which had a Chinese population of 99,000 in the 1905 census and 193,000 in that of 1930.[1]

The most interesting aspect of the history of this community is not how it came to be, but why it did not become greater; why, despite the apparent trend of the 19th century, Deli, Langkat, and Serdang did not follow the pattern of Perak and Selangor in Malaysia, with Chinese immigrants coming to form the major racial group at the end of the colonial period. The planters of Sumatra made no secret of their preference for Chinese labour over Javanese, and the massive annual influx of Chinese to Singapore and Penang between 1880 and 1930[2] would appear to have provided a ready source of supply. Yet difficulties in the way of recruiting this labour eventually persuaded the planters to substitute Javanese, who now form the largest single component of the population of the *cultuurgebied* (cultivation district).

What was the cause of these difficulties? Dutch writers have generally ascribed them to the obstructionism of British officials and the intrigues of "coolie-brokers" in the Straits Settlements.[3] Writers

Chinese Migration into North Sumatra

from the British or Malayan side who have noted the problem incidentally have been inclined to blame the Sumatra planters for giving their district a deservedly bad name among Chinese immigrants.[4] In reality, of course, the problem cannot be answered by any such categorical solutions, yet a careful examination of it is of considerable importance for an understanding of migration patterns in the Nanyang.

Before the middle of the 19th century the Chinese role in Sumatra was concentrated in the South. Srivijaya was a major collecting point for Southeast Asian exports to China between the seventh and twelfth centuries, as well as a focus for Buddhist pilgrims on their way to India. Towards the end of the 14th century wealthy Cantonese traders opposed to the Ming Dynasty (hence "pirates" in the eyes of the Zheng He expeditions) appear to have taken control of the former Srivijayan capital of Palembang. This prompted Zheng He (Cheng Ho) to intervene forcefully in 1407, take the Cantonese ruler back to China for execution, and install another Chinese or Sino-Malay dynasty in his place.[5] Palembang and Jambi were again the centre of Chinese commercial interest when junk trading to the Nanyang was licensed by the Emperor in 1567. Of the 88 Chinese ships officially sent to Southeast Asia in 1589, seven (8 per cent) were licensed to collect Sumatran pepper at the ports of Palembang and Jambi.[6] Until Dutch monopoly ambitions excluded them in the second quarter of the 17th century, the Chinese ships were the most valuable buyers of south Sumatran pepper. Many Chinese settled in Jambi and Palembang in this pepper period, acquired local wives, and became indispensable to the local economy.[7] In the following century Chinese commercial activity focused on Sumatra's off-shore islands, specifically tin mining in Bangka from around 1750 and pepper growing in the Riau Archipelago from around 1740.

Chinese were initially much less prominent in the northern half of the island. The unusually pious and orthodox Acehnese Sultan Iskandar Thani (1637–41) had explicitly excluded them from the then extensive territory Aceh controlled, allegedly because they would not give up their pigs. Although Chinese traders were again visiting Aceh by the 1680s, they initially played no part in the boom in Aceh pepper production from the 1790s. Acehnese brought their own pepper to market in Penang or sold it on the spot to American, European, or Indian buyers. Although Melaka and later Singapore Chinese frequented the East Sumatran ports between Siak and Jambi, Bugis, Arab, Indian and local craft still dominated this trade in the 1820s, and Minangkabau traders of Batu Bara that of the Deli-Asahan area further north.[8] Anderson, touring the east coast states in 1823, saw "very few Chinese" in Deli,[9] but did not think them worthy of notice elsewhere.

The growth of Chinese merchant communities in the fast-expanding entrepôts of Penang and Singapore brought about a major change which was fully evident by about 1860. Straits Chinese traders had established strong links with all the Malay states of the east coast between Siak and Temiang by the time the Dutch extended their influence to the district (1858–65). This was particularly the case in Asahan, where the import and export duties, as well as the opium and gambling monopolies, had been entrusted to the Penang merchant Boon Keng. The Dutch considered that Boon Keng's influence, and the support he could muster in Penang, were principally responsible for the Raja's resistance to Dutch overtures until 1865, when the Dutch army was sent in.[10] One of the major reasons advanced in favour of a permanent Dutch occupation of Asahan was that otherwise "the Chinese traders would spread British influence and exploit the country even more than before".[11]

Despite this early antagonism, the gradual establishment of Dutch power in the East Coast of Sumatra provided a further opportunity for Chinese enterprise. Straits-based Chinese firms continued to operate the opium, spirit, and gaming monopolies of most states, and even the import and export duties of some, including Siak and Asahan. By 1876 the Resident could report that "the trade of this Residency is exclusively in the hands of the Chinese", most of whom were connected with firms in Singapore or Penang.[12] As for Western enterprise, there was no European-owned shipping link to the East Coast of Sumatra until the Dutch mail began in 1873, and no serious commercial competition for the Chinese steamers and *tongkang* until the Ocean Steamship Company began its Singapore–Deli service in

Chinese Migration into North Sumatra

1880.[13] From the point of view of commercial connections, therefore, the East Coast of Sumatra had become as much an economic hinterland for the Straits Chinese as the Malay Peninsula.

Permanent Chinese settlement in large numbers began soon after the establishment of Dutch authority. By 1875 there were already sizeable communities at Bengkalis, where the important fishing and lumbering resources soon became a Chinese preserve; at Tanjung Balai (Asahan) and Labuan Bilik (Panai), centres of trade with the Batak districts inland; and especially in the agricultural enterprises of Deli.[14]

When the colonial government at Batavia sent its first nervous representative to Deli in 1864, there were about 20 Chinese in the place — mostly goldsmiths and small shopkeepers.[15] This official lodged at first with the Dutch pioneer of Deli, J. Nienhuys, who had arrived the previous year in search of tobacco. He had just decided to grow his own crop with hired labour, having received poor returns from buying up the inferior tobacco that the Bataks of Hamperan Perak had grown for years. Neither Bataks nor Malays would work as wage labourers, and Nienhuys resorted to bringing some Javanese *hajis* from Penang, who were probably still in debt for their passage to Mecca. As a former tobacco planter in Java, Nienhuys turned first to this familiar source of labour. However, one disappointing season was enough to make him experiment again. In 1865 he brought 88 Chinese and 23 Malays from Penang as wage labourers. This brought the pay-off. Nienhuys' 1865 crop received recognition in Amsterdam as the finest quality, and sold for the remarkable price of 1.49 guilders per half-kilogram.[16]

This success began a 25-year period of uninterrupted expansion in the Deli tobacco industry. Capital flowed rapidly into the area, which soon included Serdang and Langkat as well as Deli. Much of the capital came from nearby Penang. Chinese entrepreneurs were prominent at first, and in 1867 three of them were busy planting their leasehold with tobacco as well as copra and nutmeg.[17] But within a few years the need for large-scale investment and sophisticated technical and sales management made the tobacco industry a European preserve. Leading the field from 1869 was the

198   An Indonesian Frontier

Deli Maatschappij, a marriage of Nienhuys' local experience and the capital of the NHM.

Following Nienhuys's lead, all the new firms used Chinese exclusively for cultivating the tobacco plant, though Indians, Javanese, Bataks, and Malays were often employed for more routine labour. The Deli Maatschappij alone brought 900 Chinese from Penang when it began operations in 1869.[18] The Chinese population of Deli climbed from the 20 of 1864 to nearly 1,000 in 1867[19] and over 4,000 in 1872.[20] Every year throughout the 1870s and 1880s thousands of Chinese labourers were brought from the Straits Settlements to support the most spectacularly expanding economy of Southeast Asia.

Nienhuys and the other pioneers of the 1860s had acquired their Chinese labour through the *kongsi* system so well established in the Straits Settlements. The *kongsi*-head was allocated part of a virgin land concession and some seedlings, and the finished tobacco leaf was bought from him at the end of the year. This system was discontinued by about 1870, however, in favour of a direct contract between a European manager, assisted by his Chinese *tindals* (headmen), and the individual labourer. Advances were made to the field-worker throughout the year at half-monthly intervals, until in December he brought his crop to the European assistant who paid him according to his estimate of the quality of the crop. The planters maintained: "The first essential for a successful cultivation of tobacco is to ensure soundness of leaf ... and unless the remuneration of the labourers is based upon the condition in which he delivers his produce, the cultivation of good tobacco becomes impossible."[21] Deli thus brought the Chinese labourer into much closer relation with a European employer than any of the other major avenues of employment in the Nanyang.

Before plunging into a description of the complex pattern of Chinese labour recruitment, one must sound a note of caution. Like previous studies of the subject, this paper is based entirely on colonial sources, which give a very inadequate picture of a phenomenon whose complexity they hardly understood. This is particularly evident in the case of the reports of the Straits Settlements Protectors of Chinese, who were so burdened by the immense but routine task of registering

Chinese Migration into North Sumatra

the influx of migrants that they could give little attention to more fundamental matters.[22] The two main sources of information, the reports of the 1876 and 1890 Labour Commissions in the Straits Settlements, do supply a range of statements from Chinese involved in labour recruitment. These conceal more than they reveal, however, unless read with a full understanding of the economic and clan structure of the time, and the way each witness fitted into it. The writer is acutely aware that much of this chapter rests on the same uncertain foundation of rumour and speculation as that on which colonial officials themselves made their judgments in matters Chinese.

Following the Anglo-Franco-Chinese Convention of 1866 governing Chinese emigration, the recruitment of labourers in China and their passage to the Straits Settlements were conducted in a tolerably civilized manner. With the exception of a small and decreasing number who sailed to Singapore on Hainan junks, the migrants travelled on chartered steamers which reached Singapore in six to eight days. A firm in one of the treaty ports would publicize the coming departure of one of its chartered ships, and prospective migrants would be brought in by *khehtau* — usually men of the same area who had themselves returned from the Nanyang. By the 1866 Convention no advances could be given or contracts signed in China, and Singapore's reputation as an eldorado attracted hungry Chinese without any need for press-gang methods.

On the other hand, few emigrants could personally afford the six to eight dollars for their fare to Singapore, and therefore most were probably obligated to somebody on arrival in the Straits Settlements.[23] In many cases, no doubt, this obligation was no more than an informal one towards a relation or other associate already established in the Straits Settlements, for whom the *sinkheh* (new arrival) would work. Of the real nature and extent of such ties there can be no certain knowledge, for British officials did not concern themselves further with those who gave an affirmative answer to the question, "Have you paid your own passage?" The majority always answered affirmatively, which meant they did not have to be detained in a depot or to sign a contract at the Chinese Protectorate. Hokkiens in particular were seldom put in the official category of "unpaid passengers", because the Chinese authorities in Amoy forbade the emigration of *sinkhehs* who had not at least nominally prepaid their passages.[24]

Before the establishment of the Protectorate of Chinese in 1877 probably more than one quarter of the total immigrants were indebted to the supercargo of the ship on arrival. The *khehtau* of such migrants travelled with the *sinkhehs* he had recruited and was responsible to the supercargo for payment of their fares. On arrival in Singapore or Penang such *sinkhehs* were detained on board until the *khehtau* had arranged for a prospective employer to pay the fares. The fare on this credit basis was usually about $12, and the *khehtau* would expect a further profit for himself of $5–8. Though no written contract was signed, the *sinkheh* was then bound to his employer for at least a year by a mixture of loyalty, fear and force.[25]

The 1877 Chinese Immigrants Ordinance (superseded by Ordinance IV of 1880) provided for a category of "unpaid passengers" who were to be registered and admitted to licensed "coolie depots" which had legal power to detain them subject to government inspection. Initially this category was understood to mean those immigrants indebted to the supercargo of the ship for their passage. Most such passengers had begun their journey in Shantou. Before long, however, steamers on the Shantou run abandoned the speculative practice of carrying credit passengers, as the Hong Kong steamers had done some time earlier. The whole migrant traffic became more highly organized to cope both with this change and with the vastly increased volume of migrants in the 1880s. By 1890 recruiting firms in the treaty ports generally paid the passages of migrants in advance and recovered the sum later from a firm of "coolie-brokers" in the Straits Settlements, to whom the *sinkhehs* were consigned. An occasional variant of this practice was for the *khehtau* in charge of a group of *sinkhehs* to pay the fares and receive the due reimbursement plus profit from the consignee broker.[26]

Although the status of those who gave a negative answer to the question, "Have you paid your own passage?" changed fundamentally between 1877 and 1890, this group continued (until 1888, when official pressure in Shantou became too strong) to consist mainly of migrants from the port of Shantou, destined for the plantations of

Figure 13 Arrival of Chinese contract labour at Belawan port, c. 1903

Source: M.A. Loderichs *et al.*, *Medan: Beeld van een Stad* (Purmerend: Asia Major, 1997).

Sumatra, Sabah, Province Wellesley and Johore. This only strengthens the suspicion that the category "unpaid passengers" was determined less by the poverty of the emigrant than by the practice of the recruiting firms involved in that particular branch of the traffic. The European planters of Sumatra, North Borneo (Sabah) and Province Wellesley were dependent on the Chinese Protectorate for their labour, because they lacked the necessary direct contacts. Many, perhaps most, Chinese employers in Malaya, on the other hand, must have preferred to bypass the Protectorate. This was no difficult matter if the *sinkhehs* were instructed to state that they had paid their own passages. Official records have little to say about such systematic evasion of the regulations. It is, however, indicative of the mood on both sides that one Chinese employer did divulge his systematic frustration of the Act to the 1890 Labour Commission as if this were nothing extraordinary, and that his methods earned special commendation by that Commission. This was Gan Eng Seng, whose *sinkhehs,* destined for the Tanjong Pagar Dock Company, signed a contract in China which of course had no validity in the eyes of any government. Their passages were all paid in advance in China, but only those *sinkhehs* who could not otherwise be trusted were brought before the Protector of Chinese to sign a legally valid contract.[27]

In the view of the 1876 Labour Commission, abuses occurred less in the immigration to the Straits Settlements than in the emigration therefrom, particularly to Sumatra. Indeed abuses in recruitment for Sumatra, both real and alleged, were the main spur behind agitation leading to the establishment of the Chinese Protectorate. This agitation was begun by Chinese employers of Singapore and Johor motivated, as Eunice Thio has said, "by self-interest and perhaps philanthropy".[28] Their principal organ in this was the Gambier & Pepper Society, dominated by Teochiu planters. Its members suffered from the general labour shortage of the early 1870s, and particularly from the competition for Teochiu labourers offered by the new plantations of Deli. They petitioned government in 1871 against the forcible detention and disposition of *sinkhehs,* and followed this in 1873 with a request for "arrangements to prevent bad characters from kidnapping the newly-arrived immigrants".[29] Further pressure led at last to the

Chinese Migration into North Sumatra

203

appointment of the 1876 Commission into "the Condition of Chinese Labourers in the Colony", which heard much evidence concerning "kidnapping" for Sumatra.[30]

One of the witnesses before this Commission, Penang Police Commissioner Plunket, gave the impression that there was an organized system of kidnapping *sinkhehs* in Penang for service in Deli during the early 1870s. There were, he said, over a hundred "bad characters" in Penang whose sole occupation was to obtain labour for Sumatra, and who were constantly convicted for "kidnapping".[31] In suggesting the image of a press-gang plucking unwitting Chinese from the streets, shophouses, and brothels, Plunket is rather misleading here. All the victims of "kidnapping" brought to light by the 1876 Commission or otherwise were in fact indebted immigrants who had perforce lost some of their freedom of movement. Their wretchedness was no less because of that, but to call them victims of "kidnapping" was to confuse the issue — intentionally in the case of some interested parties.

Though always a few migrants had through tickets from China to Penang, most left their homeland with the intention of going to Singapore. If their *khehtau* succeeded in finding them work in the city or nearby in the plantations of Johore or Riau, they appear to have accepted this without much protest. If, however, there was insufficient demand from such employers, the *sinkhehs* were either forcibly detained on shore or sent on to Penang where the process was repeated. In either port they were kept under guard until somebody could be found to pay their fares. With the bill for their maintenance rising every day, abuses were frequent. *Khehtaus* used force or deception to compel the immigrants to go to a distant place of which they had heard nothing good, and to work in occupations they had never contemplated.[32]

Though most evidence before the 1876 Commission related to Singapore, there is an interesting glimpse of the system in Penang, the main base for recruitment to Deli. E. Karl, Chinese interpreter in Penang, related how "Tan Tek" (Khoo Thean Tek, sentenced to deportation in 1867 for leading the Toh Peh Kong Society during the Penang riots but later pardoned as a British subject) had a virtual monopoly over the disposition of indebted immigrants. "Tan Tek is a kind of protector of Chinese Coolies, and is paid a thousand dollars a year or more by parties in Shantou. He has a house on purpose to receive them. He is the chief of the Toh Pek Kong Society, and the most powerful man in the place."[33] According to Karl all indebted migrants were detained in the depot of "Tan Tek" until redeemed by the agents of employers. The various Penang "coolie-brokers" who supplied *sinkheh* labour for the Deli planters must therefore have been in close contact with Khoo Thean Tek. These brokers would supply labourers to the Penang agents of Sumatra tobacco firms for a cost of $40–50, of which $25–30 was an advance to the *sinkheh*. After paying the expenses of the passage, the profit of the *khehtau* and the cost of accommodation in Khoo Thean Tek's depot, the *sinkheh* would be left with only a few dollars, and the broker often tried to cheat him out of that. Whatever was received by the *sinkheh*, he had ultimately to repay the full sum fixed as the advance. The remaining $15–20 in the cost provided the profit of the broker — much higher in the case of Sumatra labourers than those for the Malay Peninsula.[34]

Almost from the beginning of the Deli tobacco plantations, they acquired an extremely bad reputation among immigrants. As a British planter with interests in both Province Wellesley and Sumatra complained in 1875:

> There exists, in the Chinese labour market, a perfect hatred of the name of 'Deli', which operates not only inimically to that particular place, but also as regards the whole Island — so much that Chinese who will ship willingly to Langkat or Serdang, in ignorance of the precise 'locale' of those places, will become perfectly mad if the word 'Deli' be heard on board.[35]

As early as 1871 this bad name was being fostered in China as well as the Straits Settlements. In that year the British Consul in Shantou sent to Singapore translations of placards erected in the streets "by certain Chinese in the habit of sending Chinese labourers here", protesting at the way *sinkhehs* were forcibly sent from the Straits Settlements to Deli and other places.[36]

Whatever the original cause of this reputation, it was greatly exaggerated by the force and deception used to make immigrants go

Figure 14 Chinese coolies tending Deli tobacco in the 1880s

Source: *Senembah maatschappij, 1889–1939* (Amsterdam, 1939).

to Deli against their will. The unpleasant nature of the migrant business attracted some of the most unscrupulous men as recruiting agents, and violence bred further violence. In 1874–5 in particular, when demand for labour greatly exceeded supply, there was a spate of complaints in the Straits press against "kidnapping" for Deli. Late in 1875 there were two cases in which labourers bound for Sumatra plantations overpowered the crews of the small steamers taking them across the Strait, and escaped with their advances. Subsequent investigation suggested that the mutineers were thugs making a business of collecting advances rather than unwary *sinkheks* deluded about their destination.[37] Tan Seng Poh, the Singapore Teochiu leader and a leading advocate of protection for *sinkhehs*, admitted: "Most of the men who take advances to go away from here are bad characters, and many ship intending to rob and run away. Singapore is relieved of many of its bad characters in this way."[38] Nevertheless, publicity obtained by these outrages only strengthened the adverse impression about Deli among Chinese.

How far did labour conditions in Sumatra justify its unsavoury reputation in the 1870s? In attempting to answer this question we are faced with some confusion as to the exact grievance against Deli. Singapore Chinese witnesses before the 1876 Commission made most play with its unhealthy climate, but also mentioned the difficulty of returning.[39] The English and Dutch commentators were in general more concerned about allegations of ill-treatment by planters.[40]

There was certainly truth in all these complaints. But it would be difficult to argue that Deli was in any important respect worse than other "frontier" communities of the time such as Perak and Selangor. The allegation of unhealthiness seems a particularly strange one. Deli was exemplary if compared with Perak, where about 3,000 tin miners died of beri-beri every year in the period 1879–82.[41] The larger tobacco plantations were in a position to provide hospital facilities for their workers, and had an interest in doing so.

There is more cause for complaint against ill-treatment by employers, though again it is difficult to find clear evidence in relative terms. Like other frontier societies, early Deli lacked an established judicial and police system, or even a code of civilized conduct. Holding complete economic power over their employees, the planters tended to assume equal judicial power. The Sultan of Deli had initially given the planters wide powers over their employees, though reserving for himself the trial of the most serious offenders. In practice almost all offences were, however, dealt with on the spot. The Sultan was certainly not lacking in goodwill towards the planters, but his police force was woefully inadequate and planters were reluctant to lose the services of both the offending worker and someone sent to guard him throughout the lengthy procedure in the capital. Abuses were to be expected, but as in the similar case of mining *towkays* in Malaya there is little recorded evidence on which to make a judgement.

Rapid expansion made government intervention long overdue by 1874, when a judicial apparatus was at last set up to regulate the immigrant population of the East Coast of Sumatra. In theory the planters were shorn of their judicial powers, which had included

Chinese Migration into North Sumatra

punishment for labourers attempting to leave the plantation. But the government machinery set up in replacement was altogether inadequate. Only 12 armed policemen were stationed in Deli, and none at all in Langkat and Serdang, where plantations were fast developing.

During the period 1874–7 Deli acquired a name for violence even in European circles. Attacks on planters and traders became a matter of frequent occurrence, culminating in the death of several planters in 1876–7. Ill-treatment of workers by planters was probably not the main cause. Gayos and Bataks initiated most of the attacks, though local Malays and runaway Chinese workers increasingly joined in as the absence of settled authority became apparent. The need for reform in labour relations was in any case glaringly apparent, and a legal commission was sent from Batavia at the end of 1876 to investigate labour conditions. It brought charges against four planters accused of ill-treatment, of whom one committed suicide soon after. At the same time considerable police reinforcements were sent to the *cultuurgebied*.[42]

On the judicial side, the 1870s witnessed a battle by the Deli planters, led by the redoubtable J.T. Cremer, against a motion introduced into the States-General by Mirandolle seeking the abolition of the penal sanction attached to labour contracts. As a result of this controversy, special labour regulations were framed for the East Coast of Sumatra in 1875, amplified in the famous "coolie ordinance" of 1880. The latter became the model for all plantations outside Java. It preserved the penal sanction (abolished in Java) but stipulated definite conditions which were, if anything, advanced for their time. All labour contracts were to be registered with government, and could not bind the labourer after three years. On expiry of the contract (or after three years if the labourer had not repaid his debt to the planter before then) the labourer was to be returned to the place where he was recruited. The employer was obliged to give regular bi-monthly advances to the worker, to provide adequate housing, water, and medical attention, and to allow him to bring his complaints before the nearest government official.[43]

On paper therefore, and probably also in practice, contract labourers were less open to ill-treatment than those in Malaya after

208 An Indonesian Frontier

the mid-1870s.[44] The 1876 Labour Commission felt bound in fairness to say that, "whatever may have been the case in former times, we believe that the welfare of the labourer is as well assured there as here, and indeed that there is far more interference on the part of the Dutch Government than there is on the part of our own to secure that welfare".[45]

This judgement ignores one vital factor. With the partial exception of those on Penang sugar plantations, Chinese contract labourers in Malaya almost never had anything to do with anyone not of their own race. Tobacco workers, on the other hand, were directly responsible to European assistant managers, from whom they received their advances and their final payment. The European planter class of Deli, moreover, was portrayed by most outside observers as unusually arrogant, "demanding a great deal in the way of servile respect for their personal dignity".[46] During the first decades of the 20th century there is enough evidence, for example in the constant attacks by workers on planters and headmen, to suggest that plantation workers in Deli were subjected to an unusual degree of personal humiliation, if not physical cruelty.[47] Probably these disadvantages were already evident in the 1870s, when evidence is scarcer. Even were this not the case, it is easy to imagine that a *sinkheh* with absolutely no experience of the "red-haired devils" felt less secure placing himself in their power than in that of an employer with shared standards of behaviour.

The final grievance commonly mentioned against Deli was the difficulty of returning. In part this complaint was simply a function of the distance from one of the centres of Chinese life — particularly Singapore.[48] In part it referred to the fact that some contract workers in Deli escaped from debt only after a very long period, if at all.

In the plantations and many of the tin fields of Malaya, the general pattern was for the *sinkheh* to work virtually without pay for a year, to pay off his passage money. After this, if he survived on the meagre diet provided, he was theoretically a free agent.[49] In the tobacco plantations, however, everything depended on the worker's performance. The most successful might leave his estate after a year with a discharge notice and as much as $100 in his pocket. The least successful might never escape from debt, until the legal

Chinese Migration into North Sumatra 209

three-year maximum clause of the "coolie ordinance" was introduced in 1880. The average return for the harvest of one cultivator in Deli was estimated at $45 (on one estate) in 1869,[50] $68 in 1874,[51] and $78 in 1882.[52] Since the crop cycle only occupied eight or nine months of the year, labourers were given other work for the remaining months at a wage averaging $6 per month. In 1882, the usual amount debited against a labourer at the end of his first year was $93 (or $78 for *laukhehs* re-engaged in Sumatra), made up as follows:

	$
Advance to *sinkhehs* in Penang (or in case of *laukhehs* $15)	30
Regular bi-monthly advances of $2	48
Special advances at Chinese New Year, etc.	7
Cost of clearing jungle before planting	5
Cost of tools, etc.	3
Total	93

In 1882, therefore, the *average* labourer in Deli could do no more than meet his debts, assuming he had incurred no additional ones, and expect five or ten dollars profit. At the lower levels prevailing in the 1870s, it is probable that the majority in fact failed to meet their commitments after one year. On the other hand, as the tobacco industry consolidated, higher productivity was achieved, until by 1890 it was acknowledged by many witnesses before the Labour Commission that Deli tobacco offered the best remuneration available to the *sinkheh*. Their evidence suggested that about 75 per cent of *sinkhehs* then made a profit in their first year, and that in the case of Teochiu labour the figure was as high as 90 per cent.[53]

The number of Chinese who left Sumatra with discharge tickets from their plantations was not great — 2,101 in 1881, compared with about 8,000 who had immigrated the previous year. But the planters argued that many re-engaged on the estates, "because they are unable in any neighbouring country to obtain equal remuneration", or remained in the area as traders. In 1881

210   An Indonesian Frontier

there were already 4,597 "free Chinese" in the *cultuurgebied* who paid the trade tax.[54]

In sum, it would appear that Chinese labourers in Sumatra were comparatively well provided for in terms of welfare services, and that the most fortunate of them were also well remunerated. The most unsuccessful or improvident, on the other hand, were liable to a much longer term of virtual servitude in an environment affording little pleasure. It was common for workers who failed to clear themselves in their first year to lose heart and take increasingly to opium. They were then likely to fall into debt to the farmers of the opium, spirit, and gaming monopolies. In such a case the three-year maximum clause of the "coolie ordinance" could not help them, since their creditors would insist on their signing a new contract and beginning the process again.[55]

These factors taken together may partly explain the bad reputation of Deli among labourers in the early 1870s. When Deli is objectively compared with other employment opportunities, however, it appears that the persistence of this reputation into the 1880s must be explained in part by the influence of Malayan Chinese employers with vested interests.

In 1875–6 the reputation of Deli was at its worst, and was accentuated by the violence so often used by *khehtaus* and brokers to compel unwilling *sinkhehs* to board the ships for Deli. The brokers in Penang required $40–50 for the supply of each *sinkheh* to the agents of Deli companies, compared with only $22–26 for labour in Penang or $32–36 for Perak.[56] The difference was not an extra inducement to the *sinkheh*. It went to the brokers as profit or possibly to some other source involved in the business. To some extent it certainly induced the least reputable brokers and *khehtaus* to use the more dangerous methods of intimidation or deceit to send the *sinkhehs* on their way. It seems likely also that this extra profit margin was an inducement to more powerful figures such as "Tan Tek" — employers of labour and society headmen — to part with labour which might have been useful to themselves.

Even with these higher costs it was impossible for the Sumatra planters to fill their labour requirements under the conditions of

Chinese Migration into North Sumatra

1875–6. In those years, therefore, they began attempting to bring Chinese directly from China, and employing Javanese more widely in the fields.[57] They were, it seems clear, saved temporarily from these difficult courses by the establishment of the Protectorate of Chinese in the Straits Settlements.

As a result of the report of the 1876 "Chinese Labourers" Commission two ordinances were passed the following year. The Chinese Immigrants' Ordinance provided for a Protector of Chinese immigrants, and the Crimping Ordinance for a Protector of Emigrants. The two offices were for all practical purposes amalgamated with the appointment of Pickering as Protector of Chinese in Singapore in May 1877, and Karl to a similar post in Penang soon after. The ordinances provided for Government Immigration Depots, where immigrants indebted for their fares would be detained under supervision until employers were found for them. Such depots were never built, however. Instead the existing depots of the "coolie-brokers" were licensed by government subject to certain standards of maintenance. Detention in unlicensed premises was made illegal. When employers were found, legally binding labour contracts were signed in the presence of the Protector, and the contracting *sinkhehs* were given some idea of their rights and duties under the law.[58]

The Protectorate broke the vicious circle of violence associated with labour recruitment for Sumatra. On the one hand, more satisfactory machinery was instituted for prosecuting against forcible and illegal abduction. On the other, a section of the labour market — that of the "unpaid passengers" — was to some extent removed from the control of the Chinese societies. In this sector a certain amount of price competition became possible, both among the *sinkheks,* who were made aware of the relatively favourable terms in the Sumatra contracts, and among the brokers, who could still expect a higher commission from the agents of the tobacco companies. Thus the supply of Chinese labour from the Straits Settlements to the plantation district of Sumatra, which had been no more than three or four thousand per year in the 1870s could expand rapidly in the 1880s (see Table 3).

TABLE 3
Labour contracts for Langkat, Deli, Serdang and Asahan made before the Protectors of Chinese, Penang and Singapore[59]

	Penang	Singapore	Total
1879	3,529	500*	4,000*
1880	6,600*	1,381	8,000*
1881	7,426	2,378	9,804
1882	5,990	1,498	7,488
1883	6,740	1,977	8,717
1884	8,540	2,464	11,004
1885	11,434	3,617	15,051
1886	12,391	4,317**	16,708**
1887	11,953	4,811	16,764
1888	10,913	7,439**	18,352**

Notes: * Estimates only, based on figures for *all* Sumatra.
**These figures include a substantial proportion of Javanese and Banjarese. The number of Indonesians signing contracts in Singapore for work in the *cultuurgebied* was 1726 in 1887, and increased in the following two years.

Opposition to Deli among interested parties continued, however. In 1880 Pickering was complaining that the *khehtaus* kept the prejudice against Sumatra alive, in order to dissuade their *sinkhehs* from accepting in Singapore "the liberal terms offered by the Deli planters". The *sinkhehs* then moved on to Penang, where "exorbitant squeezes" were possible because of the weakness of the Protectorate staff. Having refused in Singapore an advance of $24 of which the *khehtau* would have taken $16 as expenses, the *sinkheh* was compelled to accept the same contract in Penang with an advance of $30, of which the *khehtau* pocketed $26.[60] Pickering probably exaggerated here the role of the *khehtaus* as against the secret society headmen and brokers in Penang,[61] but his experience emphasized the difficulty of substituting an open labour market for the established Chinese channels of recruitment.

Chinese Migration into North Sumatra

As the largest and best organized group of European employers of Chinese labour, the Deli planters initially enjoyed the great advantage of cordial cooperation from Pickering:

> Believing that the prospects of a Chinese going to labour in Deli were really favourable [wrote Pickering], I devoted some time to visiting the Depots with the planters and their agents and issued placards to inform the immigrants and other Chinese of the advantages they would gain by engaging for Sumatra.[62]

But the Protector of Chinese was after all a British employee. His benevolent attitude soon altered under pressure from Penang employers, led by the Province Wellesley sugar magnate Khaw Boo Aun and supported by Karl.[63] In September 1881 they urged Pickering to give local employers first choice of the *sinkhehs* and prevent Deli recruiters from entering the depots until their demands were met. The *sinkhehs*, they argued, "had no real wish to go out of British territory, but were induced by delusive promises and large advances to go to Sumatra". As a result of this pressure Pickering ceased encouraging immigrants to go to Sumatra.[64]

The request of the Penang employers for first choice in the depots was refused by Pickering in 1881. The official attitude on this point appears to have weakened by 1890, however, to judge from the evidence of W. Cowan before the Labour Commission. Asked why all *sinkhehs* were not attracted to Deli by the higher wages there, he replied, "Because Province Wellesley planters were allowed to redeem coolies first."[65]

The Deli planters were particularly annoyed by Pickering's attitude on the question of through passengers from China to Sumatra. The Ocean Steamship Company, which already ran steamers from China to Singapore, opened a Singapore-Belawan (Deli) service in 1880, and offered through tickets from China to Sumatra for Chinese migrants. Pickering ruled that such migrants trans-shipping in Singapore nevertheless had to come before him to sign regular contracts. But this defeated the purpose of the Sumatra planters, which had been to keep the *sinkhehs* they had recruited in China away from the brokers, employers, and secret societies of the Straits

214　　An Indonesian Frontier

Settlements. Although they continued sending old hands to China to recruit for Sumatra, it could no longer be considered a direct emigration if all *sinkhehs* had to pass through the licensed depots of Singapore or Penang.[66]

These and other minor differences caused annoyance on both sides, but they had little to do with the crisis in the labour supply which finally decided the Deli planters to bypass the Straits Settlements altogether as a source of labour. This crisis of the late 1880s was caused in part by economic conditions, in part by the hardening attitude of officials in China.

TABLE 4
Demand and supply of Chinese labour

	Straits tin price, per pikul ($)[67]	Tobacco price Amsterdam per ½ kg[68] (guilder cents)	Immigrants landed Penang and Singapore[69]	Of whom admitted to depots as "unpaid passengers"
1881	27.74	115.0	89,803	32,316
1882	30.85	137.5	101,009	28,415
1883	30.29	134.0	109,136	26,446
1884	25.14	144.0	106,748	24,871
1885	23.53	141.5	111,456	26,391
1886	33.82	154.0	144,517	39,192
1887	36.89	121.0	166,442	42,400
1888	42.10	128.5	166,353	34,607
1889	35.52	146.0	146,820	21,213
1890	31.97	72.5	132,274	14,335

Tobacco prices were at peak levels during 1884–6, and more and more Sumatran jungle was burned to make way for plantations. Production increased steadily from 93,500 packs in 1883 to 236,300 in 1890, with a consequent demand for labour.[70] The same years

Chinese Migration into North Sumatra

witnessed the beginning of a period of sustained high prices and rapid expansion in the Malayan tin industry, which lasted from 1886 to 1895.[71] The supply of immigrant labour expanded rapidly in response to these boom conditions in 1886–7, though not rapidly enough to meet demand at the existing wage levels. The result was not, unfortunately, a rise in wages to an economic equilibrium, but spectacular profits for the brokers and others involved in the migrant business. They pushed up their premiums and commissions to unprecedented levels, especially for European employers like those in Sumatra. After 1887 immigration ceased to increase and even fell off, despite the continued high demand for labour during the following two years. The figures in Table 4 show the disparity between supply and demand in the major sectors.

The failure of the labour supply to keep pace with demand was most marked in the category judged to be "unpaid passengers", on which European employers were dependent. Most of the decline between 1887 and 1890 was in fact in this category. The main cause was to be found in the attitude of Chinese officials.

The emigration of Chinese under conditions bound to lead to indentured labour was naturally looked down upon by progressive-minded Chinese officials. The traffic in indebted *sinkhehs* was generally regarded as dishonourable, and was even sometimes referred to disparagingly as "buying and selling little pigs". It was for this reason that the Amoy authorities had made it compulsory for emigrants nominally to have paid their fares in advance. For the Sumatra plantations the most important port was Shantou (Swatow). Teochius were regarded as the best agriculturalists, followed by the Hai-lok-hongs, who are often also categorized under the broad heading of Teochius. Both groups usually emigrated from Shantou. The only other dialect group employed widely in tobacco cultivation, though less highly regarded, were Khehs, who might embark either at Shantou or Hong Kong.[72] The Sumatra planters depended for their labour first on the cooperation of the Straits Settlements Protectorate of Chinese, but ultimately on the co-operation, indifference or venality of imperial officials in Shantou, who allowed *sinkhehs* to emigrate openly in the "unpaid passengers" category.

Sporadic movements for reform on the part of senior officials in Shantou were never completely effective, largely because the whole system of emigration relied heavily on corruption and subterfuge. They could, however, seriously reduce the number of migrants arriving in the category of "unpaid passengers". Early in 1879, for example, the authorities of Chaozhou (Shantou region) forbade indebted emigration from the port, on the ground that indentured *sinkhehs* were "sold in a manner not differing much from cattle" on arrival in Singapore. Straits pressure through the British Consul in Shantou had this order revoked after a few months. But the incident substantially reduced the number of "unpaid passengers" and of contracts for Sumatra in that year.[73]

A more sustained attempt at reform in the late 1880s was largely attributable to Tso Ping-lung, the second Chinese Consul in Singapore (1881–91).[74] After unsuccessfully suggesting to the British that they ban indebted immigration to the Straits Settlements, Tso began in June 1885, to put pressure on the Chinese authorities of Chaozhou. He described to them in exaggerated terms the maltreatment of indebted migrants on arrival in the Straits. As a result a proclamation was again issued in Shantou forbidding indebted emigration, but again withdrawn after pressure from the British Consul, who had been urged into action at the behest of Pickering.[75]

Tso then turned to less direct forms of pressure against indentured labour, particularly in Deli. The Singapore daily *Lat Pau*, which he had been instrumental in founding and supporting, published two leading articles during 1886 attacking labour conditions in Deli.[76] Tso also cooperated with the authorities of Chaozhou in a series of actions against dealers alleged to have kidnapped workers from China against their will. The main target was the Shantou firm of E. Kee, the largest recruiters of Teochiu labour for the Straits Settlements. In 1886 this firm was accused of having kidnapped seven men for Singapore, who subsequently signed contracts for Deli. The men concerned denied the charge, but the pressure from their relatives in Shantou, and from officials, was such that E. Kee had to spend $500 bringing them back to China, including the expense of bribing some of them.[77] The same

Chinese Migration into North Sumatra

firm was forced to bring a *sinkheh* home from Serapong (Bengkalis) in June 1888 to testify that he had emigrated freely. Soon after this the firm was dissolved. A European agency house in Shantou was also forced to bring home two emigrants in 1888. The most devastating example to other agents, however, was the beheading of Siau Khai in Shantou in September 1888. He had been accused by two emigrants just returned from the Nanyang, of having kidnapped them years before.[78]

In all these cases the Chinese Protectors, and of course the Dutch, claimed that the charges were false, and made only for purposes of extortion. It was undeniable that widespread corruption dissipated any reforming impetus on the part of individual officials. Indeed many commentators considered that much of the huge commissions being charged by coolie-brokers in Penang and Singapore during this period went as bribes and inducements to interested parties in Shantou and Hong Kong.[79] For this, however, the Straits Settlements Government was above all responsible through its refusal to cooperate openly and emphatically with reforming Chinese officials for the termination of a recognized evil.[80]

All the main employers of *sinkheh* labour were affected by the short supply which resulted from this renewed Chinese pressure after 1885, but those who were obliged to rely on the "unpaid passengers" who came before the Chinese Protector were much the worst hit. The commissions of the "coolie-brokers" mounted steadily. In March 1885, the Deli Planters Union (DPV) resolved that all members should pay no more than $50 premium for each *sinkheh* recruited. The brokers were in too strong a position, however, and the attempt was abandoned in January 1887. Immediately the fee jumped to $60–70. By the end of that year it had risen further to $110–15 in Singapore and $125 in Penang.[81] Of this no more than $30 was ever used to cover the advance to the *sinkheh* and the expenses of the passage.

Since Sumatra tobacco growers had no alternative source to Chinese labour, and could afford to pay the premiums, their share of the indentured labour supply remained high, as is shown in Table 5.

TABLE 5
Labour contracts signed before the Protector of Chinese, Straits Settlements[82]

	All Destinations[83]	Penang and Province Wellesley	Malay States	East Coast of Sumatra	(Plus direct recruitment in China)[84]
1886	45,717	6,221	16,721	16,757	—
1887	51,859	5,464	21,397	17,489	—
1888	44,451	2,476	16,367	19,561	(+1,152)
1889	32,666	3,170	7,071	11,793	(+5,176)
1890	26,211	1,880	8,972	8,972	(+6,666)

The share going to Malayan tin mines was reduced by the gradual fall in the tin price after 1888, but probably even more by the substitution of nominally "free" immigrants for those who had been obtained from the licensed depots. The European sugar planters of Province Wellesley suffered the most severely.

The Deli tobacco industry was at the height of its prosperity in 1887–9. Previously the desire of the planters to break free from dependence on the Straits Settlements brokers had been dampened only by the extreme difficulty attending other methods. During this crisis in the labour supply they succeeded in breaking away.

The solution dearest to the hearts of the planters was to bring labour directly from China to Sumatra. This, however, necessitated the sanction of the Chinese Government. To this end Holland had in 1873 signed the Anglo-Franco-Chinese protocol of 1866 which, among other provisions, entirely ruled out any advances to the labourer, or charge against him of the cost of recruitment. J.T. Cremer, the energetic manager of the Deli Maatschappij, tried to implement these terms by travelling to China himself in 1875. He then found a general reluctance to permit emigration to Deli on any terms whatever. Cremer's conclusion was that the Deli firms should send trusted *laukhehs* (experienced migrants) back to China to persuade their friends to migrate to Sumatra without any contracts. In this way the most

Chinese Migration into North Sumatra

successful companies, particularly the Deli Mij., succeeded in influencing a growing number of emigrants to opt consciously for Deli when the scramble for labour began in the Straits Settlements.[85]

Five Sumatra tobacco concerns,[86] led again by the Deli Mij., joined forces in 1886 in a more earnest attempt to bring about direct migration. Dr J.J.M. de Groot, official Chinese interpreter in Batavia, was then making a study tour of South China. At the request of the five firms, he was instructed to try to arrange direct emigration to Sumatra at the same time.

After consultation with the planters, De Groot decided to avoid contact with the British, whom he considered to have a vested interest in opposing direct migration. Instead of working through Shantou, therefore, where the Netherlands Consul was an Englishman, De Groot decided to try to recruit Teochiu labourers through the German firm of Pasedag & Co. at Amoy, whose principal, Piehl, was the Netherlands Consul there. This firm in turn called in the assistance of Lauts & Haysloop, a German firm in Shantou, and of the German Consul in Shantou. The eventual success of the scheme owed more to German pressure on the Chinese Government than to Dutch.[87]

De Groot and his supporters quickly realized the impossibility of obtaining permission for emigration under contract — particularly from Amoy. Early in 1887 they directed their efforts to obtaining permission for emigration to Sumatra on a basis similar to that for "unpaid passengers" to the Straits Settlements. The authorities were still reluctant. Peking was anxious to force the Dutch to allow Chinese Consuls in Netherlands India, and pointed out that the strictest precautions had to be taken in the case of emigration to countries where no Chinese Consuls were stationed.

The German Consul in Canton obtained a breakthrough in late 1887, by making much of the appointment of a government adviser for Chinese Affairs at Medan, whom he portrayed as a sort of Protector of Chinese. The Viceroy of Guangdung softened to the extent of asking for a report from Shantou on the subject. Meanwhile De Groot and the German Consuls used all their influence on the higher officials of Chaozhou, and bribed some of the junior ones. As a result, official permission was obtained for free emigration to Sumatra in April 1888.[88]

The five participating Deli concerns had already signed a contract the previous February with Lauts & Haysloop for recruiting and carrying free immigrants to Deli. In May 1888 the first two ships arrived at Belawan, the *China* bringing 70 migrants from Shantou and the *Glucksburg* 68 from Amoy. The following month the *Duburg* brought 60 more from Shantou, although some had fled in Singapore where the ship had called as a result of a cholera outbreak.

The cost of chartering these three steamers — over $11,000 — fell on the five firms supporting the venture, though the migrants were under no obligation to sign contracts with these or any firms on arrival. Twenty-seven of the immigrants on the *China* signed no contracts at all, because brokers had shipped with them, and were able to prevent their signing contracts unless the brokers were given large commissions.[89] Brokers were prevented from joining subsequent ships, and few *sinkhehs* thereafter refused to sign a contract on arrival in Sumatra. Technically they were still "free" immigrants, at least as far as dealings with the Chinese Government were concerned. From the *sinkheh*'s point of view, however, the main advantage over the old system was that he could send his $30 advance back to relatives in China instead of seeing it go into the pockets of the brokers and *khehtaus*.

In the early years of direct migration the cost to the planters for each *sinkheh* brought in directly was about $100, whereas the brokers in the Straits Settlements immediately dropped their charges to $85. Nevertheless the planters were unwilling to return to their old dependence on the Straits Settlements, and hopeful that costs would drop as trade developed to fill the empty steamers on the Sumatra-China run. At their annual conference in July 1888, the Planters Union established an Immigrants' Bureau to relieve the five pioneer firms of their financial responsibility. Members of the DPV undertook to recruit labour only through this bureau, which would in turn recruit in the Straits Settlements whenever the supply direct from China was insufficient. The sum to be paid for each *sinkheh* so recruited was first fixed at $60 (or $40 for those recruited in the Straits), raised to $85 (or $50) in 1889, and finally settled at $75 (or $40) in 1891.[90] Of this amount, $20 was an advance given to the *sinkheh* on arrival at the

Chinese Migration into North Sumatra 221

plantation, and repayable by him. These sums failed to cover costs, but the losses were distributed amongst members.

In 1890 the planters ceased chartering special migrant vessels and contracted with the Hong Kong agents of the Aziatische Kustenfahrte Gesellschaft of Hamburg, which put two vessels permanently on the China-Sumatra route.[91] Lauts and Haysloop continued as recruiting agents, and in turn made an arrangement with the Shantou "coolie-hong" Heng Thye. The latter undertook to have nothing to do with the Straits brokers, and to recruit exclusively for Deli. Trusted *laukhehs* were sent home from Sumatra to assist in recruitment at a village level.[92]

Despite all these efforts, the planters never succeeded in filling their needs. The established brokers had an interest in upsetting the new system, by playing on old prejudices against Deli. Dutch commentators always claimed that agents of the Straits brokers had shipped along with 270 *sinkhehs* on the Sumatra-bound *S.S. China* in Hong Kong in March 1889.[93] When near Singapore these *sinkhehs* began to attack their *khehtaus,* claiming that they had been duped into going to Sumatra. The *China* was obliged to call at Singapore to avoid a general mutiny. There the *sinkhehs* came before the Protector of Chinese, and were lost to the Deli planters. Similar disturbances took place on two other steamers in 1889–90, but each managed to take on troops from Riau or Singapore to restore order without having to call at the British port.[94]

In China, too, there was continued pressure against emigration to Deli. The Heng Thye recruiting house, for example, was plagued by people threatening to complain to officials about the kidnapping of a relative unless they were paid to keep quiet. Early in 1890 placards were privately posted in Shantou warning that Heng Thye was about to lose his head for trafficking in men. These moves were officially denounced the following May after pressure from Hoetink, the Chinese adviser in Medan who had been sent to lobby for Deli interests in South China.[95] Despite the cordial tone of this declaration, however, Peking itself was involved in the opposition to emigration, partly because of its growing desire to place Consuls in Netherlands India. In a formal pronouncement of 4 October 1891, the Chinese

222   An Indonesian Frontier

Government imposed three conditions for the continuance of emigration: the appointment of Consuls; the abolition of opium and gambling dens in Deli; and the assurance that financial remittances would flow into China from the emigrants abroad. The last point was to be achieved by the compulsory remittance home of all the earnings of labourers above their minimum needs. This proclamation caused great alarm but little action, and was gradually forgotten after 1892.[96]

By about 1897 the direct immigration to Sumatra could be said to be on a permanent basis, no longer threatened with immediate termination by official opposition or natural disaster. But the continuing current of opposition prevented the planters from ever obtaining as full or as sure a supply of labour as they required. Attempts to begin direct migration from Hong Kong, Macao, and Hainan were unsuccessful, while the migrant ships from Amoy did not operate after 1889. Shantou had, more than ever, a monopoly of the labour supply for the *cultuurgebied*.[97]

Despite the establishment of direct migration, the planters were obliged increasingly to look to other sources to fill their labour requirements. Indian workers, so important for Malayan plantations, had never been numerous. The few Indians who signed contracts in the Straits Settlements for work in Sumatra were breaking the laws of the Indian Government. Fitful negotiations between Batavia and Calcutta in the 1870s had not succeeded in reaching agreement over the migration of workers. In 1887, as a result of the labour crisis in Deli, the Netherlands Indian Government made a more serious overture by sending a commission to India. It failed, however, to alter Calcutta's demand for a British protector of Indian labour to be resident in Sumatra.[98] This the Dutch would not allow.

Javanese labour, on the other hand, was readily available. There were established recruitment offices in Java, a huge reservoir of under-employed labour, and ample co-operation from Dutch officials. But the planters resisted switching over to Javanese, particularly for the cultivation itself, where the Chinese were regarded as being more responsive to the money incentive. In periods such as the first years of the Chinese Protectorate, when Chinese labour was readily available from the Straits Settlements, Javanese were not recruited and their

Chinese Migration into North Sumatra 223

numbers declined.[99] In the late 1880s, on the other hand, Javanese began to be employed on all tasks except cultivation. In 1887 2,210 Javanese passed through Singapore with contracts already signed for work on Sumatra plantations, and a further 1,940 "natives of Netherlands India"(Banjerese and Boyanese, as well as Javanese) signed contracts at the Singapore Chinese Protectorate for work there.[100] These numbers continued to increase until 1890, when the drastic halving of the tobacco price stopped expansion temporarily. Javanese immigration recommenced in the mid-1890s, and quickly surpassed that of Chinese. Coffee, and later tea and rubber, broadened the economic base of the plantation district after 1890, and in these new crops Javanese predominated from the beginning.

The following table[101] shows the changing composition of the plantation labour force in the East Coast of Sumatra Residency:

TABLE 6
Ethnic composition of East Coast plantation labour

	1874	1884	1890	1900	1916	1926
Chinese	4,476	21,136	53,806	58,516	43,689	27,133
Javanese	316	1,771	14,847	25,224	150,392	194,189
Indian	459	1,528	2,460	3,270	—	—

Chinese immigration had been at its peak during the period 1886–9, when more than 16,000 entered each year. For the 1880s as a whole, when labour was being recruited in the Straits Settlements, there was an average of about 12,000 indentured Chinese immigrants per year. This compares with rather less than 7,000 per year brought in by the Immigrants Bureau over the period during which it operated, 1888–1930.[102]

Though the indentured Chinese labourers gradually dwindled in number, the total Chinese population of the East Coast of Sumatra continued to grow. A more balanced community emerged, of traders, shopkeepers, small farmers, fishermen and lumbermen. It remained, however, a small minority.

224 An Indonesian Frontier

In retrospect, it appears that the greatest impediment to the Sumatran tobacco industry in recruiting Chinese labour was that the Straits Chinese who controlled most of the labour supply had no particular interest in Sumatra. In the early stages of the industry, when this disadvantage was coupled with prejudice against Deli as a strange and distant field of employment, the tobacco planters had great difficulty attracting enough labour even after paying exceptionally high commissions to the brokers in control. It seems probable that the Deli employers would have had to switch away from Chinese labour before 1880 but for the establishment of the Protectorate of Chinese in the Straits Settlements. The advantage European employers possessed was their influence with colonial governments, as opposed to the influence Chinese employers often exercised over the workers themselves. By means of the Chinese Protectorate a section of the migrant traffic was partially removed from the control of the Chinese societies, and became available to price competition among the European employers. This section was, however, limited to labour supplied by those groups in Shantou which had already established some relationships with European employers, and which it suited to work through the Chinese Protectorate. The vast majority of immigrants continued to escape the scrutiny of the Protectorate as nominally "free" migrants, and were employed for the most part on the older pattern.

The Protectorate also proved unable to provide adequate numbers to meet increasing demand in the late 1880s. The main obstacle was opposition by the Chinese Government, for whom the Deli branch of the emigration system became the main object of attack because it was the most obvious beneficiary of the open credit-ticket system.

The Deli planters probably deserved most of the criticism levelled against them for their arrogance and brutality, particularly in the early years. They showed very little interest in attempting to substitute a genuinely free and stable labour force for the rapid turnover of indentured *sinkhehs*. They were quick to point out that increases in wage levels had very little effect on labour supply, which could be increased much more cheaply by giving larger premiums to the brokers.[103] The preference constantly expressed for *sinkheh* labour

Chinese Migration into North Sumatra

over that of experienced hands suggests that planters encouraged a pattern of social and economic relationships which was actually inimical to the development of a stable labour force. Nevertheless, there were other factors at work in the labour market besides the objective conditions in Deli.

Official printed sources frequently cited include:

Straits Settlements Legislative Council Proceedings (SSLCP), especially Appendix 22 of 1876: "Report of the Committee appointed to consider and take evidence upon the Conditions of Chinese Labourers in the Colony", 3 November 1876.

Annual Reports of the Protector of Chinese, Straits Settlements, in *Straits Settlements Government Gazette (SSGG)*.

Straits Settlements Labour Commission Report, Singapore, 1890 *(SSLCR)*.

Koloniale Verslagen, The Hague.

Verzameling van Consulaire en andere Verslagen en Berigten (Consulaire Verslagen), The Hague.

10

Nineteenth-century Pan-Islam Below the Winds

ACCOUNTS of the Indonesian nationalist movement conventionally began with the cultural and educational endeavours of westernized Javanese aristocrats in the first two decades of the 20th century. The enormous popular response generated by the first mass political movement of the Archipelago, Sarekat Islam, in 1912–20 came as a surprise in this narrative, indeed almost a diversion from the main story of discovering the nation. During the important phase between the self-defense of traditional, relatively isolated, societies and modern secular nationalism, Islam was acknowledged, if at all, as a kind of proto-nationalism or pre-nationalism.[1] The dominant presumption was that the secular nation state was the end point of political movements, making aspirations towards unifying the Islamic *umma* a kind of false consciousness whose only historical value was to prefigure the successful movements towards a secular nation-state.

This presumption appears premature in the 21st century, as global identities such as various schools of Islam began to seem at least as much part of the probable future as secular nationalism. A growing number of scholars have recognized the continuing importance of intellectual communities of thought that link Southeast Asians to other centres of the Islamic world, making the pan-Islamic movements of the late 19th century more central in the story. The case for a reconsideration of these connections has now been persuasively made by Michael Laffan. He demonstrates both the importance of Cairo as

Nineteenth-century Pan-Islam

an alternative centre to Europe for modernizing intellectuals seeking to combat colonialism, and the ongoing relevance of many pan-Islamic ideals in our own day.[2]

These changes make the republication of a revised version of the 1967 article important, no longer as a lonely voice documenting a forgotten episode, but rather as supplementary data from Dutch sources on trends now seen as mainstream. No longer need we complain about the "lack of data" which Berg identified in 1932,[3] nor apologize for distracting attention from nationalism and Marxism.

The term pan-Islam became widely used by Muslim activists themselves only after the Ottoman caliphate was destroyed in the First World War, putting in question how the political unity of the *umma* would be expressed. In the early 1920s the Muslim world was preoccupied with congresses designed to rediscover a viable universal caliphate, including Ibn Saud's abortive Islamic World Congress, the Indian Khilafat movement, and the al-Islam congresses in Indonesia.[4] In the late 19th century the Ottoman sultans claimed to embody the Caliphate, and "pan-Islam" was a term used by westerners for movements of international Islamic solidarity, usually hoping for Turkish assistance.

The emphasis in this chapter is on the function of Islam as a bond which clearly distinguished its adherents from the Europeans who were beginning to dominate their lives, which made European rule ultimately intolerable because it was non-Islamic, and which provided an allegiance both broader and more persuasive than the loyalty which the commoner owed to his usually undeserving prince. A movement is taken to be pan-Islamic if it provided an ideological basis for cooperation between, or beyond, individual political units in a political struggle under the banner of Islam. This bond gained greatly in appeal by linking the seemingly weak and backward Muslims of Southeast Asia with the Caliph himself, who was popularly imagined as the most powerful ruler on earth, bound to come to the succour of his oppressed cobelievers if they could prove worthy of him. Such outbursts of pan-Islamic enthusiasm need not arise from any centrally directed international movement. Turkey was never in a position to lead such a movement, and effective organizational vehicles only arose in the later period when nationalism was becoming a powerful rival.

Islamic Solidarity

When first the Portuguese appeared in Asia, Southeast Asian society was probably almost as tolerant and receptive to new influences as it had been to Hinduism, Buddhism and Islam. Yet by attacking the Muslim trading system directly and ruthlessly, the Portuguese produced a sharp reaction in the few trading towns where Islam was already firmly established. Some important states, notably Aceh and Banten, owed most of their prosperity to refugees from centres which had fallen to the Christian newcomers, and to the diversion of Muslim trade to their new, and more aggressively Muslim, ports.

Linked to western Asia by trade, these states naturally identified their own cause with that of the Muslim world as a whole. As explained in Chapter 4 above, the Aceh Sultanate had commercial and political links with the Ottoman Sultan in the 16th century, and received Turkish gunsmiths, cannons, and soldiers in return for its "vassalage". Though these links could not be maintained thereafter, Turkish cannon and flags in Aceh, as well as the Ottoman protection of the holy places of pilgrimage, contributed to the inflated picture of Turkey's position and power in 19th-century Southeast Asia.

The religious opposition which greeted a new phase of European expansion in the 19th century was more broadly based than that in the 16th century. Not only rival traders, but all classes of society were now affected by the pervasive western influence. Islam could have been expected to deepen its hold in Southeast Asia over three centuries even without the presence of Europeans. There is no doubt that the latter fostered its expansion, however, particularly in the form of a self-consciously international desire for orthodoxy. Unable to absorb the Europeans as they had done the Indians, Indonesians found a refuge against the new culture and alien rule in Islam. Even at the beginning of the 20th century, a German missionary observed with distress how quickly tolerant animists would become opiniated Muslims under the pressure of these factors:

Nineteenth-century Pan-Islam

> What is so strange to the native in the new age is of course the atmosphere in which the European has grown up ... the equilibrium of his inner self is disturbed by the new age.
>
> In this uncertainty of soul Islam seems a very stronghold of peace, for conversion to Islam is primarily related to the vital concerns of the people. Islam offers salvation for one's innermost self, one's soul, under the very eyes of the unpleasant ruler. A domain is reserved into which European wisdom and modern technical knowledge do not penetrate, the national individuality in the shroud of a new religion.

Furthermore, Islam offered the eschatological conviction that the oppression and inferiority which marked one's status in this life would be reversed in the next.[5] If such factors weighed with animists, they also encouraged orthodox and exclusive beliefs among those nominally Muslim for generations.

Reformist movements repeatedly surged around the Islamic world in the name of greater scriptural orthodoxy and international conformity, and were always resisted by established localizations. Java represented the extreme case of localization, where the 17th-century cultural compromise with Islam had ensured the survival of Hindu mythology within a vibrant theatrical tradition, and much of the cultivation of inner spiritual strength characteristic of Indic religion.[6] Nevertheless Indonesian Muslims, however wedded to older ways, were exceptional in their readiness to admit that these were heathenish and evil, if so informed by a well-instructed *sayyid* or returning *haji*. For this reason the closer 19th-century connection between Southeast Asia and Arabia merits special attention here.

In view of the distance, and the restrictions imposed by Dutch authorities, a remarkable number of Indonesians made the pilgrimage to Mecca. In the last three decades of the 19th century there were from four to eight thousand each year, forming on average about 15 per cent of the total overseas arrivals in the Hejaz.[7] Before North Sumatra was brought into the Dutch orbit pilgrims had sailed independently from Aceh. In 1873 Dutch warships intercepted a Madras ship trying to land 270 *hajis* in that war-torn country.[8]

The holy city had a more than usual attraction for Indonesians. Snouck Hurgronje, who visited Mecca in 1885, remarked that the "Jawas" there were distinguished by their scorn for their own half-pagan country, and their naïve respect for the idealized land where all institutions were presumed to be in accordance with the law of the Prophet.[9]

The pilgrimage was the principal source of foreign ideas for 19th-century Indonesians, particularly those outside Java. Few travelled for other reasons, and the Dutch discouraged western education unashamedly. Though the majority of "Jawa" spent only a few weeks in the Hejaz, they made contact there with the remarkably large number of their countrymen residing semi-permanently in Mecca, who had come to share the international and distinctly anti-colonial outlook of the holy city.[10] This connection could only throw into sharper light the scandal of infidel rule over a Muslim people. Snouck Hurgronje tells of a Sumatran sheikh in Mecca who exploded with wrath in a letter to his cousin at home, when the latter innocently offered to help the Dutch conquer Aceh. Cowed by this outburst, the cousin promised always to pray for the success of Muslim arms in the future.[11]

Arabs and *Hajis*

As representatives of the pure source of Islam, Arab immigrants commanded a natural respect in 19th-century Southeast Asia, particularly if they were *sayyids*. Isolated Arabs had made their way east since the 17th century, and become extremely influential in such states as Aceh, Siak, Palembang, and Pontianak. Larger-scale emigration from the impoverished Hadhramaut began at the end of the 18th century, affecting Sumatra first, and Java by the middle of the 19th century. Their number remained relatively small. Netherlands India counted 20,500 persons claiming Arab descent in 1885 and 29,000 in 1905. The Straits Settlements and Federated Malay States added a further 20,000 in 1901, and the Unfederated Malay States less than 1,000, judging by later figures. But the Arabs were a distinct community with wealth and influence out of all proportion to their

Nineteenth-century Pan-Islam

numbers. The largest concentrations were in the big cities — Surabaya, Batavia, and Singapore — and in such traditional centres of Arab influence such as Palembang, Aceh, and Pontianak.[12]

Though the Netherlands Indian Government placed few restrictions on Arab immigration into Java, it obliged them, as "foreign Orientals", to live in special cantonments in the main towns, and to apply for a pass every time they wished to leave their place of residence. These annoyances, and the distrust on the part of Dutch officials which lay behind them, created a dangerous potential for discontent among Netherlands Indian Arabs.

The same was true of *haji*, who were indiscriminately regarded as potential subversives until Snouck Hurgronje championed a more intelligent approach at the beginning of the 20th century. A regulation in force between 1825 and 1852 aimed to discourage the *haji* by prescribing the enormous sum of 110 guilders for a pilgrim passport. New restrictions in 1859 required each pilgrim to obtain a certificate from his Regent showing his financial ability to make the return journey and provide for dependents at home.[13] *Haji* and *ulama* were the first to arouse suspicion whenever anti-European movements began. Thus there was a vicious circle of tension between the Government and the religious leaders. The Dutch, consequently, actively favoured the secular leaders of the *adat* against the Muslim leadership whenever there was an opportunity to exploit this division. It was common, therefore, for Indonesian pilgrims to compare notes in Mecca on the iniquities practised upon Muslims by the Dutch Government.

These various grievances combined to give the Netherlands Indian Government a reputation in the Middle East as a particularly fanatical opponent of Islam. Snouck Hurgronje was alarmed that "in the Muslim daily press our government is frequently derided as the enemy of Muslims, while in geographical textbooks used in Turkish and Arab schools the Netherlands is tersely indicated as a Power unfamiliar with the principles of tolerance, under whose yoke millions of Muslims suffer".[14]

It ought to be stressed that this was an unfairly harsh view of Dutch Islamic policy. In matters which it saw as purely religious

232   An Indonesian Frontier

Batavia was scrupulously neutral, and it did less to encourage Christian missions than most colonial governments. Indeed it was largely the absence of Christian or western schools which enabled the conservative *ulama* to retain their moral leadership throughout the 19th century.

The Turkish Consulate

The threat which the Dutch believed Pan-Islam posed to their regime was rendered much more acute by the fact that the centre of communications for their own island empire was in foreign hands. As the Colonial Minister complained in 1864, "Singapore is the gathering place not only for the many pilgrims who yearly go to Mecca from our possessions, but also for many malcontents, adventurers, etc. who, as has frequently been shown, readily choose this place as the base for activities or undertakings detrimental to Netherlands interests in the Indian Archipelago."[15] Here opponents of the Dutch regime could meet, and on occasions organize appeals to Turkey, in the secure knowledge that the Straits Government had little knowledge of, or interest in, their doings. Among the Muslims of Singapore there were men like Abubakar of Johore and the Arab families of Alsagoff and Junied, with immense wealth and impressive international connections. They were the leaders of a politically relatively sophisticated community, whose anti-colonial energies were directed exclusively against the Dutch, and never against the British.[16]

For these reasons Batavia was alarmed when Turkey appointed its first Consul in Singapore in 1864. This was a wealthy local merchant from Hadhramaut, Sayyid Abdallah al Junied. As the Dutch had feared, he did nothing to counteract the natural tendency of Javanese pilgrims and other Muslims to regard him as the spiritual and political representative of the Caliph. At his death in 1865, therefore, Holland requested that the appointment of another Muslim in his place be forbidden from London. The British too, it was argued, should be on guard against "the smouldering and easily inflammable element of fanaticism" among Southeast Asian Muslims.[17]

Nineteenth-century Pan-Islam

The Porte had apparently intended to appoint Abdallah's brother, Sayyid Junied al Junied, to the vacant office, but accepted British advice against this. Nevertheless this brother was regarded locally as "a sort of acting consul for Turkey" for several years thereafter.[18] Sayyid Muhammad Alsagoff filled a similar role in the 1880s. Britain yielded to Dutch pressure when the question of recognizing a Turkish Consul was raised in 1866, 1873 and 1884. Salisbury, however, coming to office in 1885, was willing to change this policy in return for consular concessions he wished to exact from Turkey.[19] This offer was declined, and no Consul was officially appointed until July 1901, when Haji Attaoullah Effendi took up his duties in Singapore.

Despite its severe misgivings on this issue, the Netherlands Indian Government had allowed a Turkish Consul-General in Batavia, where he could be kept under surveillance, since the 1880s.

The series of 19th-century pan-Islamic protests discussed here made very little impact on Central and East Java, for reasons which are well known enough. The alliance between the V.O.C. and the aristocracy of Mataram had succeeded there in impeding the growth of a middle-class Muslim leadership which elsewhere provided the inspiration for pan-Islam. It was, moreover, the "outer islands" which were most affected by 19th-century Dutch military, as opposed to economic expansion.

Revivalist Movements

The "Padri" movement[20] in Minangkabau, which A.H. Johns has called "the watershed of the Islamic modernist movement in Indonesia"[21] was the first clear evidence of the new Muslim dynamism in 19th-century Southeast Asia. An important party of strict Muslims had apparently existed in Minangkabau in the 18th century, but it was only galvanized into aggressive action with the return in 1803 of three hajis who had presumably been influenced by the militance of the Wahhabis in Arabia.[22] Dutch military intervention on the side of the conservative *adat* chiefs in the 1820s and 1830s gradually transformed the "Padri" cause into a patriotic one, representing broader interests than the militant puritanism with which it had begun. Although the

"Padris" were finally crushed militarily in 1837,[23] their legacy was undoubtedly important in bringing Indonesian Islam closer to that of Western Asia, and at the same time ranging its leading champions firmly in the camp opposed to Dutch rule.

Although the importance of the Wahhabis as an inspiration for the three *hajis* of 1803 is still generally acknowledged, Schrieke has left us a valid warning against overemphasizing the degree of foreign influence in the movement. The only clear evidence of cooperation between the "Padris" and Muslim forces outside Minangkabau was against the most northerly Dutch coastal positions, which were repeatedly harassed by West Coast Acehnese by sea and "Padris" by land.[24] The specter of this formidable Muslim alliance frightened the Dutch into occupying the interior as far north as pagan Batak territory. The official encouragement given in the 1860s to the Rhenische mission among the Bataks may also have owed something to government anxiety on this score.[25]

If contemporary hostility to the Dutch in Palembang, Banten, and elsewhere was connected with the "Padris", this does not appear to have been suspected in Batavia. Not until the middle of the century, with better communications, larger numbers of pilgrims, and greater Western penetration, did Dutch officials begin to refer nervously to Islamic movements with widespread ramifications. It is significant that the first Minangkabau sheikh of the Naqshibandiyah order, which Schrieke saw as the main source of a permanent Mecca-orthodox influence in Sumatra, brought a Turkish flag from Mecca when he returned a few years before 1850, so that his teaching was originally associated with Turkey.[26]

This period saw a sequence of anti-Dutch movements in South Sumatra which do appear to have some connection. A Banten revolt whose main support came from the religious leaders of the Cilegon district was crushed by Dutch troops in March 1850. Some of the *ulama* escaped, to lead another crusade in the Lampungs, which was only ended when the leader, Haji Wachia, was captured by a strong Dutch force in 1856. Palembang also was in more or less open revolt between 1848 and 1859, and the resistance there took on an increasingly religious character as it grew more desperate.[27]

Nineteenth-century Pan-Islam

The Palembang resistance received assistance from neighbouring Jambi, which had acknowledged Dutch sovereignty since 1833 while retaining the fullest autonomy. A new Sultan, Taha Safi'ud-din, neglected to declare his allegiance when he ascended the throne in 1855, and resisted Dutch attempts two years later to negotiate a more binding treaty with him. While envoys from Batavia were trying to win him round, Taha appealed to the Ottoman Sultan for a document declaring Jambi to be Turkish territory in which foreigners had no right to interfere. Taha entrusted this letter to his connections in Singapore, one of whom was provided with 30,000 Spanish dollars to undertake the journey to Constantinople. The emissary, Sharif Ali, apparently travelled only as far as Mecca, where he acquired forged letters from the Caliph authorizing the expulsion of the Dutch from Southeast Asia. Taha's letter did, however, reach its destination. The Turkish Grand Vezir asked the Netherlands Ambassador whether Jambi was independent, and when assured it was part of Netherlands India he promised to give no reply.

In November 1858 a Dutch expedition occupied Taha's capital after some sharp fighting and installed a new Sultan prepared to accept Dutch demands. Taha escaped, and after the withdrawal of Dutch troops he remained *de facto* ruler of Jambi for almost half a century. For several years he continued his attempts to have Jambi recognized as Turkish, and his agents in Singapore were reported to be raising money and arms for him there. One Arab who had been active in his cause in Singapore went to Mecca in 1861, possibly with another appeal to the Caliph.[28]

The fighting was hardly over in Jambi before the chiefs of Banjarmasin began a revolt against an unpopular Dutch-supported Sultan (1859–63). Here too the chiefs relied increasingly on the ulama to arouse popular support for their cause. In this case, it is clear, there was no question of international connections or aspirations, and the frenzied *beratib beamaal* used against Dutch troops owed more to primitive mysticism than to Islamic solidarity.[29]

Nevertheless this series of events, together with the frightening impact of the Indian Mutiny, convinced many Dutch statesmen that a pan-Islamic movement was the greatest danger to their empire.

236   An Indonesian Frontier

Consequently the 1860s were marked by considerable official nervousness. The only territorial acquisition, reluctantly undertaken, was the large but sparsely populated coast between Aceh and Siak on the east coast of Sumatra. The ruler of Asahan, the most defiant of the small states in this district, made the obvious appeal to a holy war in requesting solidarity against the Dutch from his fellow rajas. Indonesians in Mecca were also reported to have encouraged him to cooperate with Aceh in order to invoke Turkish protection more effectively. In fact, however, despite the exaggerations of some Dutch officials, it was British traders in the Straits Settlements who provided the main moral support for the slight resistance offered. In appealing to Britain for unity against the rising tide of Muslim "fanaticism", the Netherlands Government also cited the publication of some Malay pamphlets in Singapore, calling for Muslim unity in the face of European aggression against Turkey in the Balkans.[30]

The Aceh War

If the dangers of the 1860s were exaggerated by colonial officials, there is good reason to select 1873 as the year of the first religious movement against the Dutch to affect the whole archipelago. After a decade of tension Holland finally declared war on Aceh in March of that year. Its force of 3,000 men was forced to withdraw after losing its commander in an attack on the Acehnese capital. For the six months before a stronger force could be assembled, millenarian hopes of ousting the Dutch were stronger than ever before among Southeast Asian Muslims.

As a result of Aceh's early struggle against the Portuguese, militant Islam and a sentimental link with Turkey had become and remained integral elements in Acehnese patriotism. Sultan Ibrahim had renewed old ties in 1850 by sending an envoy to Constantinople to request that Aceh be considered a vassal province of the Ottoman Empire again. Flattered and gratified, Sultan Abdul Mejid had issued two Imperial *firmans,* one renewing Turkish protection over Aceh, the other confirming Ibrahim in his royal status.[31] A few years later Ibrahim

Nineteenth-century Pan-Islam

sent \$10,000 towards Turkish war expenses in the Crimea and was rewarded with the Mejidie decoration.[32]

Aceh's later relations with Turkey owed much to Habib Abd ar-Rahman az-Zahir, a Hadhramaut Sayyid who first visited Aceh in 1864 after wide experience in Arabia, Egypt, India, Europe, and Malaya. Ambitious and extremely able, he succeeded so well in his chosen task as a religious and legal reformer that within a few years his power had aroused the fear of Sultan Ibrahim. Finding his ambition checked by the Sultan's jealousy, he had gone to Mecca in 1868, and was probably behind an appeal to the Turkish Sultan in that year from 65 Acehnese "notables", requesting protection against the advances of the Dutch.[33] On this occasion the Porte appeared to have entirely forgotten the existence of Aceh, and the Netherlands ambassador was told that the appeal would be refused.[34]

In the Hejaz, if not in Constantinople, Aceh's connection with Turkey was kept alive by the flow of pilgrims. During 1872 the Turkish Pasha of Jidda, as well as some of his subordinates, repeatedly assured the Netherlands Consul that Aceh was a part of the Ottoman Empire.[35]

Abd ar-Rahman had returned to Aceh in 1869, and a year later became the most powerful man in the state as guardian of the young Sultan Mahmud, who then succeeded Ibrahim. Shortly before the Dutch invasion of 1873, however, he had again left for Mecca. He carried an appeal from Mahmud for Turkish protection, and hurried to Constantinople with this as soon as he heard about the Dutch attack.

Ably presented by this persuasive ambassador, Aceh's cause appealed to the popular Turkish mood. Sultan Abdul Aziz himself was flattered by the request for protection, while the reforming party of Midhat Pasha found it a suitably righteous anti-Western cause. For a few months the fate of Aceh became "la grande question du jour" in Constantinople, with most of the newspapers urging either diplomatic or military support.[36] But none of the major Powers were enthusiastic. Even Britain refused the encouragement it had given a similar embassy from Kashgar when that state was threatened by Russia.[37] Consequently Abd ar-Rahman was apparently told early in June that nothing could be done for his cause.

The Habib then provoked a new crisis by tracing in the Imperial archives the *firmans* of 1850 which had acknowledged a Turkish protectorate over Aceh. The radicals in the Turkish Cabinet were then able to force a decision to appeal to Holland not to renew hostilities in view of Aceh's long subordination to Turkey. Pressure from the Russian Ambassador finally reduced this to a tactful offer of mediation by the Caliph, which stated Turkey's claim to sovereignty over Aceh in such a courteous way that it could be politely brushed aside by Holland.[38] By December the issue had sufficiently subsided for the Porte to be able to dismiss Abd ar-Rahman with a minor decoration for himself and a Vezirial letter for his Sultan, summing up Turkey's attempts to help Aceh.[39]

Though Holland's worst fears were not realized, Abd ar-Rahman's activity in Constantinople had serious repercussions in Southeast Asia. Aceh and the whole archipelago were kept in touch with Turkish developments through Penang and Singapore, neutral settlements the majority of whose merchant community opposed Netherlands expansionism. The Muslim community of the two British settlements was solidly and actively behind the Acehnese. Reports on the war were given regularly after the Friday prayer in many mosques, and the leading partisans would often meet afterwards to discuss what could be done to help. Some Singapore Arabs launched an appeal among their compatriots in the Straits Settlements and Java, which was said to have raised 100,000 Spanish dollars for the Acehnese cause by the end of 1874.[40] In Penang there was an important colony of Acehnese, who encouraged their countrymen by relaying optimistic reports of probable overseas support.

Repercussions in the Region

The great excitement caused by the Dutch retreat in April 1873 was already subsiding in June, without having given rise to anything that could be called a movement. But on 9 July the Constantinople newspaper *Basiret* announced that the Ottoman Government had decided to send eight warships to Sumatra to prevent any hostile attack on Aceh, and to leave one of them permanently stationed in

Nineteenth-century Pan-Islam

Acehnese waters. The report was based on nothing more than the hopes of the pan-Islamic party and some unrelated naval movements; within 36 hours it had been officially discounted as "an absurd fiction" and the *Basiret* had been suspended for its pains.[41] But in the meantime the report had been carried throughout the world by Reuters. Official denials were less effective in Southeast Asia than in Europe. Acehnese agents in Penang sent the first report to Aceh at once, but omitted any mention of the denial.[42]

In Singapore, too, the denials failed to quell the excitement of Muslim enthusiasts. The spies of the Netherlands Consulate in Singapore were unable to keep track of the flood of inflammatory letters, verbal messages and rumours spread about the archipelago in connection with Turkish intervention in the war. Nevertheless they, with the authorities in Java, have provided the historian with sufficient evidence to show that there was a measure of organization behind the agitation of July–September 1873. Its leading spirits appear to have been Javanese *hajis* or Arabs from Java, making a living in Singapore through the pilgrim traffic or a small trade with Java. As well as writing letters to their own contacts in Java, this group organized a circular letter to the most important indigenous rulers in Java and Rhio, urging them to join the holy war against the Dutch on the arrival of the Turkish warships. The clumsy device was adopted of enclosing these letters in envelopes addressed to the Arab headmen of Batavia and Semarang, who dutifully handed them to the Dutch. The Acehnese group in Penang also provided money to send a Kelantan Arab on a mission to the native rulers in Java. This man was captured by the Dutch Resident of Surakarta before he could see the Susuhunan of that state.[43]

These early propagandists showed their inexperience in directing most of their efforts to Javanese aristocrats who were wholly dependent on the Dutch as well as indifferent to Muslims. The greatest danger to Dutch rule was in those areas in Sumatra, Borneo, and Celebes where the traditional rulers were still capable of opposition, where Islam was politically important, and where close commercial contact with Singapore was maintained. In these districts events in Aceh were followed with great interest, and rumours often circulated of impending

240 An Indonesian Frontier

risings against the Dutch. As the Resident of South and East Borneo pointed out: "That the war with Aceh produces a certain tension here, and arouses in many the hope of seeing a change of things brought about as a result, is only natural." But, he continued, news of the coming Dutch second expedition against Aceh would tend to delay any plans for rebellion until its outcome was known.[44] Thus no revolts occurred, leaders everywhere preferring to talk rebellion than to indulge in it.

The Adviser on Native Affairs to the Netherlands Indian Government was instructed to investigate the repercussions of the war in Java and Singapore only. In West Java he found many religious and secular leaders sympathetic to Aceh, but he considered the Singapore agitators unlikely to achieve much success there unless Dutch troops were again defeated in Aceh, or unless Turkey really did interfere in the war. Though the Adviser did not seriously contemplate the latter alternative, he found general belief in Java as well as Singapore that Turkey had the right as well as the strength to intervene if it wished, since Aceh was under its protection.[45]

During the period of greatest excitement there were a few Javanese who attempted to join the holy war in Aceh, as an honourable substitute for the much more expensive *haji*. Most of those who tried to do so were prevented by the Dutch blockade of the Acehnese coast, however. A group of 30 disappointed crusaders turned back to Singapore from Penang in December 1873 after failing to find a ship to take them across the Straits.[46]

Leading statesmen in Holland, and to a lesser extent in Batavia, made the mistake of seeing the 1873 agitation against them as part of a world-wide pan-Islamic movement which posed a threat to all the "Christian Powers" in Asia. The British Ambassador in The Hague found the Netherlands Government "seriously impressed with the idea that there is an extensive Mahomedan propaganda on foot".[47] An earnest appeal was sent to Britain for solidarity against this rising tide of Muslim feeling.[48] On this occasion the Foreign Office was sufficiently impressed to issue a circular to Consuls asking them to report signs of a "religious and political revival" among Muslims.[49] In fact, although a common sympathy for oppressed Muslims in various parts of the

Nineteenth-century Pan-Islam

241

world was fostered in Mecca, there was no question of a genuine world-wide movement. In India particularly there was "no reason to believe that the proceedings of the Dutch at Acheen have excited any great sympathy, or even ordinary attention, among the Mahomedans of India".[50] In Malaya, the Perak rising against the British in 1875 received no encouragement from the group of politically conscious Muslims in Penang and Singapore who had led the anti-Dutch agitation of 1873.[51] That agitation, therefore, must be seen not as part of a specifically anti-Western reaction so much as an identification with the Islamic community on the part of those who had specific grievances.

Interest in Aceh gradually subsided after the second Dutch expedition occupied the Acehnese capital in January 1874. But the hope of help from Turkey never completely died. Some individual Turkish army officers found their way to Aceh in 1875 and 1876, though they probably did not remain there long.[52] Acehnese told a French trader in 1875 that many of their leaders had resolved never to give up the fight until the Caliph interfered to settle it.[53] In the same year Singapore Muslims were excited by a rumour that a Turkish ambassador was on his way to investigate the Aceh question and in general to protect the interests of Southeast Asian Muslims.[54]

Returning to Aceh in 1876 after the failure of all his attempts to win support in Constantinople, Abd ar-Rahman az-Zahir probably destroyed most of the illusions still cherished there about Turkish power and intentions. Yet as late as 1890, when a Turkish warship on a visit to Japan created great excitement in Singapore, the hopes of the beleaguered Acehnese turned again to Constantinople. An envoy was sent to Singapore with letters requesting both the Turkish commander and Sayyid Muhammad Alsagoff to bring Aceh's plight to the attention of the Caliph. The Turkish warship had long since departed, but high hopes were placed in Alsagoff, who left on a tour of Europe shortly after receiving the Acehnese letter. Dutch officials complained that these hopes negated the effect of the special coercive measures by which they were trying finally to subdue the Acehnese.[55]

On his return to Singapore in 1892 Alsagoff sent a personal envoy to Aceh, letting the Dutch know that this was to advise submission. The mission apparently had the opposite effect, however, and an Acehnese embassy to Constantinople was soon organized. The envoy, Teuku Laota, was equipped with a Turkish sword and decoration as tokens of Turkey's earlier recognition of its protectorate over the country. Laota appears to have travelled no further than Singapore, where he was probably dissuaded from his mission by more realistic Muslims.[56] Instead the Acehnese Sultan wrote directly to Constantinople at the end of 1893. His letter fell into Dutch instead of Turkish hands,[57] and there is no record of further attempts in this direction.

Turkish Support

It was only during the reign of Sultan Abdul Hamid in Turkey (1876–1908) that the movement for a universal and effective Caliphate received consistent encouragement from the top. After the disastrous Russo-Turkish war of 1877–8 Abdul Hamid turned his back on the West and suspended the liberal constitution of 1876. Encouraged by the many manifestations of sympathy he received from the Muslim world, including Southeast Asia, he hoped to make up in Asia for the influence he could not retain in Europe. Given the endemic weakness of Turkey and the particularly acute misgovernment of Abdul Hamid's reign there could be little thought of an organized anti-European movement directed from Constantinople. The Sultan himself, however, made clear that he wished to be regarded as a sort of Pope and protector for Sunni Muslims everywhere, and this had its natural reaction among courtiers and in the Turkish press.[58]

The first fruit of this new attitude in Southeast Asia was probably a mission from Mecca in 1881. British agents in Arabia reported the departure for Singapore of two Imams and a trader who "occupy so important a position in the Mohamedan world that their movements seldom fail to have a political object".[59] The warning was passed on to the Netherlands authorities, who prevented the attempts of the two Imams to sail on from Singapore to Batavia, Padang, or Palembang. The mission was obliged to remain in Singapore for three months until requested to leave by the British. Meanwhile the Dutch arrested

Nineteenth-century Pan-Islam

30 men in Palembang, including several members of the former royal dynasty, for alleged participation in a plot to murder all the Europeans there. The chief conspirators were said to be two Turkish ex-army officers who had visited Palembang from Singapore shortly before on the pretext of trade. The role of the Meccan Imams is not clear, but the Dutch had intercepted a letter from one of them to a *haji* in Palembang immediately before the arrests. The Imam had there regretted his inability to reach Palembang, but recommended another *haji* "to take charge of the propaganda in his stead".[60]

That such a crude plot should have been consciously inspired by these highly placed Arabs is most unlikely. The so-called "propaganda" was probably directed at winning Indonesian support for Muslim or Turkish causes in western Asia. The effect of such initiatives always heightened hopes of Muslim unity in Southeast Asia, however, and to this extent Dutch suspicions may have been justified. Some Palembangers believed that Javanese Muslims were being aroused for the same cause, and had attached importance to harmless visits to Java by Muhammad Alsagoff and the Sultan of Johore in 1881.[61]

These dramatic events coincided with a new outburst in Banten, the only part of Java where discontent was habitually expressed in Islamic form.[62] Consequently Dutch officials were warned to guard against "a religious movement with political overtones".[63] Restrictions on the movement of Arabs were tightened and some districts were banned to them altogether. It is particularly at this period at the end of the 19th century that Holland gained the reputation among Muslims as the most fanatical opponent of Islam.

In the last two years of the century the occasional complaints reaching western Asia from Arabs in Indonesia burgeoned into a flood. One contributory cause was probably the concession to Japanese of European legal status in Netherlands India in 1899. A more direct cause was the pan-Islamic zeal of Muhammad Kiamil Bey, Turkish Consul-General in Batavia from 1897 to 1899.

Though enjoying natural prestige as representatives of the Caliph, previous Turkish Consuls had not gone beyond the distribution of a few Korans in an attempt to win Indonesian friends. Kiamil immediately encouraged his Arab acquaintances to regard themselves as Turkish subjects and bring their grievances to him. Eleven young Arabs left for schooling in Constantinople under his auspices. These students enjoyed royal patronage while in the Turkish capital from 1898 to 1904, and on their return insisted that they were Turks entitled to European status, producing passports to prove it.[64] Holland finally insisted on the recall of Kiamil Bey when he wrote, offering friendly assistance to the Sultan of Deli. It was later discovered that he had also tried to begin a correspondence with the Acehnese pretender Sultan — a much more serious charge.[65]

Kiamil continued to worry Dutch officials by his attempts to obtain the Turkish Consulship in Singapore in 1899 and again in 1904. On the latter occasion he was transferred to Singapore by his government, but Britain refused to give him an exequator. Besides the Dutch complaints against him, the leading Muslims of Singapore were annoyed that Kiamil had married the widow of Sultan Abu Bakar without consulting the surviving members of the Johor family.[66] The Foreign Office had already been put on its guard in 1899 by an article in the Turkish newspaper *Ikdam* which Kiamil had probably inspired. This had declared that "the most important duty of Ottoman Consuls is to strengthen the ties between the peoples of Islam wherever they may be". The appointee to the contemplated Singapore Consulate, *Ikdam* continued, should be "above all a religious man", since religion was the essential way to extend Turkish influence in such regions.[67]

The most important result of Kiamil Bey's sojourn in Batavia was to foster closer links between Southeast Asian Arabs and the Middle Eastern press. Towards the end of 1897 the Arabic *al-Malumat* of Constantinople, the *Thamarat al-funun* of Beirut, and several Egyptian newspapers acquired correspondents in Batavia or Singapore who regularly complained about the injustices to which Muslims in general but Arabs in particular were subjected by the Dutch. This press campaign aroused high hopes that Turkey would intervene to have European status given to Netherlands Indian Arabs. As *al-Malumat* jested, the Dutch authorities treated its issues like a fleet of men-of-war when they arrived in Batavia.[68]

Knowing that no such controversial material could appear in the Turkish press without tacit official approval, Snouck Hurgronje advised

Nineteenth-century Pan-Islam

taking the matter up in Constantinople rather than trying to ban the newspapers in Indonesia. The Dutch Ambassador was given the solemn assurance of Sultan Abdul Hamid in 1899 that far from encouraging pan-Islam in Indonesia he had always urged the "Jawa" to be loyal subjects of Holland. A few newspapers were obliged to print denials of the more absurd exaggerations which had appeared.[69]

Despite these assurances, the Porte was sounding out Whitehall less than a year later for support in an attempt to obtain for Turkish subjects the rights which had been given to the Japanese in Netherlands India. Frank Swettenham, in Singapore, poured scorn on the idea as part of a pan-Islamic movement, and the Foreign Office gave no support.[70] As a result the brief campaign in Turkey appears to have petered out.

Fears of an Expanding Movement

Though this movement had been almost entirely restricted to Arab circles, there was always the danger that it would spread. The propagandists were usually unclear whether they deserved Turkish protection as Arabs or simply as Muslims, and in 1900 they were preparing to publish pan-Islamic tracts in Indonesian languages to arouse wider support. The first issue of *Bintang Timur,* a Malay newspaper of Penang, claimed that since Kiamil Bey had enrolled the inhabitants of Netherlands India as Turkish subjects, they had addressed their grievances to Constantinople rather than Batavia.[71]

Such ideas appeared especially dangerous to the Dutch at the turn of the century, when their troops were beginning a systematic offensive in areas such as Aceh, Jambi, and most of Borneo and Celebes. After a series of offensives in Jambi, Dutch troops finally killed the defiant Sultan Taha in April 1904, and rounded up his remaining followers. Only five months later, however, most of the Jambi nobility were again roused to revolt by Karl Hirsch, alias Abdullah Yussuf, a Hungarian in the Turkish army, who claimed to have a special commission from the Caliph to assist in the defence of Jambi. He was quickly arrested, 19 chiefs were captured and exiled, and Jambi was again gradually subdued during the following two years.[72]

246 An Indonesian Frontier

Hirsch may have been encouraged in this mission by some Turkish officials, but he can hardly have been a fully accredited government emissary. Indeed he had already fallen foul of the Turkish Government, which had warned Britain in advance to watch his activities in Singapore.[73] Nevertheless it appears that Sultan Taha must have succeeded in bringing his grievance to the attention of the Caliph shortly before his death. In 1903 he had sent an envoy to appeal to Haji Attaullah, the first and last Turkish Consul-General in Singapore.[74] In July 1904 Sultan Abdul Hamid told the Dutch representative at his court that he wished to appeal personally to the Dutch Queen on behalf of Indonesian Muslims. He had received a petition from a chief "not far from Singapore", with a name like "Tachar", who alleged that mosques had been destroyed and Muslims oppressed. Moreover, the Sultan pointed out, Indonesian pilgrims frequently complained in Mecca about the ill-treatment they received at home. When the Dutch politely replied that this was none of the Sultan's business, he drew an analogy with the Pope's frequent representations on behalf of Catholics in Syria.[75]

Though unhistorical, such claims to a Muslim papacy had sometimes been allowed by Britain, which in the 19th century enjoyed some prestige among Muslims as the special friend of Turkey. A Turkish Consul was allowed in South Africa in the 1860s specifically to look after Muslim interests. But Holland had always felt both more nervous and more jealous of its sovereign rights, and consistently opposed all Turkish interest in its colonies. Similarly any outstanding Muslims beyond Dutch control, like those in Singapore, were automatically suspect as a potential focus of disloyalty.

In this matter as in others, the great Arabicist Christian Snouck Hurgronje gave emphatic theoretical precision to a policy which had previously been followed haphazardly by his government.[76] As an uncompromising liberal humanist, he regarded the "mediaeval" association of politics and religion as the principal enemy of peace and progress in Indonesia. Pan-Islam was the fullest and most obnoxious form of this threat: "It can stir up only confusion and unrest. At most it may cause local disturbances, but it can never in any sense have a constructive influence."[77] The government should

Nineteenth-century Pan-Islam

therefore define a religious sphere, notably including the *haji*, in which the strictest neutrality and tolerance would be maintained. On the other hand, it should abandon its qualms about crushing ruthlessly any religious leaders, like those in Aceh, who encouraged rebellion or allegiance to a foreign power.

On the positive side, Snouck Hurgronje pressed for more western education to establish a fruitful bond between the European and Asian subjects of Holland on the basis of modern Dutch culture. "The pan-Islamic idea, which as yet has little hold on the aristocracy of Java and the equivalent classes of Muslims in the outer islands, will lose any chance of achieving that in the future as soon as its members have become voluntary sharers of our culture." If the peasant masses became dangerously infected with the pan-Islamic "disease", which could happen at any time, the westernized elite would have an interest in exorcizing it.[78]

The complex and intimate relationship between Islam and nationalism in 20th-century Indonesia has already been the subject of several impressive studies.[79] Here we are concerned only to clarify the role of pan-Islam in the context of 19th-century aspirations. As Benda has pointed out,[80] the rapid appearance of a dissatisfied, Dutch-educated elite together with the eclipse of the Caliphate in Turkey, made Snouck Hurgronje's diagnosis of the Indonesian situation appear irrelevant by the third decade of the 20th century. This produced a tendency to play down the importance of pan-Islam on the part of those concerned with 20th-century nationalism. The writer hopes that this study will assist a better understanding of the reasons why a generation of Dutchmen including one as acute as Snouck Hurgronje should have been so concerned at the pan-Islamic threat.

The evidence of this chapter supports the view that the tightening bonds between Muslims in Southeast Asia and the Middle East were important in creating a sense of common purpose against the colonial masters. In most of the cases discussed the original conflict between Indonesians and Dutch was a local one not directly related to religion. But conflicts of any duration are bound to develop their own rationale, particularly when outside help is sought. Thus it was that an element of pan-Islamic solidarity was increasingly evident in many of the conflicts.

Furthermore, towards the end of the century pan-Islamic feeling appears to have heightened to the extent that a purely external stimulus was sufficient to spark off a revolt, as in Palembang in 1881 or Jambi in 1904. There is no reason to denigrate Snouck Hurgronje's estimate of pan-Islam as the most serious indigenous threat to a permanent Netherlands-Indonesian "association" in the period preceding the implementation of the Ethical Policy.

11

Merchant Imperialist: W.H. Read and the Dutch Consulate in the Straits Settlements

THERE are at least two "W.H. Read" personae in Southeast Asian historiography. One makes a dramatic entry into Indonesian and Dutch colonial history, as author of a series of telegrams in February 1873 which provoked the Dutch into a rash and disastrous attack on the independent sultanate of Aceh, thereby beginning the most bitter and costly of Holland's colonial wars. This was also the first and longest-serving Dutch Consul in Singapore, highly decorated by the Dutch crown, an influential confidant of successive Governors-General and Dutch Colonial Ministers over several decades. The odd thing about this W.H. Read is that he was not a Dutchman. Nevertheless he convinced Batavia that he could fill this most strategic of Dutch consular posts better than a Netherlands citizen.

The other W.H. Read is commemorated in the memoir he wrote in his 80s, *Play and Politics: Recollections of Malaya by an Old Resident.* Curiously, this makes no mention at all of his historic role in starting the Aceh war, and virtually none of the Netherlands Consulate which provided most of his income, status, and influence after 1873. On the contrary it portrays an unusually patriotic, even jingoistic Englishman, filled with boyish enthusiasm for the exploits of James Brooke and

Stamford Raffles, and always ready to find unorthodox but effective means to advance the bounds of British authority in Southeast Asia. This is the same Read who was a friend and supporter of James Brooke, and the one who helped bring about British intervention in the Malay States of the Peninsula in 1873–4. And yet it was the Dutch crown, not the British, which honoured him.

Of course W.H. Read lived a single life, and I believe there was a considerable consistency about it. Nevertheless it remains curious that a generally self-serving memoir found nothing to celebrate about his service of the Dutch. Was it, perhaps, that the Dutch side of his life turned gradually bitter in his older years, or did he himself feel some strain in reconciling the imperial bravado with which he chose to colour his life with his increasing reliance on a foreign government, and especially with having encouraged that government into an extremely ill-conceived and unpopular war?

W.H. Read and Singapore

William Henry MacLeod Read (1819–1909) was the archetype of the Singapore merchant, who played a leading role in virtually every aspect of the colony's life from the moment he took up residence in 1841, aged only 22. His credentials to assume this leadership could hardly have been better. His father C.R. Read had moved to Singapore from Bengkulu in 1822 on the advice of Raffles, and there joined "the pioneer European mercantile firm in the place" which A.L. Johnston had established a year or two before. C.R. Read was soon a partner in A.L. Johnston & Co., and his son "W.H." replaced him as Singapore-based partner only four months after arriving in the settlement.[1] In this role he acted as agent for a large proportion of the European ships which anchored at Singapore, including all the most significant Dutch vessels — those of the Navy, the Netherlands Trading Company (NHM) and various other companies.

In his early years, particularly before he married in 1848, Read threw himself into reinventing the social life of Europeans in Singapore, which until this period was limited (he claimed) to the

W.H. Read and the Dutch Consulate

Governor's tedious Sunday dinners, and games of fives for the young and cards for the others. With a couple of other young newcomers ("baru datangs", as he recalled them), Read established a racing track within two years, winning the first race himself; began a series of amateur theatricals in which he often played a comic female lead; organized the first Regatta in the harbour; and established a public library, of which Read was first Treasurer. In 1845 Read was the second initiate of the first Masonic Lodge in Singapore, "the Brethren of Lodge Zetland in the East" and he became its first "Provincial Grand Master".[2] It is interesting that at least one of Read's Malay associates, Sultan Mahmud of Lingga, was inducted into the Lodge in the 1850s, and the *Tuhfat al Nafis* recorded this as if it were the cause of the sultan's adopting a lifestyle "like a white man".[3]

As the most energetic of Singapore's business leaders, Read was at the forefront of the agitation which developed in the mid-1850s to place the Straits Settlements directly under British Government control rather than remain subordinate to the East India Company's government in India. He moved the key motion urging separation from India at the first Singapore public meeting on the subject on 11 August 1855.[4] He pressed for an elected municipal council with more autonomy, and served as a member of that council for 15 years and its President for six. When the Straits Settlements became a Crown Colony under the Colonial Office rather than the India Office in 1867, partly due to Read's efforts, he was appropriately appointed the first unofficial member of the colony's Legislative Council.[5] He was at that time, and for several years thereafter, also the chairman of the Singapore Chamber of Commerce. The *Straits Times* in 1873 supported the idea of putting Read's portrait in the Town Hall in acknowledgment of "his numerous, disinterested and great services to these Settlements".[6] The first colonial Governor, Sir Harry Ord, fell out badly with Read in 1869 over both local Singapore administration and what Read (and much Singapore opinion) considered Ord's insufficiently robust policy in the Malay states.[7] When in 1873 Ord departed under a hail of abuse from the Singapore press, his successor made sure to consult Read extensively.

A Muscular Imperialist

The informal memoirs which Read wrote in his old age are redolent with enthusiasm for empire. The book takes particular pride in his friendship and support for James Brooke, the "white raja" of Sarawak, and for the latter's chief military ally, Admiral Henry Keppel, as they struggled against the carping of less bold spirits.[8] When Chinese riots broke out in Singapore (notably in 1854 and 1863) Read adopted a robust policy of using Europeans and Straits-born Chinese as "special constables" to bluff the Chinese gangs into dispersing.[9] He was the most forceful champion of a more aggressive British policy of intervention in the Malay states, which he clearly believed would meet the needs of Singapore commerce, and especially his own, better than the existing policy of working through Malay figures such as the Temenggong of Johor.

Read's Peninsula strategy from the early 1850s was to support the cause of Sultan Ali, son of Sultan Hussain, whom the British arrangements for Singapore had left as nominal ruler of the old Johor-Riau empire. He quickly took possession of the Sultan's seal, and appears to have acted for some years in his name.[10] In the 1850s he sought in vain to place the Sultan in charge of Johor under a British Resident. This alliance with Sultan Ali's side of Malay politics made Read the most consistent enemy of the Temenggong family, whose scion Abubakar was eventually recognized as Sultan of Johor. Abubakar's commercial affairs were handled by Read's rivals in Singapore, Paterson, Simons & Co, who were among those lobbying for Johor to remain as an independent state closely linked to Singapore rather than being placed under colonial control in the manner Read envisaged.[11]

The conflict extended into the politics of other states of the Malayan Peninsula, where Abubakar generally sought to keep direct British influence out while Read worked with those opposed to Abubakar for more direct British commercial and political control. In Selangor in the 1860s and 1870s Read was a powerful supporter of Tengku Kudin, Yap Ah Loy, and the case for British intervention, as against Abubakar's voice on the other side of these conflicts. In 1867 he helped float the Eastern Asia Telegraph Company in London,

W.H. Read and the Dutch Consulate   253

which sought to extend the telegraph from Rangoon by land to Bangkok, Singapore, Java and Australia, and needed British involvement in the Peninsula states to reassure potential investors. Eventually Britain shifted its preference to undersea cables not subject to territorial problems. Nevertheless the momentum Read and his friends generated proved enough to persuade a new Governor of the Straits Settlements, Sir Andrew Clarke (1873–6), to intervene in Perak, Selangor and Pahang, laying the foundation for British protection of the Malay states.[12]

The Dutch Consulate

As one of the most prominent commercial agents for ships visiting Singapore, Read was a natural choice for countries wishing an inexpensive means of representation, primarily for authorizing the issuing of visas and licenses, returning the effects of deceased seamen, and similar issues. Unusually for a Singapore merchant, Read also had excellent French, as a result of having spent several of his school years in France. Much of his consular correspondence was in the diplomatic language of the day. Sweden and Norway appointed him their honorary consuls (1851–62) before the much more important Dutch consulate came his way, and he also acted as Consul for Portugal. In his memoirs Read remembers this kind of work mainly in terms of his undiplomatic derring-do, such as when he earned a reprimand from the Swedish Government for imprisoning a rebellious crew, an act for which he had no authority, in order to give them a fright.[13] Read also acted as agent in Singapore for Rajah James Brooke, and was later one of the leading associates of Alfred Dent's attempt to colonize North Borneo.

Along with his many contacts in the Peninsula Malay states, Read also had some influence in Siam, where he became a regular correspondent of both King Mongkut and the young Chulalongkorn. In Read's account this began through his association with the Siamese Consul in Singapore, Tan Kim Ching, who operated rice mills in Siam and Saigon and was Read's partner in the Selangor venture in the 1860s. In the late 1850s Tan consulted Read about King Mongkut's

254   An Indonesian Frontier

desire to escape from a disadvantageous treaty just signed with France. Read claims that his strategy of questioning the letters patent of the French Consul who had arranged the treaty proved successful, since the Consul had no power himself to sign treaties. This led to an invitation for Read to visit Bangkok, and to an ongoing correspondence thereafter, in which Read constantly urged King Mongkut to beware of French designs and to place greater confidence in Britain. In 1867, Mongkut complained in a letter to the ambassador he had sent to France, "Mr Read has written to me again from Singapore to tell me that you will meet with great difficulties from all sides while you are in France", and had urged him to trust no Frenchman. In 1871 he accompanied the young King Chulalongkorn on his first visit to Java, and was subsequently awarded the order of the Royal Siamese Throne by the king.[14]

Singapore was far more important for the Netherlands than for other European states which began appointing Consuls there. One of the merchants petitioning to open a consulate pointed out that it was the biggest port for Dutch shipping outside Europe. Singapore had become in its first 30 years the hub of shipping for Netherlands India itself. The most important shipping companies in the Archipelago were British owned, and they made Singapore their trans-shipment base between the Archipelago and international routes. Singapore was also of vital political importance as the centre where Southeast Asian Muslims gathered before embarking to Mecca on pilgrimage, and where they encountered outside ideas in conditions of relative freedom. However the Foreign Ministry appeared wholly unaware of the political potential of the consulate, which became prominent only as the Dutch moved northward in Sumatra from 1862.

Read's appointment as the first Dutch Consul in the Straits Settlements was entirely due to his close connections with Dutch business houses through his handling the local needs of their visiting ships. A group of Amsterdam shippers petitioned the Dutch Government as early as 1851 to appoint Read honorary consul, but had been refused because of standing Dutch policy not to appoint Consuls to foreign colonies lest it encourage other states to ask for consulates in Netherlands India. In 1856, however, this policy

W.H. Read and the Dutch Consulate

changed, the intention to appoint Consuls in Asia was made known, and petitions came in, suggesting various names. The most influential Amsterdam houses favoured Read, whereas Rotterdam seemed to prefer Johannes Mooyer, Singapore agent of the Hamburg firm Behn Meyer. When Batavia learned of the plans much later, the Governor-General recommended that a full-time salaried Dutch official be appointed Consul, so important did they understand Singapore to be for Netherlands India. By this time, however, the King had already appointed W.H. Read as Consul, "without cost to the state", on 6 December 1856.[15]

In these pre-telegraph days communications moved slowly. The letter of appointment as Consul reached Singapore in June 1857, and only caught up with Read in October in London, where he had been on leave since April. Read responded by urging the appointment as Vice-Consul of M.F. Davidson, Read's partner in A.L. Johnston and Co., with whom his other responsibilities in Singapore had presumably been left. Within a week the King had acted accordingly, before any of the Batavia interests which still favoured a Dutch appointment could gather their forces.[16] Davidson must have continued to act during Read's absences until February 1863, when Read took the opportunity of the Vice-Consul's impending departure for Europe to recommend a 23-year-old Dutch clerk in his office, Jean Canters, as replacement. This was again speedily decreed by the King, before the all-important NHM had an opportunity to protest. The NHM had had a permanent Dutch agent, H.J. van Hoorn, in Singapore since 1857, and had long felt that he should be appointed Dutch Consul in place of the frequently-absent Read.[17] Although Read had not felt it necessary to tell The Hague anything more about Canters than that he was a native of the Netherlands, he appears to have been previously a junior member of NHM's Singapore staff, lured to A.L. Johnston by Read to help his firm's trade with Java and its handling of Dutch ships. He made it possible for some of the consulate's business for the first time to be conducted in Dutch.

The second in importance of the British Straits Settlements, Penang, also began to have honorary consuls appointed to it in the late 1850s, as it was also an important *entrepôt* for shipping from

Sumatra and the Bay of Bengal. When the first petitions arrived in 1860 from merchants in Penang wishing to be appointed Netherlands Consul, the Foreign Ministry had learned enough to refer the question this time to Batavia. The reply from the Governor-General was that a consulate in Penang seemed not necessary yet, but the German trader Kustermann would be the best of the candidates when that time arrived.[18]

Three years later the situation changed radically and the government became eager to appoint a Consul to Penang, but it was Read's nominee who got the job, not Kustermann. In 1863 a fleet of warships was sent to the Sumatran coast opposite Penang, led by Resident Netscher of Riau, to impose Dutch authority and capture or chase away those Malay rulers and Penang Chinese merchants who were resisting that authority and hoping for British protection. Holland could not afford to alienate the British support on which the Dutch position in Southeast Asia depended.[19] Somebody was therefore needed in Penang, who could defuse the anger of the local merchants and at the same time represent Dutch interests in the *entrepôt*, destined now to be the commercial centre of the Dutch colonies on the East Coast of Sumatra.

While most of the more vocal Straits merchants and their newspapers were very hostile to the Dutch forward movement in East Sumatra, W.H. Read had endeared himself to The Hague by reporting that in practice British trade appeared not to have suffered from it. As we have seen, Read was a passionate believer in the need to extend European authority to the Malay states, and that applied as much to Sumatra (where Britain was prevented from acting by the 1824 Treaty) as to Malaya. So when Read recommended his friend H.J.D. Padday, head of the Penang merchant house of Wm Hall & Co. and chairman of the Penang Chamber of Commerce, the Minister of Colonies Franssen van de Putte was quick to agree. Read predictably advised the Dutch Ministers that "the German merchants in Penang are not very highly regarded". In recommending Read's nominee to the Foreign Minister, van de Putte pointed out:

> Mr Padday stands in relations of commerce and friendship with
> Mr Read, a point to which I attach much value in connection

W.H. Read and the Dutch Consulate

with our relations with the British Government, with respect to the extension of Netherlands Indian authority on the East Coast of Sumatra.[20]

In contrast to the off-handed way in which Read had initially been appointed without even consulting Batavia, colonial and political considerations had become central by the time Padday was appointed to the Penang consulate in September 1863. The letter of appointment to Padday spelt out that the new Consul should particularly exert himself to counter the misinformed views in Penang about Dutch intentions, and should also keep an eye on every aspect of the traffic between Penang and Sumatra. The Resident of Riau, Netscher, who was responsible for Dutch policy in the contested area of Sumatra's east coast, would keep Padday informed of that policy.[21] Netscher did make a point of visiting Penang and briefing Padday in November. He reported favourably that Padday was "generally esteemed in Penang", and that he appeared persuaded by Netscher's arguments that the Dutch advance in Sumatra could only help the Straits' trade.[22]

Padday had none of Read's assertiveness or even his imperial conviction, however, and he appears to have been of little help to Dutch interests. In February 1864 he reported apologetically on a meeting of the Penang Chamber of Commerce, of which he was chairman, which had decided to continue its protests against the Dutch occupation of East Sumatra despite Padday's having told them what Netscher had told him. The following month he departed for Europe without informing The Hague, after "commissioning" his brother as Vice-Consul which he did not strictly have authority to do.[23]

Read's lengthy absences from his post also caused some anxieties in The Hague. He had left Singapore for England in October 1863, passing through Penang where he encouraged Padday (or so he reported) to stand up to the Penang merchants. Those interests led by the NHM which sought a full-time Dutch Consul in Singapore suggested to the Foreign Ministry that Read might never return and that more orthodox representation ought to be arranged. But van de Putte rebuffed any such suggestions, adding that he intended to consult Read about Straits and Sumatran matters while the Consul was in Europe. A pencilled note from someone in the Foreign Ministry

258 An Indonesian Frontier

remarked Read "is well known to [the Ministry of] Colonies, and I think personally to the Minister".[24] Read visited The Hague in May 1864, when he appears to have strengthened further his relationship with the powerful van de Putte.[25]

Read must have returned finally to Singapore in 1865, after about 18 months in which Vice-Consul Canters had managed things. Then in July 1867 he again reported that he would leave soon for Europe on doctor's advice. Since Canters was away in Holland, he recommended his brother R.B. Read as temporary Consul until Canters' return the following February. Canters, however, never did return to Singapore, delaying several times and finally joining the Rotterdam Bank in 1869. Although W.H. Read was back in Singapore in mid-1868, the Foreign Ministry received regular petitions from the leading Dutch merchant in Singapore, J.D. Hooglandt, about the impropriety of the Netherlands being represented there by an Englishman. If he could not be appointed Consul, as he requested each time Read went on leave, he should be appointed Vice-Consul in place of the vanishing Canters. Finally in April 1869, having established with no help from Read that Canters was not returning to Singapore, the Foreign Ministry wrote to Read to propose that Hooglandt be appointed Vice-Consul.[26]

This was the moment of truth which Read had probably been expecting, when he had to persuade The Hague to trust him rather than a Dutchman. He first argued that the presence of another Dutch national in his office in the person of Sebastian Maier made the position of Vice-Consul unnecessary. When The Hague insisted that it needed a Vice-Consul it could trust, Read launched a bitter attack on Hooglandt as somebody he absolutely could not work with, since the Dutchman had systematically tried to undermine Read's business with Dutch firms.[27] The ministry recoiled from this onslaught, and the vice consulate remained unfilled until 1871, when after repeated attempts to have Maier appointed to the post Read finally carried the day with The Hague.[28] In that year Read was also given the personal title of Consul-General on the Governor-General's recommendation, despite the objections of Governor Ord at seeing his principal enemy in Singapore thus rise to the top of the diplomatic corps.[29]

W.H. Read and the Dutch Consulate

By 1872–3 Read's status with the Dutch was at its height, therefore, as Consul-General and a Knight of the Netherlands Lion (1865), and with the assistance of a Consul in Penang and a Vice-Consul in Singapore who were both his own men. On the British side it needed only a change of Governor in 1873 from the hostile Sir Harry Ord to the "new broom" Sir Andrew Clarke, to make him also the most influential private citizen in Singapore.

Read's supporters sometimes stressed that he had given his heroic services to the Netherlands at no cost to the Dutch Government. Yet it is clear that the Dutch consulate meant a great deal to Read and that he was prepared to go to considerable lengths to keep it in his own hands and that of his firm. Consuls were permitted to exact small fees for the issuing of visas and the provision of consular services for ships. For most Consuls in Singapore, however, these would only have amounted to only a few hundred dollars a year, and the main attraction of the position would have been the status and the contacts it brought, which could in turn be useful in business.

The difference in the Dutch consulate in Singapore was the traffic in Muslim pilgrims from the Indies to Mecca, all of whom passed through Singapore where they boarded overcrowded British steamers (such as that described by Conrad in *Lord Jim*) for Jidda. The Netherlands Indies Government, uneasy about what contacts these pilgrims might make in Singapore, had required that they contact the consulate for a visa. This requirement was waived in 1875, partly because more efficient procedures to control the pilgrims were set in place through the Dutch consulate in Jidda. But apparently the pilgrims were never told, and Read's consulate continued to make most of its income by exploiting the pilgrims in this way.[30] It was only in 1881, when serious preparations were being made to replace an honorary by a salaried Consul (*consul missus*), that the Dutch foreign ministry found out how lucrative this was. The large sum for a poor Javanese of 2.50 Dutch guilders (one Straits dollar) could be charged for each visa, and thousands passed through Singapore each year. The annual income of the consulate averaged $11,370 in the years 1875–80, and three quarters of this came from visas issued to pilgrims.[31] This compares with about $2,000 a year as the

Did an Englishman Start the Aceh War?

In a literal sense there is no doubt that it was Read's telegram of 16 February 1873 that was the Dutch pretext for declaring war on Aceh. This alarmist message also speeded up Dutch invasion plans to the point of recklessness, in the mistaken belief that other powers were seeking to pre-empt Dutch action. There were of course both hawks and doves in Batavia, and Read's news played beautifully into the hands of the more impetuous side. Knowing Read's boyish enthusiasm for direct action rather than legal niceties, his consistent support of European intervention and readiness to use his extensive Malay contacts to create situations likely to bring it about, we should not rule out *a priori* a deliberate attempt by Read to provoke war. It seems unlikely that war would have been much delayed even without his manoeuvres, but Dutch policy would have been more cautious.

The Sumatra Treaty of 2 November 1871 had already laid the basis for a Dutch occupation of Aceh, and created a lobby in The Hague that argued Holland would look weak if it did not get on rapidly with the job. By this treaty Britain withdrew "all objections against the extension of Netherland dominion in any part of the island of Sumatra", and specifically the guarantee of Aceh's independence in letters exchanged with the 1824 Anglo-Dutch Treaty. The Indies Government moved quickly to match these negotiations in Europe with its own strategies for advance. There were two options whereby the annexation might be accomplished — either negotiations with the Sultan to seek to turn him into a Dutch client, or protection and support of rebellious *ulèëbalang* (territorial chiefs) against the Sultan until Aceh was gradually dismembered. The trouble was that each of these policies militated against the other, and the Dutch were not well informed enough to know which was the more realistic. On the whole the Dutch Resident of Riau, Schiff, who was charged with conducting relations with Aceh and the Council of the Indies (*Raad van Indië*) in Batavia, supported the policy of negotiating with the

Sultan, while the Ministry in The Hague, James Loudon whom it sent out as Governor-General in 1872, and Read himself, favoured a policy of confrontation, and support for the Sultan's enemies.

In August–September 1871 there were already crossed purposes. The Dutch ship *Djambi* was well received in the Aceh capital, encouraging Batavia to deal with the Sultan, but at the same time the warship *Marnix* intervened to help the rebellious Indian-born ruler of Idi by chasing away the Aceh fleet blockading it to bring it to heel. Read had been the cause of the latter move, having telegraphed from Singapore that Acehnese vessels at Idi had prevented vessels under the Dutch flag from leaving Idi, and that the *Marnix* must be sent to liberate them (though none were in fact found).[32] This intervention increased the alarm in Aceh, where a series of diplomatic moves began to establish whether Aceh would have any foreign friends if it stood up to the Dutch.

Missions were first sent off to Turkey (see Chapter 9) and to the Straits Settlements to sound British opinion. As pressures mounted for a Dutch expedition to enforce a definitive treaty with the Sultanate in late 1872, the Aceh court took more urgent measures. The Indian-born *Syahbandar* (harbour-master), Panglima Muhammad Tibang, was sent to Riau with letters asking for a delay in the Dutch mission, and to Singapore to appeal to the Consuls of France, the United States, Italy and Spain to see if they might help. Resident Schiff received Tibang well in Riau and even sent him back to Aceh in a Dutch ship which called at Singapore on the way. During this Singapore stopover Tibang sought out an earlier acquaintance, Tengku Mohammad Arifin, a sophisticated Malay with fluent English and many contacts among the Europeans in Singapore. Arifin led Tibang to the American Consul, Major Studer, where the possibility of a U.S.-Aceh treaty which might keep out the Dutch was discussed. After Tibang had departed at the end of January 1873, Arifin revealed these negotiations to Read, who telegraphed the news to Batavia in terms of "betrayal" which required immediate action. The Dutch thereupon moved as rapidly as possible to send a military expedition to Aceh empowered only to accept unconditional surrender from Aceh, or to invade. The fleet arrived off Aceh on 22 March, and

Figure 15a W.H. Read

Figure 15b Tengku Mohammad Arifin

W.H. Read and the Dutch Consulate

began bombarding on the 26th as a sign that diplomacy had given way to war.[33]

Who was really responsible for the so-called "Singapore treachery", and therefore for precipitating Batavia (and of course a bewildered Aceh) into a ruinous war for which it was hopelessly unprepared? It was the Dutch case that Aceh had deceived and betrayed the Dutch by dealing with representatives of other governments. Though Tibang was a somewhat slippery character, Aceh was an independent country entitled to negotiate with others, and not obliged to report all its dealings to the Dutch. Read wanted to portray his colleague Major Studer as a villain or a fool who rashly sought to bring America to the rescue of Aceh.[34] It is true that Studer was the most enthusiastic of Singapore Consuls about the prospect of a treaty with Aceh, "knowing, as I did and do, the great benefit that would accrue to our nation from a favourable treaty".[35] But he did no more than offer to pass on to Washington any formal proposals given to him, and by no means initiated the contacts with Tibang and Arifin. In the eyes of the British Governor the real culprit was Arifin, "this rascally intriguer" who first led the Acehnese into negotiations with the American Consul, and then betrayed them to the Dutch.[36] There seems much merit in this point. But was Read merely the disinterested reporter of Arifin's information, or had he in some sense instigated a pretext for the intervention in which he profoundly believed?

Arifin claimed to have known Read since 1864, soon after he moved to Malaya from Moko-Moko in West Sumatra, grandson of the last Sultan of Anak Sungei. Since Arifin was in the service in the late 1860s of Baginda Omar, ruler of Trengganu, he may well have coordinated strategy with the pro-Sultan Ali Malay coalition which Read had established. Arifin was sent to England by Baginda Omar in 1869, but on his return from that unsuccessful mission was burdened with debts which his employer was unwilling to pay. From 1870, therefore, Arifin appears to have been a client of W.H. Read, who assisted him financially in return for information about the many Malay political intrigues in which he was interested.[37] Arifin first contacted the American Consul in mid-1872 on the pretext of asking

264   An Indonesian Frontier

him whether it was true that the United States planned to establish a naval station in Brunei as had been reported. Arifin claimed to represent "thousands of natives" who hoped that America would so intervene. Studer thanked him for the sentiment but denied knowledge of such plans. "Finding him remarkably intelligent", Studer then talked to him about other things, and had several further discussions with him in which Arifin expressed admiration for the United States and support for its playing a greater role in Malay affairs.[38]

As far as is known, Arifin had no interest in Brunei, but Read certainly did. Apart from representing the Dutch interest in the southern two-thirds of the island of Borneo, Read was the agent and enthusiastic supporter in Singapore of the Brooke regime in Sarawak, and had an active interest in the moves which led to British control of North Borneo. It seems likely that Read encouraged Arifin to sound out Studer about American intentions in Borneo and report back. Whether Arifin kept Read informed of all his conversations with Studer is unclear, but Read himself gave the impression that Arifin was under his influence. In September 1872 Panglima Tibang visited Singapore for the first time in a vain attempt to obtain British support for Aceh, and he appears to have met Arifin then. Soon after (probably in October), Arifin explained to Studer Tibang's mission, and the determination of Aceh to retain its independence and make treaties with any countries friendly to it. He asked Studer if he would negotiate a treaty on behalf of the United States, and received the reply that he would forward any such proposal to Washington.[39]

If Arifin communicated this conversation to Read, the Consul did not pass it on to Batavia. But then he had nothing incriminating to pass on, since it was his man Arifin who had made the overtures to Studer, not the Acehnese. The question is whether Read encouraged Arifin to continue to bring the Acehnese and Americans together until there was some definite evidence of Acehnese "duplicity". In late December 1872 Read left Singapore for a visit to Bangkok, and did not return until 14 February, after the discussions between Tibang, Arifin and Studer had taken place at the end of January. The fact that he found out almost immediately what Arifin had done suggests that they had a close working

W.H. Read and the Dutch Consulate

relationship, whereby Arifin was in the habit of reporting regularly to him. Read's first report claimed that in telling him the story Arifin was merely acting out of gratitude for the help Read had given him over the years, so that the information could be trusted.[40] Later, when Arifin's role was understandably coming under question in Batavia, he explained, "That Mohamed Arifin may have been at first favourable to the Acehnese, I think highly probable; though had I been in Singapore, he would not have dared to be so; as it was I had to exert a certain pressure before I obtained the information I got."[41] If Arifin really would not have dared to act in Aceh's interests rather than Read's when the latter was in town, whose interests was he acting in when he talked to Studer about Aceh the previous October? The most plausible reading, to my mind, is that Read did encourage Arifin to begin talking to Studer and reporting back to Read, and specifically to raise the Aceh issue with the U.S. Consul. Arifin's reluctance to reveal everything to Read in February may have been because he did begin to believe that Acehnese independence under American protection was a possibility, and one from which he could profit. Read reported in April that Arifin had hoped to be appointed Aceh's Consul in Singapore. Read probably had little trouble removing these illusions and substituting his own hard cash for the "empty promises"of the Acehnese.[42]

Read's letters periodically refer to amounts that he paid Arifin when he expected Batavia to pay for it. Read sent Arifin to accompany the Dutch expedition to Aceh, and also took him to Batavia in July. The Dutch became disillusioned with Arifin after meeting him in Java and wanted to get rid of this "extremely cunning intriguer",[43] but Read kept him on his payroll for as long as he remained Consul-General in Singapore. As late as 1884 Read released him to serve another highly ambiguous role in British attempts to obtain the release of British seamen of the *S.S. Nisero*, kept hostage on the west coast of Aceh after having been shipwrecked there. In this affair too he reported regularly to Read, and expressed his eternal gratitude to the Consul, "who owns my soul, after God and the Prophet".[44]

Read's despatches to Governor-General Loudon during 1873 were the very stuff of aggressive and irresponsible imperialism, attempting to maintain the momentum generated by his initial telegrams. As the First Expedition was prepared in Batavia, Read forwarded an appeal from Singapore merchants for a peaceful outcome with a contemptuous commentary. Force was the only answer to the Acehnese. "You will never be able to trust them after what has passed. The combined characteristics of Arab and Kling, who must be directly descended from the 'father of all lies', cannot be relied upon."[45] The disastrous defeat of the First Dutch Expedition did nothing to dampen his ardour. In June he seemed to be dreaming that he was commanding the troops. "This is the time now, when everybody should work double tides and throwing aside forms and ceremonies, red tape and circumlocution, act with energy for the general good of the Fatherland."[46] As the Second Expedition began he pressed for an unconditional surrender and assured Loudon that Acehnese resistance would be short-lived.[47] Unfortunately the new Governor-General seemed, at least initially, more inclined to listen to this bluster than to the extremely well-informed reporting of George Lavino, responsible for gathering intelligence on Aceh, or the sober advice of his experienced officials. How much knowledge of either Aceh or the Dutch there was in Read's belligerence is put into question by his discussions in early 1874 with the new Governor of the Straits Settlements, Sir Andrew Clarke. When an Acehnese envoy and the Maharaja of Johor proposed to Clarke some form of British intervention to end the war, Read volunteered the information that the Dutch would welcome such mediation. "He led him [Clarke] to think that the Governor-General of the Netherlands and the Civil Government were sick of the war and not over sanguine as to its results, and that its continuance was only due to the Dutch Commander-in-Chief and the military element."[48] This could hardly have been farther from the truth, as the Dutch Government quickly made clear.

Perhaps Read was already tired of his little war. As the only major recent Dutch study of the Aceh war has pointed out, Read's jingoistic memoirs were silent about this, his most remarkable political achievement, because "this turned out not to be such a jolly and profitable war as the one he had been able to unleash in Malaya".[49]

W.H. Read and the Dutch Consulate

Indeed, it was to be the most costly of colonial wars in Southeast Asia, costing 14,000 lives on the Dutch side and at least 100,000 on the Acehnese side over a period of 40 years.

The Consulates as Intelligence Bases

The importance of the consulates in the Straits changed profoundly as a result of the outbreak of the Aceh war in March 1873. In attacking Aceh, the only major Archipelago state never having been in any way under Dutch influence, the Dutch ventured into unknown territory. Aceh, like the adjacent eastern coast of Sumatra, was in the commercial sphere of the Straits Settlements and had no contacts with the Dutch except hostile ones around its borders. To mount a major attack on Aceh, and then to sustain a besieged military presence for the next 30 years, required extensive logistical support from the Straits Settlements. Since the Dutch were so poorly informed about Aceh and its external supporters, it also required a major intelligence industry to arise around the Dutch consulates.

The greatly extended role of the consulates began in an *ad hoc* manner, as the Dutch imagined that their military adventure in Aceh would be of short duration. The first, disastrous, Dutch Expedition to Aceh, which invaded the area of the capital on 8 April and retreated to its ships after losing its commander on 25 April, was accompanied by a civilian "attaché" who became the key figure in the new phase of the consulate. This was George Lavino, a Dutch national with native fluency in English, as a result of spending all his school years in England (except for two in Germany) before working for nine years as a clerk with the government in Batavia. His English was in fact considerably more fluent than his Dutch, so that all his important despatches were written in English.[50] It was presumably this fact which persuaded the Netherlands Indies Government that he would be useful to the Aceh expedition in collecting information in Singapore and Penang as the expedition made its way to the Sultanate. Having been very helpful to the First Dutch Expedition, Lavino was seen to be crucial to the subsequent expedition, which Dutch authorities determined to mobilize in Java and Europe to make good the humiliation of the First Expedition. He was reappointed in May 1873 "for the acquisition of useful information at Penang about all that may transpire between the many Acehnese residing there and the merchants of that place". He was placed under the administrative authority of Read to gather information in Penang and report regularly to Batavia on it.[51]

Two weeks earlier the Indies Government had sent another Dutch official fluent in English, J.S. Crawfurd, to help Read directly in Singapore, by circulating in both English and Malay society and finding what he could about "the course of Aceh affairs and the smuggling of contraband". Read was sent a sum of 10,000 guilders from which both Crawfurd and Lavino were each to be paid a salary of 20 guilders a day, while the remainder would serve to pay the "native spies" needed to obtain this kind of information.[52] Crawfurd was kept busy with this kind of work until October, after the Second Dutch Expedition reached Aceh. Nevertheless when Read visited Batavia in July he persuaded the colonial government to send him another man to work in Aceh intelligence. A.H. Hermans was released from his position as a clerk with the Binnenlandse Bestuur (interior administration) in mid-August 1873, and was still working with the Singapore consulate a year later when his salary was raised from 10 to 12.50 guilders a day.[53]

During the interval between the two Dutch expeditions of 1873, therefore, there were three European or Eurasian officials from the Indies on the payroll of the consulate in intelligence work. In addition many Asians were recruited as spies and informers. Determined to succeed where the First Expedition had failed, the military commanders spared no expense in locating Chinese, Malay and Acehnese informers knowledgeable enough to guide the Second Expedition to safe anchorage and landing places in Aceh, and then to a reliable route to the Sultan's palace. In June 1873 the Army Commander put the required number at five guides and five interpreters. In August Lavino proposed the names of seven experienced Penang traders to Aceh, of whom five were Chinese, one Portuguese and one Acehnese. The most valuable was Koh Beng Swie, who had been trading to the Aceh coast for 31 years, 11 of

W.H. Read and the Dutch Consulate

them as master of a small vessel. Handsomely rewarded, he had already sailed with the First Dutch Expedition in March, and his services were retained by Lavino with the generous salary of $100 a month. Except for the Acehnese trader Teungku Lebylah who declined at the last moment, all these were eventually sent with the Second Expedition, though half of them were sent back from Aceh by the army, on the grounds that they proved to know very little.[54] Lavino struggled to find other knowledgeable figures willing to serve the Dutch among the almost universally hostile Acehnese community of Penang. One proposed was a young Penang-born Peranakan Malay (with an Indian father) named Mohammad Hasan, who claimed to have been a Malay clerk (*kerani*) for the Acehnese Sultan, entrusted by the Sultan with a number of missions. Another was T. Nyah Kuala, an Acehnese aged about 50, who had acted as harbour-master of Aceh for about 20 years.[55]

Neither of these appeared in the end to have been sent to Aceh, though Lavino was constantly busy with other spies who might penetrate into the sultanate. The Minangkabau Radja Boerhanoeddin, two Peranakan Arab *hajis* from Java, and a prominent Arab official in Batavia, a Hindu from Singapore, and a Eurasian prisoner freed on condition he pose as an embittered escapee to Aceh, were all sent on to Aceh from Penang by Lavino in the guise of traders on board local pepper ships.[56] Only the first of these appears to have produced any information of value to the Dutch military. Lavino's regular reports based on his Penang sources, on the other hand, were the best resource the Dutch Army had in getting to know Acehnese strength and intentions prior to the Second Expedition. In August–September, for example, Lavino was able to send four detailed reports with accompanying charts: one of nine pages about the approaches to the Aceh fortress (*kraton*, as the Dutch called it in curious testimony to their Java-centred vision), another about the fortified Great Mosque, one of 13 pages on the geography of the Pidië region, and a fourth about the Simpang Ulim pepper-growing region where the best-equipped opponents of the Dutch were concentrated.[57] Although the Commander of the Second Expedition, General van Swieten, claimed in April 1874 that in capturing the *kraton* he had won, Lavino had already made clear the previous September that the Acehnese were laying careful plans to abandon this fortress when pressed and establishing fall-back bases in the XXII *mukims* area higher up the Aceh river.[58]

Lavino's intelligence work had become essential for the military operations in Aceh, and as the military occupation of the Aceh capital continued with no sign of peace being achieved, his position had to be regularized. In February Read suggested that he should be appointed the full-time Consul in Penang. The existing Consul, H.J.D. Padday, was on extended leave in Europe and showed little sign of returning, and his brother the Vice-Consul had just given notice of his retirement. In Read's view it would be impossible to find an English merchant in the settlement willing to act in Dutch interests, so general was the hostility there towards everything the Dutch were doing in Aceh.[59] Batavia supported this proposal, but the Foreign Minister in The Hague overruled it, "partly to avoid the possible chance of a change in the kindly disposition of the house of Padday". The absent Consul was left in place, another of his brothers, Percy, was appointed Vice-Consul, and Lavino was given the unusual position of "Agent of the Netherlands Indies Government for Acehnese Affairs" in Penang.[60] In practice Lavino had already come to perform all the business of the consulate in Penang except financial and commercial matters, operating out of a room in the Padday firm's offices. But Dutch policy was punctilious in forbidding him ever to act officially in the name of the Consul in his absence, especially in relations with British officials.[61]

In practice Percy Padday, even more than his older brothers, seemed to be a Penang merchant first, and to occupy himself as little as possible with the consulate. Lavino's busy competence made this unnecessary anyway for the most part, especially after April 1874 when an additional full-time clerk, T. de Lima, was seconded to the Penang consulate from colonial service in Batavia to help with the work.[62] Yet Percy Padday retained the power, and periodically outraged Dutch officials by the way he used it in the sensitive issue of implementation of the blockade of Aceh. Sometimes it was a question of his relaxed attitude to the shipping of "strategic" materials to Aceh; sometimes of insufficient respect to visiting Dutch military

W.H. Read and the Dutch Consulate

officials. After one such conflict in July 1874, it was agreed that Lavino had to initial all permits issued by Padday for vessels clearing to Aceh, and all consular despatches relating to Aceh.[63] After several changes among the Padday brothers which had not all pleased Read, a royal decree in 1877 named Read Consul-General for the Straits Settlements (rather than Singapore as before), so that he had authority over the Penang consulate and could ensure that the Paddays remained no more than ciphers between himself and Lavino. In 1879 Lavino himself finally became substantive Vice-Consul, and in February 1881 Consul.[64] The problematic services of the Paddays were finally dispensed with.

The intelligence service developed by the consulates during 1873 became eventually a permanent part of their work — presumably at least until many of its functions were assumed by the Indonesian consulate in 1950. In March 1874 Read pointed out on the eve of one of his departures that it would be necessary to retain the service "until peace is made with Acheh, as it will be necessary to watch the shipments of arms and ammunition, and at the same time the state of native feeling here". He further recommended that "an intelligent and faithful native" be sent to Singapore from Batavia to take control of the spy network, "as a European really trustworthy is difficult to be found here".[65] The extent of this "secret service" emerges from consular records only in the 1880s, when the monthly expenditures in Penang were recorded by Lavino. These have a rising trend, from an average 47 Straits dollars a month in 1882 to $185 a month in 1888–9.[66] By this time the Singapore expenses were probably greater, as it was the communications centre for the whole Indies, not only Aceh. Sufficient money was paid to keep a few Indonesians on permanent retainers in each city while handing out rewards of a few dollars for specific pieces of useful information. Those known to work for the Dutch consulates must have had further occasional sources of income in blackmailing their subjects. The great Dutch Islamicist Snouck Hurgronje complained in 1895 that these spies levied "gifts" even from perfectly innocent pilgrims and Arabs passing through Singapore, by threatening to denounce them at the consulate.[67]

In 1893 the Penang Vice-Consul, defending the regular information he provided on Aceh against complaints of occasional errors, described how the reports came from "spies in the service of the consulate, who are in daily contact with the Acehnese arriving here who bring the latest news from Aceh", as well as from Acehnese who visited the consulate independently and some Penang traders.[68] In Singapore the Consul-General described the extensive and constantly increasing roles of the "secret service" as follows in 1893:

> They consist mainly of lengthy conversations especially with native and Chinese informants and spies, about the movements and activities of Arabs, and people expelled from Netherlands India or otherwise indicated as dangerous; about the smuggling of war contraband and opium; while Singapore is the seat of various intrigues of which the Netherlands Indian authorities need to be informed.[69]

An 1888 appeal for more staff had added one further preoccupation to this list, in tracing the activities of Chinese secret societies, based in Singapore but active also in Netherlands possessions such as Bangka, Riau, East Sumatra and West Borneo.[70]

Occasionally allegations of particularly spectacular plots came to the attention of the consulate. One such was an apparent conspiracy involving two highly-placed Imams from Mecca, and two Turkish ex-army officers, whose letters and movements between Singapore and Palembang led to the arrest of 30 men in 1881, reported to be plotting the murder of all the Europeans in Palembang. Read was characteristically alarmed about all this, and attempted to point a finger of suspicion at two of his old enemies, (now Sultan) Abubakar of Johor and Muhammad Alsagoff of Singapore.[71] In 1883 some Germans employed in Malaya, Cramer, Schmitz, and Forker, tried to extort $50,000 from the Consul in Penang for information they claimed to have picked up at the Penang race-course. They hinted at a plot involving Europeans and Acehnese to obtain explosives from Bangkok and use them to blow up Dutch fortifications in Aceh. After a few months of excitement this was eventually dismissed as little more than a hoax.[72]

Ousting Read from the Consulate

Read's dramatic coup in revealing the activities of Panglima Tibang and Arifin and thereby providing the pretext for the invasion of Aceh gave him a unique status with officials in Batavia for many years thereafter. The great expansion and sensitivity of Dutch interests in the British colony from 1873 called for a full-time Dutch professional, but no one dared suggest replacing Read as long as the war enthusiasm was at a high pitch. He appeared to the Dutch to be a giant supporter of Dutch interests in a sea of British hostility and foreign scheming. Questioning his role seemed akin to questioning the war itself, which only began to happen among the higher reaches of colonial administration in the late 1870s.

It was the matter of visa fees for pilgrims to Mecca that forced the issue of a salaried Consul. As noted above, in 1875 the requirement that pilgrims obtain a Dutch visa in any port which had a Consul was waived. Read pointed out in March 1876 that without these fees he would not have sufficient income, and nothing was done to inform the pilgrims that the visa was no longer necessary. The press appears to have taken up this malpractice in 1880, and the Dutch Consul in Jidda forced The Hague to resolve the issue.[73] When the question of a salaried Consul was referred to Batavia, the Governor-General reiterated his satisfaction with the way the Consulate-General was run. Although he was an Englishman, Read had spared no pains to act in Dutch interests, especially during the Aceh war, and usually with good results. It was essential to have the right person in Singapore, since this was "the focus of the movements which arise in Sumatra — yes, in other parts of Netherlands India — where the attempts at resistance which we encounter are helped by word and deed". Governor-General 's-Jacob was therefore reluctant to see any change which might lose Read's services. Since the Consul-General had mentioned when on a visit to Holland in 1881 that he had no objection to being paid a salary rather than levying fees on *hajis*, the main objection to his retention was overcome. Batavia therefore sought to make Read a salaried Dutch Consul.[74]

The Ministries in The Hague were less sanguine about this approach. Already the Vice-Consul's position had been an issue,

274 An Indonesian Frontier

since Read's Dutch assistant, S.J. Maier, left that post in 1878. The position appeared to remain vacant thereafter, and the Dutch merchant Hooglandt tried again to have himself appointed Vice-Consul when on leave in Holland in 1879. Although the Ministries in The Hague appeared sympathetic, and may have begun to listen to Hooglandt's doubts about Read's loyalty to Dutch interests, the matter was again left to Read to decide. He of course refused to countenance working with a potential rival.[75] Later he attempted to nominate his nephew (and presumed successor in the firm), R. Barclay Read, as Vice-Consul.[76] This did nothing to discourage a growing impatience in the Foreign Ministry with Read's peculiar position.

Late in 1882 preparations were being made for Read to be appointed a salaried Consul, and Foreign Minister Rochussen made the necessary inquiries about the Consul's conflicting business interests. The reply from Loudon was that although A.L. Johnston was a very solid and respected firm, its commercial activities appeared to have shrunk considerably, to the point where the Netherlands consulate was its major activity. Nevertheless the firm was still the correspondent in Singapore for the Sarawak Government and the British North Borneo Company as well as a number of banks and other firms.[77] Although the Dutch had made their peace with Rajah Brooke in Sarawak, the North Borneo Company connection was too much for Rochussen. This company was at the time just beginning to make clear its claims to the northern corner of Borneo, and The Hague was highly suspicious of its activities, especially on the east coast where its claims overlapped those of the Dutch. Read should go, said Rochussen, and be replaced with a professional Dutch officer. When the Governor-General protested that Read's role in the company was not central, and that his services in Singapore were, Rochussen became more emphatic. No foreigner was fit to represent another country's interests, he argued, and if he claimed he was fit this proved he wasn't. Nevertheless the pro-Read voices carried the day, to the extent of doing nothing until Read departed Singapore on leave in March 1883.[78]

In July 1883 W.H. Read visited The Hague, where the Foreign Minister explained to him that his services would no longer be needed as a career Consul was being appointed. This appears to have come

W.H. Read and the Dutch Consulate

as a terrible blow to him, suggesting that the consulate-general had indeed become the only remaining outlet for the political instincts of a man now in his mid-60s. Back in London Read penned a bitter letter in French protesting that he had a right to more respect from the Dutch Government. Even if his resignation now was accompanied by further honours [which were notably not being considered], "elle n'en resterait pas moins une disgrace, car elle dénoterait de la manière la plus évidente, un manque de confiance qui porterait atteinte à mon honneur". He claimed that "given the nature of eastern races" the loss of face could be avoided if he returned to Singapore as Consul-General to regulate his affairs, and tendered his resignation before leaving, giving time to initiate his successor.[79]

Taken aback by this onslaught, and aware of the sympathy for Read in Batavia, the Minister relented. An "apprentice Consul" was placed in Singapore in the person of the colonial official J.A. de Vicq, but not until December 1884 did a royal decree give Read an honourable discharge at his own request, "with gratitude for the many and weighty services provided to the country by him". The same decree shifted Lavino from Penang to Singapore as Consul-General, moved J.A. Kruyt from Jidda to become Consul-General in Penang, and replaced him in Jidda with De Vicq.[80] At the same time an additional "apprentice Consul", H. van de Houven van Oordt, was detached from colonial service to work in the Straits Settlements. The other full-time official in the Straits was J.J.M. Fleury, a young Straits-born Frenchman who also spoke Dutch, English and Malay. Lavino had hired him in Penang as a Secretary of the Penang consulate from 1879, and brought him along when he moved to Singapore to fulfil a similar function there.[81]

These three consulates, in Singapore, Penang and Jidda, had become in effect a subservice of the Dutch consular corps responsible more to Batavia than to The Hague, and typically seconded from the colonial service. After nearly 30 years in the hands of an energetic and opinionated Englishman, the Singapore consulate assumed a more professional and discreet existence.

12

The Japanese Occupation and Rival Sumatran Elites[1]

THERE is a bewildering contrast between the superficial calm of the 1930s in Indonesia and the turbulence of the immediate post-war period. In addition to the enormous upsurge of anti-colonial militance, the years following the Japanese surrender were marked by an unprecedented degree of conflict amongst Indonesians, as society adjusted to the radically changed conditions of independence. In other countries occupied by Japan, notably Burma and Malaya, ethnic animosities were also unusually overt after the war. It seemed natural to ask, as Elsbree did in his pioneering essay of 1953:

> did the [Japanese] occupation, with its dissolution of existing ties, aggravate the fissures of the old order? ... Did the Japanese deliberately pursue a "divide and rule" tactic, and is their policy to be held responsible for the violent outbursts and the general increase in racial tension since the end of the war?[2]

Elsbree's own conclusion was emphatically negative. Both in intention and in fact, he argued, Japanese policy tended towards unity.[3] In the case of Indonesia, however, the majority of western scholars have continued to insist that Japanese policy was responsible for widening, or even creating, dangerous chasms between three rival elites: the secular nationalists; the Islamic leaders; and the *pamong-praja* (an aristocracy in transition to a bureacracy). Frequently this has

The extent to which this picture has found its way into the general
been explained as the consequence of deliberate Japanese divide-and-
rule tactics, maintaining counter-elites to balance what would otherwise
become a dangerously strong single Indonesian leadership.[4]

The extent to which this picture has found its way into the general
literature appears directly attributable to the work of two outstanding
scholars, A.J. Piekaar and Harry J. Benda. Piekaar, who had been
secretary to the last Dutch Resident of Aceh, wrote in 1949 the first
monograph on the Japanese occupation of Indonesia, one that remains
unrivalled in its detailed understanding of a particular region,
Aceh.[5] Since Aceh experienced a spectacular post-war crisis in which
the *ulèëbalangs* (the 102 "self-governing" hereditary rulers through
whom the Dutch had governed Aceh) were eliminated by a Muslim-
led coalition of forces,[6] it is not surprising that Piekaar emphasized
Japanese responsibility for bringing about this confrontation. Benda's
distinguished work on the Japanese occupation of Java has been still
more influential. Growing out of a thesis on Japanese Islamic policy,
Benda's central theme was the way in which the Japanese moulded
Indonesian Islam into a coherent political force and a long-run
competitor for power with the secular nationalists.[7] Like many scholars
writing in the 1950s, he also emphasized the foresight and planning
in Japanese wooing of Islam, and in the "determined policy of divide
and-rule" which he saw as motivating Japanese relations with the
three elites.[8]

The time now seems overdue to reverse this western academic
preoccupation, and return to a view closer to Elsbree's. Neither the
growing body of Japanese documents — many of them made available
in English through the labours of Benda himself[9] — nor the recollection
of prominent Japanese and Indonesians suggests that the Japanese
ever felt themselves seriously threatened by any one of the alternative
elites. The preservation of superficial tranquillity in society was a
matter of much lower priority for the Japanese than it had been for
the Dutch. The basic Japanese administrative principle was certainly
to retain the essentials of Dutch Government, including the
pamong-praja.[10] Their departure from Dutch practice in also
cultivating Muslims and nationalists was motivated not by a need
for balance but by the greater utility of the two latter groups in

mobilizing the population — whether for labour service, military recruits, and anti-Allied displays, or the eventual formation of a nominally independent government. The truly remarkable innovation of the Japanese administration was its incorporation of all available sources of leadership into various administrative, advisory, and propaganda bodies, where they had — to some extent — to work together.

If we look at the effects of these policies on Indonesian society, the trend towards unity is still more striking. Social relations between the three distinct groups had been non-existent, or at best strained, under the Dutch. As the Japanese regime progressed, they were not only obliged to make working arrangements in *Syu Sangi Kai* (residency councils), *Jawa Hokokai*, and similar bodies; they found themselves sharing a very similar predicament. All three elites became privileged in terms of the access to travel, information, and scarce resources that membership in these bodies conferred. They paid the same price in having to mediate between the heavy demands of the occupying power and the increasing misery of the population. The Japanese defeat provided another source of solidarity in the need to explain the meaning of "collaboration" to the Allies. Recent work on the revolution that followed the Japanese surrender has suggested that it was the new found solidarity of established Indonesian leaders, rather than the fissures between them, that requires explanation.[11] The most striking cleavage underlying the first year of revolution was that which divided the whole elite — in a sense embracing nationalists, Muslims, and *pamong-praja* — from the majority of the population. Popular anger at the sufferings of the wartime period found its spokesmen less among the religious or political "counter-elites" than among the *pemuda* (youth) too young to have had responsibilities under the Japanese, and to a lesser extent the handful of older leaders who had chosen non-cooperation with Japan. Although ideological and personal rivalries were not absent from the disturbances characterized as the *daulat* time or the "social revolution" of 1945–6, this unprecedented resentment against the whole group of *pemimpin* (leaders) under the Japanese[12] is a more satisfactory explanation for the phenomenon. Except when they were toppled by specific *pemuda/*

populist action, local and national leaders in authority at the Japanese surrender were generally able to retain the support of the older elite through the early revolution.[13]

It is beyond the scope of this chapter to make a detailed case for the unifying effect of Japanese policies in Java, particularly as some work leading in this direction has already been published.[14] Instead I intend to examine the situation in northern Sumatra, where the evidence against such a conclusion might appear — on the surface — very much stronger. Both in Aceh and East Sumatra, the self-governing rulers (the equivalent of the *pamong-praja* in Java) were totally eliminated from power within seven months of the Japanese surrender, in a violent "social revolution". Although *pemuda*/populist resentment certainly had a major role here as in Java, there is no denying the leadership provided by the pre-war critics of the rulers — the Islamic leadership of PUSA in Aceh, and the left-wing nationalists in East Sumatra. Practically nothing has been written about the background to these events except Piekaar's outstanding detailed study of Aceh. It is therefore not surprising that his conclusion about the Japanese effect on elite rivalry in Aceh should have gone unchallenged:

> That ... the violent resolution of the conflict between ulèëbalangs and ulamas after Japan's capitulation must be primarily ascribed to Japan's policy of divide and rule, is in our opinion not subject to doubt. The Japanese policy of balance caused the tension between both groups, which still bore a latent character under our rule, to increase so that an explosion soon appeared inevitable with the removal of a "neutral" (i.e. non-Acehnese) regime.[15]

The crucial weakness of this conclusion is its failure to take account of the explosions that occurred in both Aceh and East Sumatra in 1942, for which one-sided Dutch policies, rather than balanced Japanese ones, would appear to be responsible. Although in 1942 the "neutral" regime was merely changed, not removed, the intensity of the conflict gives no reason to suppose that Aceh or East Sumatra were better prepared for independence than in 1945. In 1942 there were already strident demands for a total reordering of the internal power balance in northern Sumatra. The conflicts of the wartime period are in fact better explained in this region by the attempts of rival Indonesian elites to manipulate the Japanese, than by Japanese manipulation of the Indonesians.

The importance of the 1942 upheavals in northern Sumatra has generally been ignored, despite the existence of significant Japanese and Indonesian accounts of them. The remainder of this paper therefore comprises an attempt to unravel the dynamics of that first round in the fight for control of northern Sumatra.

Contacting the Japanese

Northern Sumatra's proximity to Malaya and the Indian Ocean had left it open, throughout history, to "foreign" influences not filtered through the political and cultural centres of Java. Ever since its foundation in 1786, the British port of Penang was a principal focus of trade and communication for the whole region. On 19 December 1941, Penang fell to the Japanese. Almost three months elapsed before Japanese troops crossed the Malacca Straits to Sumatra. During the interval, Japanese propaganda was broadcast daily on Penang radio, usually by Sumatrans residing in the city;[16] and the opportunity existed to make contact.

The spontaneous way in which a number of Acehnese separately seized this opportunity also owes something to the "Japanese illusions" (as the Dutch wishfully called them) traditionally entertained in Aceh.[17] Throughout the long Acehnese war against Holland, resistance was encouraged by rumours of support from Turkey, France, the United States, or Britain — generally fed by the sympathy of agents of these countries in Penang and Singapore.[18] After the Acehnese Sultan had finally submitted in 1903, he was still sufficiently inspired by the Japanese victory over Russia two years later to attempt to contact the Japanese Consul in Singapore. A renewed Acehnese uprising in 1907 was evidently prompted by hopes from that quarter. In the 1930s the westernized Marxists and nationalists who led most Indonesian parties in Java rejected flirtation with the Japanese in the interests of a "common front against fascism"; but such notions in no way inhibited the leading groups in northern Sumatra.

The opportunity to contact the Japanese was there in early 1942, but who would take it? Which elements within the society of northern Sumatra would seek to ensure an advance position of favour in Japanese eyes? It is here that the question of rival elites becomes important. Social integration into the colonial order had proceeded much less far in these regions than in Java. Despite a superficial calm, the bitterness created by Dutch conquest in the Aceh war (1873–1903) and the (Karo) Batak war (1872) was still remembered. In both Aceh and East Sumatra there were strong popular forces whose opposition to the aristocratic Dutch-supported establishment was more fundamental and absolute than the rivalries of elite urban politicians in Java. In both regions, in the closing years of Dutch rule, modern organizations had arisen to focus and lead this opposition. It was the simple fact of a change of colonial masters, rather than any particular Japanese policies, that ensured that these tensions would come dangerously into the open in 1942.

The first popular mass movement of a modern type able to arise in Aceh in the wake of the military occupation was PUSA (Persatuan Ulama2 Seluruh Aceh = all-Aceh union of Islamic teachers), which in 1939 brought together the majority of active *ulama* in Aceh in a programme of developing more modern religious schools and strengthening Acehnese Islam in general. The formation of PUSA, however, came at a time when the role of the *ulèëbalangs* was being loudly called into question. In 1938–9, a movement to create a degree of administrative and symbolic unity in Aceh through the restoration of the Sultanate drew a remarkably concerted counter-attack from *ulèëbalangs*. *Ulèëbalang* defensiveness was accentuated by a simultaneous press campaign criticizing the arbitrariness of *ulèëbalang* rule and demanding the dilution of their power by local councils, the abolition of forced labour (*herendienst*), and the removal of judicial authority from *ulèëbalang* hands. Although the *ulama* leaders of PUSA carefully limited their public concern to religion and education, by 1940 the movement had created a powerful source of leadership over which the *ulèëbalangs* had no control. Its youth movement in particular became the focus of all sorts of expectations of change.[19]

282 An Indonesian Frontier

No such organizational unity existed in East Sumatra, where all the "national" political parties competed within a particularly complex web of ethnic and social tensions. Since the suppression of the Communist party in 1926, however, the continuity of the left wing of nationalism had been well-established — from Sukarno's PNI (1927) to PARTINDO (1930) to GERINDO (1937). In its militant opposition to colonialism, to the western plantations in East Sumatra, and to the Malay and Simelungun rajas who grew rich through their land concessions in these plantations, this element was persistently more radical than the leaders of these parties in Java. The moderate "common front against fascism" by which GERINDO's national executive justified its participation in official bodies was little appreciated in the militant East Sumatra branch. It was therefore the GERINDO leader in East Sumatra, Jacub Siregar, who became the focus of the movement there to contact the Japanese. Although its multi-ethnic "national" character for the most part limited GERINDO to educated town-dwellers, the party had just begun to exploit a fundamental raw nerve in the three years before the Japanese conquest. This was the tension between Karo farmers in the upland *dusun* district of the Deli Sultanate and the Dutch-backed Malay hierarchy of that state. The origins of this tension might be traced to 19th-century Dutch acceptance of the Malay picture of the land question, at the expense of the Karo; but in the 1930s it was focused by new disputes over land. Relatively recent Karo immigrants began to be discriminated against in the annual allocation of estate land for peasant crops, while all were threatened by new proposals to change the whole basis of that allocation. In 1938, Karo farmers of the Deli *dusun* formed their own peasant union, SETIA (Sarikat Tani Indonesia), with guidance from the GERINDO leaders.[20]

On the Japanese side, the organization of fifth-column work in Sumatra, as well as in Malaya and India, was in the hands of the Fujiwara-*kikan,* or *F-kikan* (F-organization). Its leader, Maj. Fujiwara Iwaichi, was a young officer with remarkably little preparation for his enormous task, and virtually no knowledge of the Malaya-Indonesian region. Nevertheless, the genuine warmth with which he responded

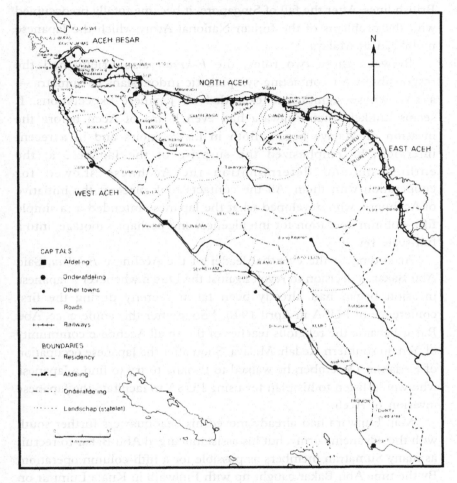

Map 5 Aceh's *ulèëbalang*-ships in the 1930s

to the pro-Japanese nationalists he came to work with in the region, and his rapid conversion to their view that Japan had a special destiny to liberate the southern countries, have led some Japanese to compare him with Lawrence of Arabia. His *F-kikan* had been hastily put together in Tokyo in September 1944 with five recent graduates from the Nakano-gakkō (military intelligence school) and some language specialists. The small group accompanied the Japanese invasion of Malaya in December 1941, making use of the Malay nationalist youth group, *Kesatuan Melayu Muda,* for sabotage and intelligence behind British lines. After the fall of Singapore, it became totally preoccupied with the problems of the Indian National Army which the Japanese mobilized in Malaya.[21]

Between these two roles, the *F-kikan* also briefly had the responsibility for contacting sympathetic Indonesians in Sumatra — a task whose significance exceeded all Japanese expectations. It seems unlikely that Fujiwara had even heard of Aceh before the invasion of Malaya began. Both in his memoirs and in a recent interview, he emphasized the surprise of the Japanese at the enthusiasm and determination the Acehnese showed for cooperation with them. All the contacts took place at the initiative of Acehnese, who developed what the Japanese intended as a simple fifth-column operation for intelligence, and perhaps sabotage, into a full-scale revolt.[22]

According to the eventual leader of the Acehnese *F-kikan,* Said Abu Bakar, a decision to revolt against the Dutch whenever a Japanese invasion began had already been taken secretly during the first conference of PUSA in April 1940.[23] Soon after this conference, Abu Bakar became the religious teacher of the small Acehnese community of Yen, in southern Kedah, Malaya. Soon after the Japanese occupation of Kedah in December, he walked to Penang to try to find a Japanese who would listen to his plan for using PUSA to facilitate the Japanese invasion of Aceh.

Maj. Fujiwara had already moved his headquarters further south with the advancing army, but his assistants urged Abu Bakar to recruit as many Sumatran members as possible for a fifth-column operation. By the time Abu Bakar caught up with Fujiwara in Kuala Lumpur on 14 January, there were five Acehnese in the party, plus a similar number from West Sumatra and a few from Inderagiri who appear to have contacted the *F-kikan* separately. An "Indonesia House" was commandeered for them in Kuala Lumpur's plush Kenny Hill. At least the younger members of the group, to judge from the memoirs of one of them, appear to have thought it all rather a lark, until some signs of Japanese military brutality made them wonder if they were heroic liberators or simply Japanese prisoners.[24]

Was there, as Piekaar suspected,[25] some Japanese promise to the PUSA in return for its support? All the evidence suggests there was no need of such a compact. Fujiwara's memoirs record Said Abu Bakar's explanation of the domestic Aceh situation in their 14 January meeting as if it were all new to him:

> the people of Aceh felt extremely resentful towards the Dutch and the *ulèëbalangs*. The *ulèëbalangs* are the confidants of the Dutch, and oppress the people, so that almost all the people distrust and even hate the *ulèëbalangs*. The people of Aceh are very committed Muslims, to the point that in the name of Islam they will endure warfare and even death. Acehnese organizations are all based on Islam. The largest is PUSA.[26]

The two men agreed that Abu Bakar's men should attempt to contact PUSA to ensure its close cooperation with the Japanese. The people so contacted would be identified by the "F" armband of the Fujiwara-*kikan;* their task would be to propagate goodwill for the Japanese, to protect bridges and vital installations from Dutch scorched-earth measures, and to provide the invading army with supplies and assistance.

There apparently was no suggestion of an Acehnese revolt against the Dutch. Fujiwara was struck at how the Acehnese — in complete contrast with the Indians, who were his major headache — made no significant demands of the Japanese in return for their services. Certainly there was no discussion of independence either for Aceh or for Indonesia as a whole, since this was explicitly forbidden by Tokyo. In his memoirs, Fujiwara admits only to an undertaking that the Japanese "would respect the happiness and the religion of the Acehnese people".[27] He knew too little about the PUSA-*ulèëbalang* rivalry to comment on it, but he did apparently add that the Japanese would not "levy taxes exorbitantly like the Dutch".[28] A letter (which fell into Dutch hands a few days before the Japanese landings) from Acehnese supporters of the *F-kikan* called for revolt in more expansive terms: "Freedom from taxation and *herendiensten* [obligatory labour for the feudal lord] had already been promised by the Japanese."[29] Since *herendienst* and other taxes were imposed through the *ulèëbalangs* it

286 An Indonesian Frontier

seems probable that the bland and vague assurances of Fujiwara were quickly translated by PUSA activists into the language of their own demand for change.

Revolt in Aceh

Impatient to begin his mission, Said Abu Bakar sailed for the Sumatran coast within a few days, in a small motorboat flying British colours. During the second half of January, three or four such boatloads of *F-kikan* activists appear to have been sent from the Selangor coast, with about six men in each — mainly Acehnese, but also a few Minangkabaus, Bataks, and others. All appear to have been picked up by the Dutch authorities and imprisoned in Medan. They adhered so convincingly to their story of being "refugees" from the fighting in Malaya that most of them were released during February and sent to their homes. The most important of them, Said Abu Bakar, was released in Aceh on 13 February, having already contacted PUSA colleagues from prison and invoked guarantees of his reliability from some of the most prominent Acehnese in government service.[30]

Abu Bakar immediately went to Seulimeum, about 25 miles upriver from Kutaraja (Banda Aceh), where he had formerly been associated with a famous "modern" Muslim school, *Perguruan Islam,* headed by Teungku Abdul Wahab. So enthusiastically was his project received that a full-scale revolt began in Seulimeum on 19 February, with a growing wave of sabotage to telephone, telegraph, and railway lines. The culmination was reached on the night of 23 February, after an intense Muslim rally at the religious school. The local Dutch official (*controleur*), Tiggelman, was killed; 5,000 guilders were seized from the post office; and the following day the local director of the Aceh railway, Graaf von Sperling, was killed while inspecting obstructions to the line nearby at Keumiroë.[31]

The inspiration and leadership for this Seulimeum revolt was in the hands of Teungku Abdul Wahab and other leading *ulama* of Seulimeum, most of whom were associated with PUSA. However, it was able to succeed so well, long before widespread resistance in Aceh, because the principal *ulèëbalang* of the region, the youthful

The Japanese Occupation and Rival Sumatran Elites 287

Panglima Polim Muhammad Ali,[32] participated fully in it. He and several other *ulèëbalangs* of Seulimeum went underground on the night of the attacks. Piekaar is probably correct[33] in suggesting that this was the reason the revolt began here, whereas Pidië — the stronghold of PUSA and centre of *ulèëbalang-PUSA* tension — remained quiet until the eve of the Japanese invasion. The PUSA leaders were not strong enough to take on the *ulèëbalangs* as well as the Dutch.

When Dutch reinforcements reestablished a tenuous control over Seulimeum and no Japanese troops appeared, there was a curious lull in acts of sabotage. The *ulèëbalangs* in other parts of Aceh, however, were increasingly aware of the danger of being caught between their Dutch allies and the rising popular rebellion, before the Japanese could halt the process. Teuku Muda Beuni, eldest son of the ruler of Blang Glumpang (Lho'Sukon, northeast Aceh), sent his brother Teuku Alibasjah off to Penang in a small boat on 13 February.[34] Other *ulèëbalangs* appear to have sent emissaries at about the same time,[35] to ensure that PUSA and other anti-*ulèëbalang* forces did not have a monopoly of Japanese favour. Teuku Alibasjah's mission was particularly successful, as he accompanied the invading Japanese forces in Aceh Besar (the Kutaraja region) and ensured that at least in that area it was the *ulèëbalangs* whom they contacted. However, still more boats arrived in Penang from local PUSA leaders in various parts of Aceh, urging the Japanese to hasten the invasion lest Aceh erupt into general violence. These emissaries, most of whom reached Penang about the beginning of March, brought the first intimation to the Japanese that the *F-kikan* had far exceeded its modest aims.[36]

On 7 March, a systematic movement of sabotage and rebellion began throughout Aceh Besar and the northern parts of Aceh's west coast. The most concerted attack came against the district headquarters of Calang, on the west coast, on the night of 9 March. This was directed by one of the most forceful Achenese *ulèëbalangs*, Teuku Sabi, who had aligned himself with PUSA and against most of his *ulèëbalang* colleagues in 1938/9 by coming out strongly for a restoration of the Sultanate. In Aceh Besar also it was the support or neutrality of the *ulèëbalangs* of the region that allowed the rebellion to assume such irresistible coordination and popularity. The leading *ulèëbalang* of

288 An Indonesian Frontier

Seulimeum had been "underground" since 24 February. On 8 March the same course was taken by the principal adviser to the Dutch provincial government, Teuku Njak Arif, after his offer to take complete responsibility for the administration was rejected. The Dutch quickly found their position in these regions untenable, and began to evacuate to the east on 10 March.

In most other parts of Aceh, where the *ulèëbalang* administration continued to support the *status quo* until the end, there was little overt violence until the withdrawal of troops. In Sigli, the Dutch Assistant-Resident was killed and the town plundered as soon as the troops left on 12 March. Along the west coast, the southward retreat of Dutch forces had to face constant attacks and obstruction, stimulated in part by the atrocities the demoralized soldiers themselves had committed in Lam No, Calang, and Tapa'Tuan.[37]

The question of who deserved the credit for inspiring this revolt, already raised by the different missions to Malaya from Aceh, became an open one as soon as the new regime was established. Teuku Njak Arif and his colleagues on the one hand, and the PUSA colleagues of Said Abu Bakar on the other, each claimed sole responsibility for the movement.[38] The PUSA claim is somewhat more convincing. Some sources even suggest that a specific plan of revolt was drawn up by the PUSA executive, though the dates given for this decision vary from December 1941 to 6 March 1942.[39] In view of the apparent non-participation of the PUSA leader, Teungku Daud Beureu'eh,[40] however, it is easier to envisage a pattern of separate initiatives by locally influential *ulama*, most of whom were associated with PUSA or its youth wing. If there was any central direction for the movement, it lay with Said Abu Bakar and a few prominent *ulama* in Seulimeum, not with the PUSA executive in Sigli.

The rebellion placed *ulèëbalangs* in a very difficult position. A few, already mentioned, were quick to support it; a few opposed it so whole-heartedly as to arrest activists and hand them over to the Dutch; most attempted to move with the wind. Outside Aceh Besar, where T. Njak Arif immediately became the leading adviser to the Japanese, PUSA *F-kikan* activists nevertheless had a clear initial advantage with the Japanese. The temporary administrative committees that the

The Japanese Occupation and Rival Sumatran Elites   289

Japanese military established as they occupied a region were dominated
by PUSA activists. This initial period of a month or two was painful
for *ulèëbalangs*. "PUSA youths, encouraged by the *ulama,* refused to
recognize the authority of the *ulèëbalangs*. Marriages were sealed without
reference to the official marriage registrars; land transactions took
place illegally. The *mukim* [subdivision] and village heads were also
pushed aside."[41] Two prominent rulers in the Meulaboh region (west
coast) were executed by the Japanese, because they had arrested
propagandists from the rebellious centre of Seulimeum — one of
whom was shot by the Dutch.[42]

Within a few months these PUSA-dominated committees were
dissolved and *ulèëbalangs* were restored to administrative power
throughout Aceh.[43] It is probable that this would have been the basic
Japanese policy under any conceivable circumstances. The *ulèëbalang*
apparatus worked efficiently, and its retention conformed to the
fundamental guidelines of the occupation to disturb Dutch methods
as little as possible. The Japanese may also have perceived that the
*ulèëbalang*s posed fewer potential problems for them than did a
popular Islamic organization. The change of regime, however, had
made the contest for power an open one. PUSA leaders naturally
believed that the machinations of influential *ulèëbalang*s had brought
about their downfall, particularly when the most prominent PUSA
leaders were imprisoned almost immediately thereafter.[44] The stakes
in this contest were already seen to be extremely high in 1942. If
one party gained exclusive access to the Japanese ear, the prospects
of the other appeared bleak.

Aron Disturbances in East Sumatra, 1942

East Sumatra did not revolt on the eve of the Japanese occupation,
nor respond with the enthusiasm of Aceh to the activity of the *F-kikan*.
Yet the basic pattern of overt confrontation between rival political
leaderships was the same. The confrontation was, moreover,
accompanied by considerably more violence than has been realized.

Two nationalist groups, somewhat mutually antagonistic, attempted
to greet the Japanese on their arrival in Medan on 13 March 1942.

The PARINDRA and *Taman Siswa* leader Sugondo formed a *Comité Indonesia* from among moderate nationalist parties, evidently in an attempt to present unified demands for concessions towards independence. However, a procession the committee organized was fired on by the police, resulting in several casualties; and the committee disbanded soon thereafter.[45] Of greater significance was Jacub Siregar's GERINDO group, which became the nucleus for the disorganized *F-kikan* activity in East Sumatra. Although GERINDO members — in concert with the few Bataks and other East Sumatrans sent by the *F-kikan* in Malaya — were able to render real service to the Japanese as informants and guides, a great deal of plunder also occurred in the name of the *F-kikan*, particularly in Pematang Siantar.[46] Masubuchi Sahei, delegated by Fujiwara to lead the *F-kikan* in Sumatra, held one meeting in late March at which plans were laid for the continued propaganda role of the *F-kikan* under Jacub Siregar. But Masubuchi quickly transferred to Aceh, where he had more pressing tasks; and it became clear that the settled Japanese administration had little use for the radical politicians of GERINDO, save as police informers.[47]

Aroused expectations were not easily laid to rest, however, particularly among the Karo farmers. When Japanese troops entered Pengkalan Brandan, they were met by a demonstration with slogans reading *hapuskan raja-raja* (abolish the rajas);[48] and there is no doubt that these sentiments were equally those of the GERINDO leadership. According to subsequent Japanese police reports,[49] the GERINDO-inspired SETIA movement among Karo farmers of the Deli Sultanate had assumed the character of a secret society shortly before the war. The land to which the Karos laid claim began to be occupied in defiance of the law by cultivation cooperatives of several men, known in Karo as *aron*. This *aron* movement assumed elaborate rituals to enforce loyalty, secrecy, and solidarity amongst the members, who were to come to one another's aid if the police attempted to eject them from the land. The movement spread rapidly during the uncertainty of the Japanese takeover. GERINDO leaders, now acting in the name of the *F-kikan*, allegedly told the Karos: "When the Japanese come, the native chiefs will be thrown out, and you can have whatever land you want."[50] One Japanese source estimated 2,000

The Japanese Occupation and Rival Sumatran Elites 291

members of the movement in 300 villages of the Pancur Batu district of Deli alone in early 1942;[51] another suggested 15,000 members altogether.[52]

Although this movement does not appear to have aroused serious Japanese concern until July 1942, it had begun to cause clashes between farmers and local authorities at least by the end of May. Violence may have begun to be reported only when village and local authorities felt sufficiently sure of the Japanese to attempt to re-impose the pre-war legal situation.

The first reported incident was in Karoland itself, rather than the ethnically mixed Deli and Langkat Sultanates. *Aron* members seized the opportunity of the Japanese conquest to occupy the unusually large irrigated land-holdings of unpopular *raja urung* (hereditary local chiefs) in Batu Karang and Tiga Nderket. When police were summoned to Batu Karang from nearby Kebandjahe on 1 June, a clash developed in which a policeman and three *aron* members were reported killed.[53]

The disturbances spread swiftly to the principal centre of pre-war tension over the land question: the Deli *dusun,* and in particular its Sunggal district. The *aron* movement came into conflict with the lower levels of the hierarchy of the Deli Sultanate by early June 1942. Village headmen (Indonesian: *penghulu*; Japanese *sonchō*) who attempted to restrain the militant Karos from taking over more plantation land were robbed or intimidated. Two were killed, on 3 and 14 June respectively.[54] The police of the Sultanate retaliated fiercely on 18 June, executing 14 members of the *aron* in the Pancur Batu region. This enraged the Karos, who surrounded the police post in their hundreds for a couple of days, until dispersed on the 20th.[55] Japanese records do not suggest that Japanese officials or police were involved at this stage; and the anger of the *aron* appeared to be directed towards the Datuk of Sunggal, his agents in Pancur Batu, and the village headmen who supported them.

Sporadic violence continued in the area into July, and the Sultanate police met increasing resistance in their attempts to suppress it. After failing in an attempt to investigate an incident near Arnhemia (the European planters' town near Pancur Batu) on 26 July, the police detained one Karo, evidently an *aron* leader, in the Arnhemia police station. Aron members quickly began to mobilize, and marched about 500 strong towards the police station.[56] It appears that the Sultanate police, perhaps encouraged by Tengku Arifin Tobo — the Indonesian head of the political intelligence section in Medan — deliberately lured the *aron* into a trap by creating the impression that the police were unarmed and unsuspecting in Arnhemia, while secretly reinforcing them.[57] That night the battle for the police station quickly became a massacre, with 21 of the attacking Karos killed and 57 wounded — according to the probably conservative Japanese report[58] — and four police wounded.

This battle, ended by the arrival of the *Kempeitai* after midnight, at last brought about direct Japanese involvement in the affair. The Sultanate establishment was now able to portray the *aron* as a subversive attack on the Japanese order, and many *aron* leaders appear to have been rounded up and executed by the *Kempeitai*. Concluding that the *aron* was "the cancer of north Sumatra",[59] the *chōkan* (governor) ordered its thorough investigation and destruction by his police-chief, Captain Inoue Tetsurō. Inoue's principal Indonesian assistant at this point was Tengku Arifin Tobo — formerly the senior Indonesian in the Dutch political intelligence service in Medan, as well as a member of the royal house of Serdang. This was Arifin's chance to pin responsibility for the movement on the militantly anti-Sultanate politicians of GERINDO, who had appeared particularly threatening to the Malay elite when mobilized in the *F-kikan*.[60] Jacub Siregar and eight other former GERINDO and *F-kikan* leaders were arrested and tortured. After imprisoning them for some months, the Japanese decided not to execute these leaders, but rather to use them — first in political intelligence and later in training nationalist guerrilla groups. The bitterness between this former GERINDO group and the Sultanate had by now become open, however, with results that were to prove traumatic during the "social revolution" of 1946.

The *aron* movement took some time to die in the Karo areas of Deli and Langkat, despite Japanese attempts to crush it by combining force with concessions on the land issue. On 7 September and 3 October there were further cases of village headmen being murdered by members or sympathizers of the *aron*.[61] Inoue reacted

The Japanese Occupation and Rival Sumatran Elites   293

to one of these incidents, at Ujong Labuhan, by publicly beheading five leaders of the village movement.[62] The last reported incident was at Bulilir, in upper Langkat, on 15 October 1942. The attempts of the Sultanate to curb illegal cultivation of forest land led to a riot in which six villagers were killed and four seriously wounded by police fire. That night a group of villagers broke into the house of the *penghulu*, whom they held responsible, killing him, his wife, and a servant. The gradual return of order, however, was indicated by the Japanese decision to try the seven Karos responsible for the night attack in the decorum of the Medan high court.[63] Nothing further was heard of the *aron* movement, but it was no coincidence that the Sunggal area of Deli, where the *aron* violence had been concentrated, again became the centre of tension from the time of the Japanese surrender in August 1945 until the "social revolution" swept away the Sultans, Datuks, and many of the village headmen seven months later.

Conclusion

Aceh and East Sumatra were two regions where Dutch rule had created an exceptionally strained polarization between the Indonesian rulers and radical "counter-elites". The violent explosion of 1942 was caused not by any Japanese policy, but by the attempt of the rival Indonesian parties to use the change of regime to advance their respective visions and claims to lead. The conflict thereby became both open and violent, greatly embittering future relations between the rival leaderships. Japanese policy was to use both for different purposes, but gradually to associate them in various bodies and organizations, particularly in the last year of the war. However, this process had not gone far enough by 1945 to avoid a renewal of conflict after the collapse of Japanese power.

13

Indonesianizing Sumatra: The Birth of the Republic

THE establishment of an Indonesian Republican government in Sumatra, between August and October 1945, was a decisive moment in the history of the island. For half a century, a colonial government had built common institutions and infrastructure linking the whole island to Batavia/Jakarta, and then in 1942–5 the Japanese had largely broken those links. When the Japanese surrendered there was a period of suspended authority, a perfect revolutionary opportunity. Those who most effectively seized it were a new generation enthusiastic about the idea of Indonesian unity and independence. With very little impetus from Java, a spontaneous series of revolutions erupted throughout Sumatra, echoing the process in Java but quite distinct from it. The central Republican government had virtually no direct means of control over Sumatra until April 1946, when a delegation under the Defense Minister Amir Sjarifuddin toured the island. The teams of *pemuda* (youth) propagandists sent from Jakarta by Sjarifuddin in September formed an earlier direct link, but they do not appear to have reached West Sumatra until the end of October[1] and North Sumatra until November. The desire on the part of the *pemuda* in Sumatra to imitate what little they knew of the Javanese example was a compelling one, but it was spontaneous and uncontrolled.

The autonomous nature of the early months of revolution in Sumatra makes it necessary to give the matter separate attention. The excellent work on the early revolution in Java by Kahin, Smail,

Indonesianizing Sumatra

Anderson and Frederick[2] has well documented the scenario there, but coverage of Sumatra remains very spotty.[3] The political balance among the actors was quite different in Sumatra. Most notably, the official Republican leadership was very much weaker in relation first to the Allies and later to the *pemuda* activists.

Japanese Policies

A major effect of the Japanese occupation of Sumatra was to decapitate all organizational activity there. On the one hand, the connection with Java was totally severed to insulate Sumatra, as far as possible, from the relatively advanced political climate of Java. On the other hand, as we will consider at the end of this section, organizational contact even within Sumatra above the residency level was made very difficult until the last six months of the occupation.

Early in the occupation a clear distinction was observable between Japanese planning for Java, and for the rest of Indonesia. Java, which was under the 16th Army, was considered capable of making political progress. The relatively sparsely-populated islands of Borneo, Celebes, and the Lesser Sundas, administered by the Japanese Navy, were to be "retained in future for the benefit of the Empire".[4] Malaya and Sumatra, united under the 25th Army, were described as "the nuclear zone of the Empire's plans for the Southern Area",[5] because of their strategic importance as well as their economic value as sources of oil, rubber, and tin. According to a Japanese policy statement of April 1942, Malaya and Sumatra were ultimately to revert to Japan,[6] and as late as December 1942 a high Japanese official saluted the inhabitants of Penang as "the new Japanese people".[7] Thus the Japanese permitted no talk of independence in Sumatra, nor any other political activity except propaganda for immediate Japanese purposes. All Indonesian political organizations there were suppressed within a few weeks of the Japanese occupation.

Only after April 1943, when Sumatra was separated from Malaya administratively, was there some reconsideration of this policy in light of the worsening war situation. But the 25th Army, which now administered Sumatra alone, fought against any concessions in the direction of independence there and took the limited steps it did only reluctantly, under pressure from Tokyo or their more hard-pressed colleagues in Java. As Gen. Shimura, who guided the Sumatra administration from January 1944, said:

> Little effort was made in this direction [independence] in Sumatra, prior to May 1945, as the demand for independence was not nearly so strong as in Java. The opinion of the Japanese Army officials in Sumatra was that the people of that country were not sufficiently developed, socially and culturally, to take on themselves the responsibilities of selfgovernment. They therefore approached the task in a "half-hearted manner".[8]

The commander in Sumatra, Gen. Tanabe, insofar as he deigned to notice Indonesian politics at all, endorsed Shimura's picture.

> Before the Japanese capitulation there was really little question of an Indonesian Independence movement, and very certainly not of help from the side of the Japanese military Government.... What this independence should consist of was not clear to me, probably something different to Manchukuo since the institution of a Volksraad is not known there. I must remark here that I have never been interested in politics, and thus I know little about it.[9]

At the first Imperial Conference on the question of Indonesia's future in May 1943, the 25th Army opposed any meaningful concessions, while the 16th Army in Java pressed for a commitment to independence. The compromise agreed upon was that no part of Indonesia would be permitted independence, but political participation could be granted to Java at once and other areas in accordance with their readiness.[10] In Java this led to the rapid establishment of advisory councils in each residency, surmounted by the Central Advisory Council for all Java headed by Sukarno. Java-wide movements had already been founded or sanctioned early in 1943 as vehicles for the nationalist politicians (Putera, to be followed by Jawa Hōkōkai), and for the Muslims (MIAI, to be followed by Masjumi). Thus a Java-wide Indonesian leadership was to a considerable extent

Indonesianizing Sumatra 297

encouraged by the 16th Army, maintaining nationalists, Muslims and *pamong praja* (bureaucracy) in tenuous balance at the all-Java level.

In Sumatra the Japanese reluctantly agreed to the establishment of regional advisory councils (*Shu Sangi Kai*) in each of the ten residencies in November 1943. The councils met only twice a year to consider a politically innocuous list of questions submitted by the Japanese *chōkan* (resident). In those residencies which were considered potentially explosive, the Japanese were careful to balance the representation of *pergerakan* (popular movement, both political and religious) against that of the *pamong praja* and *kerajaan* (traditional rulers).[11] At about the same time propaganda organizations began to be set up in some residencies as a means of controlling the erstwhile politicians and Muslim reformers of the *pergerakan* and using them as a counterweight to the administrative authority of the *kerajaan*.[12] In Palembang, Lampung, West Sumatra, Tapanuli, and Aceh, these sectional organizations were dissolved into a broader Hōkōkai, or Badan Kebaktian Rakiat (People's Loyalty Organization) in early 1945. These later organizations were modelled on the Djawa Hōkōkai headed by Sukarno, with the same double purpose of diluting the *pergerakan* while providing a broader front against the approaching Allies.[13] They differed from the Javanese model, however, in that like all other Indonesian organizations in Sumatra they were strictly confined to the residency level.

The deteriorating Japanese military position during 1944 necessitated a revision of the May 1943 policy for Indonesia, with the result that Premier Koiso publicly promised on 7 September 1944 eventual independence of the East Indies. Although the territorial limits of the future state remained undecided because of objections by the Navy as well as the 25th Army, it was decided that Sumatra as well as Java would immediately be permitted to use the national Indonesian flag and anthem already popularized before the war.[14] Mainly for this reason, the Koiso statement did have considerable impact in Sumatra, in marked contrast to previous Japanese concessions.[15] But despite the extensive use of these "Indonesian" symbols for propaganda purposes, the 25th Army continued to insist that Sumatra follow a separate path from Java. At the same time it delayed as long as possible any transfer of responsibilities to Indonesians.

The initial 16th Army plan in January 1945 for a Body for the Investigation of Indonesian Independence (Badan Penjelidik Kemerdekaan Indonesia, or BPKI) was that it should comprise "influential residents of Java and Sumatra".[16] This would have provided the first opportunity for Sumatran leaders to consult with their more advanced colleagues in Java. However, no delegates from Sumatra were included when the BPKI composition was announced on 29 April, presumably because of opposition from the Sumatra command. In the same vein General Shimura repeatedly refused permission for Sukarno to visit Sumatra because he feared that "the independence movement might get out of hand and not follow the path prescribed for it by the Japanese authorities".[17] From early 1945, however, higher military authorities were convinced that Sumatra would have to be included in a credible Indonesian state. At a series of hasty meetings held in Tokyo and Singapore between April and July 1945 to clarify Japanese policy, the 25th Army's misgivings were repeatedly overruled, and it was instructed to make rapid preparations for Indonesian independence.[18] But Tokyo conceded that although the independence of the whole former East Indies would be declared at one time, "Those areas which have not completed preparations shall gradually be transferred to the jurisdiction of the new independent nation in accordance with the progress of independence preparations."[19]

At least as late as June 1945, Sumatran leaders appeared to be understandably unsure whether the old slogan, *Sumatera Baru* (New Sumatra), or the new one, *Indonesia Merdeka* (Free Indonesia), more accurately represented Japanese plans for them.[20]

Besides sealing Sumatra off altogether from Java, the Japanese also made regular contact between residencies within Sumatra extremely difficult. Until the last two months of the occupation, all Japanese-sponsored organizations were strictly confined to the residency level, and the few non-political prewar organizations like Mohammadiah and Taman Siswa found contact beyond this level virtually impossible. Moreover, wartime conditions made communication extremely difficult

Indonesianizing Sumatra

for Indonesians even on a personal or commercial basis. The only opportunities leaders of various regions had to compare notes during the Syōnan (Singapore) Islamic Conference in April 1943, the journeys of various delegations to Japan during 1943, and the elaborate ceremonies in Bukittinggi in October 1944 to "receive" the Koiso promise.[21] These gatherings contributed little to the emergence of a Sumatra-wide leadership because of the stifling political control maintained by the Japanese in Sumatra. For example, the Acehnese Teuku Muhamad Hasan from Glumpang Payong, appointed leader of the Sumatran delegation to Japan in the second half of 1943, was arrested and executed a few months after his return.[22]

This horizontal fragmentation notwithstanding, the differences between Japanese and Dutch divide-and-rule policies are more instructive than the parallels so stimulatingly drawn by Anderson.[23] The Dutch colonial system in practice was highly centralized and subjected the Indonesian elite to economic, educational, legal, and administrative pressures which were all centripetal. Dutch strategies were based on Indonesia-wide calculations, whereby the growing power of the nationally-oriented urban intelligentsia was to be balanced by the encouragement of local political loyalties and concerns. They found ready support for this strategy among Indonesians resentful of the pace of centralization and suspicious of the larger or more advanced ethnic groups with which it brought them into contact. Japanese administration, on the other hand, was essentially fragmented. There was scarcely any coordination between the army and the navy, and not a great deal even between the 16th and 25th Armies. Even within Sumatra communication difficulties and the stress on economic self-sufficiency in each residency made it necessary for each Japanese *chōkan* to find his own solutions. Regional division became an objective fact, and the significant Japanese policies were framed at the residency level. Rather than balancing regional loyalties against each other or Java, the Japanese exploited wherever necessary the divisions *within* the residency, typically between the *pergerakan* and the *kerajaan*. This policy had serious consequences in the violent post-surrender confrontation of these balanced forces in several residencies, notably Aceh and East Sumatra. But from the standpoint of Indonesian unity, the results of three years of Japanese rule were on balance positive. Almost every social and ethnic group in Sumatra was irked by the extreme isolation of the Japanese period. Only those with long memories were particularly conscious of ethnic and regional suspicions at the war's end. The enthusiasm of youth for unity above all was heightened by the fact they had never had the opportunity to enjoy it.

Preparation for Independence

The first concession towards allowing the development of political leadership above the residency level in Sumatra was the announcement on 24 March 1945 that a Sumatran Central Advisory Council (Chuō Sangi In) would at last be set up — almost two years after that of Java. Fifteen members were elected by the ten regional advisory councils, and on 17 May the Japanese command in Bukittinggi appointed an additional 25 members. As usual, a careful balance was preserved between representatives of opposing groups in the key residencies.[24] At the end of May the *Gunseikanbu* (military administration) in Bukittinggi announced its appointees. Mohammad Sjafei,[25] founder of the experimental school at Kaju Tanam, West Sumatra, was appointed chairman of the forthcoming Central Advisory Council, with T. Njak Arif[26] of Aceh and Mr. Abdul Abbas[27] of Lampung as vice-chairmen. A substantial permanent secretariat for the Council was established headed by the leading Sumatran journalist, Djamaluddin Adinegoro,[28] who moved from Medan to Bukittinggi and resigned his elected seat in the council. These four men were built up in the Japanese-controlled press during June and July as the *Empat Serangkai* of Sumatra, comparable with the Sukarno-Hatta-Ki Hadjar Dewantoro-K.H.Mas Mansur team in Java.[29]

The Japanese prepared an agenda of questions for the Central Advisory Council concerning means of strengthening the unity and resolve of Sumatrans in the Greater East Asia War.[30] But the questions were framed generally enough to permit the braver members to voice some of their demands for more educational opportunities, lower prices, and further progress towards independence. After

Indonesianizing Sumatra

meeting from 27 June to 2 July, the Council passed a series of resolutions calling for further institutions at the all-Sumatra level, notably: (1) a preparatory committee for independence; (2) a Sumatera Hōkōkai, linking the residency propaganda organizations; (3) a higher Islamic college; (4) a liaison office to link the residency People's Guidance Bureaus; (5) a national banking system; and (6) a strong "people's army" (*Lasjkar rakjat*) built on the foundation of the Japanese-trained *Giyūgun* (army volunteers) and Heihō (military auxiliaries). Dr. Gani called for a minimum strength of 500,000 men.[31] The newspaper reports of speeches and resolutions suggested a continuing uncertainty at the meeting between Sumatera Baru and Indonesia Merdeka. On the other hand Hamka holds in retrospect: "There the spirit of unity was firm. There the spirit of wanting to divide Sumatra from a united Indonesia was clearly opposed."[32]

The Japanese appear to have indicated their readiness to implement all the resolutions of the Council.[33] They did announce the formation of a separate Sumatran Committee to Investigate the Preparation of Independence (Panitia Penjelidik Persiapan Kemerdekaan) with a heavy weighting of intellectuals calculated to bridge the gulf between *pergerakan* and *kerajaan*.[34] They also made a cautious start towards establishing a unified Islamic movement by extending the West Sumatran Madjelis Islam Tinggi (Supreme Islamic Council) to other residencies,[35] and appointed Sjech Mohammad Djamil Djambek adviser on Islamic affairs for all Sumatra.[36] But all such cautious moves were rapidly overtaken by the rush of events in August.

The last-minute attempts to create a Sumatran leadership were significant. Sjafei and Adinegoro headed an embryo Sumatra bureaucracy with contacts throughout the island, and the press made their names familiar in every residency. On 25 July they were also appointed chairman and secretary respectively of the Committee to Investigate the Preparation of Independence, and on the following day they began a speech-making tour of Sumatra.[37] In the closing months of the occupation the Japanese seem also to have recognized Dr. A.K. Gani's position as the only national-level prewar politician in Sumatra,[38] although he had been arrested and tortured during the razzia of September 1943. Hamka points out that at the Central

Advisory Council it was the unofficial gatherings of leaders from different districts, which were most important in establishing a unified approach to the problem of independence. In such gatherings, "M. Sjafei was recognized quite apart from his recognition by the Japanese as the leader to be put forward."[39] Hamka also considered Dr. A.K. Gani, T. Njak Arif, and Dr. Ferdinand Lumbantobing to have achieved positions of acknowledged leadership as a result of their strongly nationalist stand.

Inexplicably, the Japanese abandoned the leaders they had been developing when they appointed Sumatra's delegates to the Panitia Persiapan Kemerdekaan Indonesia (Committee for the Preparation of Indonesian Independence [PPKI]) in early August. Mr. Abdul Abbas was one of the delegates, but the other two were Medan intellectuals who had not even been members of the Central Advisory Council — Dr. Mohammad Amir[40] and Mr. T.M. Hasan.[41] It seems possible that the Japanese planners in Singapore or Jakarta distrusted the leadership developed by the intransigent 25th Army as too distinctly Sumatran, or too much the creatures of the Gunseikan.[42] But on either count the most logical appointee would have been Dr. Gani. Whatever the reason, the consequences were more serious than anyone would have expected.

The three Sumatran delegates arrived in Jakarta on 14 August, in the same Japanese bomber as Sukarno and Hatta. They remained to witness the dramatic proclamation of independence following the Japanese surrender and to play their part in establishing a constitution and a government. Both Amir and Hasan expressed their fears of Javanese centralism in the PPKI debates, Amir pleading "that the maximum decentralization be allowed for the islands outside Java, that governments be set up there, and that the people there be given the right to manage their domestic affairs to the widest extent".[43]

On 19 August the PPKI debated the structure of provincial government, and decided that Sumatra would constitute one province under one governor, dismissing the arguments of several members that the size and diversity of Sumatra necessitated three separate provinces, as in Java, or at least three deputy-governors in Medan, Bukittinggi, and Palembang. As Sumatran representative on the subcommittee, which had met the previous night to settle these matters,

Indonesianizing Sumatra

303

Dr. Amir was able to secure the appointment of Mr. T.M. Hasan as governor and Medan as the capital. Hasan's prewar experience in the office of the Sumatran governor was the principal reason advanced for his selection, though the importance of Acehnese support for the Republic cannot have been overlooked.[44] The third and final session of the PPKI on 22 August established the Partij Nasional Indonesia (PNI) as the state party, Komité Nasional Indonesia (KNI) at various levels as representative councils, and the Badan Keamanan Rakjat (BKR) as the armed force of the Republic.[45] The following day the three Sumatran delegates flew to Palembang on one of the last Japanese flights permitted by the Allies, with instructions to implement these decisions in Sumatra in cooperation with Sjafei and Adinegoro. Dr. Gani was specifically instructed to organize the PNI and Mr. Abbas the KNI in Sumatra.[46] Hasan as governor would appoint Republican residents, who would attempt to take the initiative in government from the Japanese.

The Obstacles

The task of the three returning delegates was a formidable one. The preparation for independence by the Japanese had been minimal in comparison with Java, and what there was had been centred in Bukittinggi. Mr. Hasan in particular had no reputation outside Medan and Aceh, and in establishing his headquarters in Medan he had to make a fresh start altogether. The various residencies remained isolated from each other, and within many of them existing social divisions had been exacerbated to the point where no cohesive action was possible.

To take advantage of these relative weaknesses on the side of the Republic, the Dutch presence was established earlier and more energetically in Medan than elsewhere in Java or Sumatra. An Anglo-Dutch Country Section (ADCS) of Force 136 was formed in Colombo early in 1945 and parachuted three small commando units into North Sumatra at the end of June. Their task was to gather information and make contacts which might be useful in Mountbatten's projected invasion of Malaya on 9 September. A fourth unit, led by

Naval Lt. Brondgeest, and like the others overwhelmingly Dutch in composition, landed near Pangkalan Brandan on 25 August. At the end of August all of these units received instructions to leave their bivouacs and contact the local Japanese commands in Kutaradja (later Banda Aceh), Rantau Prapat, Bagan Siapiapi, and Medan, respectively, in order to ensure the welfare of Allied prisoners of war and internees.[47] By 1 September Brondgeest was established in Medan's leading hotel, whence he made contact not only with the Japanese, but with the Sultans of Langkat and Deli and other prominent Indonesians who, while demanding some reforms, promised to cooperate with the Dutch.

Brondgeest quickly formed the opinion that little could be expected from either the British or Japanese, but that by acting independently with the support of local Ambonese and Menadonese the Dutch officers could control Medan and check any large-scale Republican movement until Dutch troops could land. Through his Dutch superior in ADCS, Adm. Helfrich, he obtained permission "to organize a police force to take power into our own hands over as extensive as possible an area of East Sumatra".[48] On 14 September another Dutch commando, the tough and subsequently notorious Lt. Westerling, and three Dutch sergeants were parachuted into Medan with 180 revolvers to train and equip this police force. By early October Westerling appears to have commanded a tolerably well-armed and trained force of almost two hundred men, with some hundreds more ex-POWs anxious to join it if arms could be found. The force set a watch on strategic installations such as electricity and water supply, and conducted regular patrols of Medan and the route to Belawan with a couple of commandeered Japanese armoured cars.[49] The Dutch claimed, with considerable exaggeration, that they controlled the city until the arrival of the British.[50]

During the first month following the Japanese surrender Allied radio control and air supply was much better with Sumatra than with Java. From 21 August leaflets began to be dropped in various parts of Sumatra on behalf of NICA (Netherlands Indies Civil Administration).[51] Within a few weeks of the surrender a provisional NICA administration for Sumatra, under Allied military auspices, was formed under Dr. Beck and Resident Bruggemans, both brought

Indonesianizing Sumatra

from the Dutch camp at Rantau Prapat. On 3 October about 60 key men from the prewar administration were brought from the camp to Medan to begin in secret the reconstruction of a modified *ancien régime*.[52] In West Sumatra Resident Bosselaer went even further towards re-establishing a NICA administration and attempting to send official instructions to the *demang* (Indonesian district heads).[53]

The public announcement of the Japanese surrender on 22 August was generally taken to mean that the old masters would return, and internal adjustments would have to be made accordingly. Dutch detainees in their camps were inundated with gifts and visits from Indonesian well-wishers, both genuine and opportunist. Chinese everywhere rejoiced at what they believed to be a victory for their fatherland. The *kerajaan* element, which had lost some power and status at the hands of the Japanese, made no secret of its hope of regaining both under the Dutch. The ending of the Muslim fast on 7 September became the occasion for many attempts to mend fences with outstanding pro-Dutch figures. As late as 6 October, an estimated crowd of 30,000 attended the installation of the new Sultan of Deli, whose well-known scepticism of the Republic was apparent in the official seating arrangements.[54]

Those who had more to lose by the Dutch return were initially more demoralized than militant. An Indonesian doctor who had headed the Simelungun BOMPA branch committed suicide in Pematang Siantar after having been questioned by a Swiss Red Cross team. Many others fled to other parts of Sumatra or to Java, fearing retribution from the enemies they had made through association with the Japanese. Sjafei, the pre-arranged Sumatran leader, withdrew from his Bukittinggi office to Kayu Tanam to await developments. The vast majority of the population waited in passive hope that the surrender would bring an end to the terrible shortage of food, clothing, and medical attention. The plight of plantation labourers in particular was so desperate that they would have supported anyone who could rescue them from starvation.[55]

The acute social and ethnic divisions of East Sumatra made this a particularly difficult place for Hasan and Amir to attempt to establish a government. The two leaders themselves, after driving north from

306   An Indonesian Frontier

Palembang discussing the PPKI decisions with a handful of leaders along the way, were shaken by the reports coming from their own residency. Hearing in Tarutung that the sultans were planning to arrest all those they regarded as collaborators, Dr Amir feared for his life. These reports soon proved to be based only on some meetings among the sultans, popular leaders such as the communists Karim M.S. and Luat Siregar, and the Japanese about the preservation of order in the interregnum. Nevertheless Amir withdrew quietly to Tanjung Pura during September, despite his appointment to Sukarno's first cabinet. To some friends he dismissed the whole proclamation affair in Jakarta as a *sandiwara* (play-acting).[56]

Far from leading the revolution, Medan lagged behind other centres. Although he returned to the city on 27 August, Hasan could not get the elite group to meet until 3 September. Then, and again two weeks later, they declined even to constitute a Komité Nasional because of opposition from the sultans. Real progress was not made until the end of September.[57]

The slowness of Medan accentuated the problem of all-Sumatran leadership which some PPKI members had foreseen. Both Bukittinggi and Palembang felt they had as much right as Medan to lead the Sumatran revolution. Bukittinggi's claim rested on its leadership during the last months before the Japanese surrender. During August Adinegoro was active there cabling news and advice to key men throughout the island. On 29 August Sjafei acknowledged and accepted the independence proclamation "on behalf of the Indonesian people of Sumatra", while Bukittinggi *pemuda* formed a PRI (Pemuda Republik Indonesia) executive for Sumatra as well as for West Sumatra.[58]

Dr. Gani's claim in Palembang rested on his nationalist credentials and leadership of the PNI state party. Although Sukarno had suspended this state party on 31 August, Sumatra became aware of this only much later. Gani meanwhile appointed political leaders by telegram to the executive of a Sumatran PNI, including such diverse people as the communist Karim M.S. and the Acehnese Teuku Njak Arif. At the end of November the PNI was still talking of itself as a state party led by Sukarno, though it gained little popular momentum outside Gani's South Sumatra.[59] Gani also felt that he deserved primacy because he had shown greater political initiative than the other Japanese-sanctioned leaders. When he heard officially that Hasan had been appointed Governor, Gani sent a personal messenger to Sukarno protesting that "since the beginning of the revolution not a single report has been heard about the seizure of power in the north".[60]

It has been suggested[61] that one of the reasons for the slow beginning of the independence movement in Sumatra was the different attitudes of the 25th and 16th Armies after the surrender. It is true that many Japanese in Sumatra were personally very sceptical about the chances for *merdeka* and probably conveyed this mood to their Indonesian acquaintances. It is also true that there was no Admiral Maeda in Sumatra to act as protective midwife at the Republic's birth, although there were prominent Japanese defectors to the nationalist side. But it remains true that the Japanese in Sumatra proved as reluctant as their colleagues in Java to carry out Allied instructions at the expense of a clash with the Indonesians. Gen. Tanabe's non-interference policy was well expressed in a three-point telegram to one of his officers on 7 October:

1. The Japanese Army must take a strictly neutral attitude towards the Indonesian independence movement.
2. Troop movements of the Japanese army must be directed mainly at the maintenance of law and order.
3. We must strive with all strength to avoid a conflict with the Indonesians.[62]

Mr. Hasan and Dr. Amir both noted the friendliness of the Japanese in Bukittinggi, who evidently told them on their way home from Jakarta that they would transfer all government functions to Indonesians. Gen. Tanabe, true to his military type, added, "In this revolution, make sure the army is well trained and well led, and has good Spirit."[63] At no point did the Japanese in Sumatra use force to prevent an assertion of independence in Sumatra, except where this involved a serious threat to their own security. Instances of draconian

308   An Indonesian Frontier

Japanese action, notably in Tebing Tinggi and Langsa in December, occurred after the Allied landings, either as a result of specific Allied directives or as pure revenge killing.

Establishing the Republic

The instructions of the PPKI were first revealed to the small elite of politicians and administrators prominent during the Japanese occupation and grouped together through the various Hōkōkai or their equivalents in each residency. By the end of August this group in almost every residency knew either from Amir and Hasan or by telegraph that they were expected to form a KNI, a PNI, and a paramilitary body. They did not, on the other hand, have any guidance from above as to who should take the initiative in these ventures or in governing. But where there was an obvious nationalist leadership, the Hōkōkai group transformed itself into a KNI (in Aceh in late August, in West Sumatra on 30 August, in Palembang on 3 September, and in Tapanuli in late September). Government continued much as before the surrender, with Japanese department heads continuing to come to their offices and fly the Japanese flag, though they naturally took little interest in the decisions made.

Only in Palembang was there a coherent policy by the elite group to take over power from the Japanese. Dr. Gani was one of the two *fuku-chōkan* (deputy-residents) who had taken office during the Japanese period of preparation for independence, and he had the added advantage of a credibly anti-Japanese image. He acted confidently to form a Pusat Pemerintahan Bangsa Indonesia (Government Centre of the Indonesian People) on 23 August, which obtained Japanese recognition as a subordinate authority responsible for restraining ethnic Indonesians from clashing with celebrating Chinese. From 6 September Gani began encouraging government officials to contact him directly, and on 26 September, after requesting and obtaining authorization from Jakarta, the KNI declared Gani resident and asked government officials to cease recognizing their Japanese superiors. The following two weeks saw the nationalists gradually persuade office staff, by a mixture of exhortation and

Indonesianizing Sumatra

intimidation, to defy their superiors and to force them to give up coming to the office.[64]

In Palembang it was militant *pemuda* who were responsible for intimidating senior officials into supporting the Republic during the first three nights of October. In other residencies the initiative was with the *pemuda* from the beginning. As one official publication rightly acknowledged, "these first-months of the revolution were the *pemuda* months".[65] Without the pressure they brought to bear, a viable Republican government in Sumatra before the Allied landings would have been inconceivable.

Benedict Anderson has well defined the special *pemuda* identity at the end of the Japanese occupation and the effect which Japanese models had on them.[66] In Sumatra the Japanese had done much less than in Java to mobilize youth for the war effort. But there nevertheless existed a well-defined *pemuda* elite group, old enough to have had some prewar secondary education but not to have had a stake in the prewar establishment, and trained by the Japanese for positions of special responsibility in Sumatera Baru. The most important component of this group were those who had undergone officer training as Giyūgun, Heihō, Tokubetsu Keisatsutai (police reserve to guard coasts, bridges, etc.), Tokubetsu Hikōjō Kinmutai (police reserve to guard airfields), and similar organizations. The most important of these, the Giyūgun or *lasjkar rakjat* (known as *Peta* in Java), was established in Sumatra in November 1943 as the basis of a separate Indonesian army with its own officer corps up to the rank of captain. The soldiers were trained and quartered near their home districts. The total strength in Sumatra was probably about 30,000 men at the surrender, although it was proportionately much larger in some areas such as Aceh (5,000–6,000) than in others like East Sumatra (1,400). By August 1945 the first few dozen officer trainees had reached first lieutenant rank, and a second group second lieutenant. As in Java, the combination of intense discipline and racial discrimination by the Japanese made these Giyūgun officers strongly nationalist. Many of them had agreed among themselves that in the event of an Allied invasion they would attack the Japanese first and deal with the Allies later. In July 1945 Giyūgun Lt. H. Sitompul staged an abortive revolt in the Pematang Siantar barracks.[67] Between 19 and 21 August, before any news of the surrender had been made public, all the Giyūgun were disarmed and sent back to their homes. They were too bewildered to attempt any resistance.[68]

The other source of *pemuda* leadership was the group of educated young men associated with Japanese propaganda, news, or communications media. They were the first to receive reports of the exciting developments in Java and became natural centres of the information networks which sprang up. In the atmosphere of uncertain expectancy, *pemuda* from the military, the police, and those Japanese offices gathered at certain points to exchange what news there was about the Republic in Java or the intentions of the Allies. The hostel at Fuzi Dori 6 (Jl. Jakarta) in Medan was one example. Rumours of what the Dutch intended to do to punish Japanese collaborators gradually encouraged a mood of defiance, which was sharpened in street brawls with incautiously exuberant Chinese in many towns. During September these informal gatherings and information networks were transformed into distinct organizations. Toward the end of the month leaflets advertising the proclamation began to be printed, and the *pemuda* began to show their impatience with the inactivity of the older generation of politicians.[69]

Medan was an extreme case of a residency capital where no clear leader had emerged above the conflicting interest groups during the Japanese occupation. Despite their limited contacts with left-wing politicians and Taman Siswa teachers, the Medan *pemuda* were handicapped by not even knowing until mid-September that Mr. Hasan had been appointed Republican governor. They formed their Barisan Pemuda Indonesia (BPI) on 21 September entirely on their own initiative. Their mounting determination to resist the Allied return found an appropriate focus only when the first postwar newspaper, *Pewarta Deli*, appeared on 29 September. It reproduced an Australian radio report that the Allies had put a police guard on Sukarno's home, which in the prevailing mood was taken to mean that Sukarno had been arrested and the Republic dissolved. The *pemuda* rushed from one leader to another trying to establish the truth of the matter in the course of which they put additional pressure on Hasan and the

Indonesianizing Sumatra

cautious older generation. At a mass BPI meeting the following day at the Taman Siswa School, the offending editor, Mohammad Said, was made to apologize for printing a provocative report, Hasan spoke about the independence proclamation in Jakarta, and *pemuda* and radical leaders began the public campaign for independence. The *pemuda* urged Hasan to proclaim the Republican government on the spot. He stalled discreetly on the rather artificial grounds that he carried written authority only as a *wakil mutlak* (plenipotentiary) of Sukarno rather than as Republican governor (though the appointment of governors had been announced in Jakarta in August). Hasan later telegraphed Jakarta for confirmation and received a reply on 2 October. Meanwhile Gen. Christison's statement of 1 October that the Allies would not remove the Republican government must have dispelled what doubts the older leaders still felt. Hasan got the support of the leading politicians at a meeting on 2 October and began issuing formal statements and decrees the following day.[70] One of his first acts was to appoint Republican residents who in every case except East Sumatra itself were the leaders advanced to prominence during the latter part of the Japanese period.[71]

Once the *pemuda* and the older leaders had belatedly found each other, Medan could at last begin to function as the Sumatran capital it was intended to be. The governor's decrees, publicized by the official Republican newspaper, *Soeloeh Merdeka*, beginning 4 October, were a spur to widespread action. In the remoter residencies his telegram appointing a resident was the effective beginning of the Republican movement. Where the *pemuda* were already mobilized, it provided a necessary additional legitimation for the cautious older generation. The week between the governor's taking office and the Allied landings was an extremely critical one. Mass rallies were held to salute the *Merah-Putih*, and at one office after another the flag was run up and the Japanese head discouraged from attending. The relationship between the top Indonesians and Japanese in most districts was still good, enabling them to ensure in advance that there would be no serious violence. The only weapon the Japanese attempted to use was bluff, and when the bluff was called, at least some Japanese officers appeared genuinely delighted that the Indonesians were showing some spirit.[72] By the time the 26th Indian Division occupied Medan, Padang, and Palembang (10–14 October), the government machinery of these three towns was in Republican hands, and Republican control in the remaining key areas was well on the way to being established (in Aceh by 14 October and in Tapanuli by 17 October). Republican strength in some areas had yet to be tested in relation to that of the Allies and of the separate bureaucracies operated by the generally pro-Dutch *kerajaan*. But it was a great victory that the central bureaucracies formerly under Japanese direct control were now taking orders from Republican leaders.

The same critical week saw a rationalization of the *pemuda* movement in most areas. In response to early Republican policy to form a BKR (from 5 October known as TKR — Tentara Keamanan Rakjat) as an armed force built primarily from Japanese-trained units, the *pemuda* groups split. Those with formal military training formed a TKR division in each residency, usually accepting a fair degree of control from the local Republican officials. The remaining civilians rapidly declared themselves part of an Indonesia-wide youth movement and adopted the names which had already become famous in Java. The Angkatan Pemuda Indonesia (API) of Jakarta was copied in Lampung and Jambi and by some *pemuda* in Palembang. Throughout West and North Sumatra the accepted title was Pemuda Republik Indonesia (PRI), similar to the then dominant *pemuda* group in Surabaya. All of these Sumatran organizations dutifully declared themselves branches of Pesindo (Pemuda Sosialis Indonesia) following the merging of the Java API and PRI into that new group at the Youth Congress in Jogjakarta on 9 November. In reality the Sumatran *pemuda* groups had little in common with the API/PRI/Pesindo element in Java. The network of anti-Japanese contacts organized by Sjahrir during the war among educated youth had not extended outside Java. Virtually unrepresented in Sumatra was the strongly anti-collaborationist youth, which, with a hard core of students rallying specifically behind the Sjahrir-Sjarifuddin leadership, was the most vital element of Javanese politics in the first six months of independence. The essence of API/ PRI/Pesindo in Sumatra was not a link with any of the rival Jakarta politicians in particular but a desire to embrace all youth in a common

Indonesianizing Sumatra

struggle, to reject the regional groupings of the past, and to stress as emphatically as possible a new pan-Indonesian *pemuda* identity. Changes in the titles of these groups were usually announced proudly with the words "on instructions from Java". Only Palembang was out of step with this trend. There the influence of Dr. Gani predominated in the early BPRI group which he was able to fashion later into Napindo, the powerful youth wing of the Sumatra PNI, without parallel in Java.[73]

Both the TKR and the PRI/API groups quickly organized along military lines and attempted to gather all possible arms from the Japanese. But whereas the TKR was relatively cohesive and responsive to official control, the civilian *pemuda* movement became a loose federation of fighting gangs, often competing for control of territory. Though individual members of the older political elite had varying degrees of influence over these gangs, the Republican leaders could not rely on their support during internal crises.

The balance of power between the TKR and the PRI/API varied considerably from one residency to another. In Aceh, Tapanuli, and Palembang a significant concentration of Giyūgun and early backing from the resident made the TKR relatively strong, though not in a position to dictate. The Republic was especially fortunate in Palembang because the resident also had a personal following among the civilian *pemuda*. At the other extreme the East Sumatra TKR was just one of many fighting organizations and weaker than PRI/Pesindo as a whole.

The violent phase of the revolution in Sumatra began immediately after the Allied landings in October, when the *pemuda* clashed with Dutch ex-prisoners, Ambonese, Japanese, and eventually with Allied troops themselves. Yet already by early October many of the essential features of the revolution on Sumatra were becoming clear. In comparison with Java, the central fact about Sumatra was the weakness of the Republican leadership. It was much less able to assert its authority over, or prevent internecine fighting among, those who had the guns and felt themselves, with reason, to be the vanguard of the revolution. Despite great variation among residencies, with the South approaching Javanese conditions most closely, it would be a fair generalization to say that the level of intra-Indonesian violence was considerably higher in Sumatra during the early revolution. In particular the social revolution which affected Sumatra much more profoundly than Java in late 1945 and early 1946 was beyond the power of the Republican authorities to prevent or control (see following chapter). Even more so than in Java, the revolution was made and the pace was set by *pemuda* with a rather low estimate of officialdom.

The Question of Sumatran Political Identity

Only once in history has the island of Sumatra had a meaningful legal and political identity. Its evenly-balanced major communities — Minangkabau, Batak, Acehnese, and Palembang — were brought together only by the wider authority of Batavia/Jakarta. But for precisely a decade, 1938–48, successive Dutch, Japanese, and Republican authorities did choose to treat the island as an administrative unit. One of the avowed reasons the Dutch established a governor of Sumatra in Medan was "the awareness of a Sumatran unity, already germinally present and to be further developed by the establishment of one (Sumatran) Province".[74] This was a thoroughly artificial and unsuccessful attempt to divert the Indonesian popular movement into regional channels. Its major importance was an example for later Republicans and a training ground for officials such as Mr. Hasan.

The complete and effective separation from Java under the Japanese brought quite a new situation. For three years propaganda had been directed primarily toward building *Sumatera Baru*. The Japanese 25th Army undoubtedly had the opportunity to exploit and encourage whatever Sumatran sentiments existed by building up a distinct Sumatran leadership. Fortunately for Republican unity, the Japanese were not interested in building any leadership whatever until their last two months of power, and even then to a very limited degree. Nevertheless it is not surprising that the Japanese period did encourage some leaders to think that an autonomous Sumatra was a practicable ideal. Most affected were the small elite old enough to have been members of Jong Sumatra during their student days in the 1920s and filling prominent positions under the Japanese. For the more conservative aristocratic leaders this was primarily a negative

Indonesianizing Sumatra

rejection of Java as the source of political extremism and Islamic heresy. There were, however, genuine Republicans for whom Sumatra had a positive meaning. The majority of these seem to have been Minangkabau, particularly Minangkabau living in other parts of Sumatra other than their homeland. The most outspoken example was Dr. Amir, one of the most eloquent defenders of the cultural unity of *Sumatera Baru* during the war years.[75] As deputy-governor of Sumatra from December 1945 he remained anxious to build up a highly autonomous government apparatus in Medan. After his alienation from the Republic the following April, he made Javanese domination the central theme of his criticism.

> Up till now this unitary question has not been publicly discussed. We three, who attended the meeting of the Committee for the Preparation of Independence in Jakarta in August 1945, hoped that Sumatra would obtain autonomy concerning external and internal affairs outside the Republic, but we were admonished not to form a separate state with its own departments, etc.[76]

Amir and the other members of Hasan's "cabinet", despite frequent protestations of solidarity with Java, did make their own decisions on most issues without consulting Jakarta at least until Amir Sjarifuddin's visit. Had they been stronger as a group, they would very probably have resisted the gradual erosion of their autonomy thereafter by the central government. But it was the *pemuda* who had made the Republic possible in Sumatra and who retained physical power. For the *pemuda* unity with Java was all important. Java was the heroic model for struggle, showing the way to liberation from the otherwise certain Dutch restoration.

The most striking indication of the strength of the popular, *pemuda*-inspired desire to follow Java was the experience of Aceh. Before the war it still resembled a conquered country rather than a part of the Netherlands Indies body politic. The leadership of the dominant popular force, PUSA, indisputably thought in Acehnese and Islamic rather than Indonesian terms. Yet even PUSA needed the Republican enthusiasm of the *pemuda* to escape a restoration of

Dutch and *ulëëbalang* rule. In the first year of the revolution Aceh was a model of outward loyalty to the central government.

The Dutch, in adopting their postwar federal strategy, were counting on the ethnic and regional sentiments of the older generation they knew so well. The logical superstructure for the *Negara* (member states) they later sponsored in Sumatra was an all-Sumatra grouping, to balance against Java and East Indonesia. But quite apart from its unacceptability as part of Dutch colonial strategy, the Sumatran idea was found to have no appeal in South Sumatra and little for the highly autonomous Acehnese and Batak.[77] The Muktamar Sumatra sponsored by the federalists in March–April 1949 was a predictable flop. The brief moment for Sumatran unity had passed, and Dutch pressure was unlikely to succeed in reviving it.

Appendix 1

Members of Sumatra Central Advisory Council (Chūo Sangi In)[78]

I have roughly categorized representatives of Islamic movements by (I), of political movements by (P), and of the *kerajaan*, some of whom were also moderate nationalists, by (K). Most of those not fitting into such categories were Japanese-appointed officials with no particular following. In Tapanuli the antagonism between Christian North and Muslim South took precedence over any other distinctions.

Aceh

Elected:
T. Njak Arif (K), Chairman, Aceh Council
Tgk. Mohd. Daud Beureu'eh (I), Chairman of PUSA

Appointed:
T. Tjut Hasan (K), Vice-Chairman Aceh Council
T.P.P. Mohd. Ali (K), Panglima Sagi XXII Mukims
Tgk. Mohd. Hasbi (I), Deputy Chairman of Maibkatra, and Muhammadiah leader

East Sumatra

Elected:
Djamaluddin Adinegoro (P), Editor *Kita-Sumatora-sinbun* and Vice-Chairman East Sumatra Council (resigned seat after election)
Tengku Damrah (K), Serdang royal family

Appointed:
Tengku Othman (K), Crown Prince of Deli
Raja Kaliamsjah Sinaga (K), Raja Pematang Tanah Jawa
Dr. R. Pirngadi (P), prewar Parindra leader
Hamka (I), Consul Muhammadiah Sumatra Timur
Hsu Hua Chang (Chinese), Chairman of Medan Hohkiaw

Tapanuli

Elected:
Dr. Ferdinand Lumbantobing (North), Chairman Tapanuli Council
Firman Rangkuti gelar St. Soripada Mulia (South)

Appointed:
Raja Saul Lumbantobing (North)
Haji A. Aziz (South)

West Sumatra

Elected:
Mohd. Sjafei (P), Chairman W. Sumatra Council
Chatib Suleiman (P), Vice-Chairman W. Sumatra Council

Appointed:
Datuk Perpatih Baringek (K), leader of *adat* organization
A.R. Sutan Mansur (I), Consul Muhammadiah W. Sumatra
Dr. Mohd. Djamil, non-political medical doctor

318 An Indonesian Frontier

Riau*
Elected: Aminoedin (P), Chairman Riau Council

Appointed: Orang Kaya Mohd. Djamil (K), relative of Sultan of Siak
                   Sjamsoeddin, *guncho* (district officer)

Jambi
Elected: Abdoel Manan, Chairman Jambi Council

Appointed: Abdoel Katab Makalam, Vice-Chairman Jambi Council

Palembang
Elected: Dr. A.K. Gani (P), Chairman Palembang Council and prewar
                   Gerindo leader
                   Abdoel Rozak (P)

Appointed: Tjik Mat (P)
                   Kiai Hadji Tjik Wan (I)
                   Ir. Ibrahim (P), Vice-Chairman Palembang Council

Bengkulu
Elected: Abdoellah

Appointed: Ir. Indra Tjahaja, Chairman Bengkulen Council
                   Mohd. Jasin

Lampung
Elected: Radja Pagar Alam (K)

Appointed: Mr. Abdul Abbas (P), Chairman Lampung Council
                   St. Rahim Pasaman, Head of Bureau of Popular Petitions
                   (*Koseikyokucho*)

Bangka-Billiton
Elected: M.A. Sjarif (P), Chairman Bangka-Billiton Council

Appointed: Oen Lam Seng (Chinese), Vice-Chairman Bangka-Billiton Council

---

* Mainland Sumatra only; the archipelago was united with Singapore.

Indonesianizing Sumatra

Appendix 2

Members of Panitia Penjelidik Persiapan Kemerdekaan (Sumatra)[79]

Chairman: Mohd. Sjafei   **Secretary:**   Djamaluddin Adinegoro

Members:

Aceh:
T. Njak Arif
Tgk. Mohd. Daud Beureu'eh

East Sumatra:
Dr. Pirngadi
Dr. Amir
Mr. T. Mohd. Hasan
Hamka
Tgk. Saibun Abdul Jalil Rahmat Sjah, Sultan of Asahan
Hsu Hua Chang

Tapanuli:
Dr. Ferdinand Lumbantobing
Mr. Azairin

West Sumatra:
Dt. Perpatih Baringek
A.R. Sutan Mansur
Chatib Soeleiman
Sjech Mohd. Djamil Djambek

Riau:
Aminoeddin

Jambi:
Dr. A. Sjagoff

Bengkulu:
Ir. Indra Tjahaja

Palembang:
Dr. A.K. Gani
Ir. Ibrahim
K.H. Tjik Wan

Lampung:
Mr. Abdul Abbas

Bangka-Billiton:
M.A. Sjarif

Appendix 3

First Republican Residents in Sumatra

Residency	Resident	Position during Japanese Occupation	Served until
Aceh	Teuku Njak Arif	Chairman, Aceh Council and adviser to chōkan	21 January 1946
East Sumatra	Mr. Mohd. Joesoef	Assistant to Japanese mayor of Medan	29 October 1945 (to become mayor of Medan)
Tapanuli	Dr Ferdinand Lumbantobing	Chairman, Tapanuli Council and Hōkōkai, and fuku-chōkan	September 1947
West Sumatra	Mohd. Sjafei	Chairman, W. Sumatra Council and Hōkōkai, and Chūō Sangi In.	15 November 1945 (on grounds of "illness")
Jambi	Dr. A. Sjagoff	Member PPPK (Sumatra)	December 1945 (arrested by Japanese)
Riau	Aminoeddin	Chairman, Riau Council	October 1945 (at request of KNI)
Bengkulu	Ir. Indra Tjahaja	Chairman, Bengkulen Council	May 1946 (at request of KNI)
Palembang	Dr. A.K. Gani	Chairman, Palembang Council and Hōkōkai, and fuku-chōkan	May 1946 (to become vice-governor)
Lampung	Mr. A. Abbas	Chairman, Lampung Council and Hōkōkai	September 1946 (*daulat*-ed by *pemuda*)
Bangka-Billiton	A. Sjarif	Chairman, Bangka-Billiton Council	February 1946 (Dutch occupation)

14

Social Revolution in Three Sumatran Locales

The Indonesian Revolution

THE credentials of the Indonesian "Revolution" have been doubted in more than one quarter, particularly in the period of the late 1960s and early 1970s. In Indonesia, strategists of the dominant military group at that time sought to avoid the term in favour of "war of independence", because they wanted to impose a non-revolutionary, stable format on the country while continuing to exalt the events of 1945–50 as the source of the Army's own legitimacy. Elsewhere, especially in the United States and Europe, the same period saw a fascination with the apparent success of Vietnam and China in mobilizing and feeding their populations, so that many activists, and not a few scholars, tended to redefine the term "revolution" to fit only the successful mobilization of the peasantry by a Leninist party. Both sides had constructed a political stereotype from the term "revolution", and could agree that Indonesia had not experienced it.

The concept "revolution" is one of the most central in the comparative toolkit of historical analysis. Whatever use politicians understandably make of it, historians cannot do without it as a category independent of praise or blame. A revolution is a fundamental restructuring of a political system by violent means within a relatively short span of time. Despite the enormous variety of revolutions the world has known, a certain pattern is discernible in almost all of

322 An Indonesian Frontier

them, beginning with the first defiant act of destroying the old regime, and ending with the imposition of some relatively stable new type of regime — usually one quite different from that envisaged by the leading revolutionaries of the first stage. It is the French Revolution which has given rise to by far the largest body historical analysis, and typologies of revolution usually make it the central or "classic" case, with the Russian Revolution the most influential variation. Historians differ as to how widely or narrowly they would want to draw the boundaries of the concept "revolution", but no typology would be adequate which did not include at least these two major watersheds.

Several features are common to these two revolutions, and to many others. The first stage of the revolution is an idealistic alliance of many different political elements, from the cautious to the wild-eyed, to topple the old regime. This deed, and the euphoria which immediately follows it, is exciting and exhilarating for the young — especially the young in the cities where most of the action takes place. As Wordsworth said of the French Revolution: "Bliss was it in that dawn to be alive; but to be young was very heaven." Divisions quickly appear among the former allies, and the revolution moves steadily towards the left as it becomes apparent that physical power lies with those who control the guns or the young crowds in the streets, not with the earlier leaders. Finally one element in the alliance that toppled the old regime is able to impose a settlement on the others — often aided by popular revulsion against the anarchy and violence into which the revolution has fallen.

This is the end of the revolutionary process, even if its effects are felt for decades or even centuries thereafter. The new rulers, even though they usually represent a broader section of society than the old, cannot rely on the acquiescence of a relatively passive population, as the old regime may have done. There are many elements whose revolutionary fervour cannot be satisfied by the settlement imposed, and who therefore denounce it as a "betrayal of the revolution". The new rulers have one advantage in the emotionally powerful symbols and myths of the revolution (flag, songs, slogans, martyred heroes, annual commemorations, ideals of liberty and/or equality and brotherhood). These provide a basis for a much higher degree of

Social Revolution in Three Sumatran Locales 323

unity than before, and they are manipulated by the new rulers in their quest for legitimation. Nevertheless the new society is more difficult to govern than the old, and the passions evoked by the revolution take a long time to die.[1]

The events of the late 1970s in Iran clearly fall within this "classic" type of revolution. So do the events which began in Indonesia in August 1945. The Indonesian revolution also moved quickly to the left from the proclamation until the 3 July [1946] affair; thereafter it tended to polarize into the two major forces whose conflict was resolved (temporarily) with the Madiun affair of September 1948. In terms of the purely internal revolution, this affair and the transition to guerrilla warfare that immediately followed marked the victory of one element in the revolutionary alliance — the army. This victory was of course complicated by the struggle with the Dutch and the intervention of the United Nations, so that in another sense the final "settlement" of the revolution did not take place until much later, in 1966.

The importance of the revolutionary experience in setting a path for Indonesia becomes clear if we compare post-revolutionary Indonesia with Malaysia — a country that in some respects has a similar cultural and historical background. Some of the differences are just those that we find in comparing post-revolutionary France with non-revolutionary England in the 19th century. Indonesia (like France) had an emotionally powerful set of revolutionary symbols and myths, which helped to create national pride, political centralization and ideological uniformity. Despite this, both post-revolutionary countries experienced a relatively high incidence of political violence and upheaval. Malaysia, like England, followed an unheroic, pragmatic path, in which political divisions were institutionalized rather than overridden (Malaysia, although far more homogeneous than Indonesia, retains a federal system and nine monarchs among whom the office of Head of State, Yang Dipertuan Agung, revolves).

In terms of historical analysis, in other words, it is both correct and helpful to use the term "revolution" for the events of 1945–9 in Indonesia. The concept is in fact more relevant and helpful in explaining Indonesia than in explaining Vietnam, which had the same ruling party from its independence proclamation (also August 1945)

324   An Indonesian Frontier

until today, without undergoing the same internal shifts in the revolutionary current.

We are on less firm ground when we try to define what type of revolution Indonesia experienced. Terms such as "social revolution" and "bourgeois revolution" are not very well defined. In common with other scholars I have used the label "the Indonesian National Revolution", because its most striking result was the creation of a unified nation. But as with all revolutions, the result produced is only evident some time afterwards, and differs from the initial hopes and intentions of some (perhaps all) of the revolutionaries (Who dreamed of Napoleon, or of Robespierre, when they stormed the Bastille?). At the height of revolutionary enthusiasm in early 1946 slogans like *kedaulatan rakyat* (people's sovereignty), *100 percent Merdeka* (Freedom), *milik rakyat* (people's ownership), *sama rasa-sama rata* (equality and brotherhood), and even *darah* (blood) or *darah rakyat* (people's blood) indicated some of the hopes inspired by the revolution — personal freedom, brotherhood, economic equality, and total involvement by the people in the process of government.

Social Revolution within the Revolution

The potential of the Indonesian revolution for articulating, or even achieving, a total change in social attitudes and relationships is best examined through the so-called "social revolution" which affected many parts of Sumatra and Java between October 1945 and March 1946. The term "social revolution" was initially applied by supporters of these movements to distinguish them from the political revolution to replace Dutch or Japanese governments with the Indonesian Republic. Their common element was a movement from below to overthrow the Indonesian officials who had held office under the Japanese (and, often also the Dutch) and had been confirmed in power by the new Republican government. In every case, therefore, these "social revolutions" challenged and opposed official Republican policy in their areas, although believing themselves passionately loyal in principle to the revolution and its leadership. The Republican government and the dominant Socialist Party within it bitterly opposed

Social Revolution in Three Sumatran Locales 325

all the "social revolutions". Even the most prominent Marxists (later self-proclaimed communists) in government ranks, like Amir Sjarifuddin and Abdulmadjid, condemned these violent outbreaks as an "infantile disease of leftism". A Republican delegation including these two, and led by Amir as Minister of Defence and the government's most charismatic Marxist, was brought to Sumatra in April 1946 on a British plane specifically to bring the revolution under control. "Social revolution", in other words, was a spontaneous movement from below, taking a similar form in a number of quite different areas, but without any coordination or direction between these different regions.

These movements against the local authorities began in the northern coastal districts of Java in September and October 1945, reaching a peak in the so-called "Peristiwa Tiga Daerah" in Tegal, Brebes and Pemalang. Here the traditional ruling families were captured, humiliated, or chased away; the bupatis, camats, and many of the lurahs were replaced by "revolutionary" officials [often Muslim leaders elected in mass meetings; and real power was exercised by a small committee coordinating the various *pemuda* (youth) struggle groups (*badan perjuangan*)]. In December a small civil war in the Pidië district of Aceh resulted in the total elimination of the ruling *ulëëbalang* class there; while in the early months of 1946 other parts of North and Central Sumatra experienced the same sort of anti-establishment actions, of which the most serious was in East Sumatra.

Given the broad similarity of these widely dispersed actions, there had to be some common causes: a relatively sharp polarization between the *pergerakan* (movement) and the aristocratic ruling groups; bitterness about the way the Indonesian authorities had implemented harsh Japanese demands for labour and rice; the virtual collapse of centralized authority; a relatively strong Islamic sentiment which often served to mobilize mass support and the activity of a very small number of semi-underground revolutionary (often communist) cadres.

How far did these "social revolutions" represent real mass movements of liberation, creating a new, dynamic opportunity for popular participation in the process of government and development? How far do they show what the revolution as a whole "might have been", as Benedict Anderson put it.[2] Do they represent a potential for fundamental social renewal, or only for mindless violence? Sumatra is an appropriate, though understudied, place to examine these questions, since the relatively looser hold of formal government there made possible three upheavals of different types — in Aceh, East Sumatra and West Sumatra.

Aceh

The Aceh social revolution was a head-on confrontation between two distinct social forces with rival claims to leadership. As explained in Chapter 12, the Dutch for most of their regime had relied heavily on the territorial aristocracy of *ulèëbalang,* and suppressed all opposition to it. In the last three years of their regime they relaxed this policy just enough to allow a rival leadership to emerge in the form of the Persatuan Ulama Seluruh Aceh (PUSA) (*Aceh Ulama Union*) led by Daud Beureu'eh. With the arrival of new Japanese rulers in 1942 the polarization between these two forces became intense, especially in the PUSA stronghold of Pidië, as each side attempted to use the Japanese to get the better of the other. During the Japanese regime the rivalry persisted. The *ulèëbalang* continued as government officials, while the religious leadership also made some gains in the fields of justice and propaganda. With the Japanese surrender, conflict was almost certain over control of the new independent government.

The initial Republican government under Resident Teuku Nyak Arif confirmed the *ulèëbalang* in the government positions they had occupied under the Japanese. The youth movement PRI, which began in October, was predominately of PUSA composition; while the official Republican Army, the TRI, was torn between the two elements. Conflict began in October and November over the national flag, over attempts to reverse the changes that had occurred under the Japanese, but especially over who would control the arms being seized from the Japanese. This last question led to a major battle in Sigli on 4 December in which hundreds probably died. Thereafter the two sides mustered their forces for a military showdown involving mortars, machine-guns, and thousands of *mujahidin.* In the first two weeks of January 1946, all the *ulèëbalang* strongholds in Pidië were overrun and virtually all the male defenders — including all but two of the 25 Pidië rulers — were killed.[3]

The idea that this was a "social revolution" did not occur to the participants until a month later, when the influence of Islamic communism made itself felt in the most economically polarized part of the province, the plantation district adjacent to East Sumatra. The concept of social revolution itself, and Almujahid's avowed aim to "destroy the feudal elements which still remain",[4] came from Nathar Zainuddin, a veteran Islamic communist who had considerable influence behind the scenes with younger activists particularly in this East Aceh district.[5] His star pupil was a quarrelsome former PUSA youth leader, Hussein Almujahid, who helped Nathar organize a coup against the East Aceh government leaders in Langsa on 12 February. After defeating his rivals there, Almujahid began what he called his "long march" from East Aceh to the capital, arresting all the *ulèëbalang* officials along the way. His intervention in February–March not only extended the action against the Pidië *ulèëbalang* to the rest of Aceh, but also portrayed it as a social revolutionary action against "feudal" elements, as well as an Islamic and national struggle.

The victors in this process were not Almujahid and Nathar, however, but the *ulama* and the Islamic-educated younger activists whose focus was PUSA and later PRI. Regardless of the rhetoric of the time, this really was a social revolution, which brought to power a new social class with a different ideology (Islamic populism), and made possible an enthusiastic participation by ordinary Acehnese in the process of building a newly independent society. Even those unsympathetic to PUSA and the new Islamic leadership in Aceh conceded that Aceh in the aftermath of this revolution was a model of purposefulness, unity between government and people, orderliness and cleanliness.[6] If we compare the Acehnese social revolution with the East Sumatran, below, some of the reasons for this become clear. There was a high degree of agreement in Aceh about what should be the guiding ideology of the revolution (Islam), and who should be its leaders (Daud Beureu'eh, and other respected *ulama* and intellectuals who had been sympathetic to the struggle of PUSA/PRI). The society

328 An Indonesian Frontier

was relatively homogeneous. The revolutionary action had been led not by young radicals, but by respected *ulama* who were able to impose a degree of discipline on the victorious forces. In particular they used most of the assets (reputedly 100 million rupiah) seized from the vanquished aristocrats to pay military and civilian officials, rather than squandering them in divisive quarrels as in East Sumatra.[7] Finally there was wide popular participation in the revolutionary action, including thousands of ordinary peasants, motivated sometimes by the return of the land they believed the *ulèëbalang* had taken from them, but always by a loyalty towards their *ulama*, and the recollection of the endless struggle against the Dutch *kafir*, of which the revolution was seen as a continuation.

Unfortunately these very positive results of the Acehnese social revolution were for the most part not permanent. However close they may have been to their own people, the new Islamic-educated leaders of Aceh were very far removed in spirit from the Dutch-educated urban professional people who led the government of Indonesia elsewhere. The very cohesion of post-revolutionary Aceh made it difficult to be absorbed within a unified Indonesia. A new war began in 1953.

East Sumatra

Although East Sumatra was always more "revolutionary" than Aceh in the first year after the Proclamation, it was a much more difficult society in which to bring any revolution to a stable conclusion. It was ethnically very heterogeneous, with the rajas obtaining some support from the Malay and Simalungun population but little from the more numerous immigrant groups (Javanese, Toba, Mandailing, Minangkabau, etc.).

As in Aceh, there was a high degree of polarization by the end of the Dutch regime, between the *kerajaan* (*swapraja* or *zelfbestuur* — Malay, Simalungun, and Karo rajas) on the one hand and the nationalist *pergerakan* on the other. In the same way also, the Japanese occupation kept this conflict alive. In East Sumatra, however, neither the *kerajaan* nor the *pergerakan* had acknowledged strong leaders.

Social Revolution in Three Sumatran Locales

Those who began the Republican Government in Medan in October 1945 — Mr. T. Hasan as Governor of Sumatra, Dr. M. Amir as Deputy Governor, and Tengku Hafas as Resident — could never be much more than intermediaries between the two forces. Their policy was to acknowledge the Sultans and rajas as having a place within the Indonesian Republic, and to try to persuade them to democratize internally while supporting the Republican Government externally.

In practice, after the Jalan Bali affair of 13 October 1945, and still more after many Japanese arms were captured in November, it was the *badan perjuangan* (revolutionary bodies) of the *pemuda* which held physical power especially in the towns. The most powerful among them were the radical Pesindo, led by Sarwono S. Soetardjo; the nationalist Napindo, a coalition between several groups including some Karo and Simalungun fighting units originally organized by the Japanese Lt. Inoue; the somewhat more disciplined TNI (the national army); the Islamic Sabilillah; and the Indonesian Communist Party's (PKI's) Laskar Merah — probably in that order of importance. Pressure from these *badan perjuangan* frightened the rajas into conducting serious negotiations with the Republican officials on 12 January and 3 February, about the means by which their administrations would be democratized. This came too late to save the rajas; its main result may in fact have been to speed the "revolutionaries" plans to get rid of them before their position was strengthened by democratization.

The East Sumatran "social revolution" was launched on 3 March 1946, on the instructions of a small group of leaders of Pesindo, PNI (the Indonesian Nationalist Party) and PKI working through the framework of the *Persatuan Perjuangan*. The aims of the leaders were threefold: to eliminate the rajas as potential allies of the Dutch; to seize their legendary wealth to be used in the national struggle; and lastly to advance the social revolution, by eliminating feudalism. There was tremendous revolutionary enthusiasm in the days immediately before and after the action against the rajas, notably on the part of youth groups in the towns, so that we can identify the period from mid-February to mid-April as the peak of the revolution in this area, with power almost completely in the hands of the insurgent crowds

330   An Indonesian Frontier

in the streets. "History has never experienced a revolution as intense as this Indonesian revolution", declared a Pesindo leader.[8]

The immediate objectives of the "social revolution" were quickly achieved by the *badan perjuangan* on the night of 3 March or soon thereafter. At its best, in Tanah Karo, Serdang, and some of the Simalungun *kerajaan*, the action removed the rulers neatly and without bloodshed, confining them under military guard and confiscating much of their property. In other areas, notably the spread-out southern district (Asahan, Kualuh, Bila, Panai and Kota Pinang), Langkat, and the Pane and Raya *kerajaan* in Simalungun, there was wholesale plunder and killing, of the innocent along with the guilty. In only a few instances was there resistance from the supporters of the rajas, the most significant being in Sunggal (Deli), where about 40 people may have been killed in the fighting.[9]

The positive work of creating new institutions which could embody the revolutionary ideals of equality and brotherhood was much more difficult. Two features of this period however stand out. One was the "direct democracy" system whereby huge mass rallies successfully demanded that the *kerajaan* be immediately declared abolished, and in some cases elected or ratified new office-holders on the spot. The Republican Government, in the person of Dr. Amir who was acting for the absent Governor, had little choice but to ratify all these decisions. To the higher positions of East Sumatran Resident and "pacificateur", respectively, Amir appointed two communists in the (mistaken) hope that they would be better able to restrain and guide the revolutionary forces.

Still more remarkable was the Ekonomi Rakyat Republik Indonesia (ERRI), an attempt at instant collectivization in the economic field, led by a couple of small businessmen who professed to be communists but had very little apparent experience in either politics or commerce. Since the left-wing politicians in government in Java generally preferred to concentrate on the more powerful ministries (Defence, Interior) and leave economics to moderates, this was the most ambitious experiment anywhere. It was created on 5 February 1946 in the hope of coordinating all economic activity in Sumatra, though for the meantime it was only able to mobilize economic groups like hawkers,

Social Revolution in Three Sumatran Locales

cloth-merchants and medicine sellers into cooperatives. With the "social revolution", ERRI was officially given full authority to organize the structure of the economy in every sector for the whole of Sumatra.[10]

For over a month ERRI was extraordinarily active, taking over rubber and tobacco estates, transport facilities, foreign trade and customs revenues, and almost anything else which it was able to wrest from its previous management. Its aims appear to have been twofold: to use the economic weapon to the full in the struggle against colonialism, for example by carrying out a very effective blockade of Allied occupied Medan; and to equalize the distribution of foodstuffs, cloth, and other essentials through a policy based on *sama rasa sama rata*. Unfortunately its life was too short and the situation too chaotic for a fair trial of this remarkable body, but the small amount of evidence we have on it is largely negative. Its policy of forcible requisitioning appears to have made it more enemies than friends, and it laid itself open to the charge of massive corruption.[11] Given the extraordinary speed with which it took over such vast responsibilities it is not surprising that it was judged a failure, and in practice became one of the negative points used to denounce the "social revolution".

Despite the scenes of enthusiasm with which it had begun, reaction against the "social revolution" in East Sumatra began only ten days later. Opinion began to turn against it with the news of the excesses in Asahan, where over 100 aristocrats were killed in a few days, and still more in the wealthiest state of Langkat, where seven leading aristocrats were beheaded (the first of many) and two of the Sultan's daughters raped on the night of 11 March. Two days later the political elite in Medan removed the two communists from their key positions in East Sumatra. However neither the political shuffles at the top, nor the announcement of a military government in the hands of the TRI, had much real effect on the revolutionary atmosphere. The intervention was more effective of Amir Sjarifuddin (then Minister of Defence) and other Marxists in the Republican central government, who visited East Sumatra on 9–12 April 1946 to try to bring the revolutionary turbulence back under control.

Amir's tough speeches gave encouragement to some of the "moderate" elements within the *badan perjuangan,* who were strong enough by the end of April to arrest two of the so-called "super-communists" (Joenoes Nasution, the "revolutionary Resident" of 3–13 March, was expelled from the PKI soon after his arrest), and to ban ERRI.[12]

From this revolutionary tumult in East Sumatra, however, no winner emerged (as the Islamic elite had in Aceh). The reputations of all the major leaders were damaged by the chaos of the "social revolution", so that real power devolved more and more to the separate armed youth groups led by men not much over 20. Throughout 1946 and 1947 they fought frequently with each other over territory, over control of rubber estates, and over the treasure that had been taken from the royal palaces. With "deterioration in every field", as Muhammad Radjab put it,[13] East Sumatra was one of the poorest advertisements for the Indonesian Republic, despite its great wealth. For this very reason, however, it invited eventual control from the central government — again unlike Aceh.

Within this confusing revolutionary pattern in East Sumatra, Tanah Karo stands out as one area where the "social revolution" was both orderly and popular. It seems to be the only part of East Sumatra where we can speak confidently of enthusiastic peasant participation in the struggle. Perhaps the reasons for this could be sought in the ethnic homogeneity of Tanah Karo, or in the fact that the rajas there were artificial creations of the Dutch regime, or in the hunger for education and development that was suddenly unleashed with the collapse of colonial authority.[14]

Minangkabau

The Minangkabau area of West Sumatra also experienced this social revolutionary tide, though the revolutionaries here had less success in gaining control of the government apparatus. In consequence the social revolution has been less well documented here. Our only sources for the millenarian "Baso movement", in particular, are very hostile to its radicalism.

The example of the East Sumatran social revolution was influential in West Sumatra. On 13 March, ten days after the *Persatuan Perjuangan* took control in the Medan area, Tan Malaka-style revolutionaries formed a similar group in West Sumatra. The hereditary chiefs who under the Dutch had administered the customary *nagari* communities were declared dismissed, and elections a few months later succeeded in transferring authority for the most part to popular *ulama*. As in East Sumatra, the Persatuan Perjuangan sought particularly to control the West Sumatran economy by taking over the government's authority in this area. But the arrival of Amir Sjarifuddin's delegation in April curbed this radical tide in the province after scarcely a month.[15]

As the Japanese-backed government structures dissolved at the end of 1945, authority in the Baso area east of Bukittinggi had been seized by two brothers, both rural *ulama* and followers of Tan Malaka ever since the 1927 Minangkabau rebellion. They had established an underground branch of Tan Malaka's national-communist PARI movement in Baso in the 1930s. By the early months of 1946 they had formed a militia well supplied with Japanese weapons, and killed the district head and other prominent officials in the area. According to an anti-Baso pamphlet written from the viewpoint of the "orthodox" PKI of Abdulmadjid, they attempted a radical communalization of property in each village. Members of the movement were to hold everything in common — land, food, and allegedly even women. In each village they controlled and established a "heavenly garden" (*kebun syorga*) as if to realize heaven on earth. To this communal residence the property seized from the rich was brought. "In short any property of the populace which was substantial had to be divided, made equal [*disama ratakan*]."[16]

On 13 April 1946, as the Amir Sjarifuddin team was on its way around Sumatra seeking to curb these excesses, the West Sumatran army (TNI) launched a full-scale assault on the Baso movement, accusing it of kidnap, murder and terror, and of constituting a state within a state. In three days the leaders of the movement and over a hundred of their followers were killed. A week later, after Amir's group had talked sternly to the military and civil leadership in West

334 An Indonesian Frontier

Sumatra, the leaders of the West Sumatran *Persatuan Perjuangan* were put under arrest.[17]

The Revolutionary Heritage

There is no denying the extraordinary importance of the Indonesian revolution. It was both the watershed of modern Indonesian history, and a major contribution to the eventual retreat of colonialism throughout the world. It produced profound changes in the self-confidence, the attitudes, and the political beliefs of a whole generation. It also altered the structure of Indonesian society, not only by destroying the enormous variety of local aristocratic traditions, but also by building a new, ultimately highly centralized, political system. For generations to come Indonesians will keep returning to the revolution in search of ideas about the nature of their society and their state. They will continue to find sublime ideals of freedom, brotherhood, and equality, along with instructive examples of the dangers of revolutionary enthusiasm without planning, balance and respect for human life.

15

Conflicting Histories: Aceh and Indonesia[1]

PAINFUL as it is to admit, historians are complicit in the wars of modern times. History has often been the handmaid of nationalism. The creation of a national past is usually a prelude or accompaniment to the assertion of a national destiny. The way in which Acehnese opinion has parted company with the dominant Indonesian views about the past is an unusually striking example of this phenomenon. Hasan Tiro, the prophet of Aceh's independence, might be said to be obsessed with history. This final chapter is an attempt to disentangle the way Acehnese and Indonesian memories became so bitterly ranged against one another, after the 1940s described in the previous three chapters, when enthusiasm for a common destiny was strongly expressed.

Indonesia's Memory of Aceh's Past

Once Indonesian nationalism, in the period 1926–49, defined anti-Dutch struggle as its key motif, it symbolically made a common cause with Acehnese, for whom anti-Dutch struggle was a bitter experienced reality. This involved some tension between myth and reality, since Indonesia had been shaped more by adaptations of Dutch influence than by resistance to it. By contrast Aceh's history was one long struggle to avoid absorption into the colony that became Indonesia. This struggle ironically became the exemplary case for the

336   An Indonesian Frontier

Indonesian historical consciousness constructed in the Sukarno and Suharto eras.

The textbooks written under the influence of Nugroho Notosusanto, military historian and education minister under Suharto, explicitly sought the unifying principal of Indonesian history in armed struggle against Dutch rule.[2] Acehnese warriors featured prominently in the pantheon of official national heroes, and streets in every city were named after Acehnese heroes like Teuku Umar and Chik di Tiro. A very successful film was made on the life of the female anti-Dutch warrior Cut Nyak Dien.

In the revolutionary period of 1945–9 Aceh proved again exemplary, as the only substantial region the Dutch could not or did not enter. It provided funds for the embattled Republican government, including the cost of two aeroplanes to run the Dutch blockade. To question Aceh's place in the Indonesia of this heroic myth endangers the myth itself.

There is a more fundamental sense in which Aceh was central to the making of Indonesian identity, but one less prominent in the textbooks of the Suharto era. Aceh, and its predecessor of Pasai, was the major crucible of an Islamic culture expressed in the Malay language. In a pre-Muslim era Malay had probably become an important language of trade as the vernacular of the great emporium of Srivijaya, centred in the modern Palembang and Jambi areas. But it was in Pasai in the 14th and 15th centuries that Malay became the language of Southeast Asian Islam, and in Aceh in the late 16th and 17th centuries that it was given literary substance. The most inspired Sufi writers of the period, Hamzah Fansuri, Shamsuddin as-Samatrani, Nuruddin ar-Raniri, and Abdurra'uf of Singkel (the Syiah Kuala after whom Aceh's university is named), all lived and wrote in the Acehnese capital, then the Muslim intellectual centre of the Archipelago.[3]

Acehnese appear to have written in Malay before they wrote in Acehnese. All the early Acehnese texts are in Malay or Arabic. Only in the late 17th century does there begin to be evidence of writing in Acehnese, which remained for the most part a language of speech and recitation. When Dutch-sponsored village schools were opened in the early 1900s in the face of initial Acehnese distrust, they also taught

Aceh and Indonesia

in Malay, like those in most parts of the Archipelago. Only in 1932, as the fear of Acehnese marrying their anti-foreign-rule attitude to Indonesian nationalism began to be significant, did the colonial government switch the main medium of village primary instruction to Acehnese. Many of the educated Acehnese elite protested that this was a political manoevre to isolate Aceh, that there was not enough written in Acehnese to sustain the reading habit, and that Acehnese tradition since the days of the sultanate had always been for written education to be in Malay even if Acehnese was used to explain things orally.[4] One small generation educated in the period 1932–42, but only one, would have felt comfortable writing in the complex romanized Acehnese devised by the linguists.

Aceh Distinctiveness

In these ways, and in its basic linguistic and social pattern, Aceh was a Sumatran and a Southeast Asian society. Yet there was enough distinctiveness in its historical development since the 16th century to make the separatist ideology believable when it emerged in the 1970s. In contrast with the "classical Malay" literary tradition in which Aceh played so strong a part, for example, Aceh was utterly marginal to the development of a modern Malay/Indonesian idiom and literature from the late 19th century. This was the urban "Indische" superculture of the major cities of Netherlands India, expressing itself in romanized Malay (in contrast to the Arabic script of classical Malay), and largely created in the first instance by Eurasians and Peranakan Chinese though eventually picked up as its medium by the national movement.

Up until the Dutch conquest in the late 19th century, Aceh's economic, political and cultural linkages were to the Indian Ocean and the Malayan Peninsula, not to the Java Sea world, dominated by first Java and then the Dutch. It was part of the Indian Ocean Islamic oecumene ever since Pasai was visited and described by Ibn Battuta (an Arab then acting as an envoy of Delhi) in the 14th century. Aceh's "tribute" to Ottoman Turkey, described in Chapter 4, was natural in this context, as were the contacts with France described in Chapter 8. After the Dutch Company prized the pepper-producing west coast away from Acehnese domination in the 1660s, Dutch traders ceased to visit Aceh, and allowed it to become the most important independent port on the eastern side of the Bay of Bengal.

Aceh's pepper production, first in the 16th and 17th centuries, and again in the period 1800–70 when the sultanate provided about half the world supply, gave it strong trade links to Turkey, India, England, the United States, France and Italy, all of which were appealed to diplomatically at some time. From about 1850 trade was reorganized through entrepots on the regular steamer route, so that Penang became for Aceh "the gateway to the world; yes, the world itself", according to Snouck Hurgronje. "Exclusively on the experience of Acehnese in Penang rests the general conviction in Aceh that the rule of the English would be infinitely preferable to ours."[5]

If economic or cultural logic had had their way, Aceh would have been drawn loosely into the British-influenced world centred on the Straits Settlements entrepots, perhaps as a protectorate somewhat like Brunei or Johor. But the logic of maps prevailed in Europe, where the Malacca Strait was seen as a natural boundary, despite its long role as a crossroads. In 1824 Sumatra as a whole was declared a Dutch responsibility by the colonial powers, which changed nothing in Aceh at the time, but drastically changed its destiny. When the Dutch eventually invaded Aceh in 1873, they had none of the historical leverage that derived from centuries of commercial contacts virtually everywhere else in the Archipelago. They rushed into a bungled invasion in a context of their own ignorance about Aceh and the hostility of the Penang merchants who knew it better. They were then forced to continue on an uncharacteristically militaristic course by the humiliation of that first expedition. Acehnese were dragged kicking and screaming into the Batavia-centred polity, in marked contrast to the rest of the Archipelago.

In addition, the pre-colonial Acehnese state, remembered in the graves near the palace site, the lineage of favourite rulers represented in the nine-fold seal of sovereignty (*cap sikureueng*), and a host of remembered tales and written verse epics, was uniquely central to Acehnese identity. I argued in Chapter 3 above that in Indonesian history "the state has always been essentially coastal and sustained by

Aceh and Indonesia   339

foreign resources". Most of Indonesia's ethnic identities, such as Javanese, Sundanese, Balinese, Minangkabau and Batak, were formed and sustained at a high cultural level by factors which had little to do with states in the modern bureaucratic and legal sense. But Aceh, as we saw above, was formed by the conquests of the 16th-century sultanate, and sustained by the way in which this sultanate resisted foreign domination. Aceh is alone (in competition with Batavia/Jakarta) as an identity fashioned by a coastal state over four centuries, the memory of which was still vigorous in the 20th century. If other Indonesians experienced the modern concept of state essentially through Netherlands India, for Acehnese it was the Dutch/Indonesian state that would appear the more remote and artificial, having only a century of heavily contested occupancy of the territory.

Acehnese pride in this distinct past took shape in the extremely bitter resistance to the Dutch of 1873–1914, the last part of which was focused in the Gayo area, ethnically distinct but sufficiently associated with the sultanate to resist heroically in its name. In total about 100,000 people died through war and attendant disruption on the Acehnese side, as against about 16,000 on the Dutch side.[6] Even at the most peaceful moment of the Dutch occupation during the 1930s, the Dutch Governor could warn that every Acehnese nourished "a fanatical love of freedom, reinforced by a powerful sense of race, with a consequent contempt for foreigners and hatred for the infidel intruder", so that a constant display of superior force was the only thing which kept Dutch rule intact there.[7] In response to these arguments for constant vigilance, about 4,000 troops spread around Aceh continued to give it the feel of an occupied province until almost the end of the Dutch regime.

The imposition of the hated corvée system requiring 24 days a year of labour on the conqueror's road-building schemes was a constant reminder of Acehnese defeat, and drove many into exile in Malaya. Dutch soldiers and residents had to be constantly on their guard against suicidal individual attacks by Acehnese who had decided to end their lives in trying to kill an infidel. After the war was officially over, there were still 7.5 of these attempts at what the Dutch called "Aceh-murders" (*Atjeh-moord*), on average every year in the 1910s,

Figure 16 Turkish and Portuguese guns which had guarded the Aceh citadel for centuries, being brought to the riverbank by the convict labourers who accompanied the second Dutch expedition in 1874, to be shipped in triumph to Holland

five a year in the 1920s, and 3.5 in the 1930s.[8] No doubt one factor was the popularity of the verse epic of the holy war (*Hikayat Perang Sabil*) which had been written and circulated during the anti-Dutch struggle, but even when subject to draconian Dutch bans continued to inspire suicidal heroism with a seductive vision of paradise.[9]

Rebellions were a constant theme, at least every decade under the Dutch. Southernmost Aceh returned to a state of full-scale guerrilla war in the mid-1920s, with 21 Dutch soldiers and 119 Acehnese rebels being killed in the most serious incident in 1926. Once a Japanese invasion became imminent, in early 1942, the rebellion described in Chapter 12 forced the Dutch to abandon Aceh. Although

Aceh and Indonesia

the insurgent Acehnese then welcomed the Japanese, by 1944 Acehnese pride reasserted itself in another rebellion at Bayu (Lhokseumawe), which cost the lives of 18 Japanese soldiers and over a hundred Islamic rebels. Despite this resistance, hundreds of Japanese diehards, who refused to accept the Emperor's surrender in 1945, chose Aceh to make a stand as the Southeast Asian place most certain to resist the return of Allied control.[10] After the "social revolution" described in the previous chapter eliminated the whole aristocratic/bureaucratic class from power, Aceh was sufficiently stable under the new *ulama* leadership and the Dutch saw no chance of getting any foothold there as they did in all other provinces in 1947 offensives.

Teungku Daud Beureu'eh, the PUSA leader who surged to power through the "social revolution", and became military governor of Aceh in 1948–50, led a rebellion against Jakarta's control in 1953–62 on the twin grounds of protesting Aceh's absorption into the Province of North Sumatra, and the failure of the Republic to implement Islamic law. The rebellion inspired by the then little-known Hasan Muhammad di Tiro began with his declaration of independence in 1976. The 20th century, in other words, when Indonesia was basically created out of a sprawling archipelago of many peoples, offered only a few short periods when Aceh was not disturbed by rebellion against Jakarta.

The specific idea of an Acehnese state was never far from the minds of those opposing the Jakarta *status quo*. Until his submission to the Dutch in 1903, the "pretender sultan", Tuanku Muhammad Daud, had been at the heart of resistance for 40 years. In 1938–40 the groups most dissatisfied with the power of the *uleëbalang* aristocracy in Aceh, notably including many reformist *ulama*, rallied behind the idea of a restored sultanate.[11] During the anti-Dutch revolution of 1945–9 Aceh was a model of resistance to all ideas emanating from the Dutch, including federalism, though in practice it was Acehnese who were fully in charge of Aceh. In 1953 Daud Beureu'eh's rebellion was for an Islamic State, not an independent Aceh, since he believed that was what Acehnese had fought so hard for during the revolution. Nevertheless two years later a separate *Negara Bahagian Aceh* (Aceh federal state) was established by the rebels through the Batee Kureng Declaration of 23 September 1955, under a powerful

Figure 17 The surrender of the young Sultan Muhammad Daud to Colonel van Heutsz and Captain H. Colijn, January 1903, in the "pendopo" of the Aceh Governors

Source: Paul Van't Veer, *De Atjeh-oorlog* (Amsterdam: Abeiderspers, 1969).

Aceh and Indonesia

Wali Negara (head of state — Daud Beureu'eh), a Prime Minister and a Cabinet.[12]

Acehnese Shifts of Perception

For four centuries Acehnese thought of themselves as belonging to an independent polity that competed with some comparable states like Siam and Johor, and sought to dominate others in Sumatra or the Peninsula. In a world pre-dating the 20th century dogma of equal sovereign states, they were aware of more powerful polities (all considered *negeri*, like Aceh) to which they might usefully subordinate themselves. Like many Southeast Asian states in the 15th century, Aceh's predecessor of Pasai had frequently sent "tribute" to China, and Aceh itself sent a kind of "tribute" to Turkey in the 1560s. But Aceh did differ from all other polities in the Indonesian archipelago in being outside the ambitions of the Dutch in Batavia to become the sole option as suzerain.

Hence there was no perceived difficulty in the 19th century in signing a treaty of mutual defence with the British in 1819, or in appealing to it after the Dutch attack of 1873 in a letter to the Governor of the Straits Settlements —

> for from our late ancestor's time to ours, we have never been friendly to the Dutch Government, and have always kept up connection with the English Government, neither do we like the Dutch at all. If our friend were to rule us in any way we should prefer it ten times as much, for we have been accustomed to it, from long time.[13]

A little earlier in 1868, with no sense of contradiction, a number of prominent Acehnese sent an envoy to Istanbul to ask the Ottoman Sultan "to inform all foreign peoples that we are under the protection of and subjects of the Sublime Porte, so that henceforth no other Government will be permitted to interfere in our affairs".[14] Nor was there a problem for the sultanate formally to propose a mutual defence treaty with the United States in 1873, once it became clear that the British were not going to fulfill their treaty obligations to ward off

344 An Indonesian Frontier

the Dutch. The point was that in the 19th century Aceh saw itself more as the way Burma, Vietnam or Siam did, as a traditionally independent state with multiple options for alliances, than the way the princelings around the Java Sea did in being more or less stuck with the Dutch.

As the war with the Dutch proceeded, however, leadership of the resistance passed increasingly to the most intransigent *ulama*, for whom the idiom of Islamic martyrdom was the ingredient needed to inspire courage in the face of overwhelming odds. While their war was still being fought for Aceh, not a notional Indonesia nor a Dar ul-Islam, the motive to fight now came primarily from faith in God. As Syech Saman di Tiro wrote to his less heroic fellow-countrymen in 1885:

> Do not let yourself be afraid of the strength of the kafirs, their fine possessions, their equipment, and their good soldiers... for no one is strong, no-one is rich, and no-one has fine armies than the great God (be he exalted), and no-one dispenses profit and loss than God (be he praised and exalted), and no-one gives victory or defeat than God (be he praised and exalted), the Lord of the Universe.[15]

In response to overtures from the Dutch Governor about a treaty, the same stern *ulama* appealed to him to convert to Islam, as dozens of the Europeans in his army had already done, before it was too late. "As soon as you accept Islam by pronouncing the two articles of faith, then we can conclude a treaty." Then the governor would not have to face humiliation on the battlefield and eternal punishment in Hell, but instead have access to paradise with "whatever the heart desires in the way of food, drink, fruit or women.... Why do you not consider how you will be defeated in this world and the next; how the punishment of God the Exalted awaits you in this world and the next?"[16]

Of course God did not deliver the kind of victory Teungku di Tiro expected, and a later generation had to sullenly accept the reality of Dutch rule. In the 1920s and 1930s, new grounds emerged for a restoration of Acehnese pride. The first important medium for Acehnese (and many others) to move from an Aceh or broadly Islamic

Aceh and Indonesia 345

identity to something like an Indonesian one was Sarekat Islam, which spread around the Archipelago very quickly in 1919–22. As one activist taught in a small town on the north coast, "Formerly we became *muslimin* carrying a rifle, but now that is no longer necessary, now unity (*sepakat*) is enough.... From here as far as Java unity has been achieved among the descendents of Islam."[17]

A few years later Sarekat Islam was in decline, but had planted the seed of a new belief in progress which finally convinced Acehnese of the benefits of schooling. By 1935 there were 33,500 Acehnese children attending government primary schools, a rate of participation slightly higher than Java or East Sumatra,[18] as well as a much higher participation rate in traditional Islamic schools. The novel idea began to spread among the younger generation of a nationalism centred on Indonesia rather than Aceh. One journalist pleaded in an Aceh newspaper in 1930 that Acehnese must be conscious of their nationality in this world, for "nationality (*kebangsaan*) will be a big factor also in the afterlife.... After the death of the spirit of Islam, it can return to become healthy and fertile again with the help of national feeling.... There is no other way to raise people who have become the tools of others, and who scarcely regard themselves as human any more."[19]

The high point of this trend towards identifying Indonesian nationalism as the appropriate vehicle for the historic anti-Dutch struggle of Aceh came at the end of 1945. At that point a new generation of Acehnese educated chiefly in reformist Islamic schools, and influenced by the desperate tone of Japanese propaganda at the end of the war, persuaded their reformist Muslim teachers to rally behind the new Republic.[20] In a declaration dated 15 October 1945, four prominent leaders of reformist organizations "in the name of the *ulamas* of all Aceh", declared that:

> Every segment of the population has united in obedience, to stand behind the great leader Ir Soekarno, to await whatever commands or obligations are put before them. It is our firm conviction that this struggle is a sacred struggle which is called a *Perang Sabil*. Believe therefore, fellow-countrymen, that this struggle is like a continuation of the former struggle

in Aceh which was led by the late Teungku Chik di Tiro and other national heroes.[21]

Even more full-blooded versions of this identification of Aceh's past with that of Indonesia came from the new generation of reformist Islam-educated and Japanese-influenced youth. Ali Hasjmy's passionate poems of devotion to Sukarno were one example of the genre. Another was that of a treatise on Aceh history by a 23-year-old Acehnese:

> As it was in the past, Aceh is an indivisible part of the Negara Republic Indonesia, so also its history too is one undivided part of Indonesian history, and our slogan is one nation, one language and one fatherland [the sumpah pemuda of 1928 — "satu bangsa, satu bahasa, dan satu tanah air"].

This young man, none other than Hasan Muhammad Tiro, later prophet of Acehnese independence, typed out what he claimed to be the first history of the Aceh war in "our language", Indonesian, as a contribution to fashioning "one history for one Indonesian nation".[22] Of all the youngsters fired up by the nationalist spirit of the times he was the most historically-inclined, perhaps because (as he would claim much later), an old man had come to remind him when he was a 12-year-old schoolboy, "never to forget your heritage" — that is the Tiro family of ferociously anti-Dutch *ulama*.[23] His adolescent work, written in Jogja where he had moved to continue his education after participating vigorously in the first phase of the revolution in Aceh, drew on the Dutch literature on Aceh of the 1930s. Written on the assumption that the war against Aceh had been won, these popular books by the right-wing journalist H.C. Zentgraaff, and the Military police captain H.J. Schmidt, had begun to romanticize the conflict a little, and to acknowledge the heroism of the Acehnese side as well as the Dutch.[24] The bulk of the monograph was a recitation from these books of the later stages of the war when resistance was inspired by the Tiro family, though already he took pleasure in the status of independent Aceh exchanging ambassadors with the world powers in the 19th century.[25]

Hasan Tiro's History-based Nationalism

This of course was romanticized Acehnese history in the service of Indonesian nationalism. How did Hasan Tiro get from there to his clarion call for an independent future to match an independent past?

Having moved from Aceh to the heart of the Indonesian Republic in 1946, Hasan Tiro came back to Aceh at the end of 1948 on the staff of the Deputy Prime Minister Sjafruddin Prawiranegara, who led the Emergency Government of Indonesia from Aceh in the first half of 1949. In 1950 Tiro returned to his studies in Jogjakarta, from where he obtained some kind of scholarship to the US.[26] He based himself in New York, working part-time at the Indonesian mission to the UN, presumably on the recommendation of Sjafruddin. There he grew more critical of the Jakarta leadership, sympathized with the grievances of Aceh, and formed a link with American politicians and CIA operatives interested in promoting anti-communist Indonesian leaders. When Daud Beureu'eh broke with Jakarta in 1953 and the Government followed with stern repression, Tiro issued an "ultimatum" to Jakarta to stop its "genocide" against the rebels, or he would open an office of the Republic Islam Indonesia at the UN. When Indonesia withdrew his diplomatic passport and demanded that the US expel him, Tiro was able to remain and flourish in New York with the help of his US friends.[27] Very likely these also helped him to publish the only one of his books that was properly printed and circulated, *Demokrasi untuk Indonesia* (1958), a polemic for a less centralized Indonesia.[28]

Hasan Tiro (like the revered leader of the rebellion, Daud Beureu'eh, one of whose chief lieutenants was Tiro's elder brother Zainal Abidin) had broken with the Jakarta Government, but not yet with the idea of Aceh as part of a reformed Indonesia. Yet even as Daud Beureu'eh made his peace with the Government in 1961, and as that Sukarno Government itself was overthrown by the anti-communist military in 1965–6, Hasan Tiro was drawn by his historical muse into a stand of complete independence. There was of course another factor. Huge quantities of natural gas were found in Aron, near Lhokseumawee, in 1971, and during the next six years the largest natural gas refinery in the world was built by Mobil near the site.

348   An Indonesian Frontier

Hasan Tiro had already become a successful international businessman, and certainly knew of this and may have been influenced by expectations of riches awaiting both his country and himself personally. But one should listen carefully to what aspiring leaders themselves say they are about. What Hasan Tiro wrote was all about history and hubris, and very little about gas.

Tiro's historical talks or papers in this period gradually moved him towards his support for an Aceh destined for independence by history.[29] Tiro was clearly excited by the research he had done on the *New York Times* of 1873 in the New York Public Library, and I fear perhaps by my 1969 book.[30] He later described the lecture he gave for the anniversary of the defeat of the first Dutch expedition in April 1973.

> For several generations the Achehnese[31] had forgotten this glorious day altogether, as if erased from their memories. What a shame it was. They did not even know anything about it anymore until I celebrated it for the first time in many generations, in New York, in 1973. My speech ... was meant to be a clarion call for the Achehnese to rise again to honor their dead heroes and to take their place again among the free sovereign peoples of the world.[32]

From this point Hasan Tiro himself was moving in the direction of casting himself as the prophet of a reborn and independent Aceh state. In 1976 he launched his campaign for independence in an extraordinarily Nietzschean spirit. His *Unfinished Diary* disarmingly records how he was swept off his feet by discovering Nietzsche's *Thus Spake Zarathustra* a few days before departing for Aceh. He quotes at length the chapter on "The Wanderer", about the loneliness of greatness, with its repeated litany, "You are going your way to greatness." The passage he quotes ends, "You I advise not to work but to fight. You I advise not to peace, but to victory. Let your work be fight, let your peace be victory."[33]

When he reached Aceh surreptitiously on 30 October 1976, Tiro set about his self-appointed task of preaching his view of history to influential figures. "The way to our national salvation is the recreation of Acehnese historical consciousness. I have written enough books on the subject. What I have to do now is to make our people study those

Aceh and Indonesia 349

books." He claims to have reprinted all his New York writings in the jungle and that this approach "succeeds like wild fire". It is never clear whether these were translated from English into Acehnese or Indonesian; if so copies have not come to light. On 4 December he organized a reading of the "Declaration of Independence of Acheh Sumatra", a wordy reiteration of his historical ideas that became the official charter of GAM.

> Our fatherland, Acheh, Sumatra, had always been a free and sovereign state since the world begun.... However, when, after World War II, the Dutch East Indies was supposed to have been liquidated ... our fatherland, Acheh, was not returned to us. Instead, our fatherland was turned over by the Dutch to the Javanese — their ex-mercenaries — by hasty fiat of colonial powers. The Javanese are alien and foreign people to us Achehnese Sumatrans.... 'Indonesia' was a fraud: a cloak to cover up Javanese colonialism.[34]

In addition to emphasizing the "thousand year old flag" of Aceh, Tiro issued a new calendar. Far from starting history anew like the French revolution, it marked ten holidays during the year designed to remind Acehnese of their heroes — from Sultan Iskandar Muda (d.1636) to the battles of 1910–1.[35] Tiro constantly preached this message, that the most important issue was not arms and supplies for the struggle, but

> the problem of the crisis of national identity, the problem of the study of Achehnese history.... Our true history has been subverted. When a people have forgotten their history, it is the same like a man who has lost his memory, he did not know anymore who he was and what was his name.... I cannot remember anymore how many thousand times I have had to repeat these explanations![36]

The most extraordinary of these historical outpourings was the *Drama of Achehnese History* he composed in the jungle. As his then "Minister of Education" explained in a preface, this theatrical piece, was written in spare times, in between battles, and when taking rests between inspection tours to various parts of the country.... Usually ... the only thing we heard was the sound of the Tengku's typewriter clicking which did not stop during daylight hours from 7 o'clock in the morning until 6 o'clock in the evening. We cannot use the lamp at night.

It has become a fixed tradition for the Tengku's guards that when they arrived at a new place, the first thing they did was to cut trees and to make clearing in the forest ground to establish a table and a bench for the Tengku to sit and write.

It was an extraordinary expression of Tiro's private and public passions, with a series of scenes from his version of Aceh history, each set to a piece of European classical music, since, as his off-sider claimed, Tiro "memorizes by heart major compositions of Bach, Vivaldi, Handel, Beethoven". Thus the first scene, the Dutch invasion of 1873, is set to a Brandenberg Concerto, and the last, Hasan Tiro's declaration of independence, to Vivaldi's Concerto in A Minor.[37]

Hasan Tiro took this historical passion to eccentric lengths, not just in his exceptionally westernized tastes, but in the grandiloquence with which he associated himself with the Tiro resistance leaders, and misrepresented their role to be something like that of earlier sultans, in order to allow himself to claim to embody Aceh's monarchy. After his brief period in the jungles of Aceh in 1976–9, Tiro did not return but led the independence movement from the security of Sweden. Nevertheless the simple idea he planted, that the Indonesian experience has demeaned rather than fulfilled Aceh's historical role, spread like wildfire after 1998. It seems extremely unlikely that this will evaporate, whatever the external conditions.

Transformation since 1998

After the fall of Suharto in May 1998, the atmosphere of freedom led rapidly to a situation where radical change was possible. The new President Habibie ended the military-ruled status of Aceh on 7 August 1998 and some troops were very publicly withdrawn. But far more important was his freeing of the press, which could for the

Aceh and Indonesia

first time report military actions present and past. Numerous NGOs formed in Aceh to demand restitution for the atrocities committed by the military against civilians during the campaigns against the independence movement. Publicity about these atrocities began to flood the increasingly free press.

The shift in Aceh elite opinion began to be evident in February 1999, as a campaign began for a referendum on independence (Habibie having already agreed to a referendum on East Timor). The student-led campaign obtained enough support from *ulama* and established political figures to mobilize hundreds of thousands of people (two million were implausibly claimed) at a mass rally in Banda Aceh on 8 November 1999. For the next two years the Aceh Independence Movement (GAM = *Gerakan Aceh Merdeka*) looked more and more like a government in waiting, its statements appearing regularly in the local press. Although the guerrilla forces of GAM only operated in half of Aceh's districts (primarily along the northern coast), plantations, shops and offices in a much wider area paid their contribution to its treasury, including even some government offices in the provincial capital.[38]

During the Presidencies of Habibie and Abdurrahman Wahid, covering 1998–2001, the military was officially limited to defensive actions, including self-defeating punishment of villages where attacks on the military took place. In the first half of 2000 there was an escalation of attacks by GAM, including on Aceh's second city (and natural gas headquarters) of Lhokseumawe and the Mobil/Exxon airport there. Those elements of the military in Aceh most unhappy with the internationally-negotiated initiatives towards peace, and with proposed trials of human rights violators, could only respond with anonymous assassinations, of which the most prominent victim on 16 September 2000 was Dr Safwan Idris, Rector of the Islamic University and locally popular candidate as the next Aceh Governor.

The unprecedented openness of the Abdurrahman Wahid Government created ideal conditions for the Red Cross Centre for Humanitarian Dialogue (HDC) to initiate quiet peacemaking initiatives throughout 2000 and 2001. Despite Indonesia's long-term allergy towards any form of internationalization of its conflicts, the HDC was

Figure 18 The capture of the resistance heroine Cut Nyak Dien (1848–1908) in 1905

able to broker a series of meetings from March 2000 between the Indonesian Government and representatives of GAM. The two parties agreed to a "Humanitarian Pause" in the fighting with effect from June 2000, and this spluttered on into 2001, though with limited success on the ground.

When Megawati Sukarnoputri took over the Presidency in July 2001, her warmer relations with the Indonesian military appeared to foreshadow the end of such peace negotiations. She did allow the national army (TNI) to take more offensive action against GAM in Aceh, but this in turn appeared to give her more leverage to force the military to accept the strong international pressure for negotiation. Against the odds, and despite profound disagreement between the two parties, a Cessation of Hostilities Agreement (COHA) was eventually signed in Geneva on 9 December 2002. Essentially GAM agreed to it because

Figure 19 A poster in the heart of Banda Aceh hailing the peace of 9 December 2002 between the Indonesian (RI) and the Aceh independence movement (GAM)

Source: Anthony Reid (2003).

of a promise of free and fair elections in 2004, and the Indonesian Government because the agreement accepted "as a starting point" the relatively liberal autonomy law pushed through the Indonesian Parliament, implying abandonmnent of the independence goal.

The COHA did bring relative peace to Aceh for three months, and the two sides cooperated with international facilitators in the Joint Security Commission (JSC) it established. The wide distrust and disagreement was always going to make it almost impossible for the peace to last as the deadlines approached, when GAM had to deliver on disarming, and Indonesia on implementing a fair local election (with the experience fresh in mind of having already lost one of those in East Timor). In the event the military elements bitterly opposed to the COHA managed to disrupt it before these crises were dealt with. In March and April 2003 pro-Jakarta militias controlled by the TNI attacked the JSC offices in various parts of Aceh. Since there was no protection from the army, the teams had to withdraw and the peace was in effect dead.

354   An Indonesian Frontier

Meanwhile, as the United States invaded Iraq, the TNI began mobilizing for its own "invasion" of Aceh designed to end any talk of referenda or internationalization, and at the same time to build popular support for a military solution. The invasion occurred on 19 May 2003, martial law was declared, and the negotiators for the GAM side were arrested and eventually sentenced to long prison terms for "terrorism". Far from the autonomy which had been carefully legislated for by the Indonesian Parliament, Aceh was ruled more centrally and autocratically than it had been even under Suharto.

★ ★ ★

The second half of the 20th century saw the erosion of the enthusiasm for the Indonesian idea, which had gradually developed during the first half of the century and peaked in the revolutionary period 1945–9. The events since the fall of Suharto fell out tragically for the chances of peaceful resolution, and Acehnese alienation at the time of writing appears likely to be consolidated by the heavy-handed attempts at yet another military solution. Since Aceh is now (January 2004) still closed to outside observers and press freedom drastically circumscribed, it will be a considerable time before the effects of this military crack-down are known. What seems clear is that one window of opportunity for resolving a century-long problem of Aceh's place within Indonesia has closed.

Notes

Preface
1. Barbara Watson Andaya, *To Live as Brothers: Southeast Sumatra in the seventeenth and eighteenth centuries* (Honolulu: University of Hawaii Press, 1993); Mary Somers Heidhues, *Bangka Tin and Mentok Pepper: Chinese Settlement on an Indonesian Island* (Singapore: Institute of Southeast Asian Studies, 1992); Jane Drakard, *A Kingdom of Words: Language and Power in Sumatera* (Kuala Lumpur: Oxford University Press, 1999); J.S. Kahn, *Constituting the Minangkabau: Peasants, Culture and Modernity in Colonial Indonesia* (Providence: Berg, 1993); Daniel Perret, *La Formation d'un Paysage Ethnique: Batak et Malais de Sumatra Nord-Est* (Paris: EFEO, 1995); Rita Smith Kipp, *The Early Years of a Dutch Colonial Mission: The Karo Field* (Ann Arbor: University of Michigan Press, 1990) and *Dissociated Identities: Ethnicity, Religion and Class in an Indonesian Society* (Ann Arbor: University of Michigan Press, 1993); John R. Bowen, *Sumatran Politics and Poetics: Gayo History, 1900–1989* (New Haven: Yale University Press, 1993); Lee Kam Hing, *The Sultanate of Aceh: Relations with the British 1760–1824* (Kuala Lumpur: OUP, 1995); Jorge Manuel dos Santos Alves, *O Domínio do norte de Samatra: A história dos sultanatos de Samudra-Pacém e de Achém, e das suas relações com os Portugueses (1500–1800)* (Lisbon: Sociedade Histórica da Independência de Portugal, 1999); Timothy Barnard, *Multiple Centres of Authority: Society and Environment in Siak and Eastern Sumatra, 1674–1827* (Leiden: KITLV Press, 2003).

Chapter 2
1. William Marsden, *The History of Sumatra* (London, 1783; Third revised ed. London, 1811; reprinted Kuala Lumpur: OUP, 1966); A. Eschels-Kroon, *Beschreibung der Insel Sumatra* (Hamburg, 1781); J.C.M. Radermacher, "Beschrijving van het Eiland Sumatra in zo verre het zelve tot nog toe bekend is" (Batavia: *VBG* 3, 1781).
2. C. Lekkerkerker, *Land en Volk van Sumatra* (Leiden: Brill, 1916); O.J.A. Collet, *Terres et Peuples de Sumatra* (Amsterdam: Société d'édition

356   Notes to pp. 24–31

"Elsevier", 1925); Edwin M. Loeb, *Sumatra. Its History and People* (Vienna: Institut für Völkerkunde der Universität Wien, 1935).

3. Cf. R. Roolvink, *Bahasa Jawi: De Taal van Sumatra* (Leiden: Universitaire Pers, 1975).

4. Anthony Reid & David Marr, ed., *Perceptions of the Past in Southeast Asia* (Singapore: Heinemann for Asian Studies Association of Australia, 1979), pp. 171–85, 287.

5. The best recent treatment of these issues is Jane Drakard, *A Kingdom of Words: Language and Power in Sumatera* (Kuala Lumpur: OUP, 1999), pp. 16–24. Andalas and Bukit Siguntang occur in "Sejarah Melayu" or "Malay Annals". "A translation of Raffles MS 18", trans. C.C. Brown, *JMBRAS* 25, 2 & 3. Andalas occurs as an interior kingdom in Tomé Pires, *The Suma Oriental of Tomé Pires* (trans. A. Cortesao), 2 vols. (London: Hakluyt Society, 1944), pp. 136, 155, 159–60. For Pulo Percha see A.H. Hill, "Hikayat Raja-Raja Pasai", *JMBRAS* 33, 2 (1961): 103, 170–1; Marsden, *The History of Sumatra* (1811), p. 339n.

6. John Crawfurd, *A Descriptive Dictionary of the Indian Islands and Adjacent Countries* (London: Bradbury & Evans, 1856), p. 413.

7. F.X.J.H. Brau de St. Pol Lias, *La côte du poivre* (Paris, 1891), pp. 74–5.

8. N.J. Krom, "De naam Sumatra", *BKI* 100 (1941): 22–5.

9. Drakard, *A Kingdom of Words*, pp. 122–5, 184–99; J. Kathirithamby-Wells, "Ahmad Shah ibn Iskandar and the late seventeenth century 'Holy War' in Indonesia", *JMBRAS* 43 (1970): 48–63; Marsden, *The History of Sumatra*, p. 337.

10. Leonard Y. Andaya, *The Kingdom of Johor 1641–1728* (Kuala Lumpur: OUP, 1975), pp. 250–314; Drakard, *A Kingdom of Words*, pp. 197–200.

11. Marsden, *The History of Sumatra*, pp. 376–7.

12. I owe this point to Christine Dobbin.

13. Batara Sangti, *Sejarah Batak* (Medan, 1977), pp. 24–6.

14. Masri Singarimbun, *Kinship, Descent and Alliance among the Karo Batak* (Berkeley: University of California Press, 1975), p. 6; also Anthony Reid, *The Contest for North Sumatra: Atjeh, the Netherlands, and Britain, 1868–1898* (Kuala Lumpur: OUP, 1969), p. 153.

15. Cited Reid, *The Contest for North Sumatra*, p. 269.

16. See Chapter 7.

17. Reid, *The Contest for North Sumatra*, pp. 198–201.

18. JSB, *Gedenknummer Jong Sumatranen Bond 1917–1922* (Batavia, 1922), p. 19.

Notes to pp. 31–40

19. Lance Castles, "The Political Life of a Sumatran Residency: Tapanuli 1915–1940", Unpublished PhD Thesis (Yale University, 1972), p. 175.
20. *Overzicht van de Inlandsche en Maleisch-Chineesche Pers (IPO)* (Weltevreden: Bureau voor de Volkslectuur, 1921), pp. 528–32, 568–71.
21. Ibid., 1922, II, pp. 42–4; Taufik Abdullah, *School and Politics: The Kaum Muda movement in West Sumatra (1927–1933)* (Ithaca: Cornell Modern Indonesia Project, 1971), p. 31.
22. S. van der Harst, *Overzicht van de Bestuurshervorming in de Buitengewesten van Nederlandsch-Indie, in het bijzonder op Sumatra* (Utrecht: A. Oosthoek, 1945), pp. 46–8.
23. Ibid., pp. 70–2.
24. See Chapter 13.
25. Ibid.
26. Amir, cited in Chapter 13.
27. Weekly Intelligence Summary (WIS) No. 13, Public Record Office (London), WO172/9893, 1946.
28. Anthony Reid, *The Blood of the People: Revolution and the End of Traditional Rule in Northern Sumatra* (Kuala Lumpur: OUP, 1979), p. 244.
29. Michael Van Langenberg, "National Revolution in North Sumatra: Sumatra Timur and Tapanuli, 1942–1950", Unpublished PhD Thesis (Sydney University, 1976), pp. 569, 667–8.
30. Republik Indonesia, *Propinsi Sumatera Utara* (Jakarta: Kementerian Penerangan, 1953), pp. 183–4. The movement of the North Sumatra capital to Medan after the Republican Victory in 1950 was one of the triggers for the conflict described in Chapter 14.
31. Idenberg, "Memorandum van directeur-generaal algemene zaken aan Lt. gouverneur-generaal (Van Mook), 27-ii-1947", in *Officiele Bescheiden Betreffende de Nederlands-Indonesische Betrekkingen 1945–1950*, ed. S.L. van der Wal ('s-Gravenhage: Martinus Nijhoff, 1978), vol. 7, 27 Feb. 1947.
32. Ibid., p. 577.
33. Ibid., p. 582.
34. Ibid., p. 584.
35. Van Langenberg, "National Revolution in North Sumatra", pp. 765–76.
36. Cited Republik Indonesia, *Propinsi Sumatera Utara*, p. 296.
37. Ibid., pp. 322–4.
38. Van Langenberg, "National Revolution in North Sumatra", p. 500.
39. See, for example, Koanda Sumatera, *Almanak Sumatera 1969* (Medan: Komando Antar Daerah, 1969) and Dada Meuraxa, *Sejarah Kebudayaan Sumatera* (Medan: Hasmar, 1974).

358   Notes to pp. 41–4

Chapter 3

1. Fernand Braudel, *The Mediterranean and the Mediterranean world in the age of Philip II*, trans. Sian Reynolds (New York: Harper and Row, 1972), I, p. 29.
2. Peter Bellwood, *Prehistory of the Indo-Malaysian archipelago* (Sydney: Academic Press, 1985), pp. 102–15.
3. R.H. Barnes, *Kédang; A Study of the collective thought of an eastern Indonesian people* (Oxford: Clarendon Press, 1974), pp. 28–37; F. Lebar, ed., *Ethnic groups of insular Southeast Asia. Vol. 1: Indonesia, Andaman Islands, and Madagascar* (New Haven: Human Relations Area Files, 1972), p. 126; Helen and Anthony Reid, *South Sulawesi* (Berkeley: Periplus, 1988), p. 84; Joost Coté, "The colonisation and schooling of the To Pamona of Central Sulawesi, 1895–1925", MA thesis (Monash University, Melbourne).
4. The immigration process goes on. The 1991 census of Sabah reported 139,403 Malaysian citizens of Indonesian origin, and 425,175 non-Malaysian citizens in Sabah, of whom I estimate 70% to be Indonesians, with most of the remainder Filipino. A quarter of Sabah's population were therefore recent arrivals, and these formed the majority in the eastern lowlands. *General Report of the Population Census, 1991* (Kuala Lumpur: Department of Statistics, 1995).
5. Lebar, ed., *Ethnic groups of insular Southeast Asia*, pp. 180–1; B. Sandin, *The Sea Dayaks of Borneo before White Rajah rule* (London: Macmillan, 1967), pp. 1–2.
6. Lebar, ed., *Ethnic groups of insular Southeast Asia*, p. 159; V.T. King, *The peoples of Borneo* (Oxford: Blackwell, 1993), pp. 47–8, 100–2, 116–7, 265.
7. Cited Lebar, ed., *Ethnic groups of insular Southeast Asia*, pp. 168–9.
8. B. Topin, "The origin of the Kadazan/Dusun; Popular theories and legendary tales", in *Pesta Kaamatan Peringkat Negeri* (Kota Kinabalu: Kadazandusun Cultural Centre, 1993), pp. 42–4; I.H.N. Evans, *The religion of the Tempasuk Desuns of North Borneo* (Cambridge: Cambridge University Press, 1953), pp. 187–8.
9. C. Bock, *The headhunters of Borneo; A narrative of travel up the Mahakkam and down the Barito [...]* (London: Sampson Low, Marston, Searle and Rivington, 1881), p. 234; H.J. Schophuys, *Het stroomgebied van de Barito, Landbouwkundige kenschets en land-bouwvoorlichting* (Wageningen Veenman, PhD thesis, Landbouwuniversiteit Wageningen, 1936), pp. 84–126.
10. L.M. Potter, "Banjarese in and beyond Hulu Sungai, South Kalimantan: A study of cultural independence, economic opportunity and mobility",

Notes to pp. 44–6

in J.T. Lindblad, ed., *New challenges in the modern economic history of Indonesia; Proceedings of the first conference on Indonesia's modern economic history* (Leiden, Programme of Indonesian Studies, 1993), pp. 270–9.

11. D. Henley, "Population and environment in precolonial northern Sulawesi". Paper presented at the 13th Biennial Conference of the Asian Studies Association of Australia (Perth, 13–16 July 1994), and personal communication.

12. C. Pelras, "Célèbes-sud avant l'Islam, selon les premiers temoignages étrangers", *Archipel* 21 (1981): 153–84.

13. A. Reid, "The rise of Makassar", *Review of Indonesian and Malaysian Affairs* 17 (1983): 117–60; Ian Caldwell, "South Sulawesi A.D. 1300–1600; Ten Bugis Texts", PhD thesis (Australian National University, Canberra, 1988).

14. H.G. Schulte Nordholt, *The political system of the Atoni of Timor* (The Hague: Nijhoff for KITLV, Verhandelingen 60, 1971); Lebar, ed., *Ethnic groups of insular Southeast Asia*, p. 103.

15. F. de Haan, *Priangan; De Preanger-Regentschappen onder het Nederlandsch bestuur tot 1811*, Vol. 1 (Bataviaasch Genootschap van Kunsten en Wetenschappen, 1910), pp. 381–8.

16. Th.G.Th. Pigeaud, *Java in the 14th century: A study in cultural history*, Vol. IV (The Hague: Nijhoff for KITLV, Translation Series 4, 4, 1962), p. 291.

17. F.Mendes Pinto, *The travels of Mendes Pinto,* trans. Rebecca Catz (Chicago: University of Chicago Press, 1989), pp. 20–9.

18. R.W. Hefner, *The political economy of mountain Java: An interpretive history* (Berkeley: University of California Press, 1990), p. 35.

19. A. Reid, "An 'age of commerce' in Southeast Asian history?" *Modern Asian Studies* 24, 1 (1990): 1–30; A. Reid, *Southeast Asia in the age of commerce, 1450–1680.* Vol. 2: *Expansion and crisis* (New Haven/London: Yale University Press, 1993).

20. Reid, *Southeast Asia in the Age of Commerce*, vol. 2, pp. 270–303.

21. Rijklof van Goens, *De vijf gezantschapsreizen van Rijklof van goens naar het hof van Mataram, 1648–1654*, ed. H.J. de Graaf ('s-Gravenhage, Nijhoff: Werken Linschoten-Vereeniging 59, 1956), p. 225.

22. J. Hageman, "Geschied-en aardrijkskundig overzigt van Java op het einde der achttiende eeuw", *TBG* 9 (1860): 261–419; M.C. Ricklefs, "Some statistical evidence on Javanese social, economic, and demographic history in the later seventeenth and eighteenth centuries", *Modern Asian Studies* 20, 1 (1986): 1–32.

23. Hageman, "Geschied-en aardrijkskundig", p. 267.

360   Notes to pp. 46–52

24. P. Boomgaard, *Children of the colonial state: Population growth and economic development in Java, 1795–1880* (Amsterdam: Free University Press, CASA Monographs 1, 1989), p. 166.

25. P.J. Veth, *Atchin en zijne betrekkingen tot Nederland: Topographisch-historische beschrijving* (Leiden: Kolff, 1873), Map 1.

26. B. Maloney, "Grass pollen and the origins of rice agriculture in North Sumatra", *Modern Quarternary Research in Southeast Asia* 11 (1989): 135–61; P. Bellwood, *Prehistory of the Indo-Malaysian archipelago* (Sydney: Academic Press, 1985), pp. 230–1.

27. Yoneo Ishii, *Thailand: A rice-growing society* (Honolulu: University of Hawaii Press, 1975), pp. 164–91; S. Tanabe, *Ecology and practical technology: Peasant farming systems in Thailand* (Bangkok: White Lotus, 1994), pp. 23–46; Sakurai Yumio, personal communication.

28. H.R. van Heekeren, *The bronze-iron age of Indonesia* ('s-Gravenhage: Nijhoff for KITLV, Verhandelingen 22, 1958), pp. 20–1, 63–78.

29. B.W. Andaya, *To live as brothers: Southeast Sumatra in the seventeenth and eighteenth centuries* (Honolulu: University of Hawaii Press, 1993), pp. 18–9; A. Oki, "The river trade in Central and South Sumatra in the 19th century", in T. Kato, M. Lufti and N. Maeda, ed., *Environment, agriculture and society in the Malay world* (Kyoto: Centre for Southeast Asian Studies, Kyoto University, 1986), pp. 21, 24–35.

30. C. Dobbin, *Islamic revivalism in a changing peasant economy, Central Sumatra, 1784–1847* (London/Malö: Curzon, 1983), pp. 42–3.

31. J. Kathirithamby-Wells, *The British West Sumatran Presidency, 1760–1785, Problems of early colonial enterprise* (Kuala Lumpur: University of Malaya Press, 1977), pp. 116–20.

32. A. Reid, *Witnesses to Sumatra, A travellers' anthology* (Kuala Lumpur: Oxford University Press, 1995), pp. 174, 180.

33. Andaya, *To live as brothers*, p. 230.

34. Sophia Raffles, ed., *Memoir of the life and public services of Sir Thomas Stamford Raffles [...]* New Edition (London: Duncan, 2 vols., 1835), 1: 347–8.

35. Cited in Hoven, 1927, p. 13; also Andaya, *To live as brothers*, pp. 229–31.

36. Kathirithamby-Wells, *The British West Sumatran Presidency*, p. 116.

37. *Statistisch jaaroverzicht* 1927: 36. These ethnic totals must be treated with great caution since almost 2.8 million inhabitants (20%) of the Outer Islands were given as of "unknown" ethnicity. The 1930 census is more careful to tie up such ends at the expense of creating larger and vaguer groupings. The "Palembangers" category jumped to 733,000 in that census (presumably by greatly expanding the definition of the term), while there were 83,000 Besemah, 44,000 Semendo, 67,000 Serawai

Notes to pp. 52–7

and 89,000 Rejang-Lebong, but no mention of Ogan and Komering *Volkstelling 1930* (Batavia: Departement van Economische Zaken/ Landsdrukkerij, 8 vols., 1933–6), pp. 91–2.

38. *Volkstelling 1930*, VIII, pp. 91–2; Mochtar Naim, *Merantau, Pola migrasi suku Minangkabau* (Yogyakarta: Gadjah Mada University Press, 1984), p. 31.

39. Dobbin, *Islamic revivalism*, pp. 16, 43.

40. E. Graves, "The ever-victorious buffalo, How the Minangkabau of Indonesia solved their 'colonial question'", PhD thesis (University of Wisconsin, 1971), p. 24.

41. Graves, "The ever-victorious buffalo", pp. 24–5.

42. Biro Pusat Statistik, *Penduduk Indonesia, Hasil sensus penduduk* (Jakarta: Biro Pusat Statistik, 1990), p. 22.

43. Naim, *Merantau*, p. 116.

44. Biro Pusat Statistik, *Penduduk Indonesia*, pp. 67–9.

45. W. Hoeta Galoeng, *Poestaha taringot toe tarombo ni halak Batak* (Laguboti: Zendingsdrukkerij, 1926); W.K.H. Ypes, *Bijdrage tot de kennis van de stamverwantschap der inheemsche rechtsgemeenchappen en het grondrecht der Toba- en Dairibataks* (Leiden: Adatrechstichting, 1932).

46. J.C. Vergouwen, *The social organisation and customary law of the Toba-Batak of northern Sumatra* (The Hague: Nijhoff for KITLV, Translation Series 7, 1964), p. 21.

47. L. Castles, "Sources for the population history of northern Sumatra" (*Masyarakat Indonesia* 2–2, 1975), pp. 198–209.

48. C. Cunningham, *The postwar migration of the Toba Bataks to East Sumatra* (New Haven: Yale University Southeast Asia Studies, 1958), p. 11.

49. G. Sherman, *Rice, rupees and ritual. Economy and society among the Samosir Batak of Sumatra* (Stanford: Stanford University Press, 1990), p. 234.

50. G.L. Tichelman, "Bataksch arbeidsreservaat" (*Koloniaal Tijdschrift* 25, 1936) pp. 399–403; Cunningham, *The postwar migration of the Toba Bataks*, p. 82.

51. Naim, *Merantau*, p. 49; Cunningham, *The postwar migration of the Toba Bataks*, pp. 85–7.

52. Castles, "Population history of northern Sumatra", pp. 196–8.

53. M. Joustra, *Batakspiegel* (Leiden: Van Doesburgh, 1910), pp. 53, 66, 78.

54. Naim, 1977, p. 51. Boundaries, of course, affect this ranking. When Minangkabau and Minahasans descended to their local coastal port it was still within the province dominated by their ethnic group, while Toba and Mandailing Bataks moving to East Sumatra were counted (in 1930, but not thereafter) as cross-province migrants.

55. Naim, *Merantau*, p. 49.

362   Notes to pp. 58–67

56. Cunningham, *The postwar migration of the Toba Bataks*, pp. 59, 64.

57. Usman Pelly, *Urban migration and adaptation in Indonesia: A case-study of Minangkabau and Mandailing Batak migrants in Medan, North Sumatra*, PhD thesis (University of Illinois, 1983), p. 103.

58. Biro Pusat Statistik, *Indikator kesejahteraan rakyat 1993; Sumatera Utara* (Medan: Biro Pusat Statistik, 1994), p. 35.

59. Cunningham, *The postwar migration of the Toba Bataks*, p. 78.

60. G.J. Hugo, T.H. Hull, V.J. Hull and G.W. Jones, *The demographic dimension in Indonesian development* (Singapore: OUP, 1987), p. 89; Biro Pusat Statistik, *Penduduk Indonesia*.

61. Cited by Tanabe, *Ecology and practical technology*, p. 14.

62. Michael Dove, *Swidden agriculture in Indonesia: The subsistence strategies of the Kalimantan Kantu'* (Berlin: Mouton, 1985), pp. 131–56.

63. Sherman, *Rice, rupees and ritual*, p. 19.

64. P. Gourou, *The tropical world; Its social and economic condition and its future status*, trans. E.D. Laborde (London: Longmans, 1960), pp. 6–8. [First edition 1953.]

65. P.H. van der Brug, *Malaria en malaise: De VOC in Batavia in de achttiende eeuw* (Amsterdam: De Bataafsche Leeuw, 1994), pp. 82–3 [PhD thesis, Rijksuniversiteit Leiden].

66. Brug, *Malaria en malaise*, pp. 201–6.

67. Raffles, *Sir Thomas Stamford Raffles*, p. 350; Dobbin, *Islamic revivalism*, pp. 42–3.

68. M.A. Jaspan, *From patriliny to matriliny; Structural change among the Redjang of Southwest Sumatra*, PhD thesis (Australian National University, Canberra, 1964), p. 17; Sherman, *Rice, rupees and ritual*, pp. 22–3.

69. Braudel, *The Mediterranean*, pp. 1–38.

70. Jane Drakard, *A kingdom of words; Minangkabau sovereignty in Sumatran history*, PhD thesis (Australian National University, Canberra, 1993); Castles, *Population history of northern Sumatra*, 1972.

71. Kulke 1986; Wisseman 1977; Schulte Nordholt 1993; Reid 1993a.

72. W. Collins, *Basemah concepts; A study of the culture of a people of South Sumatra*, PhD thesis (University of California, 1979), pp. 90–2.

73. J.F. Warren, *The Sulu zone, 1768–1898; The dynamics of external trade, slavery, and ethnicity in the transformation of a Southeast Asian maritime state* (Singapore: Singapore University Press, 1981), p. 208.

74. Andaya, *To live as brothers*, p. 96.

75. Castles, "Population history of northern Sumatra", p. 199.

76. Rita Kipp, *Dissociated identities; Ethnicity, religion and class in an Indonesian society* (Ann Arbor: University of Michigan Press, 1993).

Notes to pp. 69–72

Chapter 4

1. *Encyclopedia of Islam III*, pp. 1174–5.
2. *The History of Sumatra*, 3rd ed. (London, 1811).
3. Ibid., pp. 338–41.
4. Siti Hawa Saleh, *Hikayat Merong Mahawangsa*, Unpublished MA Thesis (University of Malaya, 1966). Abdullah b. Haji Musa Lubis, ed., *Kesah Raja Marong Maha Wangsa* (Kuala Lumpur: Pustaka Antara, 1965). R.O. Winstedt, "The Kedah Annals", *JMBRAS* 16, 11 (1938): 31–5. C. Hooykaas, *Over Maleise Literatuur*, 2nd ed. (Leiden: E.J. Brill, 1947), pp. 91–4.
5. H.M. Zainuddin, *Tarich Aceh dan Nusantara* (Medan: Pustaka Iskandar Muda, 1961), pp. 197–8. For another reference to Gayo origins see A.H. Hill, ed., "Hikayat Raja-Raja Pasai", *JMBRAS* 33, 2 (1960): 120.
6. Ia-lah yang meng'adahan segala isti'adat kerajaan Aceh Daru's-Salam dan menyuroh utusan kapada Sultan Rum, ka-negeri Istanbul, kerana menegohkan ugama Islam. Maka di-kirim Sultan Rum daripada jenis utus dan pandai yang tahu menuang bedil. Maka pada zaman itu-lah di-tuang orang meriam yang besar2. Dan ia-lah yang pertama2 berbuat kota di-negeri Aceh Daru's-Salam, dan ia-lah yang pertama2 ghazi dengan segala kafir, hingga sendiri-nya berangkat menyerang Melaka. T. Iskandar, ed., *Bustanu's-Salatin Bab II, Fasal 13* (Kuala Lumpur: Dewan Bahasa dan Pustaka, 1966), pp. 31–2.
7. The cannon is described in K.C. Krucq, "Beschrijving der kanonnen afkomstig uit Atjeh, thans in het Koninklijk Militair Invalidenhuis Bronbeek", *TBG* 81 (1930): 545–6.
8. This has been published only in the form of a shortened Malay prose translation by T. Mohamad Sabil, entitled "Hikajat Soeltan Atjeh Marhoem (Soeltan Iskandar Moeda)" (Batavia, 1932). H.K.J. Cowan believes the Acehnese original to be a reworking of the better-known Acehnese verse epic *Hikayat Malem Dagang*, with the addition at the beginning of this Turkish incident. *De "Hikajat Malem Dagang"*, The Hague (1937), pp. 12–13.
9. Sabil, "Hikajat Soeltan Atjeh Marhoem", pp. 3–11.
10. Snouck Hurgronje, *The Achehnese*, trans. A.W.S. O'Sullivan (Leiden: E.J. Brill, 1906), pp. 208–9. Also Mohammad Said, *Atjeh Sepandjang Abad* (Medan, 1961), p. 101. The interpretation of the mission as one of tribute rather than alliance in the version of 1891 may owe something to the events of 1873, when the Acehnese attempted to portray their country as under Turkish suzerainty.
11. Saffet Bey, "Bir Osmanli Filosunun Sumatra Seferi", *Tarihi Osmani Encümeni Mecmuasi* 11 (1912): 681–3. See Appendix for this material.

364　　　　　　　　　　　　　　　　　　　　　　　Notes to pp. 72–5

12. Sultan Selim I (1512–20) seems to be meant here. He conquered Egypt in 1517 and received as a result the submission of the Hejaz. If so it must be the result of a confusion with Selim II (1566–78), under whom the contact did take place, and the Yemen was reconquered (see below, pp. 16–7). A Turkish newspaper of 1873 similarly attributed it to Selim I; see R.H. Djajadiningrat, "Critisch Overzicht van de in Maleische Werken Vervatte Gegevens over de Geschiedenis van het Soeltanaat van Atjeh", *BKI* 65 (1911): 146. Curiously, K.C. Krucq, *op. cit.*, p. 546, appears to have made the same mistake.

13. Rashid (Turkish Foreign Minister) to Musurus (Ambassador to Britain and the Netherlands), 11 Aug. 1873, in J. Woltring, ed., *Bescheiden Betreffende de Buitenlandse Politiek van Nederland, 2de Periode*, The Hague (1962), pp. 1, 612.

14. T. Iskandar, ed., "De Hikajat Atjeh", *VKI* 26 (1958): 167 (p. 239 of MS).

15. Ibid., p. 167 (p. 238 of MS).

16. Ibid., pp. 62–4 and 157–69 (pp. 215–42 of MS). Also Djajadiningrat, "Critisch Overzicht", pp. 177–8.

17. *Hikajat Hang Toeah* (2nd ed., Balai Pustaka, Batavia, 1948), II, pp. 237–87.

18. Charles Boxer, "A Note on Portuguese Reactions to the Revival of the Red Sea Spice Trade and the Rise of Atjeh, 1540–1600", *JSEAH* 10, 3 (1969): 415–28.

19. Since the original version of this article, further Ottoman sources have been discussed in Anthony Reid, *Southeast Asia in the Age of Commerce*, II (1993), pp. 146–7, and Naimur Rahman Farooqi, "Mughal-Ottoman Relations: A study of political and diplomatic relations between Mughal India and the Ottoman Empire, 1556–1748", PhD diss. (University of Wisconsin, 1986), pp. 267–8.

20. Djajadiningrat, "Critisch Overzicht", p. 152.

21. Donald Lach, *Asia and the Making of Europe*, 1, ii, p. 107. R.B. Serjeant, *The Portuguese off the South Arabian Coast, Hadrami Chronicles* (Oxford: Clarendon Press, 1963), p. 14.

22. Boxer, "A Note on Portuguese Reactions", p. 416.

23. M.A.P. Meilink-Roelofsz, *Asian Trade and European Influence in the Indonesian Archipelago between 1500 and about 1630* (The Hague: Nijhoff, 1962), p. 145.

24. Iskandar, "De Hikajat Atjeh", p. 38.

25. Iskandar, *loc. cit.*; Djajadiningrat, "Critisch Overzicht", pp. 152–3.

26. Pinto's unreliability has been demonstrated in the case of his supposed adventures in Siam and elsewhere, but not for matters in Sumatra,

Notes to pp. 75–9   365

which were of more immediate concern to his probable informers in Melaka. His account is confirmed in general terms by some other Portuguese references (MacGregor, "Johore Lama in the Sixteenth Century", p. 82) and has been consistently followed by historians of the area.

27. F. Mendes Pinto, *The travels of Mendes Pinto*, trans. Rebecca Catz (Chicago: University of Chicago Press, 1989), pp. 19–22.

28. Serjeant, *The Portuguese off the South Arabian Coast*, pp. 76–7 and 79–80. E. Denison Ross, "The Portuguese in India and Arabia 1517–1538", *JRAS* (1922): 15.

29. I.A. MacGregor, "Johore Lama in the Sixteenth Century", *JMBRAS* 28, 2: 81.

30. Hadhrami chronicle al-Sana al-Bahir, quoted Serjeant, *The Portuguese off the South Arabian Coast*, p. 97.

31. M. Longworth Dames, "The Portuguese and Turks in the Indian Ocean in the Sixteenth Century", *JRAS* (1921).

32. *Travels of Mendez Pinto*, p. 47.

33. Ibid., pp. 45–57.

34. MacGregor, "Johore Lama in the Sixteenth Century", pp. 84–5, quoting respectively Simão de Mello, 1545, and Luis Frois, S.J., 1555.

35. H.J. de Graaf, "De Regering van Panembahan Senapati Ingalaga", *VKI* 13 (1954): 33–4; P.A. Tiele, "De Europeërs in den Maleischen Archipel", *BKI* 28 (1880): 321, Meilink-Roelofsz, *Asian Trade and European Influence*, p. 149. The main source for all these references is Diogo Do Couto, *Da Asia* (Lisbon, 1786; reprinted 1974), Decada 8; Cap. XXI, pp. 130–2.

36. At Ala'ad-din al-Kahar's death in 1571, and probably for some time previously, his son Raja Mughal was established as Acehnese viceroy in Pariaman. Judging by 18th and 19th century experience, Acehnese methods of growing pepper on virgin soil began to produce diminishing returns within less than a century as a result of soil exhaustion [v. especially J. Gould, "Sumatra — America's Pepperpot, 1784–1873", *Essex Institute, Historical Collections* 122 (1956): 207–39 and 297–319]. The old centres of Pidië and Pasai, still at their peak in Tomé Pires' time, were unimportant by the end of the century. We may, therefore, suggest a shift in the centre of pepper-growing sometime in the middle decades of the 16th century with the rapid growth of the west coast plantations.

37. Von Hammer, cited in Denys Lombard, *Le Sultanat d'Acheh au temps d'Iskandar Muda* (Paris, 1967), p.37n.

38. Tiele, "De Europeërs in den Maleischen Archipel", p. 424.

366   Notes to pp. 79–86

39. Boxer, "A Note on Portuguese Reactions", p. 418; Serjeant, *The Portuguese off the South Arabian Coast*, p. 110.
40. Farooqi, "Mughal-Ottoman Relations", pp. 267–8, 289. This petition was previously only known through its being cited in the Turkish response — see Saffet Bey, "Bir Osmanli Filosunun Sumatra Seferi", *TOEM* 10 (1912): 606–8 (for which see appendix to this chapter); Reid, *Southeast Asia in the Age of Commerce*, p. 147. Farooqi first realized that the 1566 appeal labeled in Ottoman archives as being from "The Muslims of Hindistan" was in fact from the Aceh Sultan.
41. Saffet, "Bir Osmanli Filosunun Sumatra Seferi", pp. 606–9.
42. Saffet, "Bir Osmanli Filosunun Sumatra Seferi", II, p. 680.
43. Ibid., *loc. cit.*
44. Couto, *Decada 8*, cap. 21, p. 131.
45. Couto, *Decada 8*, caps. 21 and 22.
46. As assumed by Tiele, "De Europeërs in den Maleischen Archipel", p. 425; De Graaf, "De Regering van Panembahan Senapati Ingalaga", p. 69; Djajadiningrat, "Critisch Overzicht", p. 155; Meilink-Roelofsz, *Asian Trade and European Influence*, p. 149; and Boxer, "A Note on Portuguese Reactions", p. 420.
47. Letters of L. Peres, Malacca, Nov. and 2 Dec. 1566, in J. Wicki, ed., *Documenta Indica* VII (MHSI 89, Rome, 1962), pp. 33–4 and 89. Tiele, "De Europeërs in den Maleischen Archipel", pp. 425–6, doubts the validity of this story, but he has it only from a secondary Jesuit source.
48. Wicki, *Documenta Indica* VII, p. 88.
49. Letter of C. da Costa, Malacca, 6 Dec. 1868, Wicki, *Documenta Indica* VII, pp. 529–30. Also ibid., pp. 514–5 and 574–5.
50. Wicki, *Documenta Indica VIII* (MHSI 91, Rome, 1964), pp. 489–9. F.C. Danvers, *The Portuguese in India* (London: W.H. Allen, 1894), 1, pp. 551–71.
51. *The voyage of John Huyghen van Linschoten to the East Indies* (London: Hakluyt, 1885) I, p. 110. Linschoten's wonder at the size of this cannon, "hardly to be found in all Christendom", is echoed in numerous contemporary European descriptions of Turkish artillery. For the anachronistic Turkish preoccupation with size rather than efficiency in their cannon, see C.M. Cipolla, *Guns and Sails in the Early Phase* of *European Expansion* (London, 1965), pp. 93–9.
52. De Graaf, "De Regering van Panembahan Senapati Ingalaga", pp. 34–5. MacGregor, "Johore Lama in the Sixteenth Century", p. 86.
53. MacGregor, "Johore Lama in the Sixteenth Century", pp. 86–8.
54. Such relationships were known only among petty pre-Muslim states in adjacent areas, particularly in 16th-century South Celebes. See

Notes to pp. 86–92 367

G.J. Resink, *Indonesia's History between the Myths* (The Hague: W. van Hoeve, 1967), p. 201.

55. A clear example of this rivalry appears from the Turkish merchant the Dutch encountered in Bantam in 1596, who was unable to return through Aceh because the Sultan was seizing all traders who came from Bantam. J.C. van Leur, *Indonesian Trade and Society* (The Hague: W. van Hoeve, 1955), pp. 3–4.

56. Letter of De Ribera (Macau, Oct. 1568), in Wicki, *Documenta Indica* VII, p. 514.

57. W.E.D. Allen, *Problems of Turkish Power in the Sixteenth Century* (London, 1930), p. 30.

58. E.S. Creasy, *History of the Ottoman Turks* (London: R. Bentley, 1878), pp. 224–5.

59. Allen, *Problems of Turkish Power in the Sixteenth Century*, pp. 32–3. Longworth Dames, "The Portuguese and Turks in the Indian Ocean", pp. 25–8. MacGregor, "Johore Lama in the Sixteenth Century", p. 88. Iskandar, *Bustanu's-Salatin Bab II*, p. 39.

60. MacGregor, "Johore Lama in the Sixteenth Century", p. 88. Iskandar, *Bustanu's-Salatin Bab II*, p. 39.

61. Boxer, "A Note on Portuguese Reactions", pp. 427–8.

62. *The Voyages of Sir James Lancaster to Brazil and the East Indies 1591–1603* (London: Hakluyt, 1940), pp. 94–5 and 97–8. *The Voyages and Works of John Davis the Navigator* (London: Hakluyt, 1880), pp. 142–3.

63. Augustin de Beaulieu, *Mémoires d'un voyage aux Indes Orientales, 1619–1622*, ed. Denys Lombard (Paris: Maisonneuve et Larose, 1996), pp. 199–200.

64. Ibid., p. 205.

65. See especially ibid., pp. 199–213.

66. Djajadiningrat, "Critisch Overzicht", pp. 160–1.

67. *Voyages of Sir James Lancaster*, pp. 96 and 109–11.

68. Article, "Atjeh", *Encyclopedia of Islam I*, p. 743.

69. "Bir Osmanli Filosunun Sumatra Seferi", 10, pp. 604–14; 11, pp. 678–83.

70. Tuanku Daud, who resigned the Sultanate in submitting to the Dutch in 1903, and was exiled from Aceh three years later.

71. Abdur'rauf of Singkil (c.1615–93), the national saint of Aceh. He is known as Teungku Sheikh Kuala because his *keramat*, or tomb, is at the mouth of the Aceh river. This linking of his name with the Turkish expedition seems to be gratuitous. Peter G. Riddel, *Islam and the Malay Indonesian World* (Honolulu: University of Hawaii Press, 2001), pp. 125–32.

368   Notes to pp. 92–100

72. *Osmanli Tarihi* II (Ankara, 1949), pp. 388–9.
73. I.H. Danismend, *Osmanli Tarihi Kronolojisi II* (Istanbul, 1948), pp. 380–1.

Chapter 5

1. M.A.P. Meilink-Roelofsz, *Asian Trade and European Influence in the Indonesian Archipelago between 1500 and about 1630* (The Hague: Nijhoff, 1962), p. 8.
2. *The Travels of Marco Polo,* trans. R.E. Latham (London: Penguin, 1958), p. 225.
3. Nuru'd-din ar-Raniri, *Bustanu's-Salatin, Bab II, Fasal 13,* ed. T. Iskandar (Kuala Lumpur, 1966), p. 31.
4. *The Suma Oriental of Tomé Pires,* trans. Armando Cortesão (London: Hakluyt, 1944), vol. I, p. 143.
5. See Chapter 4.
6. Cited Charles Boxer, "A Note on Portuguese Reactions to the Revival of the Red Sea Spice Trade and the Rise of Atjeh, 1540–1600", *JSEAH* 10, 3 (1969): 420. Boxer speculates, pp. 427–8, that Gujaratis operating out of Aceh were responsible for most of this shipping.
7. Teuku Iskandar, ed., *De Hikajat Atjeh.* Verhandelingen van het Koninklijk Instituut (The Hague, 1958), vol. 26, pp. 54 and 96.
8. Ibid., pp. 54 and 98. The *Bustanu's-Salatin* (Iskandar, ed., p. 33), confirms the cruelty of this ruler; "Unless he saw blood he didn't want to eat".
9. Iskandar, ed., *De Hikajat Atjeh,* pp. 54–5 and 99.
10. Francois Martin, as trans. in Anthony Reid, ed., *Witnesses to Sumatra: A Travellers' Anthology* (Kuala Lumpur: OUP, 1995), p. 58.
11. *The Voyage of Best to the East Indies,* 1612–1614, ed. W. Foster (London: Hakluyt, 1934), p. 56.
12. Augustin de Beaulieu, "Mémoires du voyage aux Indes Orientales", p. 109, in Melchisedech Thévenot, *Relations de divers voyages curieux* (Paris: Cramoisy, 1664–6), where Beaulieu states he was "allowed the rank and the access of one of his principal orangkayas". Ibid., p. 73 gives an identical phrase in a letter from Iskandar Muda.
13. Beaulieu, "Mémoires du voyage aux Indes Orientales", pp. 110–1. This and succeeding quotations are my translations from the Thévenot text. This has subsequently received a new edition, Augustin de Beaulieu, *Mémoires d'un voyage aux Indes Orientales,* ed. Denys Lombard (Paris, 1996). A section (not including the passage above) is also translated in Reid, ed., *Witnesses to Sumatra,* pp. 64–81.
14. R.H. Djajadiningrat, "Critisch overzicht van de in Maleische Werken vervatte gegevens over de geschiedenis van het Soeltanaat van Atjeh",

Notes to pp. 100–4   369

BKI 65 (1911): 161–4. *Encyclopedie van Nederlandsche-Indië* (The Hague, 1917), I, p. 74. *The Voyages and Works of John Davis the Navigator*, ed. A.H. Markham (London: Hakluyt, 1880), p. 148.

15. Beaulieu, "Mémoires du voyage aux Indes Orientales", p. 111. *The Voyages of Sir James Lancaster to Brazil and the East Indies,* ed. William Foster (London: Hakluyt, 1940), pp. 96–7. Iskandar, ed., *Bustanu's-Salatin*, p. 35. C.A.O. van Nieuwenhuijze, *Samsu'l-din van Pasai* (Leiden, 1945), pp. 19–23 and 234.

16. Iskandar, ed., *De Hikajat Atjeh,* pp. 55 and 100.

17. Beaulieu, "Mémoires du voyage aux Indes Orientales", p. 112.

18. Ibid., pp. 112–3.

19. See, in particular, the confirmation by Davis, cited in Lombard, p. 196n.

20. "this King has had great good fortune and no setbacks: all his plans have succeeded; indeed he is so fortunate... that many take him for a great sorcerer. For my part I take him to be a man of great judgement, who undertakes nothing lightly or out of season....All his designs begin with measures which appear incomprehensible until they have been carried to execution...he takes advice of no one...nor discusses with them". Beaulieu, "Mémoires du voyage aux Indes Orientales", p. 114.

21. Beaulieu, "Mémoires du voyage aux Indes Orientales", p. 44. J. Kathirithamby-Wells, "Achehnese control over West Sumatra pepper up to the treaty of Painan 1663", *JSEAH* 10, 3 (1969): 460–1.

22. Beaulieu, "Mémoires du voyage aux Indes Orientales", pp. 50–77.

23. The duties of this royal guard are described in the *Adat Aceh*, most texts of which appear to be of considerably later date although attributed to Iskandar Muda. They are described as *bodoanda* in the text published by G.W.J. Drewes and P. Voorhoeve, *Adat Atjeh*, V.K.I. vol. 24 (The Hague, 1958), p. 15; and as *hamba raja* in that of K.F.H. van Langen, "De Inrichting van hat Atjehsche Staatsbestuur onder het Sultanaat", *BKI* 37 (1888): 437–8.

24. Beaulieu, "Mémoires du voyage aux Indes Orientales", p. 103.

25. Ibid., p. 106.

26. Ibid., p. 102.

27. Ibid., p. 63.

28. Ibid., p. 103.

29. *Adat Atjeh*, p. 17.

30. Beaulieu, "Mémoires du voyage aux Indes Orientales", pp. 100–2.

31. Iskandar, ed., *Bustanu's-Salatin*, pp. 37–8.

32. Beaulieu, "Mémoires du voyage aux Indes Orientales", p. 102. Lombard, pp. 74–81.

370 Notes to pp. 104–6

33. Kathirithamby-Wells, "Achehnese control over West Sumatra pepper", p.460. Harris' English translation of Beaulieu, in *Navigantium*, I, 243, states of the orangkaya, "For besides that they have no Sallary, they are obliged to make the King a rich Present every Year." This seems to be an interpolation, no such passage appearing in the French original, p. 68.

34. Kathirithamby-Wells, "Achehnese control over West Sumatra pepper", pp. 462–3.

35. Beaulieu, "Mémoires du voyage aux Indes Orientales", p. 109. The ability of the Islamic ruler to confiscate the property of deceased subjects is also noted as a barrier to the rise of countervailing centres of economic power in Mogul India and the Abbassid Caliphate v. Barrington Moore, *Social Origins of Dictatorship and Democracy* (Boston: Beacon Press, 1966), pp. 322–3; Karl Wittfogel, *Oriental Despotism. A comparative study of total power* (New Haven: Yale Paperback, 1963), p. 77.

36. Beaulieu, "Mémoires du voyage aux Indes Orientales", p. 114.

37. Thomas Bowrey, *The Countries round the Bay of Bengal,* ed. R.C. Temple (London: Hakluyt, 1903), p. 296.

38. Beaulieu, "Mémoires du voyage aux Indes Orientales", p. 62.

39. Iskandar, ed., *Bustanu's-Salatin*, pp. 44–7, 59. Bowrey, *The Countries round the Bay of Bengal*, pp. 293–310. *The Travels of Peter Mundy in Europe and Asia*, 1608–1667, ed. R.C. Temple (London: Hakluyt, 1919), 11, pp. 335–6.

40. Bowrey, *The Countries round the Bay of Bengal,* pp. 298–9, in Aceh about 1675, describes a sort of charter by which the *orangkaya* sought to prevent the regime of the Queen returning to tyranny, but this is most easily explained in the climate of the end of Taj al-Alam's reign and the installation of a second queen. There is a need for study of the significance of female rule in 17th-century Patani and 16th-century Japara, both then at the height of their commercial importance.

41. *Reisen van Nicolaus de Graaff gedaan naar alle gewesten des werelds, beginnende 1639 tot 1687 incluis* (The Hague, Linschoten vereeniging 33, 1930), p. 13. De Graaff was in Aceh during this crisis. See also Djajadiningrat, "Critisch overzicht", pp. 187–8.

42. Iskandar, ed., *Bustanu's-Salatin*, p. 59.

43. The four principal ministers of Taj al-Alam were the Kadi, the Maharaja Sri Maharaja, the Laksamana, and the Maharaja. Their rivalries reached a peak in 1651 when a movement led by the Laksamana ousted the powerful but "pro-Dutch" Maharaja Sri Maharaja. W. Ph. Coolhaas, ed., *Generale Missiven van Gouverneurs-Generaal en Raden aan Heren XVII der V.O.C.* Vol. II (The Hague: Martinus Nijhoff, 1964), pp. 461–2, 519–22, 569.

Notes to pp. 106–10 371

44. Bowrey, *The Countries round the Bay of Bengal*, pp. 285–6.
45. "Translation of the Annals of Acheen", *Journal of the Indian Archipelago and Eastern Asia* 2 (1850): 599.
46. C. Snouck Hurgronje, *The Achehnese*, trans. A.W.S. O'Sullivan (Leiden/London, 1960), I, pp. 88–90. Also Djajadiningrat, "Critisch overzicht", p. 189; *Encyclopedia van Nederlandsche-Indië* I, p. 76.
47. Van Langen, "De Inrichting van hat Atjehsche Staatsbestuur", pp. 390–2. Compare the *mukim*, the area providing at least 40 males for the Friday prayer under Shafi law, with the *jami* organization in Hanafi areas of Western Asia; Ira Lapidus, ed., *Middle Eastern Cities* (Berkeley: University of California, 1969), pp. 69–79.
48. T.J. Veltman, "Nota over de Geschiedenis van hat Landschap Pidie", *TBG* 58 (1919): 68–70.
49. Bowrey, *The Countries round the Bay of Bengal*, p. 313.
50. *The voyages of Sir James Lancaster*, p. 136. See also Beaulieu, "Mémoires du voyage aux Indes Orientales", p. 98. Bowrey, *The Countries round the Bay of Bengal*, p. 294. Lombard, p. 61, sees the insoluble problem of rice as a reason for the eventual decline of Aceh.
51. William Dampier, *Voyages and Discoveries*, ed. C. Wilkinson (London: Argonaut Press, 1931), p. 91.
52. "There are many Indians of the Coromandel coast ... Slaves to the great men and Merchants.... To these the Acheenes owe the greatest part of their husbandry in managing their crops of Paddy, or Rice, which was hardly known on this part of the Island, till these were driven here by the famine from Fort St. David, and other places on the Coromandel Coast." Charles Lockyer, *An Account of the Trade in India* (London, 1711), p. 54.
53. Snouck Hurgronje, *The Achehnese*, p. 19.
54. Dampier, *Voyages and Discoveries*, pp. 98 and 100. Lockyer, *An Account of the Trade in India*, p. 57, also mentions these "twelve Lords, who are all absolute in their precincts". The diffusion of power among the ulëëbalangs is more fully described in Chapter 6.
55. The legal code of Van Langen, "De Inrichting van hat Atjehsche Staatsbestuur", pp. 436–7, which must, despite its self-attribution to Iskandar Muda, derive from the 18th or 19th century, gives examples of the autonomous status of the *ulèëbalangs* of Aceh Besar, particularly the three Panglima Sagi. They require no letter of confirmation from the Sultan, for their rank is entirely hereditary, unlike other officials and rulers; the Panglima Sagi are entitled to 21 gun salutes.

372   Notes to pp. 112–4

Chapter 6

1. This is a revised version of a paper initially presented at a seminar held on the occasion of the Third Aceh Cultural Festival in August 1988. I am grateful to the panitia of that Festival for making the occasion possible. This paper is also indebted to the pioneering work of Dr Takeshi Ito on unpublished Dutch sources for the history of Aceh, much of which he has kindly made available to me.

2. Clifford Geertz, *Negara: The Theatre State in Nineteenth-Century Bali* (Princeton: Princeton University Press, 1980), especially pp. 102–4.

3. Guy Tachard, *A Relation of the Voyage to Siam Performed by Six Jesuits*, trans. A. Churchill (1688, reprinted Bangkok: White Orchid Press, 1981), p. 215.

4. R.B. Pemberton, "Journey from Munipoor to Ava, and from Thence across the Yooma Mountain to Arracan", 1830, ed. D.G.E. Hall, in *Journal of the Burma Research Society* 63, 2: 43–4.

5. Willem Lodewycksz, "D'eerste Boeck", 1598, in *De eerste schipvaart der Nederlanders naar Oost-Indie onder Cornelis de Houtman 1595–1597*, ed. G.P. Rouffaer & J.W. Ijzerman, Vol. I (The Hague, 1915), p. 30.

6. *Peter Floris, his Voyage to the East Indies in the "Globe", 1611–1615*, ed. W.H. Moreland (London: Hakluyt, 1934), p. 87, also pp. 62–3.

7. As a general Southeast Asian phenomenon, these processions, festivals and contests are described in Anthony Reid, *Southeast Asia in the Age of Commerce: The Lands below the Winds* (New Haven: Yale University Press, 1988), pp. 173–91.

8. C.C. Brown, ed., "Sejarah Melayu or 'Malay Annals'", a translation of Raffles MS 18, *JMBRAS* 25 (1953): 56.

9. *Peter Floris, his Voyage to the East Indies*, pp. 33–4.

10. *De tweede schipvaart der Nederlanders naar Oost-Indie onder Jacob Cornelisz van Neck en Wybrant Warwijck, 1598–1600*, ed. J. Keuning, Vol. III (The Hague, 1942), p. 42.

11. Nuru'd-din ar-Raniri, *Bustanu's-Salatin, Bab II, Fasal 13*, di-susun oleh T. Iskandar (Kuala Lumpur, 1966), pp. 54–6.

12. Takeshi Ito, "The World of the Adat Aceh. A Historical Study of the Sultanate of Aceh", PhD thesis (Australian National University, Canberra, 1984), pp. 368–70.

13. "a king whose elephants have gold [-covered] tusks, silver on their foreheads, bells and chains of suasa [copper-gold]; a king whose elephant has a howdah of suasa" — Letter Sultan Perkasa 'Alam to Raja Yakob [King James] 1024 [1612 AD], in W.G. Shellabear, "An Account of Some of the Oldest Malay MSS now extant", *JSBRAS* 31 (1898): 127.

Notes to pp. 115–20 373

14. Sultan of Aceh to Governor-General of Netherlands India, my translation of the Dutch text in *Dagh-Register gehouden int Casteel Batavia, 1640–41* (Batavia, 1887), pp. 6–7.
15. *De Hikajat Atjeh*, ed. Teuku Iskandar ('s-Gravenhage, 1958), p. 165.
16. Ibid., p. 166.
17. Raja Ali Haji ibn Ahmad, *The Precious Gift (Tuhfat al-Nafis)*, trans. Virginia Matheson and Barbara Andaya (Kuala Lumpur, 1982), p. 143.
18. *Adat Raja-Raja Melayu*, ed. Panuti Sudjiman (Jakarta, 1983) pp. 67–81, 227–43; Reid, *Age of Commerce* 1, pp. 180–1.
19. *De Hikajat Atjeh*, pp. 55–6, 101–1.
20. Nuru'd-din ar-Raniri, *Bustanu's-Salatin*, pp. 37–8.
21. Ibid., p. 39.
22. Ibid., p. 40.
23. Ibid., pp. 41–2.
24. *Reisen van Nicolaus de Graaff, gedaan naar alle gewesten des werelds*, ed. J.C.M. Warnsinck ('s-Gravenhage, 1930), pp. 13–4.
25. For the decline in the Ottoman practice of royal processions to the mosque in the late 17th century, I am indebted to Prof. Cornell Fleischer.
26. Brown, ed., "Sejarah Melayu", pp. 58–9. The Malay text is in *JMBRAS* 26, 3 (Dec. 1938): 87–8. The fact that these Muslim feasts were not mentioned as royal celebrations in the other (Shellabear) version of the Annals, nor in the *Adat Raja-Raja Melayu*, ed. Panuti Sudjiman (Jakarta, 1983), composed in 1779, suggests that this may be a 17th-century insertion into the Raffles text based on contemporary Aceh practice.
27. *Adat Aceh dari satu Manuscript India Office Library*, transcribed by Teungku Anzib Lamnyong (Banda Aceh, PLPIS, 1976), pp. 25–46. The list of court rituals is summarized in Denys Lombard, *Le Sultanat d'Atjéh au temps d'Iskandar Muda 1607–1636* (Paris, 1967), pp. 144–6.
28. C. Snouck Hurgronje, *The Achehnese*, trans. A.W.S. O'Sullivan (Leiden, 1906), I: 208–13. The credibility of this tradition is further undermined by the fact that Acehnese political contacts with Turkey were strongest in the 1560s, whereas the Maulud celebration was not introduced to Turkey itself until 1588. *Shorter Encyclopaedia of Islam* (Leiden/London 1961), p. 366.
29. In the 19th century, by contrast, this was much less popular a feast in Aceh than Maulud or Idulfitri — Hurgronje, *The Achehnese*, I, p. 243.
30. *Adat Aceh*, pp. 34–46; Ito, "The World of the Adat Aceh", pp. 231–8.
31. *Adat Aceh*, p. 45.
32. Ito, "The World of the Adat Aceh", p. 243.

374 Notes to pp. 122–8

33. *The Travels of Peter Mundy in Europe and Asia, 1608–1667*, ed. Sir Richard Temple, Vol. III, Part I (London, 1919), pp. 121–3. In this and subsequent English quotations I have modernized the English spelling.
34. Ito, "The World of the Adat Aceh", pp. 217–23.
35. Cited in ibid., p. 220.
36. Daghregister of P. Willemsz, Aceh, 1642, as translated in Ito, "The World of the Adat Aceh", p. 221.
37. *Adat Aceh*, pp. 25–6. Also Ito, "The World of the Adat Aceh", pp. 218–20.
38. *Adat Aceh*, pp. 28–31. Also Ito, "The World of the Adat Aceh", pp. 224–6.
39. Account of S. de Weert, 1603, trans. in Ito, "The World of the Adat Aceh", p. 227.
40. *Adat Aceh*, pp. 46–8. Also Ito, "The World of the Adat Aceh", pp. 209–11.
41. Journal of Ralph Croft, in *The Voyage of Thomas Best to the East Indies 1612–14*, ed. Sir William Foster (London: Hakluyt Society, 1934), pp. 171–2. Cf. pp. 168–9 for the procession of 26 June.
42. Note that in Siam the same pattern was followed with magnificently-decorated galleys on the river instead of elephants, the royal letter being carried in the finest galley.
43. *The Voyages of Sir James Lancaster to Brazil and the East Indies, 1591–1603*, ed. Sir William Foster (London: Hakluyt Society, 1940), pp. 91–2. For similar procedures subsequently see "Narrative of Copland, 1613", in *The Voyage of Thomas Best*, p. 52; Wybrant van Warwijck, "Historische Verhael vande Reyse gedaen inde Oost-Indien" (1604), p. 30, in *Begin ende Voortgangh van de Vereenighde Neederlandtsche Geoctroyeerde Oost-Indische Compagnie*, ed. Isaac Commelin (Amsterdam, 1646; reprinted Amsterdam, 1974); Daghregister Pieter Sourij, 1642, Algemene Rijksarchief [henceforth ARA] KA 1051 bis, f.554.
44. Brown, ed., "Sejarah Melayu", p. 55; *Peter Floris, his Voyage to the East Indies in the "Globe", 1611–1615*, ed. W.H. Moreland (London: Hakluyt Society, 1934), pp. 33–4.
45. *The Voyage of Thomas Best*, p. 52; *The Voyages of Sir James Lancaster*, p. 93.
46. *The Voyages of Sir James Lancaster*, p. 99.
47. This phenomenon is discussed more fully in Reid, *Age of Commerce 1*, pp. 183–91.
48. Nuru'd-din ar-Raniri, *Bustanu's-Salatin*, p. 33.
49. *Hikayat Atjeh*, p. 97.
50. "Pantjagah (Iskandar Mudah) rode a wild elephant, standing upright when the elephant ran obediently; and rode a horse while squatting, and

Notes to pp. 129–34

jerked his foot from the right side of the horse to the left side, and waved his sword to right and left, and tied his head-cloth while the horse ran straight on. It was the custom that Pantjagah exercised like this on Thursday and on Monday" — *Hikayat Atjeh*, p. 158.

51. Thomas Stamford Raffles, *History of Java* (London, 1817) 1, p. 347.
52. *The Voyage of Thomas Best*, pp. 210–11.
53. De Reis van de vloot van Pieter Willemsz Verhoeff naar Aze 1607–1612, ed. M.E. van Opstall (The Hague, 1972), 1, p. 240.
54. *The Voyage of Thomas Best*, p. 52, also p. 158.
55. *The Travels of Peter Mundy* III, i: 126–30. See also Jan van der Meulen (Aceh) to Governor-General 13 Feb. 1638, ARA VOC 1131, f.1198.
56. Daghregister Pieter Sourij, 1642, ARA KA 1051 bis, f.555; Daghregister of Vlamingh van Oudtshoorn, 1644, ARA VOC 1157, f.578.
57. Godinho de Eredia, *Eredia's Description of Malaca, Meridional India and Cathay*, trans. J.V. Mills (Singapore: MBRAS, 1930; reprinted Kuala Lumpur, 1997), pp. 242–5.
58. *De oudste reizen van de Zeeuwen naar Oost-Indië, 1598–1604*, ed. W.S. Unger ('s-Gravenhage, 1948), pp. 71–2. Davis' account is on p. 55 of the same volume.
59. Ibid., p.81.
60. *The Voyage of Thomas Best*, p. 55.
61. Ibid., p. 210.
62. Standish narrative, in ibid., p. 159.
63. Ibid., pp. 55 and 210.
64. Daghregister Pieter Sourij, 1642, ARA KA 1051bis. f.567.
65. Ibid.
66. Ibid., f.568.
67. Daghregister P. Willemsz, 1642, ARA KA 1051bis, ff. 512 and 524.
68. Francois Martin de Vitre, *Description du premier voyage faict aux Indes Orientales par les francois en l'an 1603* (Paris, 1604), pp. 44–5. A Persian traveller in the 1680s noted that Aceh possessed "a magic spring. If someone is afflicted with a particular disease ... the magic waters cure the sick person immediately" — *The Ship of Sulaiman*, trans. John O'Kane (London, 1972), p. 179. Also William Dampier, *Voyages and Discoveries* (1699, reprinted London, 1931), pp. 95–6.
69. *Hikajat Atjeh*, p. 165.
70. Ibid., p. 165.
71. *The Voyage of Thomas Best*, p. 213. Lombard, *Le Sultanat d'Atjéh au temps d'Iskandar Muda*, p. 130.
72. Nuru'd-din ar-Raniri, *Bustanu's-Salatin*, pp. 49–52. See also L.F. Brakel, "State and Statecraft in Seventeenth Century Aceh", in *Pre-colonial State*

376   Notes to pp. 134–40

Systems in Southeast Asia, ed. Anthony Reid and Lance Castles (Kuala Lumpur: MBRAS, 1975), pp. 59–63, and Robert Wessing, "The Gunungan in Banda Aceh, Indonesia: Agni's Fire in Allah's Paradise?", *Archipel* 35 (1988): 157–94, both of whom analyze the Taman Ghairah as an essentially Indic conception with Mount Meru (the Gunungon) at its centre.

73. Lombard, *Le Sultanat d'Atjéh au temps d'Iskandar Muda*, p. 132; L.F. Brakel, "State and Statecraft", p. 61; Wessing, "The Gunungan in Banda Aceh", pp. 171–8.

74. *Adat Aceh*, p. 49.

Chapter 7

1. Akin Rabibhadana, *The Organization of Thai Society in the Early Bangkok Period, 1782–1873* (Ithaca, NY: Southeast Asia Program, Cornell University, 1969); Arthur Phayre, *History of Burma* (London: Trubner, 1883), pp. 136–41; M.C. Ricklefs, *Jogjakarta under Sultan Mangkubumi* (London; New York: Oxford University Press, 1974), pp. 18–21. On the other hand it is gratifying to note that the parallelism we emphasize here was also noted by Victor Lieberman, *Burmese Administrative Cycles: Anarchy and Conquest c. 1580–1760* (Princeton, NJ: Princeton University Press, 1984), pp. 271–92.

2. Rabibhadana, *The Organization of Thai Society* pp. 29–37.

3. This argument is set out in a fuller and more nuanced manner in Anthony Reid, *Southeast Asia in the Age of Commerce, c. 1450–1680*, Vol. II: *Expansion and Crisis* (New Haven: Yale University Press, 1993), particularly chapters 4 and 5. It is contested for the Mainland states in Victor Lieberman, *Strange Parallels: Southeast Asia in Global Context, c. 800–1830* (Cambridge: Cambridge University Press, 2003), notably pp. 15–21.

4. J.M. Gullick, *Indigenous Political Systems of Western Malaya* (London: University of London, Athlone Press, 1958); D.E. Brown, *Brunei: The structure and history of a Bornean Malay Sultanate* (Brunei, 1971); C. Snouck Hurgronje, *The Achehnese* (Leiden: E.J. Brill, 1906), 2 vols.; John Crawfurd, *Journal of an Embassy from the Governor-General of India to the Courts of Siam and Cochin China* (London, 1928; reprinted 1967), H.J. Friedericy, *De Standen bij de Boegineezen en Makassaren* ('s-Gravenhage, 1933).

5. Augustin de Beaulieu, "Memoires du Voyage aux Indes Orientales du General Beaulieu, dressés par luy-mesme", in *Relations de divers voyages curieux*, ed. Melch. Thévenot (Paris, 1666), 11, pp. 102–3.

6. Snouck Hurgronje, *The Achehnese*, I, p. 88.

7. Ibid., p. 144.

Notes to pp. 141–3

8. F.C. Danvers, *The Portuguese in India*, 2 vols. (London: W.H. Allen, 1894), vol. 1, pp. 480–1, based on Faria y Sousa, *Asia Portuguesa*; Sebastiao Rodolfo Dalgado, *Glossario Luso-Asiatico*, 2 vols. (Coimbra: Imprensa da Universidade, 1919–21), vol. 2, s.v. ORABALAO.

9. Hoesein Djajadiningrat, *Atiehsch-Nederlandsch Woordenboek* (Batavia, 1934), II, p. 196.

10. T. Iskandar, ed., *De Hikajat Atjeh* ('s-Gravenhage, 1958), pp. 96–9; T. Iskandar, ed., *Bustanu's-Salatin* (Kuala Lumpur: Dewan Bahasa dan Pustaka, 1966), p. 33.

11. *The Suma Orientol of Tomé Pires*, trans. A. Cortesão (London, 1944), 1, pp. 138–45; *The Book of Duarte Barbosa*, trans. M.L. Dames (London, 1921), II, pp. 182–5.

12. Iskandar, ed., *De Hikajat Atjeh*, pp. 53–4, 64–5, 90–5, 169–83; Iskandar, ed., *Bustanu's-Salatin*, p. 32; Hoesein Djajadiningrat, "Critisch Overzicht van de in Maleische Werken vervatte gegevens over de Geschiedenis van bet Soeltanaat van Atjeh", *BKI* 65 (1911): 154–8, 173–4; *The Voyages and Works of John Davis*, p. 153.

13. Iskandar, ed., *De Hikajat Atjeh*, p. 96.

14. Beaulieu, "Mémoires", p. 63.

15. See Chapter 5. Beaulieu, "Mémoires", pp. 58–63; *Pieter van den Broecke in Azie*, ed. W. Ph. Coolhaas ('s-Gravenhage, 1962), I, pp. 175–6; *The Voyage of Thomas Best to the East Indies, 1612–1614*, ed. W. Foster (London, 1934), p. 172.

16. G. Tichelman, "Een Atjehsche Sarakata (Afschrift van een besluit van Iskandar Muda)", *TBG* 73 (1933): 368–73; Tichelman, "Samalangasche Sarakata", *TBG* 78 (1938): 351–8.

17. Koloniaal Archief, The Hague (henceforth K.A.) 1051bis, "Daghregister" of P. Soury (1642), ff.568v.-9r., 581v.-2r.; ibid., "Copie daghregister" of P. Willemsz (1642–3), f. 506v., 517v.; K.A. 1059bis, "Copie daghregister" of A. van Oudstschoorn (1644), f. 574r., 579v.; K.A. 1100, "Originele missive" of D. Schouten, 16 Sept. 1655, f. 277v.; *Daghregister Batavia*, 1663, pp. 633–4; ibid., 1664, pp. 110, 120.

18. K.F.H. van Langen, "De Inrichting van het Atjehsche Staatsbestuur onder het Sultanaat", *BKI* 34 (1888): 390–1.

19. Iskandar, ed., *Bustanu's-Salatin*, p. 36; Van Langen, "Inrichting", pp. 390–2; *Voyage of Thomas Best*, pp. 171, 175n3; "Oost-Indische Reyse onder den Admirael Wijbrandt van Waerwijck", pp. 12, 14, in *Begin ende Voortgangh van de Vereenighde Nederlantsch Geoctroyeerde Oost-Indische Compagnie* (Amsterdam, 1646), 4 vols.

20. Drewes and Voorhoeve, ed., *Adat Atjeh*, *VKI* 24 (1958): 114b–5b.

21. Snouck Hurgronje, *The Achehnese*, I, p. 85.

378   Notes to pp. 143–7

22. K.A. 1051 bis, "Copie daghregister": of P. Willemsz. (1642–3), f.503r.
23. *Adat Atjeh*, pp. 110a–1b.
24. K.A. 1127, "Verbael" of B. Bort (1660), f. 340v.
25. *Reisen van Nicolaus de Graaff naar alle gewestern des werelds, beginnende 1639 tot 1687 incluis* ('s Gravenhage, 1930), p. 13.
26. Thomas Bowrey, *The Countries round the Bay of Bengal*, ed. R.C. Temple (London, 1903), p. 296; Iskandar, ed., *Bustanu's-Salatin*, p. 59.
27. Bowrey, *The Countries*, p. 296.
28. *Daghregister*, Batavia, 1641–2, pp. 96, 123; K.A. 1051 bis, "Copie memorie" of J. Compostel, 10 Aug. 1642, f.594r.-v.; ibid., "Copie daghregister" of P. Willemsz., f.508r.; Iskandar, ed., *Bustanu's-Salatin*, pp. 60, 62–3.
29. K.A. 1060, "Verbael van Attchin" (1644–5), f.167v.; K.A. 1123, "Raport" of B. Bort, 29 Jan. 1660, f.515r; K.A.1127, "Verbael" of B. Bort, ff.364r.–5r.; *Daghregister*, Batavia, 1663, pp. 201–3, 633–4; ibid., 1664, p. 480. K.A.1051bis, "Copie memorie" of J. Compostel, f.593r.
30. K.A.1051bis, "Copie memorie" of J. Compostel, f.593r.
31. *Bouwstoffen voor de geschiedenis der Nederlanders in den Maleisch Archipel*, ed. J.E. Heeres ('s-Gravenhage, 1895), vol. 3, pp. 345–6; S. Arasaratnam, "Some Notes on the Dutch in Malacca and Indo-Malayan Trade, 1641–1650", *JSEAH* 10, 3 (1969): 486.
32. K.A.1051 bis, "Copie daghregister" of P. Willemsz., f.527r.
33. Ibid.
34. G.W.J. Drewes, ed., *Hikajat Potjut Muhamat: An Acehnese Epic* (The Hague: KITLV, 1979), pp. 98–107.
35. Beaulieu, "Mémoires", p. 103.
36. Ibid., pp. 41, 44, 97.
37. Tiele, P.A., "De Europeërs in den Maleischen Archipel", *BKI* 36 (1887): 244–5, 247 n.2; Kathirithamby-Wells, "Achehnese Control over West Sumatra up to the treaty of Painan, 1663", *JSEAH* 10, 3 (1969): 458–9.
38. K.A.1127, "Verbael" of B. Bort, ff.320r.-45r., 374r.-84r.; Kathirithamby-Wells, "Achehnese Control", pp. 467–77.
39. Thomas Best, *The Voyage of Thomas Best to the East Indies, 1612–1614*, ed. W. Foster (London, 1934), pp. 65, 67–8, 179–80; *Letters received by the East India Company from its servants in the East*, ed. F.C. Danvers and W. Foster, 6 vols. (London, 1896–1902), vol. 2, pp. 287–8; vol. 3, pp. 129, 188, 191, 220, 222, 226, 235; vol. 4, pp. 22, 125–7, 166–7; vol. 5, pp. 30–1, 171–2; *Jan Pietersz. Coen. Bescheiden omtrent zijn bedrijf in Indië*, vol. 7, pt. 1, ed. W. Ph. Coolhaas ('s-Gravenhage, 1953), p. 396; K.A. 1127, "Verbaell" of B. Bort.

Notes to pp. 147–52

40. B.W. Andaya, *Perak, the Abode of Grace: A Study of an Eighteenth-Century Malay State* (Kuala Lumpur, 1979), pp. 42–9; K.A. 1040, "Copie Missive", J. Harmansz., 3 Apr. 1639, f.1234.

41. K.A. 1127, "Verbaell" of B. Bort, f.320r.-v., 324r.-6r., 335r.-6v., 340v.-1r.; *Bouwstoffen*, vol. 3, pp. 498–9, 501–3; *Corpus Diplomaticum Neerland-Indicum*, ed. J.E. Heeres ('s-Gravenhage, 1907–31), vol. 1, pp. 345–7, 528–32; vol. 2, pp. 165–8; Kathirithamby-Wells, "Achehnese Control", p. 479.

42. K.A. 1068, "Copie daghregister" of J. Truijtman (1649), f.222r.-v.

43. Snouck Hurgronje, *The Achehnese*, p. 87. *De "Hikajat Malem Dagang". Atjehsch Heldendicht*, ed. H.K.J. Cowan (Leiden: KITLV, 1937).

44. Drewes, ed., *Hikajat Potjut Muhamat*, pp. 45–7.

45. See Chapter 4; William Dampier, *Voyages and Discoveries* (London: The Argonaut Press, 1931), p. 91.

46. J.B. Morelli, cited in A. Meersman, *The Franciscans in the Indonesian Archipelago* (Louvain, 1967), p. 123n.

47. De Premare to de La Chaise, 17 February 1699, in *Lettres édifiantes et curieuses, écrites des missions étrangères (de la Compagnie de Jesus)*, new ed. by Y.M.H. de Querbeuf (Paris, 1780–3), vol. 16, p. 348.

48. Reid, "Trade", pp. 53–5.

49. Drewes, ed., *Hikajat Potjut Muhamat*, p. 163.

50. William Marsden, *The History of Sumatra*, 3rd ed. (London, 1811), p. 457. Van Langen, "De Inrichting", p. 404. Reid, "Trade", p. 54.

51. Malay borrowings in Achenese are today characteristic of the language of the ruling class of *ulëëbalang* — another indication of the origins of this class in the cosmopolitan and cultured capital (information from Mark Durie.)

52. Anthony Reid, *Slavery, Bondage and Dependency in Southeast Asia* (New York: St. Martin's Press, 1983), pp. 13–4, 170–2. Dampier, *Voyages*, pp. 98–9.

53. E.g. Marc Bloch, *Feudal Society*, trans. L.A. Manyon (London, 1961), p. 446; Perry Anderson, *Lineages of the Absolutist State* (London: N.L.B., 1974), p. 407.

Chapter 8

1. E.S. de Klerck, *De Atjeh-oorlog* (The Hague, 1912), pp. 209n and 435–6.

2. Ch. Schefer, ed., *Le Discours de la Navigation de Jean et Raoul Parmentier de Dieppe* (Paris, 1883). For a recent survey of early French travel literature on Indonesia, see Denys Lombard, "Voyageurs Français dans

380   Notes to pp. 152–5

l'Archipel Insulindien XVIIème, XVIIIème et XIXème s.", *Archipel* 1 (1971): 141–68.

3. François Martin, *Description du premier voyage faict aux Indes Orientales par les francois en l'an 1603* (Paris, 1604). A section of this rare book has been translated in *Witnesses to Sumatra*, ed. Anthony Reid, pp. 55–63.

4. J.E. Heeres, "Franschen in de Maleischen Archipel", *Encyclopaedie van Nederlandsch-Indië* (The Hague, 1899–1905), 1, p. 246.

5. Iskandar Muda to Louis XIII, Radjab 1030H (June, 1621), quoted in Denys Lombard, *Le Sultanat d'Atjeh au temps d'Iskandar Muda 1607–1636* (Paris, 1967), p. 246.

6. Alexander Hamilton, *A New Account of the East Indies* (London: Argonaut Press, 1930), 11, p. 83.

7. Sultan Abdul Jalil Shah to Louis XV, n.d., Bibliothèque Nationale, Manuscrits Malayo-Polynésiens, No. 223.

8. H.H. Dodwell, *Dupleix and Clive: The beginning of empire* (London, 1920), pp. 16–7.

9. Thomas Forrest, *A Voyage from Calcutta to the Mergui Archipelago, lying on the East Side of the Bay of Bengal* (London, 1792), pp. 51–2.

10. Henri Moris, ed., *Journal de Bord du Bailli de Suffren dans l'Inde, 1781–1784* (Paris, 1888), p. 194.

11. Ibid., p. 200.

12. John Bastin, *The British in West Sumatra (1685–1825)* (Kuala Lumpur: University of Malaya Press, 1965), pp. 71n and 113n.

13. Auguste Toussaint, *Deux Siècles d'Histoire (1735–1935)* (Port Louis, 1936), pp. 173–83.

14. E. Netscher, *Padang in het laatst der XVIIIe eeuw,VBG* XLI (2) (Batavia/The Hague: 1880), pp. 56–73.

15. Toussaint, *Deux Siècles d'Histoire*, pp. 172–3.

16. Bastin, *The British in West Sumatra*, p. 117n.

17. C.N. Parkinson, *War in the Eastern Seas, 1793–1815* (London: Allen & Unwin, 1954), pp. 210–1.

18. Ibid., p. 365. William Marsden, *The History of Sumatra* (Reprint, Kuala Lumpur: Oxford University Press, 1966), pp. 368–9.

19. One Frenchman with the standard Muslim convert's name, Abdullah, took a prominent part in an attack on a French brig at Pidië by Acehnese pirates in 1793. H.R.C. Wright, *East-Indian Economic Problems of the Age of Cornwallis and Raffles* (London: Luzac, 1961), pp. 260–1. Deserters from French privateers were also noticed in Aceh in 1810. Campbell to Edmonstone, 24 July 1810, FCCP 18 July 1811 in Straits Settlements Factory Records [henceforth SSFR], vol. 31.

Notes to pp. 156–7 381

20. Eroplong (Padang) to Paris, 23 Aug. 1858, citing *Le Moniteur* 104 (14 April 1858); Ministère des Affairs Etrangères [henceforth M.A.E.], Pays-Bas, Correspondence Politique des Consuls, no. 5. Official knowledge of Batakland in this period was hardly sufficient to justify such emphatic denials. An intriguing detail which may or may not be connected with the de Molac story is that Roman Catholic elements were very marked in the Batak pormalim sect, which became known to Europeans only about 1900. These elements are usually attributed solely to the Italian traveller Modigliani, who visited the Batakland in 1891. Elio Modigliani, *Fra I Batacchi Indipendenti* (Roma, 1892), of which the relevant sections are translated in Reid, ed., *Witnesses to Sumatra*, pp. 199–209. Also Gentilis Aster, *Een Volk Ontdekt Christus. De Katholieke Missie onder de Bataks op Sumatra* (Voorhout, 1959), pp. 104–112.

21. Campbell to Edmonstone, 24 July 1810, FCCP 18 July 1811 in SSFR 31.

22. Ibid. Lee Kam Hing, *The Sultanate of Aceh: Relations with the British, 1760–1819* (Kuala Lumpur: OUP, 1995), pp. 123, 126.

23. ENI III, p. 531.

24. Madeleine Ly-Tio-Fane, "Pierre Poivre et L'Expansion Française dans l'Indo-Pacifique", *BEFEO* 53 (1967): 453–510. B.E. Kennedy, "Anglo-French Rivalry in India and the Eastern Seas, 1763–1793", unpublished PhD (Australian National University, 1969), pp. 254–60. John F. Cady, *The Roots of French Imperialism in Eastern Asia* (Ithaca: Cornell University Press, 1954), pp. 11–2.

25. D.G.E. Hall, *A History of South-East Asia* (London: Macmillan, 1960), pp. 422–4.

26. Ibid., pp. 364–70. Kennedy, "Anglo-French Rivalry in India and the Eastern Seas", pp. 266–76. Cady, *The Roots of French Imperialism*, pp. 11–2.

27. Lee, *Sultanate of Aceh*, pp. 63–7. D.K. Bassett, *British Trade and Policy in Indonesia and Malaysia in the late eighteenth century* (Hull Monographs on Southeast Asia, No. 3, 1971), pp. 63–71.

28. Daendels to Minister of Colonies, 23 Aug. 1809, in J.K.J. de Jonge, *De Opkomst van het Nederlandsch Gezag in Oost-Indië*, vol. 13 (The Hague, 1888), p. 414.

29. Macalister to Sultan of Aceh n.d. (July 1809), and other correspondence in A.C. Baker, "Some Account of the Anglo-Dutch Relations in the East at the Beginning of the 19th Century, Based on the Records preserved in the Colonial Secretary's Office in Singapore, and in the Resident's Office, Malacca", *JSBRAS* 64 (June 1913): 2–6.

382   Notes to pp. 157–61

30. Lee, *Sultanate of Aceh*, pp. 132–40.
31. D.C. Boulger, *The Life of Sir Stamford Raffles* (London: H. Marshall, 1897), p. 91.
32. Memorandum to Lord Minto (Mar. 1810), cited C.E. Wurtzburg, *Raffles of the Eastern Isles* (London: Hodder & Stoughton, 1954), p. 101.
33. *Biographie Générale* (Paris, 1855–66), 29, cols. 422–4 (Langlès). L.C. Damais, "The Contribution of French Scholars to the Knowledge of Indonesian History", *Madjallah Ilmu-Ilmu Sastra Indonesia* 4, No. 3: 140.
34. Coudé to Descourvières, 26 Apr. 1782, in Adrien Launay, *Histoire de la Mission de Siam 1662–1811. Documents Historiques* (Paris, 1920), 11, p. 311.
35. Archive of the Société des Missions Etrangères [henceforth S.M.E.], vol. 887, ff. 81-3 and 103-8. Also Launay, *Mémorial de la Société des Missions Etrangères*, pp. 172–3. 1 am very grateful to Fr. Guennou and the S.M.E. for permission to use this archive.
36. *General College Third Centenary* (Penang, 1965), p. 19.
37. Florens to Directors, 16 July 1826 and 20 June 1829, S.M.E. 888, ff. 11 and 172. Although a Portuguese Franciscan mission had cared for some of the foreign traders in Aceh between 1671 and about 1703, it would be difficult to conceive a less promising field. C. Wessels, "Uit de missiegeschiedenis van Sumatra. Atjeh in the 16e en 17e Eeuw", *Historisch Tijdschrift* XVIII (1939): 14–6.
38. Boucho to Directors, 24 May 1829, S.M.E. 888, ff. 154-5.
39. Ibid. ff. 154-6. Boucho's scanty information was reasonably accurate. Both North and South Nias recognize Lowalangi (or Lubulangi) as the sky god from whom men derive life. The lord of the underworld is Latura, and it seems that Boucho's Cekhou must be one of many locally important evil spirits. "A pecularity of Nias law consists in the severity with which offences against women are dealt with ... Sexual morality ... had diminished upon their becoming Christians." E.M. Loeb, *Sumatra — Its History and People* (Vienna, 1935), pp. 141–57. Also *Encyclopedie van Nederlandsch-Indië* III, 23.
40. Boucho to Dubois, 16 Dec. 1831, S.M.E. 888, ff. 239-41. Bruquière letter, 22 Aug. 1831, S.M.E. 892, ff.735-6.
41. Vallon to Boucho, 1–21 Jan. 1832, S.M.E. 888, ff. 267-72.
42. Bérard to de Copse, 29 Feb. 1832; Vallon to Boucho, 1 Mar. 1832; S.M.E. 888, ff. 281-7. Bérard's letter from Padang failed to mention the Nias colony there, however.
43. Bérard to Embrecht, 15 June 1832, S.M.E. 888, ff.313-4.

Notes to pp. 161–4 383

44. Embrecht to Supries, 2 Jan. 1833, S.M.E. 888, f.415. Emphasis in original.
45. Adrien Launay, *Mémorial de la Société des Missions Etrangères* (Paris, 1911–6), II, pp. 36–7 and 613.
46. Bérard had pleaded for cloth to be sent from Penang, because he feared "their state of nudity would make them unapproachable". Bérard to de Copse, 29 Feb. 1832, S.M.E. 888, f. 284.
47. Vallon in fact embarked for Nias in a Chinese vessel from Natal, and never visited Padang. This may be a confusion with Bérard's very difficult voyage from Padang to Natal.
48. *The Martyr of Sumatra: A Memoir of Henry Lyman* (New York, 1856), pp. 389–90.
49. Bérard letters of 29 Feb., 5 and 18 Mar., 12 Apr. and 15 June 1832, S.M.E. 888, ff.281-4, 289-93, 297-8, and 313-4.
50. Candalph to Directors, 29 Nov. 1834, S.M.E. 888, f.591.
51. *Idem*, ff. 591-3. Lyman, *The Martyr of Sumatra*, pp. 390–1. J.H. van der Velden, *De Roomsch-Katholieke Missie in Nederlandsch Oost-Indië 1808–1908* (Nijmegen, 1908), pp. 60–4. A.I. van Aernsbergen, *Chronologisch Overzicht van de werkzaamheid der Jezuiten in de Missie van N.O.-I. 1859-1934* (Bandung, 1934), pp. 46–52.
52. Th. Muller Krüger, *Sedjarah Geredja di Indonesia* (2nd ed., Djakarta, 1966), pp. 235–6. Another Catholic priest, the Dutch Caspar de Heselle, died in Nias in 1854. He was already mortally afflicted with fever on arrival, and could not commence work. Van der Velden, p. 154.
53. C.D. Cowan, "Early Penang and the Rise of Singapore 1805–1832", *JMBRAS* 23, II (1950): 153. For the American pepper-trade see James W. Gould, "Sumatra — America's Pepperpot 1784–1873", *Essex Institute, Historical Collections* 92 (1956): 83–152, 203–51, 295–348; and J.D. Phillips, *Pepper and Pirates, Adventures in the Sumatra Pepper Trade of Salem* (Boston, 1949).
54. Reports of Captain Larocque de Chanfray n.d. (1840), and Captain Le Comte, 21 June 1843, in M.A.E. Mémoires et Documents, Asie 23, ff. 32 and 135 respectively. Besides pepper, some French ships also appear to have purchased Nias slaves for Bourbon plantations in the 1830s. Lyman, *The Martyr of Sumatra*, p. 377. Melchior Yvan, *Six Months Among the Malays, and A Year in China* (London: J. Blackwood, 1855), p. 2.
55. Martin was decorated by the French Government in 1843 for the way he had upheld the name of France in his long association with the Atjeh pepper coast. Report of Le Comte, *loc.cit.*, ff.135-6. Melchior

384 Notes to pp. 165–71

Yvan, pp. 151–9, gives a colourful portrait of Martin, whom he met in Penang in 1843.

56. Martin to Commissaire de Marine, Marseilles, 16 Nov. 1839, M.A.E. Mémoires et Documents, Asie 22, ff.243-6.

57. *Idem*, f.245.

58. *Idem*, f.246.

59. Marine to Affaires Etrangères, 30 Apr. 1841, citing letter of Bourbon Government of July 1840, M.A.E. Mémoires et Documents, Asie 23, ff.20-2.

60. Cady, *The Roots of French Imperialism*, pp. 17, 25 and 29.

61. Report of Captain le Comte, 21 June 1843, M.A.E. Mémoires et Documents, Asie 23, f.135.

62. Jean-Paul Faivre, *L'Expansion Française dans le Pacifique, 1800–1842* (Paris, 1953), pp. 367–82.

63. Marine et Colonies to Affaires Etrangères, 30 Apr. 1841, and reply 8 June 1841, M.A.E. Mémoires et Documents, Asie 23, ff. 20-1 and 48-9.

64. Affaires Etrangères to Instruction Publique, 8 Oct. 1843, M.A.E. Mèmoires et Documents, Asie 23, ff. 97-8.

65. Damais, "The Contribution of French Scholars", pp. 140–1.

66. Report of Laroque de Chanfray, captain of the brig *Le Lancier*, n.d., M.A.E. Mémoires et Documents, Asie 23, ff.24-31.

67. Captain Le Comte of the corvette *La Fortune* discovered in Meulaboh in 1843 that the Acehnese who had piloted *Le Lancier* to Seunagan in 1840 was afraid to visit Banda Aceh because of the Sultan's anger. M.A.E. Mémoires et Documents, Asie 23, ff.134-5.

68. Report of Roy, captain of frigate *La Magicienne*, 5 Oct. 1840, M.A.E. Mémoires et Documents, Asie 23, ff.250-3.

69. His grandfather was Sultan Ala'ad-din Muhammad Shah (1781–95), who had visited Ile de France as a youth and received de Suffren's fleet in 1782.

70. Sultan Mansur Shah to King Louis-Philippe 15 Jumadi II, 1256H (14 Aug. 1840). Dulaurier's French translation of 24 Apr. 1841, from which this extract is taken, is in M.A.E. Mémoires et Documents, Hollande 152, ff.159-60. I was unable to locate the Malay original.

71. Report of Le Comte, 21 June 1843, M.A.E. Mémoires et Documents, Asie 23, ff. 130-1.

72. *Idem*, f.137.

73. *Idem*, f.138.

74. King Louis-Philippe to Sultan of Aceh, 2 Jan. 1843, reproduced in E.S. de Klerck, *De Atjèh-oorlog* (The Hague, 1912), p. 435.

Notes to pp. 172–5   385

75. Berchou to Guizot, 12 Aug. 1845, M.A.E. Mémoires et Documents, Asie 23, ff.273-4.

76. Affaires Etrangères to Berchou, 6 Sept. 1845, M.A.E. Mémoires et Documents, Asie 23, f. 276. Président du Tribunal de Commerce, Rouen, to Ministre de l'Agriculture et du Commerce 6 Dec. 1846, M.A.E. Mémoires et Documents, Asie 24, ff. 13-14.

77. Sultan Ibrahim to President of France 15 Rabi I, 1265H (8 Feb. 1849), M.A.E. Mémoires et Documents, Hollande 152, f.161. This is my translation from the Malay text, of which a romanized version follows in an Appendix.

78. Anthony Reid, *The Contest for North Sumatra* (Kuala Lumpur: University of Malaya Press, 1969), p. 84. J. Woltring, ed., *Bescheiden Betreffende de Buitenlandse Politiek van Nederland: Tweede Periode, 1871–98*, I (The Hague, 1962), pp. 612–3.

79. Mohammad Ghauth to Louis Napoleon 21 Jumadi 1, 1268H (12 Mar. 1852), French translation in M.A.E. Mémoires et Documents, Hollande 132, f.167.

80. Alix Desgranges, Professor of Turkish at the Collège de France, translated from the Arabic text of Ibrahim's letter, assuming it to be identical with the Malay text. If so, his translation was unusually free. M.A.E. Mémoires et Documents, Hollande 152, ff.161-5.

81. Affaires Etrangères to Lemoyne, 20 Apr. 1852, M.A.E., Egypte, Depêches Politiques des Consuls, Alexandria, 24, f.69.

82. Dutch Ambassador, Paris, to Buitenlandse Zaken, 1 and 2 Nov. 1852, Archive of Buitenlandse Zaken dossier 3076. Also De Klerck, pp. 208-9.

83. Berchou to Affaires Etrangères n.d. [1853], M.A.E. Mémoires et Documents Asie 24, ff.11-12.

84. The Correspondence of these consuls is in M.A.E. Pays-Bas, Correspondence Politique des Consuls, No. 5 (1857–69).

85. A. de Pina, *Deux Ans dans le Pays des Epices* (Paris, 1880), p. 200.

86. Ibid., p. 315.

87. Reid, *The Contest*, p. 85. Later, in America, Moreno referred to the two letters and the sword from France, which Sultan Ibrahim has asked him to translate and explain.

88. Alexander, "Korte Levensschets van de Arabier Habib Abdoe'r Rahman Alzahir", *De Indische Gids* 2, II (1880): 1010 and 1016. See also my translation of the same memoirs in *Indonesia* 13 (1972): 45 and 54–5. An 1873 visit to France was certainly imaginary, and it seems probable that the earlier one was also based on Sidi Muhammad's experiences rather than the Habib's own.

386 Notes to pp. 175–9

89. Anthony Reid, "Indonesian Diplomacy: A Documentary study of Acehnese Foreign Policy in the Reign of Sultan Mahmud, 1870–4", *JMBRAS* 62, 2 (1969b): 79–82; see Chapter 11.

90. Affaires Etrangères to Gabriac (The Hague), 19 Apr. 1873, M.A.E. Pays-Bas, Depêches Politiques 672, f.102.

91. Thiers to Gabriac, 27 Apr. 1873, *loc. cit.*, f.119.

92. Reid, "Indonesian Diplomacy", pp. 90–1.

93. Affaires Etrangères to Bresson (The Hague), 9 Aug. 1873, M.A.E. Pays Bas, Depêches Politiques 672, ff.242-3.

94. Marine et Colonies to Affaires Etrangères, 6 May 1873, *loc. cit.*, ff.150-1.

95. Affaires Etrangères to Duchesne de Bellecourt (Batavia), 8 Oct. 1873, M.A.E. Pays-Bas, Depêches Politiques des Consuls 8, ff.292-3.

96. D.V. McKay, "Colonialism in the French Geographical Movement 1871–1881", *Geographical Review* 33 (1943): 218.

97. Ibid., pp. 216–7.

98. Francois-Xavier-Joseph-Honoré Brau de Saint-Pol Lias (1840–1914) trained as a lawyer in Paris, and worked for five years (1868–73) in the Banque de France. Thereafter he devoted himself entirely to publicising the geographical and colonial movements. A prominent member of the Paris Société de Géographie, he was also a founder of the Société des Etudes coloniales et maritimes (1873), and the Société de Géographie Commerciale. The convening by the latter society of a *Congrès Internationale de géographie commerciale* in 1878 was largely at his initiative. He founded various French companies to operate in Sumatra, Malaya and Indo-China, and travelled to Java and Sumatra (1876–7); Sumatra and Malaya (1880–1); and Burma, Indo-China and Malaya (1884). His numerous writings depict the opportunities in these countries in glowing colours.

99. Brau de St.-Pol Lias, "Deli et les Colons-explorateurs Français", *Bulletin de la Société de Géographie* 14 (1877): 326–7.

100. Brau de St.-Pol Lias, *Chez les Atchés. Lohong* (Paris: Librairie Plon, 1884), p. xi.

101. Brau de St.-Pol Lias, *Pérak et les Orang-Sakèys* (Paris, 1883), p. 21.

102. Brau, *Chez les Atchés*, pp. xii–xxii.

103. Ibid., p. x. Also Brau de St.-Pol Lias, *De France à Sumatra* (Paris: H. Oudin, 1884), pp. 79–80.

104. Brau, "Deli", pp. 298–327; *De France à Sumatra*, pp. 48–54; *Pérak*, pp. 6–9. W.H.M. Schadee, *Geschiedenis van Sumatra's Oostkust* (Amsterdam, 1918–9) 11, pp. 103–4, notes that the Bedagai area was only officially opened to planters in 1882.

Notes to pp. 180–4

387

105. K.F.H. van Langen, "Atjeh's Westkust", *Tijdschrift van het Aardrijkskundig Genootschap* [henceforth *T.A.G.*], 2e série, 5 (1888), 11: 230–1. Th. J. Veltman, "Goud-exploitatie in Atjeh", *T.A.G.* 2e série, 23 (1906) 11: 935–8.

106. The brochure, *Eenige Beschoutvingen over goud en de aanzvezigheid daarvan ter Sumatra's Westkust* by Reinier D. Verbeek, is described in *T.A.G.* 2 (1877): 377–8.

107. Lavino to Governor-General, 13 Mar. 1877, A.R.A. Consulaatsarchief, Penang 102.

108. Van Langen, "Atjeh's Westkust", p. 231. Brau, *Côte du Poivre* (Paris: FXJH, 1981), pp. 9–10.

109. Brau, *Côte du Poivre*, p. 10.

110. K.F.H. van Langen, "Steenkolenbergen in het voormalige rijk van Meulaboh", *De Indische Gids* 2, II (1880): 671.

111. Van Langen "Atjeh's Westkust", p. 231. Rinn (Singapore) to Affaires Etrangères, 13 Dec. 1877, M.A.E. Correspondence Politique des Consuls, Angleterre 55, ff. 35-9.

112. Brau, *De France à Sumatra*, pp. 42–3, 50–6 and 307–8; *Pérak*, pp. 9–12.

113. Schadee, *Geschiedenis van Sumatra's Oostkus*, II, p. 196.

114. Brau, *De France à Sumatra*, pp. 56–9.

115. Ibid., pp. 59–61.

116. Ibid., p. 44.

117. Reid, *The Contest*, pp. 201–7.

118. Brau, *Côte du Poivre*, pp. 17–9; *De France à Sumatra*, pp. 182–3.

119. Netherlands Indies press cuttings on the Wallon affair, translated in Rinn (Batavia) to Affaires Etrangères, 15 Apr. 1880, M.A.E. Depîches Politiques des Consuls, Pays-Bas 9, ff.64-5.

120. Rinn to Affaires Etrangères, 15 Apr. and 9 May 1880, M.A.E. Depêches Politiques des Consuls, Pays-Bas 9, ff. 59-65 and 98-100.

121. Paul Fauque, *Rapport sur un voyage à Sumatra (province des Siaks et province d'Atchin)* (Paris, 1886), p. 19. Also Brau, *Côte du Poivre*, pp. 12–17. Rinn to Affaires Etrangères 15 Apr., 7 and 9 May 1880, M.A.E. Depêches Politiques des Consuls, Pays-Bas 9, ff. 59-100.

122. K.F.H. van Langen, "De 'Nisero-kwestie'", *De Indische Gids* 6, II (1884): 461. A. Pruys van der Hoeven, *Mijne Ervaring van Atjeh* (The Hague, 1886), pp. 26–7.

123. Brau, *Côte du Poivre*, passim.

124. Brau, *Pérak*, passim. M.J. Errington de la Croix, *Les Mines d'Etain de Pérak* (Paris, 1882). J. Sig. D. Rawlins, "French Enterprise in Malaya", *JMBRAS* 49, 11 (1966): 52–3.

388   Notes to pp. 185–8

125. Brau, *Chez les Atchés*, passim; *Pérak*, pp. 192–3 and 294–5.

126. Brau, *Côte du Poivre*, p. 236.

127. Rinn to Affaires Etrangères, 8 Jan. 1881, M.A.E. Depêches Politiques des Consuls, Pays-Bas, ff. 140-1.

128. Paul Fauque, *Rapport sur un voyage à Sumatra*, pp. 4–9 and *De France à Sumatra (Journal de Bord)*, pp. 1–13. These two official reports to the Ministre de l'Instruction Publique are bound together though separately paginated.

129. Fauque, *Rapport sur un voyage à Sumatra*, pp. 14–24.

130. Portales-Gargier (Batavia) to Affaires Etrangères, M.A.E. Depêches Politiques des Consuls, Pays-Bas 9, f. 240.

131. Extracts from journal of Captain Roura, Nov. 1883, in Parliamentary Papers, House of Commons, 1884, 87, pp. 305–6. Reid, *The Contest*, pp. 222–3.

132. Weld to Derby 20 April 1885, copy C.O. to F.O. 27 Apr. 1885, F.O. 37/699.

133. Reid, *The Contest*, pp. 260–2. Weld to Granville, 8 July 1886, C.O. 273/140.

134. Veltman, "Goud-exploitatie", pp. 934–5.

135. *Penjedar* (Medan), 1 Jan. 1940, p. 11. J. Jongejans, *Land en Volk van Aceh Vroeger en Nu* (Baarn, 1939), pp. 203–4.

136. Auguste-Jean-Baptiste-Marie-Charles David was born in Toulon in 1842, and entered military service in 1859. He served in the Spahis Cochinchinois in Indo-China (1863–8), and earned the Croix de la Légion d'honneur as a Captain in the Franco-Prussian War (1870–1), being wounded three times. Thereafter he worked as a banker in Paris until 1883, when an embezzlement charge forced him to flee. After a year in Java and three months back in Paris, he departed in December 1884 for his remarkable exploits in Vietnam. From that point he styled himself le Baron David de Mayréna, this last name being one his father, a naval officer, had adopted to distinguish himself from other members of the family. In 1890 he adopted another title, Comte de Maas, in addition to his royal one, Marie I, roi des Sedangs. Detailed biographies are: Jean Marquet, "Un aventurier du XIXe siècle: Marie Ier, roi des Sedangs (1888–1890)", *Bulletin des Amis du Vieux Hué* 14, nos. 1 & 2 (1927); Gerald Hickey, *Kingdom in the Morning Mist: Mayrena in the Highlands of Vietnam* (Philadelphia, 1988).

137. Bernard Bourotte, "Essai d'histoire des populations montagnards du sud indochinois jusqu'à 1945", *Bulletin de la Société des Etudes Indochinoises* 30, 1 (1955): 61.

Notes to pp. 188–95   389

138. Marquet, "Un aventurier du XIXe siècle", pp. 11–4.
139. Ibid., p. 14. Engagement between Sellière and Mayréna 16 Mar. 1885, copy in Buitenlandse Zaken to Kolonien, 7 Sept. 1883, A.R.A. Kol. Kab. E10, dossier 6162.
140. Marquet, "Un aventurier du XIXe siècle", p. 17.
141. Ibid., pp. 16–62. Bourotte, "Essai d'histoire des populations", pp. 61–2.
142. Marquet, "Un aventurier du XIXe siècle", pp. 86–93.
143. Ibid., pp. 93–105. Lavino (Singapore) to Pijnacker Hordijk 21 Feb., 11 and 31 Mar., 29 Apr. 1890, copies G.G. to Koloniën 5 May 1890, Kol. Kab. B8 dossier 6196. Hugh Clifford, who was an official in Pahang at the time of Mayréna's death, provides an engaging portrait of him in his *Heroes in Exile* (2nd. ed., London: J. Murray, 1928), pp. 61–87.
144. The original text in Arabic script is in M.A.E. Mémoires et Documents, Hollande 152, f.161.

Chapter 9
1. The 1930 census was the last to record ethnicity until the Indonesian census of 2000. This, however, published data only in terms of the eight largest ethnic groups in each province, and Chinese did not reach the 387,000 needed to qualify in the ethnically very divided North Sumatra Province. The Chinese of East Sumatra undoubtedly grew slowly in numbers after 1930, concentrated in the city of Medan, and declined markedly as a proportion of population. From the 325,000 recording as Buddhist in the 2000 census for North Sumatra, one would presume the number of self-defining Chinese to be about 370,000. This would be 3.2% of the population of the Province, or 4.2% of the former East Coast Residency.
2. Between 1882 and 1932 the annual influx fell below 100,000 only in the years 1918–19.
3. W.H.M. Schadee, *Geschiedenis van Sumatra's Oostkust* (Amsterdam: Oostkust van Sumatra-Instituut, 1918–19), II, pp. 34–5. H.J. Bool, *De Chineesche immigratie naar Deli* (Utrecht, 1904), pp. 1–2.
4. R.N. Jackson, *Pickering, Protector of Chinese* (Kuala Lumpur: Oxford University Press, 1965), pp. 70–2. Ng Siew Yoong, "The Chinese Protectorate in Singapore 1877–1900", *JSEAH* 2, 1 (1961): 99.
5. Ma Huan, *Ying-yai Sheng-lan; The Overall Survey of the Ocean's Shores [1433]*, trans. J.V.G. Mills (London: Hakluyt Society, 1970, reprinted Bangkok: White Lotus, 1997), pp. 98–100. Barbara Andaya, *To Live as Brothers: Southeast Sumatra in the Seventeenth and Eighteenth Centuries* (Honolulu: University of Hawaii Press, 1993), p. 41.

390 Notes to pp. 195–8

6. Anthony Reid, *Southeast Asia in the Age of Commerce*, Vol. II: *Expansion and Crisis* (New Haven: Yale University Press, 1993), pp. 18–9.
7. Andaya, *To Live as Brothers*, pp. 55–6.
8. John Anderson, *An Exposition of the Political and Commercial Relations of the Government of Prince of Wales' Island with the States on the East Coast of Sumatra from Diamond Point to Siak* (Penang, 1824), pp. 22, 37, 39. William Milburn, *Oriental Commerce*, revised ed. (London, 1825), p. 375. J.H. Moor, *Notices of the Indian Archipelago, and Adjacent Countries* (Singapore, 1837), pp. 101–2. John Anderson, *Mission to the East Coast of Sumatra in* 1823 (Edinburgh/London: W. Blackwood, 1826), pp. 172, 352–3, 394–6. For an ethnic breakdown of 18th-century Melaka shipping on eastern Sumatra see Anthony Reid and Radin Fernando, "Shipping on Melaka and Singapore as an index of growth, 1760–1840", *South Asia* 19 (Special Issue, 1996): 64–75. These records show that both Batubara and Siak did have significant resident Chinese traders in the 1760s and 1770s, though these may have moved to Singapore or Penang by the time of Anderson's visit.
9. Anderson, *Mission*, p. 296.
10. C.A. Kroesen, "Geschiedenis van Asahan", *TBG* XXXI (1886): 105 and 111.
11. M. Hamerster, *Bijdrage tot de Kennis van de Afdeeling Asahan* (Amsterdam, 1926), p. 50, Schadee, *Geschiedenis* I, pp. 141–2.
12. *Koloniaal Verslag*, 1876, p. 18.
13. *Verzameling van Consulairte en Andere Verslagen en Berigten (Consulaire Verslagen)* (The Hague), 1876–86: Consular reports, Penang and Singapore. Holland destroyed Acehnese vessels after declaring war on Aceh in 1873, leaving this field almost equally in the hands of Chinese traders. The war, however, prevented the establishment of resident Chinese traders in any numbers, while it also gave a larger role to the European firm which acted as provisioner for the Dutch forces.
14. *Koloniaal Verslag*, 1875, p. 18.
15. J.A.M. Cats baron de Raet, "Vergelijking van de vroegeren toestand van Deli, Serdang en Langkat met den tegenwoordige", *TBG* XXXIII (1876): 30.
16. Schadee, *Geschiedenis* I, pp. 171–7.
17. De Raet, "Vergelijking van de vroegeren toestand van Deli", p. 31.
18. Schadee, *Geschiedenis* I, p. 181.
19. De Raet, "Vergelijking van de vroegeren toestand van Deli", p. 33.
20. Schadee, *Geschiedenis* I, p. 186. A much more accurate figure was the number of Chinese employed on Western plantations — 4,476 by the end of 1874. *Koloniaal Verslag*, 1875, p. 196.

Notes to pp. 198–203   391

21. Planters' Committee to Read, 31 May 1882, *The Deli Coolie Question* (Singapore, 1882), pp. 10–1.

22. Moreover, the early Protectors of Chinese were not men of outstanding ability or imagination. Significantly, they took no part in the various attempts during the late 19th century to reform the system of immigration. See, for example, Powell's strained defence of the status quo, in *Straits Settlements Labour Commission Report* [henceforth *SSLCR*] (Singapore, 1890), pp. 69–72.

23. This is the impression given by the *SSLCR*, 1890, pp. 8–11, though earlier sources were more ready to accept the category of "paid passengers" at face value. See especially Report of Protector of Chinese 1883, Annual Reports of the Protector of Chinese, Straits Settlements, *Straits Settlements Government Gazette* [henceforth *SSGG*], 1884, pp. 453–4.

24. Reports of Protector of Chinese for 1878 and 1883, *SSGG*, 1879, p. 113 and 1884, pp. 453–4.

25. "Report of the Committee appointed to consider and take evidence upon the Condition of Chinese Labourers in the Colony", 3 Nov. 1876, *Straits Settlements Legislative Council Proceedings* [henceforth *SSLCP*], Appendix 22, pp. ccxlii–iv.

26. The Protectorate of Chinese continued to base its classification on the *sinkheh*'s answer to the question, "Have you paid your own passage?" so that the change in the organization of the traffic was not officially noted until June 1890. The Court of Appeal then reverted to the original definition in a judgment on a case of forcible detention. Since no *sinkheh* was any longer indebted to the ship on arrival, the effect of this judgment was to remove the legal power of depot-keepers to detain any immigrants. The *status quo ante* was restored by Ordinance I of 1891. *SSLCR* 1890, pp. 8–12. Report of Protector of Chinese for 1990, *SSGG*, 1891, pp. 1084–5.

27. *SSLCR*, 1890, p. 62 of evidence. On this question, as on others, the Chinese Protectors in Singapore and Penang were curiously obscure. On the other hand W. Cowan, Acting Secretary for Chinese Affairs in Perak, told the 1890 Commission: "The men who come down nominally as free passengers are really in debt to the brokers." *Ibid.*, p. 128.

28. E. Thio, "The Singapore Chinese Protectorate: Events and Conditions leading to its establishment, 1823–1877", *Journal of the South Seas Society* xvi (1960): 64.

29. *SSLCP*, 1873, Appendix 33.

30. *SSLCP*, 1873, pp. 139–49. Thio, "The Singapore Chinese Protectorate", pp. 64–5. Jackson, *Pickering, Protector of Chinese*, pp. 49–64. Another,

392   Notes to pp. 203–6

and more obviously self-interested, lobby against "kidnapping" for
Sumatra was the sugar planters of Province Wellesley. Petition of
25 Oct. 1876, *SSLCP* 1876, Appendix 23.

31. *SSLCP*, 1876, Appendix 22, p. cclxxxi. See also the evidence of
Captain Ellis, *ibid.*, p. cclxvii, and the divergent views expressed in
the Legislative Council Meeting of 9 Sept. 1873, *SSLCP*, 1873,
pp. 140 and 149.

32. 1876 Report on Chinese Labourers, *SSLCP*, 1876, Appendix 22,
pp. ccxliii–iv.

33. Ibid., p. ccixxx. Though smaller numerically than the Ghee Hin in
Penang, the Toh Peh Kong included most of the wealthy merchants,
mainly Hokkien. C.D. Cowan, *Nineteenth-Century Malaya* (London:
Oxford University Press, 1961), p. 48.

34. Lavino to Wiggers van Kerchem, 5 Oct. 1876. Consulaat Penang
102, Algemeene Rijksarchief, The Hague. 1876 Report on Chinese
Labourers, *SSLCP*, 1876, Appendix 22, pp. ccxlvi–vii, cclxvii–viii and
cclxxx.

35. Walter Knaggs to Lavino, 23 Aug. 1875, copy in Bylandt to Willebois,
28 Sept. 1875, Buitenlandse Zaken Dossier Atjeh, Algemeene
Rijksarchief.

36. Statement of Colonial Secretary in Legislative Council meeting of
9 Sept. 1873, *SSLCP*, 1873, p. 141. I am indebted to Dr Eunice Thio
for this reference, and much incidental help.

37. Singapore report in *Vezlameling van Consulaire en andere Verslagen en
Berigten*, 1876, p. 113. Schadee, *Geschiedenis van Sumatra's Oostkust*, II,
pp. 14–5. Schadee asserts that the offenders in one of the mutinies
were part of a group who had already escaped from contract labour in
Deli in order to collect a second advance in Penang, and so repeat the
offence.

38. *SSLCP*, 1876, Appendix 22, p. cclix.

39. Ibid., p. cclxvi (Tan Hong Moh): "They don't like going to Deli because
it is very hot, and they don't get back from there, and if they fall sick
they don't get enough treatment." Ibid., p. cclxvii (Lim Kah Kway):
"They don't like going to Deli because the water is bad and makes
their bodies swell up."

40. Walter Knaggs to Lavino, 23 Aug. 1875, *loc. cit.* Lavino to Wiggers van
Kerchem, 5 Oct. 1876, *loc. cit. Koloniaal Verslag*, 1875, p. 196. Ibid.,
1876, p. 198.

41. Annual Report on Revenue and Expenditure of Perak for 1882, *SSGG*,
1883, pp. 1105–6. See also Wong Lin Ken, *The Malayan Tin Industry
to 1914* (Tucson: University of Arizona Press, 1965), p. 74.

Notes to pp. 207–8

42. Schadee, *Geschiedenis van Sumatra's Oostkust*, II, pp. 10–8 and 32–4. *Koloniaal Verslag*, 1878, p. 22. Lavino to Van Lansberge, 4 Feb. 1877, Consulaat Penang 102, Algemeene Rijksarchief.

43. Schadee, *Geschiedenis van Sumatra's Oostkust*, II, pp. 33–9. A. Vandenbosch, *The Dutch East Indies: Its Government, Problems, and Politics* (Los Angeles: University of California Press, 1944), pp. 285–7. J.H. Boeke, *The Structure of the Netherlands Indian Economy* (New York, 1942), p. 142. The highly controversial penal sanction gave rise to an extensive literature, some of which is reviewed in A.D.A. de Kat Angelino, *Colonial Policy* (The Hague: M. Nijhoff, 1931), II, pp. 497–531.

44. Only after 1889 did the governments of the British-protected Malay states issue a series of ordinances to protect labour, which were "honoured more in the breach than in the observance". Government had much less contact with employers in Malaya than in Sumatra, and was reluctant to interfere in a field where it had so little experience. Wong, *The Malayan Tin Industry to 1914*, pp. 73–4. For agricultural labour the Straits Settlements were brought up to the standard of Sumatra by an ordinance of November 1891, *SSGG*, 1891, p. 2582.

45. *SSLCP*, 1876, Appendix 22, p. ccxlvi.

46. P. Endt, *Wanderarbeiterverhaeltnisse*, 1919, quoted in Bruno Lasker, *Human Bondage in South-east Asia* (Chapel Hill: University of North Carolina Press, 1950), p. 221.

47. The attacks on plantation personnel, numbering as many as 80 in 1929, are listed in the annual *Kroniek* of the Oostkust van Sumatra-Instituut. For impressions of conditions in Deli during the early decades of this century see Lasker; W.F. Wertheim, *Indonesian Society in Transition: A study of social change* (The Hague: W. Van Hoeve, 1956), pp. 250–3; Ladislao Szekely, *Tropic Fever. The Adventures of a Planter in Sumatra*, trans. Marion Saunders (London: W. Hamilton Limited, 1936). A similarly critical opinion of 1888 is quoted in A.G. de Bruin, *De Chineezen ter Oostkust van Sumatra* (Leiden, 1918), p. 81. In complete contrast, however, is the enthusiasm of an official British report of 1900. *Parliamentary Papers, House of Commons*, 1900, LXXXVII, p. 103. It seems possible that the predominance of Javanese labour in 20th-century Deli may have encouraged more servility in labour relations, as opposed to an earlier pattern borrowed from the Straits Settlements.

48. The tobacco industry in Sabah suffered from all the difficulties of early Deli when trying to establish itself in 1888–90, including remoteness; Tongkah (Siam) suffered from similar factors in 1876. *SSLCP*, 1876, Appendix 22, p. cclxiv.

394 Notes to pp. 208–13

49. Ibid., pp. cclix–x. *SSGG*, 1883, p. 1105. *The Deli Coolie Question*, pp. 19–20. Wong, *The Malayan Tin Industry to 1914*, pp. 71–6. *SSLCR*, 1890, p. 24 of evidence.

50. *Straits Times and Singapore Journal of Commerce*, 24 Apr. 1869.

51. *Koloniaal Verslag*, 1874, p. 211.

52. *The Deli Coolie Question*, pp. 5–6.

53. *SSLCR*, 1890, pp. 8, 13–4, 16–7, 24, 108 of evidence. Also Wong, *The Malayan Tin Industry to 1914* , p. 67.

54. *The Deli Coolie Question*, pp. 9–10.

55. *SSLCR*, 1890, p. 16. Most observers stressed the rapacity of the Chinese *tindals* in endeavouring to keep unlucky workers in debt; e.g. the Imperial Chinese Commission of 1886, *SSGG*, 1887, pp. 243–4; and John Parker (1888), quoted in De Bruin, *De Chineezen ter Oostkust van Sumatra*, p. 82. And for a later impression see Szekely, *Tropic Fever*, pp. 176–7.

56. Lavino to Wiggers van Kerchern, 5 Oct. 1876, Consulaat Penang, 102, Algemeene Rijksarchief. The brokers also charged $50 for *sinkhehs* recruited to work for the Dutch army of occupation in Aceh before 1877. As was the case for Deli, $25 of this was listed as an advance to the *sinkheh* which the latter was obliged to repay, but almost all of this advance was used to meet the expenses of the *khehtau*. *Consulaire Verslagen* 1878, p. 758. This differential was maintained throughout the 1880s. In 1890 brokers were charging $35–38 for Teochiu *sinkhehs* if for Province Wellesley, and $80–90 if for Sumatra or Sabah. The 1890 Labour Commission considered the profit of the brokers was roughly double in the case of Sumatra and Sabah, but that most of the differential went to meet extra expenses in China. *SSLCR*, 1890, p. 17.

57. See below, pp. 314 and 318.

58. Wong, *The Malayan Tin Industry to 1914*, pp. 69–71. Jackson, *Pickering, Protector of Chinese*, pp. 66–70.

59. Compiled from Annual Reports of the Chinese Protectorate in *SSGG*, and Annual Reports of the Netherlands Consulate in Penang in *Consulaire Verslagen*.

60. *SSGG*, 1881, pp. 354–5.

61. The Deli Planters Committee were nearer the mark, when regretting their inability to recruit large numbers in Singapore, "for it appears that the connexions, between Penang and the Hong Kong coolie Hongs, are so strongly established as to direct the stream of emigration via the northern port". *The Deli Coolie Question*, pp. 6–7.

62. Minute by Pickering, 13 June 1882, ibid., pp. 13–4.

63. The planters of Province Wellesley were always in the vanguard of opposition to what they called "crimping", which meant anything from

Notes to pp. 213–5

enticing labourers away from their plantations to Deli before the expiry of their contracts to merely recruiting at the expense of the Province Wellesley recruiters. See the petition from eleven Province Wellesley sugar planters to the Legislative Council, 25 Oct. 1876, *SSLCP*, 1876, Appendix 23. The presence of Khaw Boo Aun in this delegation may suggest that he, as a Teochiu and a Ghee Hin leader, could not rely on labour through the sources controlled by the Toh Peh Kong. For Khaw see C.S. Wong, *A Gallery of Chinese Kapitans* (Singapore: Ministry of Culture, 1963), pp. 81–3.

64. *The Deli Coolie Question*, pp. 14–5.

65. *SSLCR*, 1890, p. 130 of evidence.

66. Bool, *De Chineesche immigratie naar Deli*, p. 6. *The Deli Coolie Question*, pp. 6–7, 14, 17–8. Another cause of friction was the tendency of Sumatra planters to send back to the Straits Settlements labourers whom they considered unfit. In justification of thus breaking their side of the contract, the planters claimed that substitutions were often made after the contracts had been signed. After an ultimatum from Pickering in 1881, a system of medical inspections for all labourers signing contracts was evolved. The Kapitan China of Labuan (Deli) was charged with checking against substitutions on arrival there. Old or sick relations of the workers could come without medical certificates only if they comprised no more than 15% of the total contract workers. Finally in 1886 the Protectorate agreed to provide photographs of all those signing contracts. Bool, *De Chineesche immigratie naar Deli*, pp. 2–3. P.W. Modderman, *Gedenkboek uitgegeven ter gelegenheid van het Viftig Jarig Bestaan van de Deli Planters Vereeniging* (Batavia, 1929), pp. 33–4, *SSGG*, 1887, p. 244.

67. Ibid.

68. Schadee, *Geschiedenis van Sumatra's Oostkust*, II, pp. 20 and 181.

69. Annual Reports of Protectorate of Chinese, in *SSGG*.

70. Schadee, *Geschiedenis van Sumatra's Oostkust*, II, pp. 20 and 181.

71. Wong, *The Malayan Tin Industry to 1914*, Appendix A, tables 'c' and 'e'.

72. The occupational structure of the different dialect groups in northern Sumatra differed widely. While Teochius, followed by Hakkas, predominated on the estates, there was always a substantial number of Hokkiens in trade. As a result of the gradual integration of Deli into the economy of Netherlands India, where Hokkiens were the largest and longest-established group, they numbered 24.3% of Chinese in the *cultuurgehied* by 1930. Cantonese came to the area mainly as craftsmen, and by 1930 formed 21.1% of the total, as against 21.8% Teochius. Hakkas were active in small trade as well as estate labour.

396   Notes to p. 216

Though only 8.7% of the Chinese in the *cultuurgebied* in 1930, they had long held a virtual monopoly of official positions throughout northern Sumatra — as *kapitans china*. This tradition probably began with the predominance of Chang Chen-hsun (alias Thio Tiau Siat), a Batavia Hakka who went to Aceh as contractor to the Dutch army, and by 1877 was farming most of the government monopolies of the east coast.

The Chinese communities of the Bengkalis district (Kampar, Siak, and Rokan), occupied in fishing, lumbering, and trade, were overwhelmingly Hokkien (82% in 1930). The smaller group of Chinese in Aceh (21,795), on the other hand, was predominantly Hakka (40.8%) and Cantonese (27.7%) in 1930.

Though Chinese secret societies were forbidden in Netherlands India, branches of Penang societies certainly existed among plantation workers of the *cultuurgebied*. In the period 1881–4 there was a series of violent incidents between the Ghee Hin, which in Sumatra represented primarily Teochius, Hakkas, and Hailams, and the Ho-seng, representing Hokkiens and Hakkas from Fiu-chew. Sterner measures were taken in 1884 to suppress these societies. De Bruin, *De Chineezen ter Oostkust van Sumatra*, pp. 38–52. Bool, *De Chineesche immigratie naar Del,* pp. 27–82. Schadee, *Geschiedenis van Sumatra's Oostkust*, II, pp. 45–6. Lavino to Governor-General, 17 Feb. 1877 and 22 Apr. 1884. Consulaat Penang 102, 13, Algemeene Rijksarchief. Wen Chung-chi, *The Nineteenth-Century Imperial Chinese Consulate in the Straits Settlements: Origins and Development*, unpublished thesis (University of Singapore, 1964), pp. 235–8.

73. *SSGG*, 1879, pp. 113–4. Ibid., 1880, pp. 225 and 751.
74. The first consul, and one of the first Chinese representatives abroad, was Hoo Ah Kay ("Whampoa"), the greatly respected Singapore merchant, who had been made a C.M.G. and a member of the Legislative and Executive Councils by the British. During his tenure from 1877 to his death in 1880 he did nothing to disturb the British authorities. Tso by contrast was a bright young Chinese official and scholar, though unusually well versed in Western affairs. Wen, *The Nineteenth-Century Imperial Chinese Consulate*, pp. 86–9.
75. Ibid., pp. 121–3. *SSGG*, 1886, p. 133.
76. Bool, *De Chineesche immigratie naar Deli*, p. 4. Modderman, *Gedenkboek uitgegeven ter gelegenheid*, p. 45. The increased hostility towards Deli about this time may have owed something also to the tour of two Chinese Government Commissioners, who visited Deli among other places in 1886. There is a wide discrepancy between the favourable

Notes to pp. 216–9

impression which they told Pickering they had of Deli (*SSGG*, 1887, pp. 243–4) and the extremely critical one quoted by Wen Chung-chi (p. 132) from a Chinese printed source of 1928.

77. *SSGG*, 1887, p. 244.

78. Ibid., 1889, p. 221.

79. Pickering, in *SSGG*, 1889, pp. 222–3. *SSLCR*, 1890, pp. 17 and 19, and pp. 14–5 of evidence.

80. Pickering's 1883 report (*SSGG*, 1884, pp. 453–4) looked forward to the banning of indebted immigrants, who were subject to so many abuses. Subsequently, however, neither he nor his successors reverted to the subject, even when the "unpaid passengers" became an unimportant fraction of the total arrivals in the 1890s. On the contrary, the British Government refused to take up the recommendations of the 1890 Labour Commission for a cooperative Anglo-Chinese regulation of the migrant traffic, on the grounds that the credit-ticket system would never obtain official Chinese recognition. Wong, *The Malayan Tin Industry to 1914*, p. 69. The reports of the Protectorate suggest that a genuine concern to assist Chinese immigrants in its earliest years gradually gave way to a defence of its own vested interests, which included the fees (25 cents on contracts for British Malaya, $1 on those for elsewhere) accruing as a result of the indentured labour system.

81. Bool, *De Chineesche immigratie naar Deli*, p. 4. *Consulaire Verslagen*, 1887, p. 435; 1888, pp. 790 and 1073.

82. From annual reports of Chinese Protectorate in *SSGG*.

83. These figures are larger than those in the final column of Table 4 because they include (a) 3,000–5,000 Indonesians each year, (b) some *laukhehs* who had already worked for some time in the Nanyang. The only region taking an increasing number of contract labourers during this period was Sabah, where tobacco was being established. Taking fewer than 500 before 1888, Sabah recruited 3,028 in that year, 6,321 in 1889 and 7,223 in 1890. *SSGG*, 1891, p. 1087. Wong, *The Malayan Tin Industry to 1914*, p. 67.

84. See below, pp. 219–21.

85. Bool, *De Chineesche immigratie naar Deli*, pp. 5–6. Schadee, *Geschiedenis van Sumatra's Oostkust*, II, pp. 35 and 44.

86. The Deli Mij., the Deli Batavia Mij., the Tabaksmaatschappij Arendsburg, the Amsterdam Deli Compagnie and Messrs Naeher & Grob.

87. Commercially Germany was the country most interested in breaking British predominance in Asian trade. Germans also had a large share in Deli tobacco. Among the 688 European residents of Sumatra's East

398   Notes to pp. 219–26

Coast in 1884 were 390 Netherlanders, 123 Germans, and 88 British. Schadee, *Geschiedenis van Sumatra's Oostkust*, II, p. 41.

88. Bool, *De Chineesche immigratie naar Deli*, pp. 6–10. Schadee, *Geschiedenis van Sumatra's Oostkust*, II, pp. 219–20.

89. Bool, *De Chineesche immigratie naar Deli*, p. 11.

90. Bool, *De Chineesche immigratie naar Deli*, pp. 28 and 40. Modderman, *Gedenkboek uitgegeven ter gelegenheid*, pp. 50–4. *Consulaire Verstagen*, 1889, II, pp. 35–6; 1890, II, pp. 37–8. The planters differentiated between so-called "first class coolies" recruited in Swatow, who were mainly Teochiu, and "second class coolies", recruited locally, who were usually Hakkas or Hokkiens, and were often *laukhehs* rather than *sinkhehs*.

91. Bool, *De Chineesche immigratie naar Deli*, p. 26. Jebson & Co. (Hong Kong) took over this contract in 1904, and the K.P.M. in 1914.

92. Bool, *De Chineesche immigratie naar Deli*, pp. 11–2.

93. In a proclamation of May 1890, the Provincial authorities of Kwangtung endorsed this by stating the disturbance on the *China* was solely the work of the Straits brokers. Bool, *De Chineesche immigratie naar Deli*, p. 17.

94. *Consulaire Verslagen*, 1890, II, p. 37. *SSGG*, 1890, p. 847. Bool, *De Chineesche immigratie naar Deli*, p. 13.

95. Bool, *De Chineesche immigratie naar Deli*, p. 17.

96. Ibid., pp. 19–21.

97. Ibid., p. 22.

98. Schadee, *Geschiedenis van Sumatra's Oostkust*, II, pp. 223–4. *Consulaire Verslagen*, 1888, p. 790.

99. *Koloniaal Verslag*, 1880, p. 192. Schadee, *Geschiedenis van Sumatra's Oostkust*, II, p. 44.

100. *Consulaire Verslagen*, 1888, p. 1076. Also Schadee, *Geschiedenis van Sumatra's Oostkust*, II, p. 223; *SSGG*, 1891, p. 1087.

101. From *Kolonial Verslagen*, relevant years.

102. The majority of these were brought directly from Swatow. After 1899 the Immigrants Bureau ceased to recruit from the Straits Settlements, though planters who were not members of the D.P.V. continued to do so in small numbers.

103. Bool, *De Chineesche immigratie naar Deli*, p. 24; Boeke, *The Structure of the Netherlands Indian Economy*, pp. 74–5.

Chapter 10

1. H.J. Benda, *The Crescent and the Rising Sun. Indonesian Islam under the Japanese Occupation, 1942–1945* (The Hague: W. van Hoeve, 1958), p. 131; W.F. Wertheim, *Indonesian Society in Transition: A Study of Social*

Notes to pp. 227–31

Change (The Hague: W. van Hoeve, 1959), p. 318. The version in which this chapter was first published, as the author's first academic article in 1967, was influenced by the same mind-set.

2. Michael Francis Laffan, *Islamic Nationhood and Colonial Indonesia: the umma below the winds* (London/New York: Routledge Curzon, 2003).

3. C.C. Berg, "Indonesia", in *Whither Islam?*, ed. H.A.R. Gibb (London: V. Gollanck, 1932), p. 262.

4. The Indonesian role in these matters is well covered in Laffan, *Islamic Nationhood*, pp. 202–14.

5. Gottfried Simon, *The Progress and Arrest of Islam in Sumatra* (London: Marshall Brothers, 1912), pp. 38–9.

6. The debate over how to read the Javanese variants of Islam was enlivened by Clifford Geertz, *The Religion of Java* (Glencoe: Free Press, 1960), and continued in M.C. Ricklefs, "Six Centuries of Islamization in Java", in *Conversion to Islam*, ed. Nehemia Levtzion (New York: Holmes & Meier, 1979), pp. 100–29; Mark Woodward, *Islam in Java: Normative piety and mysticism in the Sultanate of Yogyakarta* (Tucson: University of Arizona Press, 1989); Robert Hefner and Patricia Horvatich (ed.), *Islam in an Era of Nation-States* (Honolulu: University of Hawaii Press, 1997).

7. J. Vredenbregt, "The Haddj, Some of Its Features and Functions in Indonesia", *BKI* 118 (1962): 140–52.

8. Lavino to Read, 21 July 1873, Algemeen Rijksarchief, Consulaat Penang 100.

9. C. Snouck Hurgronje, *Mekka in the Latter Part of the Nineteenth Century*, trans. J.H. Monahan (London: Luzac & Co., 1931), pp. 220–30.

10. There were estimated to be 10,000 such residents in the 1920s, though an official count in 1937 revealed only 3,113, of whom 1,400 were students; G.-H. Bousquet, *La politique musulmane et coloniale des Pays-Bas* (Paris, 1938), pp. 38–9.

11. Snouck Hurgronje, *Mekka*, pp. 259–61. See also Laffan, *Islamic Nationhood*, pp. 62–76.

12. L.W.C. van den Berg, *Le Hadhramaut et les colonies arabes dans l'archipel Indien* (Batavia, 1886), pp. 105–20. J.A. Morley, "The Arabs and the Eastern Trade", *JMBRAS* 22, 1 (1949): 156. C. Snouck Hurgronie, "L'Arabie et les Indes Néerlandaises", *Revue de I'Histoire des Religions* 57 (1908): 74–5. *Encyclopedia van Nederlandsch-Indië* (The Hague, 1917), II, p. 3.

13. Vredenbregt, "The Haddj", pp. 98–103.

14. C. Snouck Hurgronje, *Nederland en de Islam*, 2nd ed. (Leiden: E.J. Brill, 1915), p. 73. A different motive for antagonism towards Holland among a small group of Western-educated Turks was revealed in the semi-official

400   Notes to pp. 232–4

Constantinople newspaper *La Turquie,* in May–July 1873. This dwelt less on religious grievances than on the evils of the forced cultivation system, in a manner similar to that of European liberals.

15. Van de Putte to Cremers, 1 Nov. 1864, Algemeen Rijksarchief, Kol.Kab. F11, Dossier 5971.

16. For a discussion of this community see W.R. Roff, "The Malayo-Muslim world of Singapore at the Close of the Nineteenth Century", *JAS* XXIV, 1 (1964): 75–90.

17. Van de Putte to Cremers, 4 Jan. 1866; also Read to Cremers, 31 July 1865; A.R.A., Buitenlandse Zaken Dossier 3076.

18. Read to Loudon, 23 June 1873, copy Koloniën to B.Z., 6 Sept. 1873, Buitenlandse Zaken Dossier Atjeh.

19. Foreign Office to Colonial Office, 13 Apr. and 20 July 1885, C.O. 273/137.

20. So called by Europeans, presumably because they first heard the Islamic party described by analogy with the priests of the Portuguese. Contemporary Malays referred to them only as *orang puteh,* in reference to the white robes commonly associated with Muslin fervor. An Indonesian work refers to the "Padris" only as *kaum muda Islam,* thus associating them with modernism; Dawis Datoek Madjolelo and Ahmad Marzoeki, *Tuanku Imam Bondiol* (Djakarta/Amsterdam, 1950), pp. 61–2 and *passim.* The best discussion of the Padris to date is in Christine Dobbin, *Islamic Revivalism in a Changing Peasant Economy: Central Sumatra 1784–1847* (London: Curzon Press, 1983).

21. A.H. Johns, "Muslim Mystics and Historical Writing", *Historians of South East Asia,* ed. D.G.E. Hall (London: Oxford University Press, 1961), p. 42.

22. Madjolelo and Marzoeki, *Tuanku Imam Bondiol,* pp. 46–7. R.A. Kern, "Padri", *The Encyclopedia of Islam, III* (Leiden/London, 1936), p. 1018. B. Schrieke, "Bijdragen tot de Bibliografie van de huidige godsdienstige beweging ter Sumatra's Westkust", *TBG* 59 (1919–21): 249–57. Schrieke's emphatic contention that the "Padris" were not Wahhabis is no doubt strictly correct, in view of the paucity of communication with Arabia and the very different conditions with which reformers in Minangkabau were faced. His argument does not, however, appear to destroy the orthodox view that the three Minangkabau hajis were to some extent inspired by the example of the Wahhabis, then threatening Mecca and Medina from their base in Nejd.

23. In addition to Dobbin, *Islamic Revivalism,* the military aspect of the war has received voluminous treatment in H.M. Lange, *Het Nederlandsch Oost-Indisch Leger ter Westkust van Sumatra (1819–1845),* 2 vols.

Notes to pp. 234–6   401

('s Hertogenbosch, 1852); H.J.J.L. de Stuers, *De Vestiging en uitbreiding der Nederlanders ter Westkust van Sumatra*, 2 vols. (Amsterdam, 1849–50); and the more balanced series of articles by E.B. Kielstra in *BKI* 36 (1887): 7–163; *BKI* 37 (1888): 216–380; *BKI* 38 (1889): 161–249, 313–79, 467–514; *BKI* 39 (1890): 127–221, 263–348; *BKI* 40 (1891): 254–330, 622–706.

24. E.S. de Klerck, *De Atjeh-oorlog* (The Hague, 1912), pp. 145–51, 163–6.

25. This kind of official concern was much clearer in the case of the later NZV mission to the Karo-Bataks adjacent to the plantation belt of East Sumatra — Rita Smith Kipp, *The Early Years of a Dutch Colonial Mission: The Karo Field* (Ann Arbor, 1990).

26. Schrieke, "Bijdragen", pp. 262–6. The importance of the Naqshibandiyah-tariqah in fostering more exclusive attitudes during the second half of the 19th century has at last been systematically investigated by Martin van Bruinessen, *Tarekat Naqsyabandiyah di Indonesia* (Jakarta: Mizan, 1992). Its growth in Bantam during the 1880s and its connection with anti-Dutch movements there was of concern to the Dutch Consul-General in Singapore, who noted that it counted about 500 members there in 1888. *Verzameling van Consulaire en andere Verslagen en Berigten*, 1889, pp. 56–7.

27. E.S. de Klerck, *History of the Netherlands East Indies* (Rotterdam: Brusse, 1938), pp. 11, 279–84. Once more the international connection is not well established. The Dutch did, however, take action in 1857 against a rumour circulated in Sumatra by returning hajis, to the effect that some *ulama* in Mecca had received a revelation that the Prophet was weeping over the advance of the Christian Powers in Asia. Orfeur Cavenagh, *Reminiscences of an Indian Official* (London: W.H. Allen, 1884), pp. 355–6.

28. Note by Bureau A: "Turksche bemoeijing in den N.I. Archipel", n.d. (1864), A.R.A., Kol.Kab.H 10, Dossier 5970. Rochusscn to Van Goltstein, 4 Sept. 1858; Van Zuylen van Nyeveldt to Goltstcin, 30 Sept. 1858; A.R.A., B.Z. Dossier 3076. J. Tideman, *Djambi* (Amsterdam: Koninklijke Vereeniging, 1938), pp. 31–3.

29. *Encyclopedie van Nederlansch-Indië* I, pp. 135–6 and 274. W.A. van Rees, *De Bandjermasinsche Krijg van 1859–1863* (Arnhem, 1865), pp. 31–51, 165–6, 180–3, 284–6.

30. Hasselman to Van Zuylen van Nyeveldt, 6 Sept. 1867, A.R.A. Kol.Kab. x9, Dossier 5994. *De Atjeh-oorlog*, pp. 294–5. C.A. Kroesen, "Geschiedenis van Asahan", *TBG* 31 (1886): 107n.

31. Heldewier to Gericke, 19 and 26 June 1873, Buitenlandse Zaken Dossier Atjeh.

402   Notes to pp. 237–41

32. De Klerck, *De Atjeh-oorlog*, pp. 216–7.
33. Ibid., pp. 461–2. Alexander, "Korte levensschets van de Arabier Habib Abdoe'rRahman Alzahir", *De Indische Gids* 2, II (1880): 1008–20, trans. in Anthony Reid, "Habib Abdur-rahman az-Zahir (1833–1890)", *Indonesia* 13 (April 1972): 37–60. Habib Abdur-Rahman's role in Aceh diplomacy is covered in Anthony Reid, *The Contest for North Sumatra* (Kuala Lumpur: OUP, 1969).
34. Keun to Roest van Limburg, 2 Dec. 1868 and 3 Feb. 1869, A.R.A., B.Z. Dossier 3076.
35. J. Woltring, *Bescheiden Betraffende de Buitenlandse Politick van Nederland*, Vol. I (1871–4) (The Hague: R.G.P., 1962), p. 420.
36. Ibid., p. 541. R.H. Davison, *Reform in the Ottoman Empire 1856–76* (Princeton: Princeton University Press, 1963), p. 276. Constantinople press clippings of May–July 1873 in Buitenlandse Zaken, Dossier Aceh.
37. Elliot to Granville, 8 May 1873, F.0. 78/2267.
38. Woltring, *Bescheiden Betreffende*, pp. 612–4. Heldewier to Gericke, 7 and 23 July 1873, Buitenlandse Zaken, Dossier Atjeh.
39. Heldewier to Gericke, 1, 6, 15 Dec. 1873, Buitenlandse Zaken, Dossier Atjeh.
40. Maier to Loudon, 22 Nov. and 14 Dec. 1874, copies to Lavino, Algemeen Rijksarchief, Consulaat Penang 99.
41. Davison, *Reform in the Ottoman Empire*, p. 276. Heldewier to Gericke, 11 July 1873, Buitenlandse Zaken, Dossier Atjeh.
42. Lavino to Read, 5 Sept. 1873, A.R.A., Consulaat Penang 100.
43. Enclosures in Governor-General to Koloniën, 27 Sept., 7 and 15 Oct. 1873, A.R.A., Kol.Kab. D38, Dossier 6042. Series of letters, July–Sept. 1873, in A.R.A., Consulaat Singapore 100.
44. Tramp to Loudon, 26 Nov. 1873, copy Governor-General to Koloniën, 19 Dec. 1873, A.R.A., Kol.Kab. A9, Dossier 6047.
45. Secret Report of K.H. Hall, July 30, 1873, copy Governor-General to Koloniën, 16 Aug. 1873, A.R.A., Kol.Kab. Q30, Dossier 6040.
46. Read to Loudon, 17 Dec. 1873, copy Governor-General to Koloniën, 16 Aug. 1873, A.R.A., Kol.Kab.Q30, Dossier 6040.
47. Harris to Granville, 22 July 1873, F.O. 37/534.
48. Woltring, p. 586.
49. Circular to Consuls in Muslim countries, 22 Aug. 1873, F.O. 83/414.
50. Government of India to Argyll, 2 Oct. 1873, copy India office to Foreign Office, 3 Nov. 1873, F.O. 37/519.
51. Lavino to Van Lansberge, 25 Nov. 1875; Maier to Van Lansberge, 16 Nov. 1875; A.R.A., Consulaat Penang 102 and 99 resp. The only phenomenon in the Peninsula bearing a resemblance to the type of

Notes to pp. 241–3

403

Islamic movement described in this paper was the rebellion led by Orang Kaya Bahman in Pahang (1891–5). Beginning, as so often, with the personal grievance of a chief, the movement gained considerable popular support even in neighbouring Trengganu and Kelantan as the result of a religious appeal against the British. This appeal certainly owed much to the inspiration of a famous Trengganu religious leader, Ungku Sayyid, and some Pahang hajis, but on the other hand Malaya's East Coast was isolated from the main stream of the 19th-century Muslim awakening. On the popular level magical charms and mystical formulae appear to have been more important than Islamic solidarity. See W. Linehan, "A History of Pahang", *JMBRAS* 14, pt. 2 (1936): 139–68; and for some colourful anecdotes, Hugh Clifford, *Bush-whacking* (Edinburgh/London: W. Blackwood, 1901), pp. 64–8.

52. Maier to Willebois, 18 Sept. 1875, Buitenlandse Zaken Dossier Aceh. Read to Van Lansberge, 16 Mar. and 1 Apr. 1876, copies to Lavino, A.R.A., Consulaat Penang 99.

53. Maier to Read, 8 May 1875 (private), extract in Bylandt to Willebois, 12 June 1875, Buitenlandse Zaken Dossier Aceh.

54. Maier to Van Lansberge, 24 July 1875, copy to Lavino, A.R.A., Consulaat Penang 99. The rumour apparently derived from Turkey's announcement of its intention to appoint an ambassador to Peking to protect Chinese Muslims.

55. Sultan Daud to Alsagoff, r8 Ragab 1307H (10 Mar. 1890), trans. Governor-General to Koloniën, 12 Sept. 1890; Van Assen to Van Teijn, 13 Sept. 1890, copy G-G. to Koloniën, 26 Sept. 1890; A.R.A., Kol.Kab. H16, Dossier 6198.

56. Deijkerhoff to Pijnacker Hordijk, 17 Mar. 1893, copy G-G. to Koloniën, 30 Mar. 1893, A.R.A., Kol.Kab. N8, Dossier 6219. Enclosures in Smith to Meade, 30 May 1892 (private), and Smith to Ripon, 19 Oct. 1892, C.O. 273/180 and 273/183.

57. *Ambtelijke Adviezen van C. Snouck Hurgronie*, ed. E. Gobée and C. Adriaanse (The Hague, 1957–9), I, pp. 153–7.

58. T.W. Arnold, *The Caliphate* (Oxford, 1924), pp. 173–7. C. Snouck Hurgronje, *The Holy War "Made in Germany"*, trans. J.E. Gillet (New York, 1915), pp. 23–7.

59. Weld to Kimberley, 18 and 28 May 1881, C.O. 273/108.

60. Weld to Kimberley, 27 Aug. 1881, C.O. 273/109.

61. The Dutch Consul-General in Singapore, W.H. Read, always suspicious of Alsagoff, had a similar impression. He pointed accusingly at the hospitality the Sayyid had extended to some of the Palembang conspirators and to the anti-Dutch leaders in Jambi, and alleged that he

404 Notes to pp. 243–5

had promised support to the latter. Weld to 's-Jacob, 4 Oct. 1881 (most confidential), private Singapore letterbook III, Singapore Museum.

62. Banten, like Aceh, inherited the legacy of a flourishing 17th century mercantile emporium and Muslim center. Conquered by force alone in 1682 and again after a revolt in 1751, the inhabitants of the northern coastal plain in particular were ever prone to express their discontent over miserable economic conditions by revolting under religious leadership. The minor outbreak of 1881 was one of several, marking a gradual rise in tension from the preaching of Haii Abdul Karim in 1872, and the activity of the Naqshibandiyah-tariqah, to the violent climax of July 1888, when all the European men in Cilegon, including an Assistant-Resident of Serang, were assassinated. Most of the leaders of the revolt were hajis, one of them a son of Haji Wachia. The effect of the Cilegon affair on contemporary Dutch opinion was considerable; it cost "not only the lives of a small group of Europeans established there, but also the normal working of the intelligence of a much more important number of Europeans in the Indies". C. Snouck Hurgronje, "Vergeten Jubilés" (1923), *Verspreide Geschriften* (Bonn/Leipzig, 1924–6), IV, ii: 429. Also *Encyclopedie van Nederlandsch Oost Indië* (The Hague, 1918–38), I, p. 166. Snouck Hurgronje, *Verspreide Geschriften* IV, i: 249–56. A similar incident had occurred in the supposedly "pacified" part of Djambi in May 1885, when three Europeans had been killed by two *hajis*.

63. Lavino to Rochussen, 22 Aug. 1881, Buitenlandse Zaken Dossier Atjeh.

64. *Ambtelijke Adviezen*, II, 1617, 1619–20, 1737–8.

65. Ibid., p. 1662.

66. Ibid., pp. 1740–1. *Bescheiden betreffende de buitenlandse politiek van Nederland,* Period 3, ed. C. Smit (The Hague, 1957), I, pp. 166–7, and II, 250–11, 280–1. Mitchell to Chamberlain, 6 Jan. 1899, GD/C 7, Singapore Museum. Enclosures in C.O. to Singapore, 14 and 19 July 1904, COD/C 41, Singapore Museum. After the death of Haji Attaoullah in 1903 and the subsequent British veto of Kiamil, successive German Consuls acted as Turkish Consuls-General in Singapore.

67. Trans. in C.O. to Singapore, 30 Mar. 1899, COD/C 3r, Singapore Museum.

68. *Ambtelijke Adviezen*, II, pp. 1620–42.

69. Ibid., pp. 1647–52. Enclosures in B.Z. to Koloniën, 11 Mar. 1899, A.R.A., Kol.Kab.P 4, Dossier 6260.

70. Swettenham to Chamberlain, 6 July 1900, GD/C 8, Singapore Museum.

71. *Ambtelijke Adviezen*, II, p. 1640.

72. *Koloniaal Verslag*, 1905, p. 43. *Encyclopedie van Nederlandsch-Indië*, 1, p. 612. At the same period four Turkish instructors were reported to be

Notes to pp. 246–52

assisting in the defence of Boni (Celebes). *Ambtelijke Adviezen*, II, p. 1743.

73. Ibid., pp. 1741–4. Musurus Pasha to Lansdowne, 29 June 1904, copy C.O. to Singapore, 6 July 1904, COD/C 41, Singapore Museum.
74. *Ambtelijke Adviezen*, II, 1662.
75. Smit, II, pp. 271–4, 328–9, 364–6, 443–5.
76. We are still in need of a full appraisal of the work of Snouck Hurgronje for a better knowledge of the foundations of the ethical policy. The excellent essay of Benda in *The Crescent and the Rising Sun*, pp. 19–31 would appear somewhat to exaggerate the obscurantism of Dutch policy-makers before Snouck Hurgronje.
77. Snouck Hurgronje, *The Holy War "Made in Germany"*, X, p. 27.
78. Snouck Hurgronje, *Nederland en de Islam*, p. 99 and *passim*. Also "Over Panislamisme", 1910, *Verspreide Geschriften*, ed. A.J. Wensinck (Leiden, 1922), I, 378 and *passim*.
79. Among others Benda, *The Crescent and the Rising Sun*; Deliar Noer, *The Modernist Muslim Movement in Indonesia 1900–1942* (Kuala Lumpur, 1973); C. van Dijk, *Rebellion under the Banner of Islam* (The Hague: Martinus Nihhoff, 1981); Takashi Shiraishi, *An Age in Motion: Popular Radicalism in Java, 1912–1926* (Ithaca: Cornell University Press, 1990).
80. Benda, *The Crescent and the Rising Sun*, p. 31.

Chapter 11

1. Charles Burton Buckley, *An Anecdotal History of Old Times in Singapore* (1902, reprinted Kuala Lumpur: University of Malaya Press, 1965), pp. 76 and 367.
2. W.H. Read, *Play and Politics. Recollections of Malaya, by an Old Resident* (London: W. Gardner, 1901), pp. 4–6; Buckley, *An Anecdotal History of Old Times in Singapore*, pp. 367–8.
3. Raja Ali Haji, *Tuhfat al Nafis (The Precious Gift)*, ed. Virginia Matheson and Barbara Andaya (Kuala Lumpur; New York: Oxford University Press, 1982), pp. 287 and 405.
4. Buckley, *Anecdotal History*, p. 623.
5. Ibid., pp. 367–8; *Who Was Who 1987–1915* (London, 1935), p. 589.
6. *Straits Times*, 11 Oct. 1873.
7. *Straits Times*, 1873; C.N. Parkinson, *British Intervention in Malaya 1867–1877* (Kuala Lumpur, 1964), pp. 31, 66 and 119.
8. Read, 1901, pp. 56–77.
9. Song Ong Siang, *One Hundred Years of the Chinese in Singapore* (1923, reprinted Singapore: University of Malaya Press, 1967), pp. 87–8, 124–5.

406 Notes to pp. 252–8

10. Ibid., pp. 13–6.
11. C.H.H. Wake, "Nineteenth Century Johore: Ruler and Realm in Transition", PhD diss. (Australian National University, 1966), pp. 297–8.
12. Khoo Kay Kim, *The Western Malay States 1850–1873* (Kuala Lumpur: OUP, 1972), pp. 103–4; Read, *Play and Politics*, pp. 24–7; W.D. McIntyre, *The Imperial Frontier in the Tropics, 1865–75* (London: Macmillan 1967), pp. 144–9, 203; C.N. Parkinson 1964, pp. 119–23; Col. R.H. Vetch, *Life of Lieut. General the Hon. Sir Andrew Clarke* (London 1905), pp. 149, 172–3. Read's role in this British forward movement is more fully described in the original version of this chapter, published in *Empires, Imperialism and Southeast Asia: Essays in Honour of Nicholas Tarling*, ed. Brook Barrington (Clayton: Monash Asia Institute, 1997), pp. 34–59.
13. Read, *Play and Politics*, pp. 85–90; *Who Was Who*, p. 589.
14. Read, *Play and Politics*, pp. 38–48; A.L. Moffat, *Mongkut, the King of Siam* (Ithaca, NY: Cornell University Press, 1961), pp. 119, 121 and 123.
15. Consideratiën en advies van het B.Z., 5 Dec. 1856, and correspondence there enclosed; Departement van Kolonien [henceforth Kol.] to Department van Buitenlandse Zaken [henceforth B.Z.] 6 May 1857; both in B.Z 3050, Algemene Riksarchief, The Hague [henceforth ARA].
16. Read to B.Z., 8 Oct. 1857; NHM to B.Z. ,13 Oct. 1857; both in B.Z. 3050, ARA
17. Read to B.Z., 5. Feb. 1863 and attached documents; NHM to B.Z., 24 Nov. 1863; both in B.Z. 3050, ARA.
18. B.Z. to Kol., 10 Feb. 1860; Kol to B.Z. 21 Sept. 1860; both in B.Z. 3050, ARA.
19. Anthony Reid, *The Contest for North Sumatra: Atjeh, the Netherlands and Britain, 1858–1898* (Kuala Lumpur: University of Malaya Press, 1969), pp. 30–41.
20. Kol. to B.Z., 22 Aug. 1863; also Kol. to Governor-General of Netherlands India [henceforth GGvNI], 22 Aug. 1863; both in B.Z. 3050, ARA.
21. B.Z. to Paddy 25 Sept. 1863, B.Z. 3050, ARA.
22. Netscher to GGvNI, 27 Nov. 1863, 3050, ARA.
23. H.J.D. Padday to B.Z., 4 Feb. 1864, 10 Mar. 1864; B.Z. to King of Netherlands, 21 Apr. 1864; W.C.S. Padday to B.Z., 26 Sept. 1865; all in B.Z. 3050, ARA.
24. B.Z. to Kol., 26 Nov. 1863; Kol. to B.Z., 15 Dec. 1863; both in BZ. 3050, ARA.
25. Reid, *The Contest*, p. 53.
26. B.Z. to Read, 21 Apr. 1869, & attached letters, in B.Z. 3050, ARA.

Notes to pp. 258–66 407

27. Read to B.Z., 16 June 1869; B.Z. to Read, 6 Aug. 1869; Read to B.Z., 8 Oct. 1869; all in B.Z. 3050, ARA.
28. B.Z. to Read, 2 Dec. 1869 and 3 May 1869; Read to B.Z., 14 Mar. 1870 and 20 Oct. 1870; all in B.Z. 3050, ARA.
29. GGvNI to Kol., 24 Dec. 1870, B.Z. 669, ARA. F.O. to C.O. 17 May 1871, C.O. 273/53. Public Record Office, London [henceforth PRO].
30. Kruyt [Consul Jidda] to B.Z., 30 Sept. 1880, B.Z. 669, ARA.
31. R.B. Read (Acting Consul-General) to B.Z., 28 Mar. 1881, B.Z. 669, ARA. In 1881 $8,694 came from pilgrim visas in a total consular income of $11,868. The only other major items were $1,364 as a commission taken by the consulate in arranging repairs to Dutch warships, and $823 charged to Dutch steamers visiting Singapore as tonnage.
32. E.S. de Klerck, *De Atjeh-oorlog* (The Hague, 1912), p. 350; Reid, *The Contest*, pp. 79–96; Reid, "Indonesian Diplomacy", pp. 74–114; Paul Van't Veer, *De Atjeh-oorlog* (Amsterdam, 1969), pp. 43–8.
33. Klerck, *De Atjeh-oorlog*, pp. 359–95; Reid, *The Contest*, pp. 79–96; Anthony Reid, "Indonesian Diplomacy. A Documentary Study of Atjehnese Foreign Policy in the Reign of Sultan Mahmud, 1870–74", *JMBRAS* (1969a): 74–114; Van't Veer, *De Atjeh-oorlog*, pp. 43–8.
34. Read to GGvN1, 6 Mar. 873, B.Z. Atjeh I, ARA. Read comments on Ord letter, 19 Mar. 1873, Consulate Singapore 100.
35. Studer to Hale (Washington), 18 Mar. 1873, U.S. Consular Despatches, Singapore.
36. Ord To Kimberley, 24 Mar. 1873, CO 273/65, P.R.O.
37. Anthony Reid, "Tengku Mohamed Arifin, Envoy Extraordinary", *Peninjau Sejarah* (Kuala Lumpur, 1968), pp. 31–4.
38. Studer to Hale (Washington), 18 Mar. 1873, U.S. Consular Despatches, Singapore.
39. Ibid.
40. Read to N.I. General Secretary, 20 Feb. 1873, Consulaat Singapore 8.
41. Read to GGvNI, 7 July 1873, B.Z. Atjeh, ARA.
42. Reid, "Tengku Mohamed Arifin", pp. 35–9.
43. Army Commander to GGvNI, 2 Aug. 1873, Kol.Kab. Q30 1873, Dossier 6040, ARA.
44. Read to GGvNI, 8 Sept. 1873, Kol.Kab. Q30 1873, Dossier 6040, ARA. Various notes in an Arifin file of 1873–76 in Consulaat Singapore 100.
45. Read to GGvNI, 11 Mar. 1873, B.Z. Atjeh, ARA.
46. Read to GGvNI, 3 June 1873, B.Z. Blokkade Atjeh, ARA.
47. Read to GGvNI, 14 Oct. 1873 and 10 Feb. 1874, B.Z. Blokkade Atjeh, ARA.

408   Notes to pp. 266–72

48. Vetch, 1905, p. 129; Reid, *The Contest*, pp. 160–1.
49. Van't Veer, *De Atjeh-oorlog*, p. 23.
50. Lavino to B.Z., 28 Jan. 1882, Consulaat Penang 11.
51. Stortenbecker to Read, 1 May 1873, Consulaat Singapore 100.
52. Stortenbecker to Read, 30 Apr. 1873, Consulaat Singapore 100.
53. Stortenbecker to Read, 2 Aug. 1873, Consulaat Singapore 100. Besluit GGvNI 2 June 1874, in GGvNI to Kol., 2 June 1874, Kol. Kab. 25 August 1874, ARA 1052.
54. Army Commander to Lavino, 30 June 1873; 30 Aug. 1873; 19 Dec. 1873; Consulaat Penang 99. Lavino to Army Commander, 5 Aug. 1873; 2 Oct. 1873; and 11 Nov. 1873, Consulaat Penang 100.
55. Lavino to Army Commander, 18 Sept. 1873 and 2 Oct. 1873, Consulaat Penang 100.
56. Reid, *The Contest*, pp. 93n and 97n; Lavino to Chef van het bureau voor de Krijgstoerustingen op Sumatra, 8 Aug. 1873; 12 Aug. 1873; 23 Aug. 1873; 3 Oct. 1873, in Consulaat Penang 100. Lavino to Read, 8 July 1873; 19 Sept. 1873, in Consulaat Penang 100. Army Commander to Read, 13 July 1873, Consulaat Singapore 100.
57. Lavino to Army Commander, 29 Aug. 1873; 2 Sept. 1873 (twice); 15 Sept. 1873, in Consulaat Penang 100.
58. Lavino to Read, 19 Sept. 1873, Consulaat Penang 100.
59. Read to GGvNI, 19 Feb. 1874, Consulaat Singapore 9.
60. Besluit of the GGvNI, 16 July 1874, and attached documents, Consulaat Penang 46.
61. Government Secretary of N.I. to Lavino, 26 July 1874, Consulaat Penang.
62. Besluit of the GGvNI, 12 Apr. 1874, Consulaat Penang 14.
63. Lavino to Secretary-General of N.I., 27 June 1874; Lavino to Padday, 27 June 1874, both in Consulaat Penang 100. Read to B.Z., 17 Feb. 1876, ARA, B.Z. Atjeh.
64. Lavino to B.Z., 11 Apr. 1881, Consulaat Penang 11.
65. Read to Secretary-General of N.I., 18 Mar. 1874, Consulaat Singapore 9.
66. Three-monthly accounts of "secret expenses" presented to N.I. Department of Finance in Consulaat Penang 12, 13, 14 and 20.
67. E. Gobee and C. Adriaanse (eds.), *Ambtelijke Adviesen van C. Snouck Hurgronje* (The Hague 1957–59), p. 1603.
68. J.A. de Vicq to GGvNI, 4 Feb. 1896, Kol. A14/no.45, Dossier 6239, ARA.
69. Lavino to B.Z., 7 Mar. 1893, B.Z. 669, ARA.
70. Lavino to B.Z., 19 Apr. 1888, B.Z. 669, ARA.
71. Discussed more fully in Chapter 9 above.
72. Fleury to Governor Atjeh, 13 Feb. 1883; Fleury to Read, 20 Feb. 1883; 6 Mar. 1883; all in Consulaat Penang 12.

Notes to pp. 273–7 409

73. Kruyt to B.Z., 30 Sept. 1880; 20 Nov. 1881, both in B.Z. 669, ARA.
74. GGvNI to Kol., 29 Dec. 1881. B.Z. 669, ARA.
75. Read to B.Z., 9 Mar. 1880, B.Z. 669, ARA.
76. Read to B.Z., 7 Oct. 1881, B.Z. 669, ARA.
77. Rochussen (B.Z.) to van Bylandt (London), 28 Sept. 1882; 28 Oct. 1882; Bylandt to Rochussen, 9 Oct. 1882; 31 Oct. 1882; 8 Nov. 1882, all in B.Z. 669, ARA.
78. B.Z. to Kol., 3 Jan. 1883; De Braun to Rochussen (private), 5 Jan. 1883; GGvNI to Kol., 7 Mar. 1883; B.Z. to Kol., 16 and 19 Apr. 1883; all in B.Z. 669, ARA.
79. Read to B.Z., 24 Aug. 1883, B.Z. 669, ARA.
80. Koninklijk Besluit, 14 Dec. 1884, B.Z. 669, ARA.
81. Lavino to B.Z., 29 Jan. 1887, B.Z. 669, ARA.

Chapter 12

1. The author is greatly indebted to a number of Japanese colleagues who made it possible, during a short visit to Japan in August 1973, for him to locate and use important Japanese sources concerning the occupation in northern Sumatra, and to interview Japanese concerned in those events. The debt is especially great to Shiraishi Saya, who guided, translated, and advised; most of the translations from Japanese sources are hers. I also wish to acknowledge the late Professors Itagaki Yoichi and Nagazumi Akira, the late Fujiwara Iwaichi, Azuma Toru, Ichikura Tokusaburo, Prof. Masuda Ato and Dr. Nishihara Masashi. Indonesians who have helped me with information and guidance are more numerous, and not all would wish to be mentioned. I would nevertheless like to mention particularly the late Said Abu Bakar, whose exciting tale led me into many new paths.
2. Willard H. Elsbree, *Japan's Role in Southeast Asian Nationalist Movements* (Cambridge: Harvard University Press, 1953), p. 12.
3. Ibid., pp. 120–32, 141–5, 163.
4. In addition to Piekaar and Benda, discussed below, see Benedict Anderson, *Some Aspects of Indonesian Politics under the Japanese Occupation, 1942–1945* (Ithaca: Cornell Modern Indonesia Project, 1961), pp. 22–3; J.D. Legge, *Indonesia* (Englewood Cliffs: Prentice-Hall, 1964), p. 132; and, to some extent, G. McT. Kahin, *Nationalism and Revolution in Indonesia* (Ithaca: Cornell University Press, 1952), pp. 110–4.
5. A.J. Piekaar, *Atjeh en de oorlog met Japan* (The Hague: Van Hoeve, 1949).
6. On this clash, the "Cumbok war" of Dec. 1945/Jan. 1946, see Abdullah Arif, "The affair of the Tjumbok traitors", Anthony Reid, trans. and ed.

410   Notes to pp. 277–9

Review of Indonesian and Malayan Affairs 4/5 (1970/1): 29–65; Anthony
Reid, *The Blood of the People: Revolution and the End of Traditional Rule
in Northern Sumatra* (Kuala Lumpur: Oxford University Press, 1979),
pp. 195–204.

7. Benda, *The Crescent and the Rising Sun*, especially pp. 186–9 and 199–
204. Also *Continuity and Change in Southeast Asia: collected journal articles
of Harry J. Benda* (New Haven: Yale Southeast Asia Studies, 1972),
pp. 44–5, 77 and 151–2.

8. Benda, *The Crescent and the Rising Sun*, p. 199; also Benda, *Continuity
and Change*, p. 173.

9. H.J. Benda, J.K. Irikura and K. Kishi, ed., *Japanese Military Administration
in Indonesia: Selected Documents* (New Haven: Yale Southeast Asia
Studies, 1965).

10. "Principles governing the administration of occupied southern areas,
20 Nov. 1941", in ibid., p. 1.

11. There is a similar striking contrast between the unity presented by the
AFPFL in Burma and the Vietminh in Vietnam in 1945, and the
seemingly hopeless divisions of the pre-war national movement in these
two countries. The specificially anti-Japanese character of these two
movements in 1945, however, makes comparison with Indonesia difficult.

12. Nationalists themselves frequently complained of this: "The reputation
of the leaders is ruined in the eyes of the people", said Ki Hadjar
Dewantoro in June 1945, cited in Bernhard Dahm, *Sukarno and the
Struggle for Indonesian Independence* (Ithaca: Cornell University Press,
1969), p. 304. "What the masses are saying ... is frequently not very
nice. There are some who say, 'Our leaders are now living the good
life but we are just as poor as ever'", Mohammad Hatta, Aug. 1943,
trans. William Frederick in *The Putera Reports. Problems in Indonesian-
Japanese wartime cooperation* (Ithaca: Cornell Modern Indonesia Project,
1971), p. 61.

13. On the "social revolutionary" upheavals of 1945–6, see Benedict
Anderson, *Java, in a time of revolution, occupation and resistance, 1944–
1946* (Ithaca: Cornell University Press, 1972), pp. 16–189 and 332–69;
John Smail, *Bandung in the Early Revolution 1945–1946. A study in the
social history of the Indonesian revolution* (Ithaca: Cornell Southeast Asia
Program, 1964), pp. 99–146; Reid, *The Blood of the People*, pp. 185–251;
Anthony Reid, *The Indonesian National Revolution, 1945–1950* (Melbourne:
Longman, 1974), pp. 14–7 and 59–76.

14. Dahm, *Sukarno*, pp. 261–6; and *History of Indonesia in the Twentieth
Century* (New York: Praeger, 1970), p. 93. See also George S. Kanahele,

Notes to pp. 279–84   411

"The Japanese Occupation of Indonesia: Prelude to Independence", PhD thesis (Cornell University, 1967), pp. 241–2. Harry Benda himself (*Continuity and Change in Southeast Asia*, p. 72), described a situation in Java very like that presented below for Sumatra, though without drawing the same conclusion.

15. Piekaar, *Atjeh en de oorlog met Japan*, p. 332. Despite my difference here, one must admire the astonishing level of fairness towards the Japanese regime shown by Piekaar, given the circumstances under which he was writing.

16. These broadcasts, for an hour each evening, were directed by the veteran Sumatran nationalist Mohammad Samin (bin Taib), well-remembered both in East Sumatra and Aceh for his prominence as Medan leader of Sarekat Islam, editor of the radical *Benih Merdeka*, and legal agent, until hobbled by government restrictions in 1921. He moved to Penang in the late 1930s, where he wrote for such journals as *Sahabat* and *Suara Malaysia*. At the Japanese conquest he emerged as leader of a *Persatuan Indonesia Merdeka* (Indonesian independence association) with another Minangkabau, Haji Thamin. Interviews with Nip Xarim and Ghazali Yunus.

17. Piekaar, *Atjeh en de oorlog met Japan*, p. 183.

18. See Chapter 10.

19. Piekaar, *Atjeh en de oorlog met Japan*, pp. 14–24. Reid, *The Blood of the People*, pp. 7–37; James T. Siegel, *The Rope of God* (Berkeley: University of California, 1969), pp. 83–133. H. Ismuha, "Lahirnja Persatuan Ulama Seluruh Atjeh' 30 Tahun Jang Lalu", *Sinar Darussalam* 14 (June 1969): 43–7, and 15 (July 1969): 33–9.

20. Politiek Verslag S.O.K., June 1938, pp. 3–7, mailr. 766 geh/38, in the colonial archive of the Ministerie van Binnenlandse Zaken, The Hague; Reid, *The Blood of the People*, pp. 70–3.

21. Joyce C. Lebra, *Jungle Alliance. Japan and the Indian National Army* (Singapore: Asia Pacific Press, 1971), *passim*. Fujiwara Iwaichi, *F-kikan* (Tokyo: Hara Shoba, 1966), *passim*.

22. Fujiwara, *F-kikan*, p. 149. Fujiwara interview, 23 Aug. 1973.

23. Said Abu Bakar interview.

24. Abdullah Hussain, *Terjebak* (Kuala Lumpur: Pustaka Antara, 1965), pp. 27–41. Also Fujiwara, *F-kikan*, pp. 149–51; Nakamiya Goro, "Sumatora muketsu senryo no kageni" [Behind the bloodless occupation of Sumatra] in Shukan Yomiuri, *Nihon no himitsu sen* (Tokyo: 1956), pp. 93–6. I have discounted Fujiwara's claim to have first met Abu Bakar in Taiping, since it is not supported by other sources.

412 Notes to pp. 285–8

25. Piekaar, *Atjeh en de oorlog met Japan*, p. 179.
26. Fujiwara, *F-kikan*, pp. 200–1.
27. Ibid., pp. 201–2. Hussain, *Terjebak*, pp. 44–6, records a different speech by Fujiwara, in which the subordinate role of the *F-kikan* was still more explicit. The group was told frankly that it was to be a fifth column, whose role was to enable "a country to be conquered easily, causing few victims among its inhabitants".
28. Fujiwara interview, 23 Aug. 1973.
29. Cited Piekaar, *Atjeh en de oorlog met Japan*, p. 145.
30. Hussain, *Terjebak*, pp. 47–85. Fujiwara, *F-kikan*, pp. 275–6. "Verslag van Atjeh ... tot 15 January 1946", in Spits to Van Mook, 26 Feb. 1946, Archive Ministerie van Zaken Overzee, 21/1. Interview. The Dutch sources — including Piekaar, *Atjeh en de oorlog met Japa*, p. 61 — include the famous Seulimeum ulama, Sjech Ibrahim, in the group of *F-kikan* members who came from Malaya in the guise of refugees. Said Abu Bakar and Fujiwara, however, give him no place in the *F-kikan*, because he returned to Aceh before the Japanese occupation of Singapore.
31. Piekaar, *Atjeh en de oorlog met Japan*, pp. 63–7. T.M.A. Panglima Polim, *Memoir (Tjatatan)* (Kutaraja: stenciled, 1972), pp. 3–5.
32. Panglima Polim (or Polem) was the title of the principal *ulèëbalang* of the *sagi* of the XXII *mukims*, the largest of the three *sagis* that made up Aceh Besar. Since its foundation in the 17th century, the dynasty was always one of the most powerful in Aceh. Muhammad Ali's father (d.1941) had led resistance against the Dutch in the period 1898–1903, but subsequently became a highly respected part of the Dutch administration.
33. Piekaar, *Atjeh en de oorlog met Japan*, pp. 77–9 and 84–5.
34. Ibid., p. 142. Fujiwara, *F-kikan*, p. 273. Interviews.
35. *Asia Raya* (Jakarta), 19 Oct. 2602 [1942] published a fanciful tale of 50 emissaries from *ulèëbalangs* in Aceh. However, one figure in this account — T. Muhammad of Jeuniëb (Samalanga, North Aceh) — may really have been sent to Penang by the ruler of Jeuniëb, whom Piekaar, (pp. 132–3) notes suddenly aligning with PUSA in February 1942, evidently to insure himself with the Japanese. T. Njak Arif is sometimes also credited with having sent envoys to Penang, though I have seen no hard evidence.
36. Fujiwara, *F-kikan*, pp. 273–4. Piekaar, *Atjeh en de oorlog met Japan*, pp. 145 and 178. Nakamiya Gorō, "Sumatora", p. 96.
37. These events are carefully chronicled from the Dutch side by Piekaar, *Atjeh en de oorlog met Japan*, pp. 85–106 and 120–88.

Notes to pp. 288–90 413

38. The PUSA view appears to have been first advanced in an article in *Pewarta Deli* (Medan), 7 May 2602 [1942], cited in Piekaar, *Atjeh en de oorlog met Japan,* pp. 170–6. An extreme *ulèëbalang* view, apparently conveyed to Parada Harahap, appeared in *Asia Raya* (Jakarta), 19 Oct. 2602. In general, published Japanese sources give an exaggerated view of the PUSA role, apparently because a common source for these accounts is a paper prepared by Said Abu Bakar.

39. Piekaar, *Atjeh en de oorlog met Japan,* p. 177, citing the *Pewarta Deli* article (21 Dec.); Fujiwara, *F-kikan,* pp. 274–5 (mid-Dec.); and Nakamiya Gorō, p. 97 (6 Mar.).

40. In a 1969 interview, Daud Beureu'eh categorically denied that PUSA organized the 1942 revolt. He explained the PUSA envoys to Malaya as an insurance against the certainty that the Japanese would work through the *ulèëbalangs* unless PUSA had good relations with them. Ismuha, in *Sinar Darussalam,* 15 July 1969, p. 36, chronicles the history of PUSA without claiming credit for the revolt, beyond the spontaneous participation of members of the youth group, *Pemuda* PUSA.

41. Piekaar, *Atjeh en de oorlog met Japan,* p. 190.

42. Ibid., pp. 158–61.

43. In one case noted by Piekaar, *Atjeh en de oorlog met Japan,* pp. 138–9, the PUSA activist who had become the strong-man of the Lhokseumawe district was apparently dismissed because of an unfavourable report from the local Dutch official!

44. Ismuha, *Sinar Darussalam,* p. 37, clearly implies that these arrests of Daud Beureu'eh and others occurred because of hostile reports by other Acehnese.

45. Interviews with Sugondo Kartodiprodjo, 29 July 1972 and Selamat Ginting, 22 Aug. 1971. Hussain, *Terjebak,* p. 89. Dr. Amir's notes of 14 June 1946, I.C. 005966 in Rijksinstituut voor Oorlogsdocumentatie — which have been used by Kanahele, "The Japanese Occupation of Indonesia" (pp. 28–9 and 259), among others — state that this *Comité Indonesia* urged the Japanese to abolish the Sultanates. This was strongly denied by Sugondo, and appears to result from a confusion with the *F-kikan* on Amir's part.

46. Willem Brandt, *De Gele Terreur* (The Hague: Van Hoeve, 1946), pp. 22–4; Tengku Luckman Sinar, "The East Coast of Sumatra under the Japanese heel", *Sumatra Research Bulletin* 1, 2 (1972): 29; Inoue Tetsurō, *Bapa Djanggut* (Tokyo: Kōdansha, 1953), p. 77.

47. Hussain, *Terjebak,* pp. 91–4. Abdullah Jusuf interview, 17 Aug. 1972. *Asia Raya,* 10 June 2602 [1942] reported that the Indonesian political

414   Notes to pp. 290–4

parties of Medan dissolved themselves on 7 June, after thanks were
expressed for their help in defeating the Dutch army.

48. Haji Abdul Malik Karim Amrullah [Hamka], *Kenang-kenangan Hidup*
(Kuala Lumpur: Pustaka Antara, 1966), pp. 197–8.
49. Sumatora Gunseikanbu, Keimubu, "Sumatora ni okeru chian-jō no
ichi-kōsatsu", 27 Nov. 2602 [1942], (stenciled document in Tokugawa
papers of Japanese Defence Agency), pp. 40–48. This Japanese report
was translated by Saya Shiraishi, and published in "Rural Unrest in
Sumatra, 1942: A Japanese Report", ed. Anthony Reid and Shiraishi
Saya, *Indonesia* 21 (Apr. 1976): 115–33. See also Inoue, *Bapa Djanggut*,
pp. 54–5.
50. Inoue, *Bapa Djanggut*, p. 54.
51. Keimubu, "Sumatora ni okeru", p. 47.
52. Inoue, *Bapa Djanggut*, p. 55.
53. Table in Keimubu , "Sumatora ni okeru". Interviews. One important
source of land conflict in the affected parts of Karoland was the
re-allocation of land which had followed irrigation works in the 1930s.
54. Inoue, *Bapa Djanggut*, p. 55.
55. Table in Keimubu, "Sumatora ni okeru".
56. Keimubu, "Sumatora ni okeru", pp. 36–8.
57. Tengku Luckman Sinar, "The East Coast of Sumatra", p. 34.
58. Keimubu, "Sumatora ni okeru, p. 39.
59. Inoue, *Bapa Djanggut*, pp. 52–3.
60. Both Inoue, *Bapa Djanggut*, p. 55 and Tengku Arifin (cited in Tengku
Luckman Sinar, "The East Coast of Sumatra", pp. 34–5) attribute
to Arifin the linking of the GERINDO leadership with the *aron*
disturbances. Although I have questioned a number of GERINDO
leaders on the matter, it seems impossible to establish what truth there
was in the allegation, beyond the stimulus GERINDO undoubtedly
gave to the earliest phase of the Karo movement in 1938–9.
61. Table in Keimubu, "Sumatora ni okeru".
62. Inoue, *Bapa Djanggu*, pp. 70–2.
63. *Sumatora Shinbun* (Medan), 11 Mar. 2603 [1943]. Table in Keimubu,
"Sumatora ni okeru".

Chapter 13

1. The Sumatran commander, General Tanabe, testified that these
pemuda landed in South Sumatra in early Sept. Rijksinstituut voor
Oorlogsdocumentatie, Indisch Collectie [henceforth I.C.], 059351.
However, they appear to turn up first in Palembang only on 1 Oct., in

Notes to pp. 295–6   415

West Sumatra on 30 Oct., and in Aceh about 25 Nov. Kementerian Penerangan, *Republik Indonesia Propinsi Sumatera Selatan* (Jakarta: n.p., 1954), p. 41. Kementerian Penerangan, *Republik Indonesia Propinsi Sumatera Tengah* (Jakarta: n.p., n.d.), pp. 94–5. *Semangat Merdeka* (Kutaradja), 27 Nov. 1945.

2. G. McT.Kahin, *Nationalism and Revolution in Indonesia* (Ithaca: Cornell University Press, 1952); John R.W. Smail, *Bandung in the Early Revolution 1945–1946: A study in the Social History of the Indonesian Revolution* (Ithaca: Cornell Modern Indonesia Project, 1964); Benedict R.O'G. Anderson, *Java in a Time of Revolution, Occupation and Resistance, 1944–1946* (Ithaca: Cornell University Press, 1972). William Frederick, *Visions and Heat* (Athens: Ohio University Press, 1989).

3. The few notable works are on specific regions: Anthony Reid, *The Blood of the People: Revolution and the End of Traditional Rule in Northern Sumatra* (Kuala Lumpur: OUP, 1979); Audrey Kahin, *Rebellion to Integration: West Sumatra and the Indonesian Polity* (Amsterdam: Amsterdam University Press, 2000), three chapters (Aceh, East Sumatra and West Sumatra) in *Regional Dynamics of the Indonesian Revolution: Unity from Diversity*, ed. Audrey Kahin (Honolulu: University of Hawaii Press, 1985); and several unpublished theses, notably Michael van Langenberg, "National Revolution in North Sumatra: Sumatera Timur and Tapanuli, 1942–1950" (Sydney University, 1976).

4. Army-Navy Agreement, 26 Nov. 1941, in Benda, Irikura, and Kishi, ed., *Japanese Military Administration in Indonesia: Selected Documents* (New Haven: Yale University Southeast Asia Studies, 1965), p. 7. Also ibid., p. 29.

5. Instructions on the administration of Malaya and Sumatra, April 1942, in ibid., p. 169.

6. Ibid., p. 169.

7. *Penang Shimbun*, 19 Dec. 1942.

8. Interrogation of General Shimura, I.C.009403. Also I.J. Brugmans, H.J. de Graaf, A.H. Joustra, and A.G. Vromans, ed., *Nederlandsch-Indië onder Japanse Bezetting: Gegevens en documenten over de jaren 1942–1945* (Francker: Wever, 1960), p. 584.

9. Interrogation of General Tanabe, I.C.059351.

10. Waseda Daigaku, Tokyo, Okuma Memorial Social Sciences Research Center (team led by Nishijima), *Japanese Military Administration in Indonesia* (Washington: U.S. Dept. of Commerce, Clearing House for Federal Scientific and Technical Information, Joint Publications. Research

416 Notes to pp. 297–300

Service, 1963) [henceforth Nishijima 1963], pp. 122–4 and 372. Benda, Irikura, and Kishi, ed., *Japanese*, pp. 237–40.

11. Nishijima, *Japanese Military Administration*, pp. 171–2. *Kita-Sumatora-sinbun* (Medan), 11 Nov. 1943. This balance was particularly necessary in Aceh, East Sumatra, and West Sumatra, as all of those residencies had experienced tensions between the two groups at the time of the Japanese invasion.

12. The East Sumatran body, formed on 28 Nov. 1943, was known as BOMPA (Badan Oentoek Membantu Pertahanan Asia). In Aceh Maibkatra (Madjelis agama Islam untuk bantuan kemakmuran Asia Timur Raja di Atjeh) had been established for Muslim leaders in March 1943. Tapanuli had its Bapen (Badan Pertahanan Negeri) and West Sumatra its Giyugun Kōen-Kai. The suspicion of all politicians in Palembang following mass arrests in September 1943 evidently prevented the formation of such a body there.

13. *Kita-Sumatora-sinbun*, 26 Nov. 2063 [1943]. Kementerian Penerangan, *Republik Indonesia Propinsi Sumatera Utara* (Jakarta: n.p., 1953), p. 21. *Propinsi Sumatera Tengah*, pp. 79–80. *Propinsi Sumatera Selatan*, pp. 33–4. A.J. Piekaar, *Atjèh en de oorlog met Japan* (The Hague and Bandung: W. van Hoeve, 1949), pp. 205–6 and 240–1.

14. Nishijima, *Japanese Military Administration*, pp. 373–80, 642–4; Benda, Irikura, and Kishi, ed., *Japanese*, pp. 240–62.

15. Hadji Abdul Malik Karim Amrullah [Hamka], *Kenang-kenangan Hidup* (2nd ed., Kuala Lumpur: Pustaka Antara, 1966) pp. 239–44. Dr. Amir's notes, 14 June 1946, I.C.005964.

16. Benda, Irikura, and Kishi, ed., *Japanese*, p. 263.

17. Interrogation of General Shimura, I.C.009405.

18. Interrogation of General Tanabe, I.C.OS9351, and General Hamada, I.C.0593S3. Benda, Irikura, and Kishi, ed., *Japanese*, pp. 265–74.

19. Decision of Supreme War Guidance Council, 17 July 1945, in Benda, Irikura, and Kishi, ed., *Japanese*, p. 274.

20. See for example the speeches hailing the Sumatra Chuō Sangi In, in *Kita-Sumatora-sinbun*, 27 June 2605 [1945].

21. *Atjeh Sinbun* (Kutaradja), 7–14 Nov. 2604 [1944].

22. Piekaar, *Atjèh en de oorlog met Japan*, pp. 214, and 231–2.

23. Benedict R.O'G. Anderson, "Japan: 'The Light of Asia'", in Josef Silverstein, ed., *Southeast Asia in World War II: Four Essays* (New Haven: Yale University Southeast Asian Studies, 1966), p. 17.

24. See appendix for the composition of the Chuō Sangi In.

25. Engku Mohammad Sjafei (1901–69), adopted son of a prominent Minangkabau teacher and writer, Marah Soetan, was educated in the

Notes to pp. 300–1   417

Bukittinggi teachers' college. Subsequently in Batavia, and in Europe (1922–4), he was especially drawn to the study of painting and educational theory. In 1926 he founded his Indische Nationale School (I.N.S.) for teachers in Kayu Tanam, West Sumatra, where the curriculum stressed self-expression and the arts and attempted to embody specifically Indonesian values. Politically Sjafei was associated with Indische Partij/Insulinde before visiting Europe and Hatta's PNI-baru thereafter. He was chairman of the West Sumatra Shū Sangi Kai (1943–5) and Hōkōkai (1945), the first Republican resident of West Sumatra (1945), and was later named Minister of Education (June–Oct. 1946).

26. Teuku Njak Arif (1900–46), educated at the Bukittinggi Teachers' College and the OSVIA in Serang, was the Panglima Sagi of the XXVI Mukims in Aceh Besar. He established himself as the most prominent Acehnese nationalist during his period in the Volksraad (1927–31). Despite his uncompromising opposition to some aspects of the Japanese regime, he was recognized by 1943 as the principal Acehnese spokesman. He was the Republican resident of Aceh until he was removed during the anti-*ulèëbalang* action of Dec. 1945.

27. Mr. Abdul Abbas, of Mandailing origin, obtained his law degree in Holland. He was the prewar Parindra leader in Lampung and became Chairman of the Lampung Shū Sangi Kai, and first Republican resident of Lampung until he was *daulat*-ed by the pemuda in Sept. 1946.

28. Djamaluddin Adinegoro (1903–?) was given the former name, but adopted the latter. Born in Sawahlunto, the son of a District Chief, he was closely related to both Dr. Amir and Muhammad Yamin. He studied medicine in Batavia (STOVIA) and journalism in Munich (1925–9). From 1931 he was chief editor of the leading Indonesian daily in Sumatra, Pewarta Deli, and for many years a member of the Medan *gemeenteraad* (city council). He was the only resident Sumatran in a potential Indonesian Cabinet presented to the Japanese in Mar. 1942 by the leading nationalist parties. The Japanese appointed him editor of the *Sumatera-sinbun* (later *Kita-Sumatora-sinbun*) and vice-chairman of the East Sumatra Shū Sangi Kai. *Atjeh Sinbun*, 29 May 2605 [1945]; Nishijima, *Japanese Military Administration*, p. 342.

29. Ali Hasjmy, in *Atjeh Sinbun*, 24 July 2605 [1945].

30. *Atjeh Sinbun*, 28 June 2605 [1945].

31. Ibid., 29 June, 3 July, and 31 July 2605 [1945]; *Penang Shimbun*, 11 July 1945.

32. Hamka, *Kenang-kenangan Hidup*, p. 263.

33. *Penang Shimbun*, 11 July 1945.

418   Notes to pp. 301–2

34. *Atjeh Sinbun,* 28 July 2605 [1945]. For the membership of this body, which never met, see Appendix.

35. E.g. to Riau in May 1945; *Atjeh Sinbun,* 31 May 2605 [1945]. The Madjelis Islam Tinggi in Bukittinggi continued this role after the proclamation, and succeeded in holding an all-Sumatra Islamic conference in Dec. 1945.

36. *Atjeh Sinbun,* 29 May 2605 [1945].

37. Ibid., 19 July 1945; *Propinsi Sumatera Selatan,* p. 35. The plan was for a two-month tour of Sumatra from South to North, but the only major centre they reached before the surrender was Palembang on 1–4 August where their visit gave rise to a local independence investigating committee.

38. General Shimura stated that Sjafei, Adinegoro, and Gani "were the Sumatrans' leaders in all negotiations with the Japanese", I.C.009402. Dr. Adnan Kapau Gani (1909–68), a Minangkabau, studied medicine in Jakarta. He was founder and chairman of Gerindo, the major socialist party (1937–41), and secretary of the political federation GAPI (1941). He moved from Jakarta to Palembang in 1940. The Japanese initially distrusted him, presumably because of his association with Amir Sjarifuddin, and imprisoned him for several months in 1943. He rapidly returned to prominence after the Koiso statement, as chairman of the Palembang Shū Sangi Kai, deputy to the Japanese chōkan, and eventually the first Republican resident in Palembang. He entered the Republican Cabinet as economic minister in October, 1946, and was deputy premier in 1947.

39. Hamka, *Kenang-kenangan Hidup,* p. 262.

40. Dr. Mohammad Amir (1900–49), another Minangkabau, studied medicine in Batavia (STOVIA, 1918–23) and Utrecht (1924–8), specializing in psychiatry. From his student days he was a prominent essayist and an editor of *Jong Sumatra* (1917–22) and later *Penindjauan.* He appears not to have been a party man after the failure of the moderate Partai Rakjat Indonesia in 1930, though sympathizing with Parindra. Like many Indonesian intellectuals he was attracted to the theosophist movement in the 1920s, but became more involved than most, and married the daughter of Ir. Fournier, the leading Dutch theosophist in Java. He lived in Medan from 1934 and from 1937 was personal physician to the Sultan of Langkat. He appears to have been valued by the Japanese because of his links with both *pergerakan* and *kerajaan* and because his Dutch wife made him especially vulnerable. He was appointed minister without portfolio in Sukarno's first cabinet, and deputy-governor of Sumatra from Dec. 1945 until his defection from the Republic the following April.

Notes to pp. 302–4

41. Teuku Mohammad Hasan (born 1906), eldest son of the ulëëbalang of Pineuëng, in the Pidië district of Aceh, obtained his law degree from Leiden (1933). From 1936 he was attached to the commission investigating administrative decentralization in the outer islands, and in 1938 transferred to the new office of governor of Sumatra in Medan. Studious and devout, his relations with Medan *ulama* were good, though he was not completely trusted by the Acehnese PUSA. During the Japanese occupation he was concerned mainly with rice production and distribution, but became a confidant of the East Sumatra chōkan during 1944–5 and was eventually appointed Kōseikyokuchō (head of bureau dealing with petitions).

42. Dr. Amir stated that Yamaguchi, head of political affairs in Sumatra, was piqued that the choice of delegates had been made in Singapore or Jakarta without reference to the 25th Army: I.C.005966. On the other hand *Propinsi Sumatera Tengah*, p. 83, claims it was the 25th Army who obstructed Sjafei's departure for the PPKI.

43. Muhammad Yamin, ed., *Naskah persiapan Undang-Undang Dasar 1945* (Jakarta: Jajasan Prapantja, 1959), I, pp. 410 and 419. I have here translated from the seemingly more coherent text in Iwa Kusuma Sumantri, *Sedjarah Revolusi Indonesia* (Jakarta: n.p., 1963), p. 132. Dr. Amir's importance in stressing the need for a rapid independence proclamation is emphasized by Mohammad Hatta, *Sekitar Proklamasi 17 Agustus 1945* (Jakarta: Tintamas, 1969), pp. 21–22.

44. Yamin, *Naskah persiapan*, I, pp. 439–40, 450–3; Hatta, *Sekitar Proklamasi*, pp. 61–2. Interviews.

45. Koesnodiprodjo, ed., *Himpunan undang2, peraturan2, penetapan2, pemerintah Republik Indonesia, 1945* (Jakarta: Seno, 1951), pp. 117–20.

46. Dr. Amir's notes, 14 June 1946, I.C.005966; *Propinsi Sumatra Selatan*, p. 37; Hamka, *Kenang-kenangan Hidup*, p. 279.

47. Tweede Kamer, Staten-Generaal, Netherlands, *Enquête-commissie regeringsbeleid 1940–1945, militair beleid: terugkeer naar Nederlandsch- Indië* (The Hague: Staatsdrukkerij en Uitgeverijbedrijf, 1956), 8A and B, pp. 585, 590, 593, and Appendix p. 126; Conrad E.L. Helfrich, *Memoires* (Amsterdam: Elsevier, 1950), II, pp. 237–8. Both Helfrich and the *Enquête-commissie* report state that Brondgeest's unit was dropped on 15 Aug., but I have followed Brondgeest's written submission to the Enquête-commissie on this.

48. Brondgeest in *Enquête-commissie*, p. 588.

49. Ibid., pp. 588–94; Helfrich, *Memoires*, II, pp. 237–8; Raymond Westerling, *Challenge to Terror* (London: W. Kimber, 1952), pp. 38–50. While Helfrich states and Westerling implies a strength below 200 for the police force,

420   Notes to pp. 304–9

Brondgeest claimed that the 800 men of the 26th Indian Division landed on 12 Oct. were "fewer than I now had at my own disposal".

50. Helfrich, *Memoires*, II, p. 269, whose purpose was polemical, claimed that the force "completely controlled Medan and its immediate environs. There was peace and order." Another Dutch commando, who spent four days in Medan at the beginning of October en route to become Allied representative in Aceh (5 Oct.–15 Nov.), said of it, "The situation there was tense, but was controlled by a very able police commandant — Raymond Westerling." "Contact met Atjeh", *Vrij Nederland*, 19 Jan. 1946.

51. Seksi Penerangan, Dokumentasi Komite Musjawarah Angkatan 45, Daerah Istimewa Atjeh, *Modal Revolusi 45* (Kutaradja, 1960), p. 28; *Propinsi Sumatera Utara*, p. 39.

52. Enquête-commissie, pp. 585–6; Willem Brandt, *De Gele Terreur* (The Hague: W. van Hoeve, 1946), pp. 215–9; Oostkust van Sumatra Instituut, *Kroniek, 1941–1946* (Amsterdam, 1948), pp. 45–6 and 52.

53. Enquête-commissie, p. 598. Mohammad Said, *Empat Belas Boelan Pendoedoekan Inggeris di Indonesia* (Medan: Kantor Berita Antara, 1946), p. 32.

54. *Pewarta Deli*, 6 Oct. 1945 and interviews. Allied (British and Dutch) and Japanese representatives were given places of honour, while the new Republican governor was seated only in the front of the public section.

55. Piekaar, *Atjèh en de oorlog met Japan*, pp. 246–7; Brandt, *De Gele Terreur*, pp. 208–9; Insider [S.M. Amin], *Atjeh Sepintas Lalu* (Jakarta: Archapada, 1950), pp. 5–7; *Propinsi Sumatera Utara*, p. 22; Hamka, *Kenang-kenangan Hidup*, pp. 270–7; *Propinsi Sumatera Tengah*, p. 255; Abdullah Hussain, *Peristiwa* (Kuala Lumpur: Pustaka Antara, 1965), pp. 33–4.

56. Dr. Amir's notes, 14 June 1946, I.C.005967. Interviews.

57. "Pamandangan Mr. Teuku M. Hasan", in *Amanat Satoe Tahoen Merdeka* (Padang Panjang: Penaboer, 1946), p. 60; *Propinsi Sumatera Utara*, p. 27.

58. *Propinsi Sumatera Tengah*, pp. 84–5, 500 and 544.

59. *Propinsi Sumatera Selatan*, pp. 50–1, and 189; *Semangat Merdeka*, 17, 20, and 29 Nov. 1945.

60. *Propinsi Sumatera Selatan*, p. 40.

61. *Aneta I.D.D.*, 31 May 1946, pp. 21–2.

62. Interrogation of General Tanabe, I.C.059351.

63. Interview.

64. *Propinsi Sumatera Selatan*, pp. 37–41.

65. *Propinsi Sumatera Tengah*, p. 87.

66. Anderson, *Java in a Time of Revolution, Occupation and Resistance*, pp. 1–35.

Notes to pp. 310–27   421

67. *Kita-Sumatora-sinbun*, 18 and 25 Nov. 2603 [1943]; Piekaar, *Atjèh en de oorlog met Japan*, pp. 219 and 238; *Propinsi Sumatera Tengah*, pp. 79–80. Interviews. Aceh and West Sumatra were the first residencies to provide Giyūgun, though the remainder followed by early 1944.

68. *Modal Revolusi* 45, pp. 64–5.

69. *Propinsi Sumatera Tengah*, pp. 87–9 and 542–9; *Propinsi Sumatera Utara*, p. 29; *Modal Revolusi* 45, pp. 41–2, 54–6, 65–6, 72–3. Interviews.

70. *Propinsi Sumatera Utara*, pp. 29–30; *Mengenangkan Hari Proklamasi* (Medan, 1956), pp. 84–5; M.K. Djusni and Aminuddin Nasir, "Kenang-kenangan Repolusi dikota Medan", (typescript); Mohammad Said in *Dobrak* (Medan), 25 Aug. 1970. Interviews. I am indebted to Michael van Langenberg for the typescript source.

71. For details of the first residents, see Appendix.

72. See especially Hussain, *Peristiwa*, p. 71.

73. *Republik Indonesia Propinsi Sumatera Tengah*, pp. 542–9; *Republik Indonesia Propinsi Sumatera Selatan*, pp. 49–50.

74. S. van der Harst, *Overzicht van de bestuurshervorming in de Buitengewesten van Nederlandsch-Indië, in het bijzonder op Sumatra* (Utrecht: A. Oosthoek, 1945), p. 46.

75. E.g. *Kita-Sumatora-sinbun*, 27 June 2605 [1945].

76. Dr. Amir, "Nieuw Sumatra", *De Opdracht*, Oct. 1946, p. 9. After the transfer of sovereignty Mohammad Sjafei also became one of the leading critics of Javanese centralism. G.S. Maryanov, *Decentralization in Indonesia as a Political Problem* (Ithaca: Cornell Modern Indonesia Project, 1958), p. 41.

77. Directeur-Generaal voor Algemene Zaken to Lt. Gouverneur-Generaal, 27 Feb. 1947 (Bundle 22/6 in the postwar Indonesian archive in The Hague).

78. Sources: *Kita-Sumatora-sinbun*, 27 June 1945; *Atjeh Sinbun*, 19 May 1945.

79. *Atjeh Sinbun*, 28 July 1945.

Chapter 14

1. For an extended analysis along these lines, a classic work is Crane Brinton, *The Anatomy of Revolution* (London: G. Allen & Unwin, 1953).

2. Benedict R.O'G. Anderson, *Java, in a Time of Revolution, Occupation, and Resistance, 1944–1946* (Ithaca: Cornell University Press, 1972), p. 409.

3. Reid, *The Blood of the People*, pp. 185–211. Abdullah Arif, "The Affair of the Tjumbok Traitors" (edited translation by Anthony Reid), *Review of Indonesian and Malayan Affairs* 4/5 (1972): 29–65.

422   Notes to pp. 327–36

4. Insider [pseud. S.M. Amin], *Atjeh Sepintas Lalu* (Jakarta: Archapada, 1950), p. 22.
5. For Nathar, and his brother-in-law Xarim MS, the most prominent Sumatran communist, see Reid, *The Blood of the People*, pp. 79–80, 154–5, 173–4, 208–9.
6. *Atjeh Sepintas Lalu*, 1950, p. 23; Muhammad Radjab, *Tjatatan di Sumatera* (Jakarta, 1949), pp. 47–50. Dutch intelligence reports of 1947–7 acknowledged the same orderliness, and formed the basis for the Dutch decision to leave Aceh alone in their military action of 1947.
7. Nazaruddin Sjamsuddin, "The Course of the National Revolution in Atjeh, 1945–1949", MA thesis (Monash University, 1974), p. 175.
8. *Soeloeh Merdeka*, 17 Feb. 1946.
9. Reid, *The Blood of the People*, pp. 218–33.
10. *Soeloeh Merdeka*, 7 Mar. 1946.
11. For example, *Merdeka*, 1 June 1946; *Soeloeh Merdeka*, 20 and 30 Apr. 1946.
12. Reid, *The Blood of the People*, pp. 233–45.
13. Radjab, *Tjatatan di Sumatera*, p. 30.
14. Ibid., p. 24. Reid, *The Blood of the People*, pp. 255–6.
15. Audrey Kahin, "Struggle for Independence: West Sumatra in the Indonesian National Revolution, 1945–1950", PhD diss. (Cornell University, 1979), pp. 136–8, 178–89; Audrey Kahin, "West Sumatra: Outpost of the Republic", in *Regional Dynamics of the Indonesian Revolution: Unity from Diversity*, ed. Audrey Kahin (Honolulu: University of Hawaii Press, 1985), pp. 156–7.
16. Soeara Proletar (pseud), *Pembongkaran Tiga Rahasia Penting* I (Silungkang, 1946), pp. 14–20.
17. Kahin, "West Sumatra", p. 157; Anthony Reid, "The Revolution in Regional Perspective", in *The Indonesian Revolution: Papers of the Conference held in Utrecht, 17–20 June 1986*, ed. J. van Goor (Utrecht: Instituut voor Geschiedenis der Riksuniversiteit te Utrecht, 1986), pp. 191–3.

Chapter 15
1. An earlier version of this chapter was presented as a public lecture at the Australian Defence Force Academy, UNSW, Canberra, on 21 Nov. 2002.
2. Katherine McGregor, "Claiming History: Military Representations of the Indonesian Past in Museums, Monuments and other Sources of Official History from Late Guided Democracy to the New Order", Unpublished PhD diss. (Melbourne University, 2002).

Notes to pp. 336–46

3. The best short survey of this writing is now in Peter G. Riddell, *Islam and the Malay-Indonesian World: Transmission and Response* (Honolulu: University of Hawaii Press, 2001), pp. 101–38.

4. "Atjeher" [pseud. H.M. Zainuddin], "Soal Bahasa dalam sekolah desa di Atjeh", *Penjedar* III, 3 (18 Jan. 1940): 47–8; Memorie van Overgave [henceforth MvO] A. Ph. Van Aken, Gouverneur Atjeh, Mar. 1936, pp. 137–8, in Mailr.504x/36.

5. *Atjeh Verslag* of C. Snouck Hurgronje, 1893, as translated in Reid, *The Contest*, p. 269.

6. Reid, *The Contest*, p. 296.

7. MvO Van Aken, 1936, p. 1.

8. Reid, *The Blood of the People*, pp. 9–11.

9. The best study of this phenomenon is Ibrahim Alfian, *Perang de Jalan Allah: Perang Aceh 1873–1912* (Jakarta: Sinar Harapan, 1987), esp. pp. 105–136. See also A. Hasjmy, *Hikayat Perang Sabi Mendjiwai Perang Atjeh lawan Belanda* (Banda Atjeh: Pustaka Faraby, 1971); James Siegel, *The Rope of God* (Berkeley: University of California Press, 1969), pp. 75–7.

10. Reid, *The Blood of the People*, pp. 185–6.

11. A.J. Piekaar, *Atjeh en de oorlog met Japan*, pp. 14–6; Reid, *The Blood of the People*, pp. 28–9.

12. The Piagam Batee Kureng is reproduced in S.M. Amin, *Sekitar Peristiwa Berdarah di Atjeh* (Jakarta: Soeroengan, 1956), pp. 293–5.

13. Sultan Mahmud of Aceh to Governor of the Straits Settlements, 4 Safar 1290H (3 Apr. 1873) — official translation; in Anthony Reid, "Indonesian Diplomacy. A Documentary Study of Atjehnese Foreign Policy in the Reign of Sultan Mahmud, 1870–1874", *JMBRAS* 42, 2 (1969): 74–114.

14. Petition to Turkey from the Nobles of Aceh, n.d. [1868].

15. Letter from Teungku Syech Saman di Tiro to *ulèëbalang* in the Dutch-occupied zone, Sept. 1885, in H.C. Zentgraaff, *Atjeh* (Batavia, n.d. [1938]), p. 17 (my translation).

16. Letter from Teungku Syech Saman di Tiro to Resident K.F.H. van Langen, Sept. 1885, in Zentgraaff, pp. 18–9 (my translation).

17. Testimony of Nja' Gam, 23 Apr. 1921, in Mailrapport 1259 x/21; ARA.

18. MvO van Aken, 1936, p. 135; *Atlas van Tropisch Nederland* (1938), p. 9.

19. Anon., "Islam dan Nationalisme", in *Soeara Atjeh*, 1 Apr. 1930.

20. This was certainly made easier by Hatta's prudent choice of an Acehnese as first Republican governor of Sumatra.

21. "Maklumat ulama seluruh Atjeh", 15 Oct. 1945, in *Modal Revolusi '45*, p. 61.

424 Notes to pp. 346–51

22. Hasan Muhammad Tiro, *Perang Atjeh, 1873–1927 M*, stencilled, Jogjakarta, Apr. 1948.

23. Hasan di Tiro, *The Price of Freedom*, p. 2.

24. H.C. Zentgraaff, *Atjeh* (Batavia: De Unie, n.d. [1938]); H.C. Zentgraaff and W.A. van Goudoever, *Sumatraantjes* (Batavia: Java-Bode, n.d. [1936?]); Col. M.H. du Croo, *Marechaussee in Atjeh: Herinneringen en ervarngen van den eersten Luitenant en Kapitein van het Korps Marechaussee van Atjeh en onderhoorigheden, H.J. Schmidt, van 1902 tot 1918* (Maastricht: Oost en West, 1943).

25. Hasan Muhammad Tiro, *Perang Atjeh*. This stencilled monograph also advertised another 1948 work of the teenage Hasan Tiro, a translation of the Cairo professor Abd al-Wahhab Khallaf's Arabic textbook on Islamic law (fikh), rendered into Indonesian as *Dasar-Dasar Negara Islam*.

26. M. Isa Sulaiman, *Sejarah Aceh: Sebuah Gugatan Terhadap Tradisi* (Jakarta: Pustaka Sinar Harapan, 1997), p. 328n.

27. Ibid., pp. 328–9.

28. Hasan Muhammad Tiro, *Demokrasi untuk Indonesia* (n.p., Penerbit Seulawah Aceh, 1958).

29. Though none of these is easy to find in libraries, New York papers cited in Tengku Hasan di Tiro, *The Price of Freedom: the unfinished diary of Tengku Hasan di Tiro* (n.p., State of Acheh Sumatra, 1982), p. 11, include *The Political Future of the Malay Archipelago* (1965), *Acheh in World History* (1968) and *One Hundred Years Anniversary of the Battle of Bandar Acheh* (Apr. 1973), on the anniversary of the Dutch retreat from Aceh after their first setback.

30. My dissertation focusing on the diplomatic history of the Aceh-Dutch War was published in 1969 as *The Contest for North Sumatra: Atjeh, the Netherlands, and Britain 1858–1898* (Kuala Lumpur: OUP, 1969).

31. In his reaction against Indonesian language and its spelling conventions, Hasan Tiro preferred the English spelling style of "ch".

32. Hasan di Tiro, *The Price of Freedom*, p. 62. Sources close to Hasan Tiro declare that he also met with Daud Beureu'eh in 1973 to consider how to revive the idea of Aceh independence.

33. Ibid., pp. 3–4.

34. The Declaration is in ibid., pp. 15–7.

35. Ibid., p. 53.

36. Ibid., pp. 50–1.

37. Tengku Hasan M. di Tiro, *The Drama of Achehnese History; 1873–1978. A Play in VIII Acts*. Ministry of Education, State of Acheh, 1979 [stencilled].

38. This information is based on interviews during my January 2000 visit to Banda Aceh.

Glossary

[Malay/Indonesian terms except where noted as Acehnese (Ac); Chinese (Ch); Dutch (D)]

aron (Karo)	cultivation cooperative; radical land-occupying movement
badan perjuangan	struggle unit (politicized armed forces in revolution)
biduanda	royal retainer
cultuurgebied (D)	cultivation district (of East Sumatra)
dalam	royal enclosure, citadel
Darul Islam	House of Islam; rebel movement for an Islamic state
daulat	sovereignty; as revolutionary verb, to impose the people's sovereignty (*kedaulatan rakyat*) on an official
hamba raja	royal slave or retainer, often as guards
hikayat	chronicle; Acehnese verse epic
hulubalang	war leader — see *ulèëbalang*
imam	leader of the Friday prayer, in Aceh head of *mukim*
hari raya	great day, holiday
hari raya puasa	feast at end of fasting month; *idulfitri*
kadi	religious official or judge
kafir	unbeliever
kerajaan	kingdom, indirectly ruled states of Netherlands India
kerkun	scribe
khehtau (Ch)	headman, labour supervisor
kongsi (Ch)	partnership, [Chinese] company
Laksamana	admiral; in Ndjong (Aceh) title of the *ulèëbalang*
laukheh (Ch)	experienced labourer, signed for a second labour contract
Maharaja	king; in Lhokseumawe (Aceh) title of the *ulèëbalang*
mandi Safar	ritual bathing in the month of Safar

Glossary

Mantroë (Ac)	minister; cf Malay *Mantri*
mujahidin	Islamic warriors
mukim	parish; in Aceh a territorial unit of a few villages
nagari	Minangkabau district under Dutch
orangkaya	merchant-aristocrat (lit. "rich man")
panglima	governor, war-leader
pamong praja	Java aristocracy in process of bureaucratization
pemuda	youth (activist in revolution)
pergerakan	(nationalist) movement
penghulu	head
Persatuan Perjuangan	Struggle Front (a radical coalition supportive of Tan Malaka)
raja	ruler
sagi	district of Aceh Besar (lit. corner)
sama rasa sama rata	equality and brotherhood (lit. same feeling same level)
senenan (Javanese)	weekly Monday tournament of jousting
sinkheh (Ch)	new arrival
suasa	gold-copper alloy
syahbandar	port official
tindal	headman
ulama (pl. of Ar. *'alim*)	learned in Islam, religious teacher
ulèëbalang (Ac)	lit. war-leader (Malay *Hulubalang*); Aceh territorial chief

Index

Abdul Abbas, Mr, Lampung politician, 34, 35, 300, 302, 303, 318, 319, 320, 417
Abdul Aziz, Turkish traveller, 92
Abdul Hamid, Sultan of Turkey (1876–1908), 242, 245, 246
Abdul Mejid, Sultan of Turkey, 173, 236
Abdulmadjid, 325, 333
Abdul Muis, 17
Abdurrahman Wahid, President of Indonesia, 20, 351
Abu Bakar, Said, 284–8, 413
Abubakar, Maharaja, later Sultan, of Johor, 232, 252, 272
Aceh, xiii–xiv, 6–8, 14, 17, 19, 20, 26, 29, 37, 39
   and France, 152–6, 159, 164–7, 168–75
   and independence struggle, 335–54
   and Islam, 228–30, 344, *see also* Aceh War
   and Japan, 280–9
   and social revolution, 326–8, 316
   and Turkey, 69–93, 94–111, 140–50
   and the USA, 343
   Darus-Salam, 70–1, 95, 133
   festivals in, 112–30
   gold in, 180–8
   Independence Movement, *see* GAM
   language, 17, 336, 337

War, against the Dutch (1873–1903), 28, 70–1, 95, 133, 175–7, 236–8, 249, 260, 273, 280–1, 335–6
Aceh Besar, 95, 96, 97, 107, 108, 109, 110, 149, 226–87, 371, 412
adat, 231, 233
   Aceh, 103, 112, 113, 119, 123, 124, 143, 369, 373, 374, 376, 377, 378
   Raja-raja Melayu, 115, 373
Adinegoro, Djamaluddin, 34, 35, 301, 317, 319, 417, 418
Adityavarman, ruler of Central Sumatra (1356–75), 3, 4, 50
agriculture
   highlands, 43, 48, 49, 56, 60, 61
   lowland deltaic, 45, 46, 60
Ahmad Shah ibn Iskandar, 27
Alexander the Great, 27, 69
Ala'ad-din, Sultan of Aceh (1781–95), 154
Ala'ad-din Mansur Shah, Sultan of Aceh (1838–70), 88, 169, 193, *see also* Ibrahim, Sultan
Ali, Sultan of Johor-Riau empire, 252
Ali Beg (1580–9), 87
Ali Mughayat Syah, Sultan of Aceh (1516?–30), 5, 74, 95
Ali Riayat Shah, Sultan of Aceh (1571–8), 85, 88, 98, 123
Alisjabana, Takdir, 17

428   Index

al-Kahar, Ala'ad-din Ri'ayat Shah,
    Sultan of Aceh (1539–71), 6,
    70, 74, 75, 77–80, 83, 85, 89,
    91, 97, 98, 141
Almujahid, Hussein, 327
al-Mukammil, Ala'ad-din Ri'ayat
    Syah Sayyid, Sultan of Aceh
    (1589–1604), 100, 101, 125,
    127, 137, 142, 145
Alsagoff, Sayyid Muhammad, 232,
    233, 241, 243, 272, 403
American: pepper-traders, 164–6,
    196
    consul in Singapore, 166, 175–6,
       261–5
    gunboats, 170
Amin, S.M., Mr, 37
Amir, Dr M., 30, 35, 36, 302, 303,
    306, 307, 308, 315, 319, 325–
    30, 417, 418, 419, 420, 421
Amir Sjarifuddin, Mr, Indonesian
    Defence Minister, 17, 36, 294,
    315, 325, 331, 333
Andalas, 26
Angkatan Pemuda Indonesia, see API
Anglo-Dutch Country Section, 303,
    304
Anglo-Dutch Treaty, of 1824, 11, 14,
    256, 260
    of 1871, 14, 260
Anglo-Franco-Chinese Convention
    of 1866, 199
ani-ani, 49
anopheles mosquito, 45, 62, 63
API, 312, 313
Arabs, 148, 230–2, 233, 234, 239,
    243
    scholars, 27, see also Habib
    sources, 24
    traders, 8, 78, 94, 164, 196
    travellers, 5, 26

arak, 127, 131, 132
Arifin, Tengku Mohammad, 261–5,
    273, 407, see also Habib Abdur-
    Rahman
Army, 329, 332
    BKR, 303,329
    TNI, 333, 352, 353, 354
    TRI, 35, 326, 331, see also badan
       perjuangan
aron, 290, 291, 292–3, 347
Aru, 5, 77, 78, 83, 84, 97
Asahan, 13, 29, 50, 196, 197, 212,
    235, 331
Austronesian languages, 41

Badan Penjelidik Kemerdekaan
    Indonesia, see BPKI
badan perjuangan, 329, 330, 332, see
    also API and RRI
Banda Aceh, 14, 19, 26, 37, 74, 96–
    8,113, 125, 147, 169, 170, 171,
    172, 286, 351, 376, 424
Bangka, 20, 195
    and tin, 10
Banjarese, 42, 43, 44, 61, 358
Banten, 45, 87, 113, 228, 234
Barisan Pemuda Indonesia, see BPI
Barus, 3, 5, 48, 57, 146
Basilan (S. Philippines), 151,168
Baso movement (Minangkabau),
    332–4
Batak or Bataks, xiv, 6, 17, 19, 28,
    31, 38, 42, 55, 56, 64, 65, 66,
    147, 155, 162, 197–8, 207, 234,
    290, 314, 316, 339, 355, 356
    Aceh's wars against, 7, 75, 77
    Karo, xiv, 6, 16, 28, 51, 55, 58,
       59, 66, 67, 290–3, 328, 330,
       332
    Karo-Batak War (1872), 281
    kings, 45, 64

Index

Mandailing, 15, 16, 51, 58, 66, 328, 361
Toba, 6, 15, 16, 19, 28, 32, 34, 51, 54, 55, 56, 57, 58, 59, 66, 67, 328, 361, 362
Batam, Riau Archipelago, 20, 59
Batang Hari river, 3, 4, 8, 26
Beaulieu, Augustin de, 99–103, 153, 370
Bengkulu, 10, 11, 22, 50, 51, 52, 154, 155, 156, 157, 250, 318, 319, 320
Berchou, Noel, Nantes trader, 172, 174
Besemah, see Pasemah
betelnut, 14, 97
Beureu'eh, Teungku Daud, 288, 317, 319, 326, 327, 341, 343, 347, 413
Body for the Investigation of Indonesian Independence, see BPKI
Boon Keng, Penang merchant, 196
Borobudur, 3
Bowrey, Thomas, 106, 108, 109, 370, 378
BPI, 310, 311
BPKI, 298
Boucho, Fr Jean-Baptiste, 159–60
Bourbon: Island 158, 164, 165–7, 170, see also Réunion dynasty, 158
Brau de St.-Pol Lias, F-X-J-H., 178–86, 386
British, competition with Dutch, 8, 10, 194, 196, 219
Chartered Companies, 182
consuls: in Sumatra, 29
in China, 204, 216
Brooke, Rajah James, 249, 252, 253, 274

Budi Utomo, 30
Bugis, 44, 148
Bukit Barisan, 1, 48, 61
Bukit Siguntang, 26
Bukittinggi, 18, 33, 35, 37, 300
Burma (Pegu), 112, 136, 137, 157, 170
Bustanu's-Salatin, 70, 73, 95, 104, 106, 114, 116, 368, 370, 374, 375, 377

camphor, 3, 97
Camus, Mustaffa, Turkish envoy, 80
cannons, 117, 123, 138, 140, 228
Cantonese, 195, 395–6
Cessation of Hostilities Agreement (COHA: 9 December 2002), 352, 353
China, 3, 27, 195, 204, see also raja Cina
consuls, 216, 221–2, 396
emigration policy, 215–7, 221–2
Chinese: population in Sumatra, 194, 198, 389, 390
immigration, 194, 197–225
labour, 13, 55, 194–5, 198–9, 201, 204, 208, 214–7, 222–4
miners, 10, 180
traders, 10, 195–7
Chinese Immigrants Ordinance (1877), 200, 211
Chinese Protectorate, in Straits Settlements, 198, 199, 200, 201, 211, 212, 215, 217, 218, 219, 221–4, 391, 395, 397
chokan (Japanese governor) 296, 297, 299
cholera, 63, 220
Christian: conversions, 15–6, 56, 66, 163–4
missions, 158–64, 234

Index

Chulalongkorn, King of Siam (1868–1910), 253, 254
Chulia (Tamil Muslims) merchants, 10, 156
Chuo Sangi In, see Sumatran Central Advisory Council
Clarke, Sir Andrew, 253, 259, 266
colons explorateurs, 179, 180, 181, 182
Constantinople (Istanbul), 69, 79, 84, 172–3, 176, 235, 236, 237, 238, 241, 242, 244, 245
Crawfurd, J.S., 268, 356
Crimping Ordinance, 211
cultuurgebied (cultivation district), 194, 207, 210, 212, 222
Cut Nyak Dien, Acehnese female warrior, 336, 352

dalam (Aceh citadel), 102, 116, 120, 131, 151
Dampier, William, 108–9
Dar al'Isyki River, 133, 134
Dar ul-Islam, 19, 344
Deli, 13, 88, 179, 182, 184, 186, 194, 196–7, 202–25, 292–3, 304
Deli Maatschappij, 198, 218, 219, 397
Deli Planters Union (DPV), 217, 220
Dongson bronzes, 50
Dulaurier, Edouard, 168
Dutch: competition with British, 8, 10
  administration, 16, 18, 38, 40, 59, 257, 260
  conquest of Sumatra, 2, 11–6, 57, *see also* Aceh war
  East India Company, 8, 10, 15, 64, 337, *see also* VOC
  Ethical Policy, 248
  Protestant Mission, 66

East Timor referendum, xiv, 20
Economy of Sumatra, 21–2, *see also* ERRI
elephants, 1, 8, 112–26, 148, 372, 374
  fights, 127, 128, 129, 130
  hunting, 114
English East India Company, 8, 10, 64, 154, 251
ERRI, 330–2
Errington de la Croix, M.J., mining engineer, 182, 183–4

F-*kikan*, 282, 283, 284, 286, 287, 288, 289, 290, 292, 411, 412
Fauque, Paul, 185–6
Female rule in Aceh, 8, 106–11, 148, 370
  in Patani, 370
Firearms, 138, *see also* cannons
First Dutch Expedition, 267, 268, 269
Fort Marlborough, 10, 154, *see also* Bengkulu
French: adventurers, 154–7, 181–4, 188–90
  Asian policies, 151–8, 165–78
  consuls, 29, 156, 167, 174, 183
  missions, 15, 151–2, 153, 158–63
  revolution, 322–4
  trade, 152, 158–9, 164–6, 171–2, 174–5
Fujiwara Iwaichi, Major, 282–6, 290, 409, 411, 412, *see also* F-*kikan*

GAM, 20, 351–4
  and "Declaration of Independence of Acheh Sumatra", 349
Gambier & Pepper Society, 202
Gani, Dr A.K., 34, 35, 301–20, 418
Gayo, xiv, 6, 28, 70, 207, 339, 355

Index

431

GERINDO, 282, 290, 292, 414, 418
German: consuls, 219
gold, 2, 3, 8, 15, 97, 148
  coins, 5
  exploration for 180–8
  gold-bearing areas, 3, 180
  in Aceh ritual, 114, 116–7, 124–6, 372
Gunongan Menara Permata
  (monument), 71, 96, 134, 376
Gunseikanbu (Military
  Administration), 34, 300, 302

Habib Abdur-Rahman az-Zahir,
  175, 176, 180, 237, 238, 241, 402
Habibie, B.J., President of
  Indonesia, 20, 350, 351
haji, 161, 197, 229, 231, 234, 239,
  240, 243, 247, 269, 273, 400,
  see also pilgrimage
Haji Attaullah (Turkish Consul
  General in Singapore), 246
Haji Wachia, 234, 404
Hakka (Kheh), 215, 395–6
Hamilton, Alexander, 153
Hamka, writer and Muhammadiah
  activist, 17, 301,317, 319, 414,
  416, 418
Hamzah Fansuri, 336
Hang Tuah, 73
Hasan, T.M., 302–8, 315, 328
Hatta, Mohammad, 17, 31, 37, 302,
  410
Heutsz, J.B. van, 14
hikayat, 132
Hikayat Aceh, 73, 98, 100, 115, 128,
  133, 364, 368, 369, 373, 374,
  377
Hikayat Malem Dagang, 104, 147,
  363

Hikayat Marong Mahawangsa, 70,
  363
Hikayat Meukota Alam, 71
Hikayat Perang Sabil, 340
Hikayat Pocut Mohammad, 146, 378,
  379
Hindu-Javanese: centres, 46
  concepts, 96
Hokkien, 395–6
hulubalang, 98, 102, 119, 141, 192,
  see also uleëbalang
Husain, Acehnese envoy, 80, 84, 90
Hussain, Sultan of Johor-Riau
  empire, 252

Ibn Battuta, Arab travel-writer, 5,
  24, 66, 337
Ibrahim, Sultan of Aceh (1838–70),
  169, 170, 171, 172, 173, 175,
  236, 237
  Letter to President of France,
    191–3, *see also* Ala'ad-din
    Mansur Shah
Idul Adh, 119, 120, 121
Idulfitri, 119, 122, 123, 373
imam, 107, 108, 123, 143, 242, 243,
  272
Indian Mutiny, 235
Indian Ocean, 1, 5, 7, 70, 74, 151,
  154, 156, 158, 280, 337, 365
  Turkish initiatives in, 75–85, 87–8
Indian: traders, 3
  labourers, 222–3
  slaves, 109, 371
Indische Partij, *see* NIP
Iskandar Dzul Karnain, *see*
  Alexander the Great
Iskandar Muda, Sultan of Aceh
  (1607–36), 7, 69, 71, 73, 88,
  100–8, 114, 115, 116, 123–48,
  153, 349, 368–71, 373, 374, 376

cruelty of, 104–5
Iskandar Thani, Sultan of Aceh
  (1637–41), 7, 71, 96, 106, 114–
  7, 120, 127, 129, 134, 143–5, 195
  funeral of, 117, 118
Islam, 2, 3–6, 15, 66, 78, 83, 86, 88,
  134, 143, 226, 227, 228, 229,
  239, 243, 247, 277, 336, 345,
  399
  Islamic festivals, 117–24
  Islamization, 15, 66, 94
  Sabilillah, 329, see also Pan Islam,
    Sarekat Islam
Islamic World Congress, 227
Istanbul, see Constantinople

Jambi, 3, 8, 12, 24, 48, 52, 65, 195,
  196, 235, 245, 248, 318, 319,
  320, 336
Janissaries, 77, 87, 88, 102
Japanese: Occupation, 18, 19, 34,
  67, 276–93, 294–5, 419
  25th Army, 33, 34, 35
  and policies in Sumatra, 295–8,
    302–20
Japara, Queen of, 85
Jauhar al-Alam, Sultan of Aceh, 157
Java, 229, 240
  Javanese labourers, 194, 222–3
  Javanese migrants, 13, 55
  model, 45–8, 51
Java War of 1825–30, 48
Jesuit sources, 83, 84
Johor, 7, 69, 70, 78, 115, 153, 202,
  203, 252
Joint Security Commission (JSC),
  353
Jong Java, 30
Jong Sumatranen Bond (JSB), 17,
  30, 31, 32, 35, 39, 356
Junied Sayyid Abdallah al, 232

Junied Sayyid Junied al, 233

kabupaten, 53, 55
kadi, 142
Karo, see Batak
Kamalat Syah, sultana of Aceh, 109
Kedah, 7, 70, 159
Kempeitai, 34, 292
kerajaan, 297, 299, 301, 305, 328,
  330, 418
Kerinci, Lake, 49, 50, 65
Kesatuan Melayu Muda, 284
khehtau, 199, 200, 203, 204, 210,
  212, 220, 221
Khoo Thean Tek, 203, 204, 210
king/kingship, 8, 96, 112, 122, 124,
  125, 126
  Buddhist king, 2, 3
  Bugis kingship, 44
  Minangkabau, 64
KNI (all-Sumatra representative
  council), 36, 37, 303, 308
kora-kora expeditions, 42
kris, 7, 124, 138
Kurtoglu Hizir Reis, Admiral of
  Suez, 80, 85, 91, 93

Labour Commission, Straits
  Settlements: 1876, 201, 203, 206,
  208, 211
  1890, 201, 209, 213
Lampung, 22
Lamri, ancient port-state, 5, 26, 95
Langkat, 13, 194, 204, 292–3, 304
laukhehs (experienced migrants),
  209, 218, 221
Lavino, George, 267–71, 275, 408
L'Etoile, Francis, country trader,
  156–7
Lhokseumawe, 5, 21, 27, 146, 341,
  347, 351

Index

433

Louis Napoleon, Emperor of France, 173–4
Louis Philippe, King of France, 151, 169, 172–3, 191
Lumbantobing, Dr Ferdinand, 34, 302, 317, 319, 320

Ma Huan, 66
Madiun Affair of September 1948, 323
Maharaja Lela, Sri, 98, 103
Majapahit, 3, 24, 25, 46, 51, 73
Malacca, *see* Melaka
Malacca Straits, *see* Straits of Malacca
malaria, 45, 62, 63, 362
"fever", 161, 162
Malay
classical literature, 17, 86, 89, 337
ethnic group, 328
labour on plantations, of Sumatra, 197, 198, 203–9
language, 2, 13, 17, 24, 26, 43, 158, 164, 168, 175, 336–7
system of writing, 5
Mandailing, *see* Batak
mandi Safar, 129, 131, 132, 134
Mansur, Dr Tengku, 39
marga, 54
Marsden, William, xiii, 23, 26, 27, 69, 70, 356, 380
Martin, Captain, Marseilles pepper-trader, 164–6, 169, 383–4
Mataram, 46, 48, 86, 112, 136, 137, 233
Maulud, 119, 132, 373
Mauritius (Ile de France), 154, 155, 158
Mayrena, Charles David de, 188, 189, 190, 388, 389

Mecca, 14, 84, 176, 229, 230, 232, 235, 236, 242, 259, 272, 401
pilgrimage to, 11, 230, 259–60, 273, 407
Medan, 21, 29, 33, 35–6, 221, 292
and independence, 300, 303–12
Megawati Sukarnoputri (president of Indonesia), 20, 352
Melaka, 5, 7, 11, 26, 71, 73, 75, 77, 80, 98, 105, 119, 126, 196, 366, 378
Acehnese attack on, 77, 78, 82, 83, 84
combined Acehnese and Japara's attack on, 85
Dutch capture of (1641), 105, 145
Sultanate, 73, 114
Melayu, 24
Meulaboh, 10, 183, 186
Migration, *see* outmigration, Chinese, Javanese
Minangkabau, xiv, 3, 4, 6, 8, 10, 11, 13, 15, 17, 19, 27, 28, 30, 31, 32, 33, 34, 38, 42, 51, 52, 53, 64, 67, 70, 78, 138, 147, 180, 196, 233, 234, 314, 315, 328, 332–4, 339, 355, 361, 418
Yang di Pertuan Sakti, 26, 27
modernization, 65, 68
modernizing project, 66, 67
Mohammadiah, 298
Mongkut, King of Siam (1851–68), 253, 254, 406
Muara Takus, 3
Muhammad Daud, Tuanku, Sultan of Aceh, 341, 342
Muhammad, Sultan, also known as Mehmed III (1595–1603), 73
Muhammad Ghaut, Acehnese envoy, 172, 173, 193

Muhammad Kiamil Bey, 243, 244
mukim (parish), 107, 108, 109, 110,
141, 142, 146, 147, 148, 270,
289
Musi river, 8, 9, 26, 51

Nagarakertagama, 24, 25
Napindo, 329
Napoleonic Wars, 11, 155, 157
Naqshibandiyah order, 234
Natal, 155
Nathar Zainuddin, 327, 422
nationalism
Malay, 26
Indonesian, 17, 18, 20, 31, 32,
33, 226, 335, 337
Javanese, 31
Sumatran, 24, 30–3
nationalist historiography, 24–5,
226
Negara Bahagian Aceh (Aceh
Federal State), 341
Negara Sumatra Timur (NST), 39
Netherlands India, 194, 219, 221,
223, 235, 240, 243, 245, 254,
255, 273, 315, 337
government, 231, 236, 257, 259,
260, 267, 268, 270, 339
Netherlands Indies Civil
Administration, *see* NICA
Netherlands Trading Company, *see*
NHM
Netscher, Elisa, Dutch Resident of
Riau, 257
New Order, 19
NHM, 250, 255, 257
Nias, 41–2, 159–64
NICA, 304, 305
Nienhuys, Jacob, Dutch planter, 13,
179, 197

NIP, 32
Nisero affair, 186–8, 265
Notosusanto, Nugroho, 336
Nur al-Alam, Sultana of Aceh
(1675–8), 107, 108
Njak Arif, Teuku, 300, 302, 306,
317, 319, 320, 326, 417
Nur, Iskandar, 17

Ocean Steamship Company, 196,
213
Opium, 156, 196
Opium War, 168
orangkaya, 97, 98, 99, 100, 101, 102,
103, 104, 105, 106, 107, 132,
142, 143, 144, 145, 146
Orangkaya Laksamana, 100, 103
orang laut, 65
orang mardika (freemen), 64
orang ulu, 52
Ord, Sir Harry, First Colonial
Governor of Singapore, 251,
258, 259
Ordinance IV of 1880, 200, 207,
209, 210
origin myths, 41, 42, 51
Ottoman Sultan, 5–7, 69, 72, 79,
84, 119, 227, 228, 235, 238
outmigration, 21, 41, 42, 43, 44, 48,
52, 54, 55, 56, 58, 59

Padang, 7, 10, 12, 17, 29, 31, 33, 50,
68, 146, 154, 155, 156, 161,
163, 174, 242, 312, 380, 381,
382
Padang Lawas, 50
Padday, H.J.D., Dutch Consul,
Penang, 256–7, 270–1
Padris, 11, 12, 28, 234
Padri movement, 15, 55, 233

Index

Padri War (1820–41), 13, 52, 163
Pagurruyung, 11, 26, 27, 50, 51
Pahang, 7, 116, 144, 253
pahlawans, 71
Painan Treaty, 10, 369
Palembang, 2, 3, 8, 9, 11, 13, 17, 20,
  21, 24, 27, 29, 33, 34, 35, 48,
  50, 65, 68, 195, 230, 231, 234,
  235, 242, 243, 248, 272, 297,
  336, 414, 418
  and independence, 302–20
  people, 52
pamong-praja, 276, 277, 278, 279,
  297
pan-Islamic or pan-Islam, 86, 227,
  232, 245, 246, 247, 248
  front against the Portuguese, 85
  movement, 226, 227, 235, 240,
  245
  party, 239
panglima, 102, 107, 146, 147
Panglima Polem, 107, 108, 110,
  148, 412
Panitia Penjelidik Persiapan
  Kemerdekaan, *see* PPKI
Pararaton, 25
PARINDRA, 290
PARTINDO, 282
Pasai, 5, 48, 73, 74, 75, 77, 87, 95,
  97, 98, 114, 141, 146, 147, 336,
  337, 343, 365
  kings, 96
Pasemah, xiv, 49, 50, 51, 52, 362
pasisir, 46, 48
pergerakan, 297, 299, 301, 325, 328,
  418
pemuda, 36, 37, 278, 294, 295, 306,
  309, 310, 311, 313, 314, 315,
  325, 329
Pemuda Indonesia, 32

Pemuda Republik Indonesia, *see*
  PRI
Penang, 10, 29, 157, 158, 159–60,
  187, 196, 238, 239
  as trade centre for Sumatra, 164–
  5, 197, 198, 202, 212, 213,
  214, 217, 218, 338
  Collège Général, 159, 160
  consulates in, 255–8
  role in Aceh War, 267–71, 275,
  338
pepper, 5, 6, 7, 8, 10, 14, 21, 51, 74,
  75, 78, 87, 97, 104, 138,
  140,141, 145, 152, 164, 165,
  166, 174, 181, 187, 195, 196,
  269, 338, 370, 383
  pepper-growing areas or regions,
  7, 8, 10, 79, 102, 138, 170,
  180, 337
  traders, 158–9, 164–6, 171–2,
  174
Perak, 184, 185, 194, 206, 253
Perlak, kingdom of, 5
Persatuan Perjuangan, 329, 333,
  334
Persatuan Ulama2 Seluruh Aceh, *see*
  PUSA
Pesindo, 312, 313, 329, 330
Pickering, William, 212, 213, 389,
  391, 394, 395, 397
Pidië, port state, 5, 75, 95, 98, 108,
  114, 141, 142, 145, 146, 147,
  269, 287, 325, 327, 365
Pilgrimage to Mecca (*haji*), 11, 230,
  259–60, 407, *see also* Mecca
Pires, Tomé, 96, 356, 368, 377
PKI, 31, 329, 332, 333
PNI, 35, 282, 303, 306, 308, 329,
  417
Poivre, Pierre, 156

Index

Polo, Marco, 3, 5, 24, 66, 95, 368
Population: Sumatra, 21, 51–4, 55–8, 194, 389
Java, 52
Portuguese: Aceh's wars against, 6, 7, 77, 84, 236
arrival of, 5, 6, 228
and Melaka, 74, 78, 87, 97, 141
strength of, 6
PPKI, 301, 302, 303, 306, 308, 319
pribumi, 21
PRI, 306, 312, 313, 326, 327
PRRI, 19, 40
Ptolemy, 2
PUSA, 279, 281, 284–9, 315, 326, 327, 341, 412, 419

Raffles, Thomas Stamford, 48, 51, 119, 129, 158, 250, 356, 360, 362, 375, 382
railway, 68
in Java, 29
in Sumatra, 17, 29
raja or rajas, 13, 14, 18, 37, 64, 98, 110, 112, 166, 183, 187, 328, 329
and Acehnese political system, 141, 146, 147
Raja Cina, 69, 70
Raja Kecil, 27, 153
Raja Rum, 69, 71, 73
Raniri, Nurud-din ar-, 70, 116, 117, 134, 374, 375, *see also Bustanu's-Salatin*
Read, W.H., Dutch Consul in Singapore, 249–75, 403, 407, 408, 409
reformasi, 20
Republican Government of Indonesia, 18, 36

Revolutionary Government of the Republic of Indonesia, *see* PRRI
Réunion, 155, 158, 182, *see also* Bourbon
Rhenisch Mission Society, 15, 164
Riau, 20
Dutch Resident of, 257, 260
Roura, Edouard, 176, 180–1, 187–8
Rubber, 13
Rum, 27, 69, 70, 73, 86, *see also* Constantinople, *Raja Rum*
Rusli, Marah, 17

sagi, 105, 107, 108, 109, 141, 148, 412
Salah-ad-din, Sultan of Aceh (1530–9), 74
Samudra, 5, 24, 27, 355, *see also* Pasai
sarakata, 142, 144
Sarekat Islam, 31, 32, 226, 345, 411
sayyids, 229, 230, 232, 233
script: Arabic, 5, 6, 89, 336, 337
Indic, 6
Second Dutch Expedition, 266, 268, 269, 340
Sejarah Melayu, 114, 119, 126, 372, 373, 374
Selim II, Sultan of Turkey, 72, 80, 81, 83, 84, 90, 91, 93
senenan, 127, 128
SETIA (Sarekat Tani Indonesia), 282, 290
Seunagan (West Aceh), 169, 171, 180
Serdang, 13, 194
Shamsud-din, Sheikh of Pasai, 73, 100
Shantou (Swatow), 200, 204, 215–7, 219, 220, 221, 222, 224

Index

Sharif Ali, emissary, 235
Siak, xiv, 27, 48, 78, 196, 355, 390
Siam, 112, 113, 127, 132, 136, 139, 158, 159, 253–4
Sibolga, 10, *see also* Tapanuli
Sidi Muhammad, Acehnese envoy, 173–4, 385
Sinan Pasha, 72, 80
Singamangaraja XII, 28
Singapore, 175, 183, 185, 187, 190, 196, 231, 232, 235, 238, 239, 240, 241, 242
and Aceh, 240–1
and consuls in, 249, 253–5
and Japanese occupation, 280, 284, 298–9
as coolie recruitment centre, 194, 198–225
as regional trade centre, 164, 167
Read's role, 250–75
Singasari Inscription of 1286, 27
sinkheh (new arrival), 199, 200, 201, 203, 204, 205, 208, 209, 210, 211, 212, 213, 214, 215, 216, 217, 220, 221, 224
Singkil, 169–70
Siregar, Jacub, 290, 292
Sjafei, Mohammad, 34, 35, 301, 306, 317, 319, 320, 416, 418
Slavery, 65, 109
in Nias, 159–60, 163
Snouck Hurgronje, Christian, 107, 246–8, 271, 338
Social Revolutions of 1945–6, xiv, 18, 67, 321, 322, 324, 325, 334, 341, 422
Société des Missions Etrangères, 158, 162, 382, 383
Soetan Sjahrir, 17, 312
South Indian raid in 1025, 3

Spice trade, 78, 79, 137–8, 151, 152, 156, 368
Srivijaya, 2, 3, 24, 26, 27, 48, 195, 336
State of East Sumatra, *see* NST
STOVIA Medical School, 30, 417
Straits of
Malacca, 2, 3, 24, 43, 65, 86, 97, 145, 156, 157, 280, 338
Singapore, 69
Sunda, 24
Straits Settlements, 13, 171, 194, 198
and Protectors of Chinese, 198–225, 391
and role in Dutch Aceh War, 230, 236, 238, 251, 253, 254, 255, 261, 266, 267, 271, 275, 338, 343
Studer, Major, American Consul, 261, 263, 264, 265
Suez canal project, 85
Sufi, 336
brotherhoods, 10, *see also* Naqshibandiyah
Suffren, Admiral de, 154, 156
Suharto, xiv, 19, 20, 336, 350, 354
Sukarno, 35, 282, 296, 302, 306, 307, 310, 311, 336, 345, 346, 347
Suleiman Pasha, 75, 77, 89, 91
Suleiman the Magnificent, Ottoman Sultan, 6, 77, 79, 80, 83, 84, 86, 87, 91
Sultan Agung, 46, 136, 139
Sultan Zainal Abidin, 128
Sultanate
Aceh, 6–8, 71, 95, 110, 112, 164, 165, 170, 228, 249, 355, 381
Riau-Johor, 11, 252

Sumatera Baru, 33, 298, 314
Sumatran identity, 2, 17–9, 20–1,
    23–33, 36–40, 314–6
Sumatra Research Bulletin, 23, 413
Sumatran Central Advisory Council,
    34, 300, 302, 317
Sunni Muslims, 242
surau (prayer-hall), 10
Suvarna-dvipa (gold-land), 1
Suwarna-bumi (gold-land), 2, 27
Swatow, see Shantou
syahbandar (port officials), 104, 261
Syonan (Singapore), 33, 299

Taha Safi'ud-din, Sultan, 235, 245,
    246
Taj al-Alam, Safiyyat al-Din, first
    female ruler of Aceh (1641–75),
    106, 107, 108, 127, 129, 132,
    142, 144, 145, 148, 370
Taman Ghairah, 134
Taman Siswa, 290, 298, 310, 311
Tan Malaka, 333
Tan Tek, *see* Khoo Thean Tek
Tapanuli Residency, 16, 20, 28, 31,
    32, 37, 40, 51, 55, 56, 57, 59,
    68, 75, 194, 297, 308, 313, 317,
    319, 320, 357
    port (Sibolga), 155, 161, 162
Taprobana, 2
tarekat, 10
Teochiu, 215, 395, 396, 398
    labour or labourers, 202, 216
    leader, Tan Seng Poh, 205
    planters, 202
Teuku Laota, 242
Teuku Umar, 187–8, 336
Teunom (West Aceh), 180, 181,
    183, 186–8
    Teuku Imam Muda of, 181, 183

Tibang, Muhammad, 175, 176, 261,
    263–4, 273
Tin-mining, 10, 195, 206, 215, *see
    also* Perak, Bangka
Tiro, Hasan Mohammad, xiv, 20,
    34, 35, 36, 37, 302, 303, 306,
    307, 308, 310, 315, 317, 319,
    329, 335, 341, 346–50, 424
Tiro, Teungku Syech Saman di
    (Chik di Tiro), 336, 344, 346
Toba: Lake, 1, 48–9, 54, *see also*
    Batak
tobacco, 11, 13, 21, 179, 197, 205,
    206, 208, 209, 211, 214, 217,
    218, 223, 224, 397
Toh Peh Kong Society, 203, 204,
    392
Toraja, 44, 67
towkays, 206
trade or traders: Arab, 8, 78, 94, 196
    British, 10, 156
    Chinese, 94, 160, 196, 390
    Muslim, 5, 6, 7, 74, 78, 80, 102,
    152
    Tamil, 10, 156
    Turkish, 84
transmigrants, 17, 56, *see also*
    outmigration
trans-Sumatra highway, 17, 30
travelers: Arab, 5, 26, *see also* Ibn
    Battuta
    French, 26
    Muslim, 2, 80
    Turkish, 84, 92, *see also* Abdul
    Aziz
Trengganu, 153, 263
Trumon, 160–1, 170
Tso Ping-lung, second Chinese
    Consul (1881–91), 216
Tuhfat al Nafis, 251, 405

Index

Turkey, 27, 69–93, 97, 117, 119, 172,
173, 176, 227, 228, 340, 343
and Aceh War, 261–3
and Pan Islam, 232–3, 234, 235,
236, 237, 242, 244
Turkish Caliph, 17, 72, 227, *see
also* Ottoman

ulama (religious scholar), 14, 92,
143, 231, 232, 234, 281, 286,
288, 289, 327, 328, 333, 341,
344, 345, 346, 351, 401
ulèëbalang (local chiefs), 8, 18, 92,
102, 107, 109, 110, 140–9, 172,
180, 181, 183, 260, 277, 281–9,
316, 325–8, 341, 371, 379, *see
also hulubalang*

Ulèëlheuë, 29
umma, 226, 227
US-Aceh treaty, 261

Vietnam, 157, 168
VOC, 46, 63, 64, 138, 145, 152,
233
Volksraad, 31

Wahhabis, 11, 233, 234, 400, *see also*
Padris
Wallon, French gold-explorer, 181–5

Xarim, M.S., 31–2

Zainal Abidin, Sultan of Aceh, 128
Zheng He (Cheng Ho), 195